Putting Down Roots

paskwāwi masinahikewina / Prairie Writing

ISSN 2818-1379

Brenda Macdougall and Robert Innes, Editors

paskwāwi masinahikewina / Prairie Writing series publishes books both academically rigorous and accessible to the public that relate to the contemporary experiences, histories, and knowledges of prairie Indigenous societies. It supports the work of new and established scholars who are examining how prairie Indigenous peoples understand and shape their own worlds..

2 *Putting Down Roots: Métis Agency, Land Use, and Women's Food Labour in a Qu'Appelle Valley Road Allowance Community,* by Cheryl Troupe

1 *Bead Talk: Indigenous Knowledge and Aesthetics from the Flatlands,* edited by Carmen Robertson, Judy Anderson, and Katherine Boyer

Putting Down Roots

Métis Agency, Land Use, and Women's Food Labour in a Qu'Appelle Valley Road Allowance Community

Cheryl Troupe

UMP
University of Manitoba Press

Putting Down Roots: Métis Agency, Land Use, and Women's Food Labour
in a Qu'Appelle Valley Road Allowance Community

29 28 27 26 25 1 2 3 4 5

University of Manitoba Press
Winnipeg, Manitoba, Canada
Treaty 1 Territory
uofmpress.ca

Cataloguing data available from Library and Archives Canada
paskwāwi masinahikewina/Prairie Writing, ISSN: 28181379 ; 2
ISBN 978-177284-102-2 (PAPER)
ISBN 978-177284-104-6 (PDF)
ISBN 978-177284-105-3 (EPUB)
ISBN 978-177284-103-9 (BOUND)

Cover photograph of Margaret Pelletier Harrison's rug by Cheryl Troupe.
Cover and Interior Design by Galley Creative Co.

Printed in Canada

The University of Manitoba Press acknowledges the financial support for its publication program provided by the Government of Canada through the Canada Book Fund, the Canada Council for the Arts, the Manitoba Department of Sport, Culture, and Heritage, the Manitoba Arts Council, and the Manitoba Book Publishing Tax Credit.

This book has been published with the help of a grant from the Federation for the Humanities and Social Sciences, through the Awards to Scholarly Publications Program, using funds provided by the Social Sciences and Humanities Research Council of Canada.

Funded by the Government of Canada | Canada

For Bob, George, and Margaret

Contents

Illustrations

Tables

Figures

Foreword

THIS IS SUCH a great tahpacimowin history story of a community full of deep cultural knowledge and wisdom told by those people who were known as otipaimsowauk, the people who owned themselves. In older times, a storyteller would tell us a story reminding us, the listeners, of someone or something long forgotten or almost forgotten that needed to be remembered. Among us listeners, that someone would reciprocate by sharing a memory. This was the memory you, Cheryl, invoked in me.

Her name was Chee stah way pie sees, meaning Little Echo, and everybody was always happy when they saw her coming down the road. She lived way out on the edge of the road allowance about half a mile from Pimtutinow, the crooked hill. She was a real happy woman, very kind and gentle. You could always hear her coming long before you saw her because she would walk to the top of Pimtutinow and shout out what she was coming to do, and her echo would reverberate over the hills. I was checking my rabbit snares when I heard, "Me, I am going to visit Zubutt, Zubutt, Zubutt, zubutt, zubutt."

I listened to the echo only for a few moments, then raced through the bush to the road, and like everybody else, when I saw her coming, I followed her, and sure enough, she stopped at Zubutt's house and went inside. I arrived shortly after her, all breathless and was invited in to share a cup of sugared tea. I didn't care about the tea, I wanted to see what Chee stah way pie sees had made and was gifting to Zubutt. I didn't want to miss anything because I had heard the old ladies talking once and they had said that to witness a story being made and then, to tell it, was a great gift and I had promised myself that if I should ever be blessed to have that happen to me I would tell it so good I would not miss a detail.

I knew that Chee stah way pie sees liked giving presents away better than anybody else I knew. And she made such nice ones too and they always suited the people she gave them to. Just like this Zubutt she was going to visit. That woman she loved tin cans. All kinds of tin cans. Big ones, small ones, skinny ones, fat ones, and even them little round tin and cardboard snuff boxes 'cause they were just the right size for needles and all kinds of small things. I know that sounds kind of weird, but you should have seen what that Zubutt did to those cans. She was always buying paint with every spare dollar she could get hold of and when she had enough, she would paint all them tin cans in all kinds of beautiful colours. Virgin Mary blue, Chinese red, sunshine yellow, spring green, and one time she even found purple paint. Imagine that. Purple just like the purple the bishop wears for special masses and stuff.

Sometimes she even painted flowers on the cans or tied twine or store string and pretty ribbons around them. They were so beautiful. When they were all finished to her liking she would give them to the women who loved them because everybody was poor in our community and very few people had nice things to make themselves or a home look special. Like vases to put wildflowers in or pretty containers to store things like scissors and awls and packages of needles. Zubutt's gifts always had a special place on a shelf or windowsill or in the middle of the table. Just an ordinary tin can all painted up could make a poor little house real happy looking.

She even made aprons and clothes from flower sacks once and dyed the white cloth in pots of boiling berries, plants, and even moose blood, all of which turned into rich colours just like the paint she bought at the store. Someone driving past her house saw all that pretty cloth on her clothesline, blowing proud in the wind, and they told someone at the store and pretty soon everybody was excited and wondering what she was making and for who? She made stuff for the men, too, not just for the women. One time, she made a pair of leather cuffs with brass studs on them, and not long after, we saw an old man wearing them to protect his shirt cuffs on Sundays. A year later she made him a studded vest to go with his cuffs.

She made bells with pretty ribbons for the horses' neck yokes, and the horses, they seemed to know how good they looked, and they always danced and pranced as they went past a house, and people would stop what they were doing to look at them and wave.

She made leggings and belts for the young girls. They'd be all beaded or embroidered with silk threads and really show off someone's nice legs when they were dancing. She was just a good woman that Zubutt who held people up with her presents and made good stories for us to tell about them. And you know those stories always made us all feel good and helped us remember the old way of helping each other through hard times. Stories are very important for our people. Stories give us teachings and laws. They tell us the history of our old times and how we used to do things. They tell us why the hill was called Pimtutinow and about people like Chee stah way pie sees who came down the hill and road to give a story away and always did it with an echo song so we wouldn't forget to hold that person up.

Oh, I'm sorry, I almost forgot to tell you what Chee stah way pie sees gave Zubutt for a special present because I got so busy telling you about Zubutt's tin cans. Chee stah way pie sees gave her a big can of Coldwell Banker House Paint. Yes, Chinese Red, because it was the hardest one to find in our country and because red is a sacred colour in the Old Ways and the favourite one of our people.

So, to all of you, I give you this story of Chee stah way pie sees and Zubutt to hold up Cheryl Troupe for this wonderful book. And I send maarsii's to the Spirit World for uncles George Klyne and Bob Desjarlais, who took Cheryl out on the land and gave her these foundational stories, and to Margaret Harrison who lovingly hooked her a rag rug map and mentored her through our people's language, customs, values, and deep love of place. We are so much richer for their gifts.

With love and deep respect,
Maria Campbell

Gabriel's Crossing,
Batoche, Saskatchewan.
17 February 2024

Acknowledgements

THIS BOOK HAS been a long time coming and would not have been possible without the guidance, support, and encouragement of many people.

First and foremost, I owe an enormous debt of gratitude to Margaret Harrison, Bob Desjarlais, George Klyne, and their families for helping make this book a reality. Thank you for trusting me enough to share your time and stories. I am also indebted to Pauline Anderson, Dorothy Desjarlais, Mary Desnomie, Dorothy Fayant, Murray Hamilton, Irma Klyne, Deborah Pelletier, Isador Pelletier, Joan Pelletier, Roger Pelletier, Roy Poitras, Joanna Potyondi, Calvin Racette, Norma Welsh, Joe Welsh, Bev Worsley, and many others I have had the pleasure to get to know and learn from. Many of these individuals have unfortunately now passed on, but their stories live on in this book. I have tried to care for each of the stories they have shared with me in a respectful way. Any errors are mine alone.

Thank you to Maria Campbell for your friendship, mentorship, and teachings. You have taught me so much about the importance of being in community and how to respectfully and meaningfully do this work. Thank you for the miles we have shared and for always encouraging and believing in me. I am so grateful for the visiting that we have done along the way.

I would also like to extend my gratitude to Karon Shmon, Amy Briley, David Morin, Darren Prefontaine, and the team at the Gabriel Dumont Institute for your support and encouragement. Your contributions to Métis scholarship, though often overlooked, are immense and sincerely appreciated.

Thank you to my colleagues at the University of Saskatchewan both during my time as a student and now as faculty. Thank you to colleagues and mentors Geoff Cunfer, Erika Dyck, Valerie Korinek, Jim Clifford, Ben Hoy, Katie Labelle, Winona Wheeler, Sarah Nickel, Mary Jane Logan McCallum, and others who offered invaluable insight, thoughtful critique, and constant encouragement throughout various stages of this work. Your expertise and feedback helped shape this manuscript into its final form.

Thank you to Michelle Desveaux, Laura Larsen, Glenn Iceton, Carling Beninger, and Jessica DeWitt for creating time and space for writing, for reading early drafts of this work, and most importantly, for support, reassurance, and encouragement.

Thank you to Jill McConkey, Barbara Romanik, and the team at UMP for believing in my work and making it a reality. Thank you to Patrick Farrell, Matthew Kunkel, Neil Soiseth, Rhianne Billard, and Ben Hoy for various editorial and production work, including drafting of maps and charts.

Last but certainly not least, I want to express my deepest gratitude to Jason, Keeler, and my family. I could not have done this without your unwavering support, love, and, most of all, your patience. Maarsii.

Introduction

ROAD ALLOWANCES ARE the narrow strips of land between township sections set aside in Canada's Dominion Land Survey for future road building. No more than one chain width or sixty-six feet wide, this land was never intended for settler occupation or agriculture. These road allowances, along with survey adjustments called correction lines that compensated for the convergence of lines of longitude, as well as unoccupied but surveyed Crown land on the margins of First Nations reserves and land on the outskirts of developing towns and cities, became home to displaced Métis in the late nineteenth and early twentieth centuries.[1] These spaces have become known as road allowance communities, and the Métis who lived there as "road allowance people." The term has since been popularized by Métis author Maria Campbell in her collection of translated oral stories, *Stories of the Road Allowance People.*[2]

In the late nineteenth century, Métis struggled to adapt to new social, economic, and political environments brought about by the decimation of the buffalo, removal from the land, and the influx of settlers. Despite such challenges, Métis connections to the land and to one another were not severed. Instead, they used gaps and spaces in the colonial survey system to find land to live on, remain within familiar territory, and avoid being governed by the state. Relocating into makeshift and temporary settlements on unoccupied Crown lands, they formed communities where they could maintain kinship networks and cultural practices.

While seemingly peripheral and marginal, these spaces should be understood as sites of opportunity where Métis remained tied to the land in distinct ways, where they resisted outside pressures and intrusions into their everyday lives, and where Métis women's work in food production was central. As the Métis have demonstrated, road allowance communities should be understood as sites of resistance and resilience where liminality and poverty are not synonymous with atrophy.

This framing challenges how we think about Métis history and forces us to rethink how Métis resistance is understood. It moves beyond the efforts of recognizable leaders Louis Riel and Gabriel Dumont who have loomed large in prairie history and the accounts of the collective actions of Métis patriots fighting for recognition of land rights in both 1869–70 at Red River and 1885 in the North-West Territory. Indeed, road allowance communities and the actions, experiences, and stories of those who lived there reveal a different type of resistance that is more than a struggle for recognition of land rights.[3] This reframing requires us to look at these communities through the lens of women's work—particularly in food production—and to consider their resilience and resistance embedded in their everyday actions to maintain culture, family systems, commonly held values, and connections to the land.

The Métis families who lived on the road allowances in southern Saskatchewan's Qu'Appelle Valley until the mid-twentieth century are part of a distinct Indigenous nation that shares a collective, place-based history tied to the western prairies.[4] These families were part of a late eighteenth- and early nineteenth-century buffalo hunting economic tradition that saw large groups of Métis moving out of and through the Red River and Pembina regions and on the western plains in a seasonal rotation following the buffalo herds.[5] Métis families recognized and relied upon kinship relationships between extended families to create sprawling networks that came together and broke apart as buffalo herds and natural resources dictated. Métis economic, social, and political traditions were deeply connected to the hunt and the prairie landscape. This cohesion gave rise to a growing political consciousness that already in 1816 declared the Métis to be a unique nation, distinct from their First Nations and European relatives and neighbours, with its own common cultural expressions, language, and markers of identity defined by mobility, kinship relationships, and geography.[6]

By the 1850s, Métis buffalo hunters regularly followed the herds west into the Qu'Appelle Valley. At the time, the region was firmly Nêhiyawak (Cree) territory, extending from the Cypress Hills across the Wood and Moose Mountain areas towards the confluence of the Qu'Appelle and Assiniboine Rivers.[7] The Nêhiyawak granted Métis access to the territory and hunting privileges based on trade, kinship, and political alliances, including their participation in the Nêhiyaw-Pwat, or Iron Confederacy.[8] This was a political and military alliance amongst Nêhiyawak, Nahkawinniwak (Saulteaux), Nakota (Assiniboine), and Métis bands across western Canada and the northern United States. Their enemies were the A'aninin (Gros Ventre), Siksika (Blackfoot), Dakota, and Mandan/Hidatsa.[9] The Dakota and the Métis had been enemies until the Battle of Grand Coteau in 1851 when, overpowered by Métis forces, the Dakota withdrew, ending any long-standing disputes and creating peace between these long-time adversaries.[10]

By this time, complex environmental and economic factors were already starting to impact buffalo numbers.[11] Consequently, as the Métis sought to be competitive and meet market demands, their intensified and expanded hunts overtaxed an already declining population.[12] Within a decade many found it necessary to spend the winter in the Valley to continue accessing the diminishing herds. Wintering further afield from the Red River and Pembina region was common for most Métis buffalo hunters by this time and gave rise to year-round settlements across the prairies. By the late 1860s, a community of interrelated extended Métis families formed in the Qu'Appelle Valley close to the Qu'Appelle River and the Pasqua, Echo, Mission, and Katepwa Lakes known collectively as the Qu'Appelle or Fishing Lakes. Here the Métis supported themselves through the buffalo hunt for as long as possible, relying on fish, other hunted game, and food gathered or grown, as well as through trade with, and wage labour for, the Hudson's Bay Company.

The end of the bison economy in the 1870s brought significant changes for the Métis, including forced changes to their subsistence-based economy and imposition of Canadian government policy to open the west for settlement. Encroaching policy and impending settlement increased land pressure and exacerbated Métis anxiety over the Canadian government's lack of recognition of their rights. This led to two armed Métis resistances, first at Red River in 1869–70 and later in the South Saskatchewan River region in 1885. These have been well documented and have pointed to the displacement, dispossession, diaspora, and erasure of the Métis from the landscape.[13] Indeed, the government's Dominion Land Survey carved up the prairies into digestible units, manageable for settler farm families, while accompanying homestead policies set out the processes by which land would be occupied and used.

Successful settlement first required the removal of First Nations and Métis from the land. While the government recognized First Nations' land rights and dealt with them collectively through treaties, Métis' rights and land tenure practices were ignored.[14] This omission from treaty agreements allowed the government to deal with the Métis separately through distinct policies. These policies and Métis scrip processes—coupons redeemable for unoccupied surveyed land or money meant to extinguish any existing Métis land rights—failed to secure Métis land tenure and, as I argue here, forced many to live on land they did not own, displaced and dispossessed within territory their families had used and occupied for generations.

The division of land into an orderly township grid conflicted with Métis land tenure practices that prioritized access to water and resources along with proximity to family.[15] Métis in the Qu'Appelle Valley, like in other settlements across the prairies, struggled to maintain occupancy over their plots of land within the new and larger Canadian liberal framework.[16] The geometric precision of the provincial boundaries and the imposition of the township grid system left little room for the Métis.

The margins or allowances to compensate for the application of a precise two-dimensional grid system over the topographical features of the landscape became sites of resistance and resilience and not merely places for mathematical correction of the colonial survey. When attempting to take up land either through homestead policy or through the exchange of scrip, the Métis often selected land based on proximity to family and not for its agricultural potential, demonstrating their desire to maintain a subsistence-based rather than agricultural lifestyle. For instance, when settling in the Batoche region in present-day Saskatchewan, Métis took up land in long narrow lots fronting the South Saskatchewan River, initially chosen for proximity to water, hay, and wood lots. When surveyed, good agricultural land was made available in neighbouring municipalities, but Métis prioritized kinship relationships over economic opportunity, choosing the safety of family and community and remaining within recognizable kinship groupings over relocation to adjoining townships with access to better agricultural land.[17]

By the early twentieth century, Qu'Appelle Métis, like others across southern and central Saskatchewan, faced pernicious anti-Métis racial discrimination from growing Euro-Canadian settler society in response to Métis actions during the 1885 North-West Resistance. They also increasingly felt the imposition of Euro-Canadian values and government policy. With few options, many relocated to newly surveyed unoccupied Crown land, forming road allowance communities that were unique to the provinces of Saskatchewan, Manitoba, and Alberta, and by the early 1950s numbered in the hundreds.[18]

Histories of these spaces are limited and, when available, have largely looked at these communities in terms of their poverty, marginalization, ill health, and social problems. Scholarship has positioned road allowance communities as a drain on municipal and provincial welfare coffers and at odds with development of settler society.[19] Framing the Métis as Canada's "forgotten people," Bruce Sealey and Antoine Lucier contend that "the first half of the twentieth century did not belong to the Métis," instead they faced racism and discrimination, living at the margins of society as they attempted to survive as small-scale farmers or by living off the land in traditional ways.[20] Indeed, by the time the province of Saskatchewan was created in 1905, the Métis "were being engulfed by an unsympathetic settler society, whose ability to monopolize social and economic power cast disdain upon [Métis] values and their way of life."[21] For the Métis, "it was a life of almost total destitution and poverty, and apart from the social and racial condemnation it sometimes aroused, it met with little public sympathy and government inaction."[22] By the 1930s, as the Great Depression intensified so did Métis poverty and reliance on government relief. Municipal and provincial governments, overwhelmed by the financial responsibilities that accompanied the Métis, contemplated how to remove them from the road allowances.

The election of Tommy Douglas and the Co-operative Commonwealth Federation Government (CCF) in Saskatchewan in the 1940s ushered in a new period of intensive surveillance and ill-conceived government attempts to alleviate Métis poverty and remove them from the road allowance. Métis removal experiences then "became a horrific and untold story of bullying, cheating, burning [of homes], and forceful removal."[23] By the 1950s, most road allowance communities disbanded as individuals and families moved into cities and towns searching for employment and education opportunities. Increasing municipal pressure and conflict with settlers displaced others.[24]

Viewing this history through this lens of poverty masks the inner workings of Métis kinship networks and the level of community building and cultural continuity taking place. A new narrative, found in Métis stories, voices, and memories, is revealed when road allowance communities are considered in terms of resilience and resistance. Oral histories, community histories, and individual memoirs overwhelmingly demonstrate that these communities were not merely peripheral spaces where Métis lived as squatters on Crown land, but places where families lived according to a Métis worldview and culturally thrived despite economic poverty.[25] In these spaces, Michif language and Métis cultural traditions flourished.[26] Kinship relationships provided mutual aid and support and were of the utmost importance. Living close to one another helped maintain cultural traditions and practices such as visiting, storytelling, celebrating, and food sharing, and ensuring that all family members were well cared for and had enough to eat. Food united people and was an integral part of all Métis gatherings and celebrations. Families continued relying upon a subsistence lifestyle of fishing, trapping, and gathering wild foods supplemented by small-scale agriculture and wage labour when available. When Métis engaged in the settler economy, it was as labourers for local farmers, and they worked hard clearing fields or picking rocks or potatoes for meagre wages. Often, families worked as an economic unit, with women helping in the fields and maintaining more domestic responsibilities of caring for the children and Old People. Women's labour was crucial in harvesting, preparing, and preserving food and medicines for their families. Women's kinship networks and their food-based labour defined and anchored these families to the land. The Métis, women specifically, adapted to economic, political, and social changes and demanded recognition of their rights as they resisted government oppression, surveillance, and imposition into their daily lives.

Gender is central to this story. While scholarship on Indigenous women's contributions to eighteenth- and nineteenth-century fur trade economies has flourished since the 1980s, popular and academic narratives of the West continue to privilege men's stories.[27] Until recently, scholars have argued that women's work in prairie settlement and as rural labourers has been invisible, or added as an afterthought.[28] Yet, settlement of the western prairies could not have been possible without female homesteaders and other women's participation in almost every aspect of prairie life.[29] Studies of rural wage labour tend to be celebratory works, charting the progress or success of prairie communities with little analysis of the role women or children who played critical roles in creating and maintaining the rural economy.[30] Likewise, studies of Indigenous labour have also focused on the masculine, obscuring Indigenous women's contributions and assuming that Indigenous men "were the main or sole family breadwinner and that their work counted for more than that of women."[31] The exclusion of a gendered analysis in Indigenous history is an important oversight.[32] A history of economic systems from which Indigenous women are absent mistakenly suggests that women either played no significant economic role or "that their exclusion from the economy was natural and not also part of the experience of colonization."[33] A gendered lens allows for the inclusion of the myriad forms of Métis women's economic labour, including their artistic production, which from the early days of the fur trade was a critical component of the economy.[34] *Putting Down Roots* firmly inserts Métis women and their labour into this discussion of gender roles and rural labour in the prairie settlement period. It explores the degree to which Qu'Appelle Métis women were taking up small-scale agriculture, acquiring and maintaining homestead lands, farming within a family context, and providing their wage labour well into the twentieth century, which allows for a comparison of experiences of Métis women alongside First Nations and settler women's experiences.

Contrary to the earlier scholarship that has emphasized Métis poverty and displacement, this book considers how Métis people have cultivated individual and collective relationships to the land. Métis, like other Indigenous peoples, demonstrated a sophisticated understanding of their environments and modified and actively managed and humanized landscapes.[35] Métis subsistence activities allowed families, at least initially, to live autonomously and temporarily outside the watchful eye of government.

Métis women's food labour proved indispensable to the family economy; studying food systems offers a unique point of entry for understanding the everyday lives of the Métis and their connections to the Valley environment.[36] Food and stories about food appeal to the senses and to memory. As food historian Warren Belasco reminds us, "food indicates who we are, where we came from and who we want to be."[37] Indeed, for the Métis, food harvesting, production, and consumption is integral to identity, shaping how the Qu'Appelle Métis organized, structured, and understood themselves and the world around them.

Food production and consumption are also gendered and political. This work reveals women's significant contributions to the family subsistence economy through food harvesting, production, preparation, and preservation activities, adding to what is known about women's roles during these times of change. This work also explores how food affected social, political, and economic relationships, and power dynamics within Métis extended families and between the Métis and the state. Food is also an important lens for examining relationships to power and conflict.[38] In particular, how conflict between the Métis and municipal, provincial, and federal land policy, wildlife conservation policies, and relief measures restricted Métis land use, harvesting practices, access, and control over food resources.

This work explores Indigenous responses to settler colonialism, increased regulation and surveillance of Indigenous economies and livelihoods, and the erasure of Indigenous peoples from the landscape. It adds nuance to how we understand the development of the North American conservation movement in the late nineteenth and early twentieth centuries, the resulting impacts of government intervention and surveillance on subsistence livelihoods, and how local populations, including Indigenous peoples, resisted, responded to, and challenged this imposition. It reveals how governments, in redefining legitimate land use and land tenure, met with social unrest and resistance by local populations criminalized for their activities.[39] Qu'Appelle Métis consistently challenged state intervention into their livelihoods, and actively advocated for land use, access, and tenure in strategic and conscious ways grounded in an Indigenous worldview, their understanding of place, and recognizable political approaches to maintain their subsistence economy. Métis land use practices supported and reproduced Métis cultural understandings and were intimately connected to identity. Indeed, in their move to the road allowance Métis were resilient in taking back a connection to the land through deliberate reconstruction of cultural knowledge linked to kinship, women's labour, and their foodways.

Putting Down Roots demonstrates that Métis experiences in the Qu'Appelle Valley were complicated as they countered local, regional, and national intrusions.[40] The community's experience is one of continuity and change wherein they adapted their subsistence activity and livelihoods in flexible ways, responding to and resisting various government policy and legal and ideological interventions while prioritizing connections to familiar landscapes. This work refocuses this history on Métis experiences of displacement well into the twentieth century, challenging the understanding that the impacts of colonialism happened early and all at once and suggesting instead that the process and impacts of settler colonialism in the Qu'Appelle Valley ratcheted up over the course of more than a century.

This work traces the history of the Qu'Appelle Valley Métis and examines how road allowance communities persisted. I do this by scrutinizing the land-based food systems that connected families and reinforced gender roles in the community. Qu'Appelle Métis women quite literally "put down roots" in their gardens, growing what they needed to feed their families, while maintaining and reproducing cultural knowledge that anchored their families to the land. Occupying this territory, Qu'Appelle Métis people found individual and collective ways to resist settler colonialism. This study fits within a growing body of community-level studies examining specific prairie Métis communities in the late nineteenth and early twentieth centuries that reveal individual and everyday experiences from which we can better understand broad cultural, social, political, economic, and demographic continuity and change.[41]

Although I am Métis, the Qu'Appelle Valley is not my community. My work is the result of community-engaged research grounded in relationships, cultural protocols, and the lived experience and worldview of Métis people. It emerges from personal and professional relationships created and maintained with Métis community members over the past two decades. I am privileged to have received permission to share this history. My work explores the innovative and overlapping use of Indigenous research methods, oral history interviews, genealogical reconstruction, archival research, and Historical Geographic Information Systems methodologies to provide new approaches and insights into the relationship between individuals, their stories, and familiar places.

Chapter 1 introduces Métis storytellers Bob Desjarlais and Margaret Harrison, demonstrating how they ground themselves in specific places and families, and how they understand themselves through their stories, kinship, and connections to place. Their stories are foundational to this work and serve as the jumping-off point for elucidating the broader narrative of Métis history in the Qu'Appelle region that follows.

I consider Métis social, economic, and political structures from 1850 to 1870 in Chapter 2, with close attention to gender roles in food production and shifts in seasonal mobility and settlement patterns brought about by the decline of the buffalo herds. Women's labour in feeding their families and supplying the fur trade anchors this story in women's kinship networks and brings readers into the Métis' world through women's everyday work. Looking closely, and spatially, at women's activities reveals their centrality in creating and maintaining stability within their families and communities.

Chapter 3 firmly establishes agency and resilience as central to Métis values and reveals how women's strength and stability made political action possible. The narrative moves forward in time and closely examines the shift towards year-round occupation in the Valley region as a period of economic adjustment, political action, and relocation within recognizable and familiar territory. I have chosen to use the term "Halfbreed" in this chapter because this is how these families regularly referred to themselves and how some continue to do so today. Continued use of the term should be understood as an act of resistance by the Métis—an act of claiming and re-claiming, challenging the legacy of racism, removal, and erasure that they survived. I explore ideas of conflicting land tenure and how the Métis asserted their political autonomy, independence, and land rights within Canada's developing national framework. These ideas continue in Chapter 4, by considering the extent to which Métis were becoming agriculturalists from the 1880s onward and examining continued efforts to assert Métis sovereignty and secure title to the land they occupied. Chapter 4 also observes the Métis' determination in resisting increased government intervention into their lives through the Dominion Lands Act, Dominion Land Survey, Homestead Policy, and the scrip system that served to limit Métis land ownership and dispossess them well into the twentieth century. A close examination of Qu'Appelle Métis experiences with the scrip system and efforts to secure land title is the focus of Chapter 5. This chapter acts as a turning point in the narrative, after which Qu'Appelle Métis experienced widespread displacement from their lands.

Chapter 6 explores the movement of Métis to the surveyed and unoccupied Crown land that surrounded the Qu'Appelle Lakes, arguing that this relocation to "the road allowance" was not a passive acceptance of defeat and a retreat to the periphery, but a reassertion of Métis agency and affirmation of their deep connections to the Valley environment. Métis families consciously tried to remain within familiar territory and live within recognizable community structures that privileged kinship relationships and responsibilities. When engaging in the settler economy, they did so in ways that reinforced and reproduced identity and cultural knowledge. A close review of economic activity reveals that Métis families, when possible, continued working as economic units, and women laboured in creating, sewing, and selling handmade items, gathering and selling Seneca roots and berries, and working as domestics to bring much-needed income into the family.

Métis women's everyday work and the social and cultural context of food production, gathering, preparation, and sharing are the heart of Chapter 7. Reaffirming women's central and continued role in Métis families and communities, this chapter assesses consistency and change in family structure and gender roles into the twentieth century, paying attention to food harvesting and production.

Chapter 8 examines Métis agency in interactions with state agents, such as conservation and fisheries officers. It reveals that as Métis faced increased surveillance and regulation of their livelihoods, they responded by adjusting their harvesting practices and finding ways to challenge and skirt government interference to maintain their subsistence practices. Métis activism followed familiar political strategies and for the first time, publicly included women. Women's inclusion recognizes their agency, their growing public role in their families and communities, to show that they too were often courageous challenging increased state intrusion into their lives.

Métis experiences in accessing municipal and provincial relief from 1930 to 1940, the subsequent rehabilitative efforts of Saskatchewan's CCF government under the leadership of Tommy Douglas, and government efforts to remove Métis from the road allowances are the focus of the last chapter. It reveals how these interventions brought Métis lives under direct government surveillance and firmly into public view, increasing the racism that they already faced from their settler neighbours and for many, ultimately severed Métis connections to the land and broke apart extended family settlements, leading to the dissolution of the road allowance settlement in the Qu'Appelle Valley.

Métis throughout Canada have consistently demonstrated agency and resiliency in their actions and have always operated within a particular worldview that privileges kinship relationships, deep connection to the land, and the strength and significance of women. How these families moved, spatially organized themselves, and utilized the resources of the Qu'Appelle Valley was fundamental to how they understood themselves in this space. Each time these families moved within the Valley region, they strategically adapted to changing economic, social, and political situations in ways that reinforced the reproduction of Métis identity and cultural knowledge. These families were not passive in their adaptation, rather they recognized and responded in individual, collective, and familiar ways to settler colonialism, government surveillance, and regulation over their lands and livelihoods. This activism was made possible by Métis women's labour, particularly their food-based labour, and the cultural grounding they provided within their families and communities.

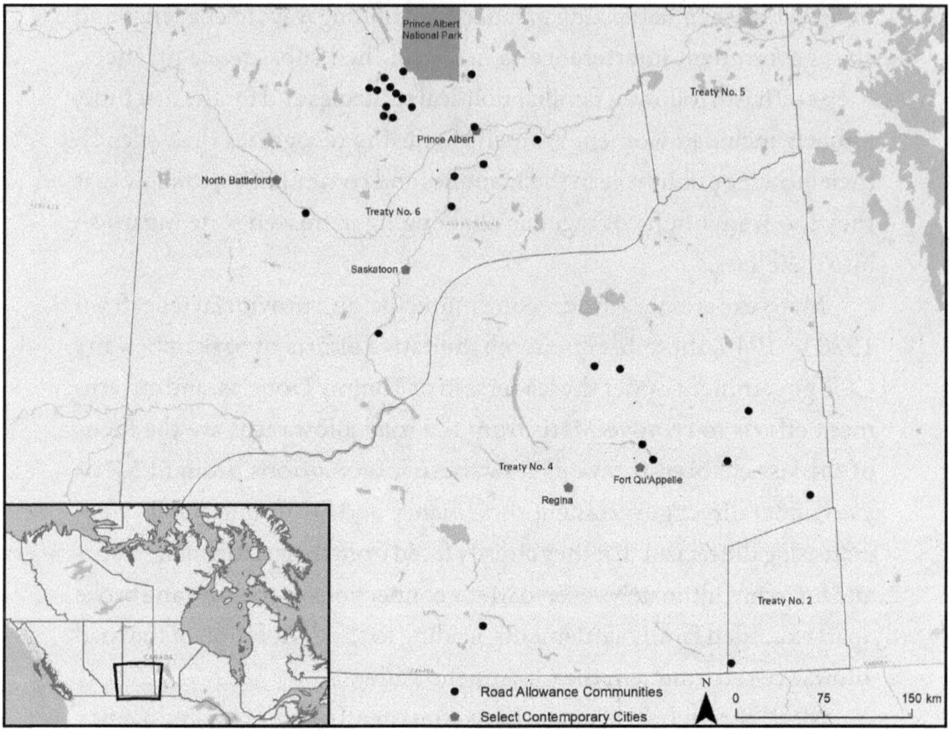

Figure 1. Road Allowance Communities in central and southern Saskatchewan to 1950 (select). Map courtesy of Cheryl Troupe and Matthew Kunkel.

Chapter 1

"Down There in the Valley": Introducing Bob and Margaret

STORIES ARE PLACE-BASED. They connect people to the places that are important to them. Stories define people's relationships to the land and explain their presence on it. Métis filmmaker and oral historian Christine Welsh argues that oral history and stories are "deeply rooted in the land; [they] provide a continuity that helps to nurture and sustain the people and their way of life. In it, we find the expression of their culture, values and worldview."[1] Similarly, anthropologist Keith Basso maintains that we can learn much about a people by how they speak about their familiar places.[2] In his work on the Western Apache, he asserts that "whenever community members speak about their landscape—whenever they name it and tell stories about it, they represent it in ways that are compatible with shared understandings of how they know themselves to occupy it."[3]

Stories give Indigenous peoples a sense of identity and belonging and situate them within their lineage, establishing their relationship with the rest of the natural world.[4] Place is central to how people share their stories

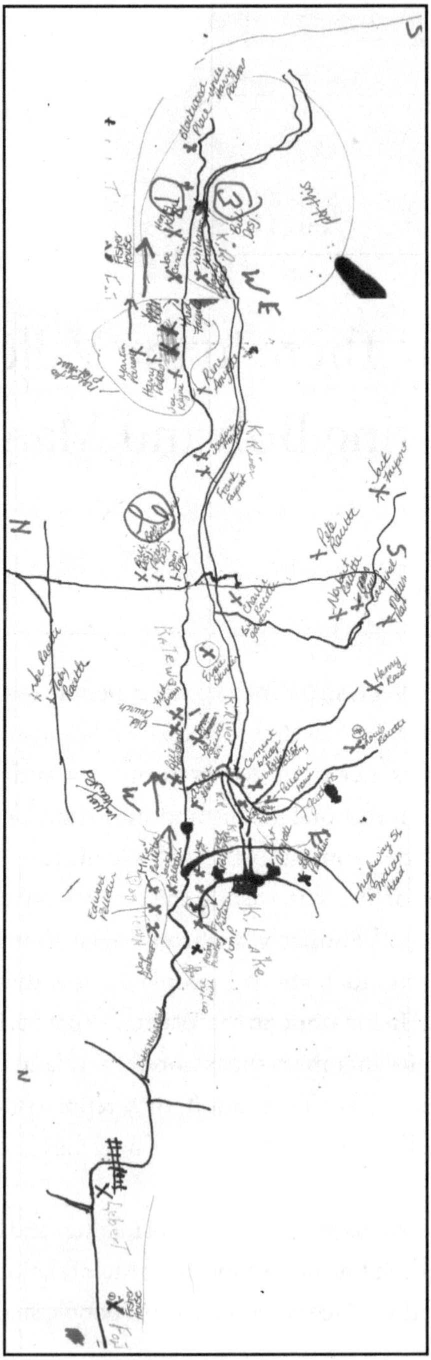

Figure 2. Bob Desjarlais's Map. Courtesy of Cheryl Troupe.

and understand themselves, their history, and their experiences within specific places. For those who grew up in the road allowance settlements along the four Qu'Appelle Lakes, their stories are permeated by themes of family, community, and the Valley landscape. Many stories regularly begin with the simple phrase, "down there in the Valley," as if locating both the storyteller and the listener in that space before the story begins.

My work on this book began with the stories of two Michif Li Vyeu from the Qu'Appelle Valley—Bob Desjarlais and Margaret Harrison.[5] During our time together, each gifted me a map of the Qu'Appelle Valley through which they shared their stories. Bob's map is a hand-drawn representation of the road allowance settlement at the east end of Katepwa Lake where he grew up. In red, blue, and black ink, he marked the location of relatives' homes as he remembered them. An accomplished textile artist, Margaret gifted me a hooked rag rug in 2014.[6] She practises Métis-style floral embroidery and is one of a few remaining Métis women who continue to make hooked rag rugs. Her mother, grandmother, and aunties were well-recognized artists in the Qu'Appelle Valley for their sewing work and hooked rugs, and they passed this expertise on to her. The rug is not in the typical Métis floral design but a pictorial of the Valley landscape and her home along the shore of Katepwa Lake. These maps are mnemonic devices for sharing Bob and Margaret's stories, helping anchor their stories to the landscape. Importantly, these place-based representations provide insights into resistance, resilience, agency, and kinship in Qu'Appelle Métis communities. My relationships with Bob and Margaret and the stories and maps they have shared are the foundation for the Qu'Appelle Valley history that follows.

I first met Bob Desjarlais in the early 2000s when I was working with the Gabriel Dumont Institute in Saskatoon, Saskatchewan. A colleague, Calvin Racette, suggested that I meet with his uncle Bob for a research project I was working on. A member of the extended Desjarlais and Racette family, Bob was a well-recognized storyteller amongst the Qu'Appelle Valley community and holder of cultural and community knowledge. He introduced me to the Qu'Appelle Valley. Bob's trust in

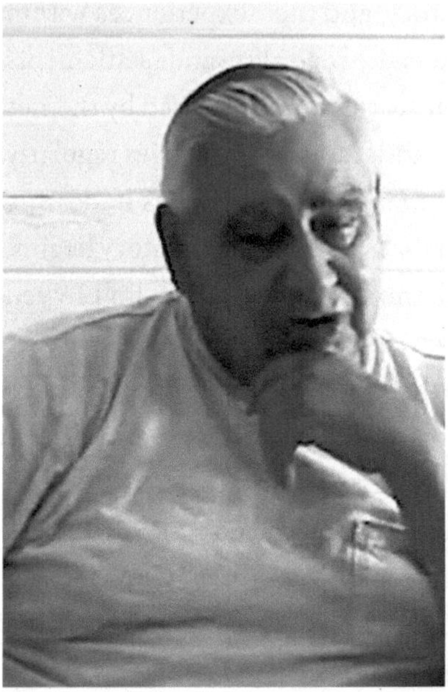

Figure 3. Bob Desjarlais. Image courtesy of Gabriel Dumont Institute Archives.

Figure 4. Margaret Pelletier Harrison. Photograph courtesy of Margaret Harrison.

Figure 5. Margaret Pelletier Harrison's Rug. Photograph courtesy of Cheryl Troupe.

Calvin facilitated our first visit to Bob's home and set the foundation for our relationship. Over the next three years, I spent time getting to know him, listening to stories of his family and community, and visiting places important to him, all the while asking questions, listening, and laughing. He passed away in 2004.

Bob always graciously shared his stories, and we developed a strong friendship. Often, as I listened to his soft voice, he would speak to me with an expression of Michif kinship, saying, "you know my girl, someone should write these stories down." Expressing the relationship between us and bringing me into his kinship circle, he shared his wish that I record his stories and family and community history. He gave me my assignment and permission to share his stories. I have a responsibility to tell them and care for them.

Bob gave me his map of the Katepwa Lake road allowance settlement in 2002 following a drive we had made through the Valley that summer.[7] As he spoke, I jotted down names and what bits of information I could. Bob's map represents the community as he remembered it growing up in the 1940s and 1950s. Using the map, he told stories of family and community history, kinship relationships, and cultural and land use practices. He also spoke of Métis resistance: not just familiar stories of the 1885 North-West Resistance but of how Métis from the road allowances in the Valley confronted and responded to economic, social, and political changes and the ongoing settler colonial intrusion into their lives.

Around this time, I also met and began working with Margaret Harrison. She also grew up in the Katepwa Lake road allowance community and was a member of the extended Pelletier, Racette, and Cardinal families. She and Bob are closely related: her mother, Adeline, and Bob's mother, Florence, were sisters. Like Bob, Margaret expressed her desire to share these stories and gave me permission to do so. In 2009, we hosted a traditional food harvesting and preparation workshop in Lebret as part of a diabetes prevention program I was facilitating for the Regina Qu'Appelle Health Region. Margaret opened the day with a prayer and spoke briefly about the efforts of women in her family and community.

Dedicating the day to "the women of the Valley," she named these women and spoke passionately about their contributions to their households and families. Honouring the memory of these women, Margaret read a short piece she had written:

> Some of the women who lived in the Métis road allowance community at Katepwa Lake from 1940–1955 included: Rosanna Parisien and her daughters Mary, Lorraine, Bernice, and Cecilia; Cora Pelletier and her daughter Ernestine; Vitaline Pelletier (Cardinal) and her daughters Philomene, Clara Wells, and Josephine; Adeline Pelletier and her daughters Mary and Margaret.
>
> We honour these women and remember their hard work to keep their families healthy. They gathered all kinds of berries: saskatoons, pin cherries, raspberries, strawberries, gooseberries, and chokecherries. They picked rose hips and wild mint for tea and many wild plants for their medicine. Their supplies spread throughout the Valley, so by wagon, buggy, or walking it took a bit of travel for women to do their gathering.
>
> These women worked hard every day. They had to haul water from a well near the lake and then some had to haul it back up the hill to where they lived. Rosanna and Cora hauled water from the lake to wash their clothes if there wasn't a lot of rainwater caught. Others lived close to the well and lake, but the walk to get simple drinking water was still a daily gathering.
>
> Whether it be the gathering of wood for their stove to cook, can, and preserve their fruit, crushing chokecherries with rocks, drying berries, stewing, or frying to enjoy for the season to come, they were always preparing for a new season.[8]

When she finished, she handed me the piece of paper she read from and, echoing Bob's words, shared her wish that I acknowledge these women for their hard work. This book is my attempt to share these stories in a respectful, humble, and meaningful way.

My relationships with Bob and Margaret evolved and are grounded in the practice of visiting, often around kitchen tables over food and pots of tea. Visiting—the practice of talking, conversing, and getting to know one another—should be viewed as a cultural and ethical protocol for Métis research.[9] It is a recognizable social practice in Métis communities that helps build, renew, and strengthen relationships. It is through visiting that trusting relationships are built and maintained. Visiting elevates Métis voices, allowing their words, stories, and experiences to be heard. As a research practice, it has the power to unsettle "historical inaccuracies about Indigenous people, such as their being lazy, dependent, uneducated, and worthless, and restores diplomacy by asserting an ethics of care, transparency, and accountability to our kinship relations."[10] The stories Bob, Margaret, and other Qu'Appelle Métis shared about themselves and their families demonstrate resistance and resilience, challenging and dismantling colonial systems that have historically oppressed Métis peoples.

Bob and I spent time visiting in a local coffee shop, driving around Fort Qu'Appelle to run errands, or just driving through the Qu'Appelle Valley sharing stories. Often, friends of his joined us at the coffee shop. Bob and his friends regularly teased me, and I'm sure they told some jokes and funny stories specifically for my benefit. Listening to them share their stories, I gained insight into a wider range of family and community stories and was able to develop personal relationships with other community members who also became my teachers. One of these was Bob's friend and cousin, George Klyne. George also grew up in the Valley and his recollections often added to and validated Bob's stories and vice versa.

My relationship with Margaret developed in much the same way. However, we also spent time together attending cultural events, picking berries, and driving through the Valley picking plants and medicines and visiting friends and relatives. I have called on her extensively as a cultural teacher in my personal and professional life. She has been an invaluable resource for me and a large part of my cultural learning. She taught me how to embroider, make hooked rugs, and prepare various traditional Métis foods. Margaret also shared valuable teachings about the significance of women in providing for their families, working hard, persevering and making do, parenting, childrearing, and taking care of their Old People.

These personal and research relationships are a central component of Indigenous research, where research sources can also be cultural teachers, requiring a level of commitment, trust, and respect that is often lifelong.[11] These relationships are rooted in getting to know one another and gaining a mutual entry into each other's lives. This may take the form of personal service or apprenticeship and may require that the student do their own cultural learning.[12] In her collection of Métis oral stories, *Stories of the Road Allowance People,* Maria Campbell describes her long-term personal commitment to her teachers not only through cultural protocols of offering tobacco and gifts, but "by being a helper or servant to the teachers" and by "re-learning and re-thinking [her] language."[13] To fully understand and share these stories, Campbell did her own cultural work to earn the trust and respect of her storyteller teachers. I strive to do the same.

Developing strong relationships with Bob, Margaret, and others in the Qu'Appelle Valley Métis community has taken time, commitment, and trust. It required my own cultural learning and engaging with this history through the lens of Métis values of family, community, and kinship. Bob passed away before I began the dissertation on which this book is based, but our time together continues to guide my research practice and cultural learning and is foundational to this work. Likewise, Margaret has been, and continues to be, one of my most significant teachers and mentors and remains an ongoing source of cultural teachings, knowledge, and community history.

There is an inherent responsibility in these relationships to be accountable and respectful and to be guided by reciprocity. This includes being mindful of and how I care for, share, and protect the stories shared with me. Not all stories are for the public; some are sensitive and difficult to tell and unsettling to hear. But, sometimes, this complexity is what makes them important to tell. I have sought guidance and direction about how to share difficult and potentially unsettling stories. I have made decisions, in conversation with storytellers, their families, and my own cultural teachers, about what stories should be, or more importantly, should not be, shared. It is my responsibility to uphold the wishes of those I am in relation with. This has been a process of renegotiation, double-checking, and checking in, and has involved frank conversations about how to balance being both an insider and outsider to this research. As a Métis woman, an insider, it has been essential for me to think critically about the processes and relationships created during this research, and how to capture and present data according to culturally appropriate, responsive, and meaningful ways. As an outsider to the Qu'Appelle Valley, I must be equally mindful of these considerations and acknowledge that I do not have an insider's first-hand connection to these stories and spaces.

Conversations with storytellers and their families and community members directed me to interview individuals recognized as holding particular family, local, and community knowledge important for this research. As a result, decisions about interviewees and what elements of Qu'Appelle Métis histories to include or exclude were driven by the community.[14] I recreated family genealogies to help identify individuals, family groupings, and community formation patterns and processes over time and place into the mid-twentieth century. Genealogical reconstruction is a framework used to detail families and communities and is increasingly employed by scholars to explore Métis social, economic, and cultural traditions, examine gender, and ground individuals and histories in specific families, communities, and spaces.[15] Locating oneself this way is a well-recognized and culturally appropriate practice among the Métis, and arguably all Indigenous peoples, to understand one's relation to their communities.

To complement these stories and genealogies, I used Historical Geographic Information Systems (HGIS) methodologies, a computer-based approach that organizes different types of data with a geographic indicator or a land location, to create maps and examine and analyze patterns. I created a HGIS dataset from archival records to spatially analyze and map individual, family, and community demographics, movement, economic activity, and land use and tenure in specific geographic locations at multiple points across time.[16] These methods allow me to tell place-based stories and visually demonstrate spatial understandings and connections to specific places. They demonstrate the cultural, historical, and contemporary associations with place that existed and still exist for these families. This is particularly important for telling Indigenous stories and oral histories that are deeply rooted in local landscapes and that connect us to our families, communities, culture, values, and worldviews.

I combine these stories, genealogies, archival data, and maps in a process called "deep mapping" to reveal meanings embedded in specific places.[17] Deep mapping is the detailed collection and layering of different types of data that moves beyond conventional two-dimensional maps by asking, not only what is in a place but also why, how, and whose experiences have created a *sense* of place. Deep mapping captures how people think about space and how they create meaning about specific places. It connects multiple and varied stories of specific places, representing diverse perspectives, revealing how different individuals and groups have thought about these places at different points in time, and allowing for the construction of intersecting spatial stories about important places.

Grounding Bob's Map

Having spent his formative years on the Katepwa Lake road allowance, Bob Desjarlais told stories that focused largely on his family and memories of growing up in the Valley. He spoke at length about kinship relationships, how these families spatially organized themselves, their social and cultural practices, and the economic history of his own family and broader Valley community. Central to Bob's extended family grouping were female kinship relationships where women played strong, crucial roles, particularly around food production and harvesting. Families grew large gardens, harvested wild plants, and fished and hunted small game. While women were mostly responsible for the gardens, men helped with preparing the ground for planting and children pulled weeds and hauled water. Women processed, prepared, and preserved food—contributing significantly to the family diet. They were also responsible for ensuring food was shared among the community, with older women often directing the male hunters when to hunt so that the Old People would not go hungry. These complementary roles for men and women echoed the division of labour when families hunted buffalo on the plains, suggesting that they relied on traditional practices and understandings in how they related to their environment. Bob spoke about particular women, such as his Koohkoom Maross and Koohkoom Flora, healers and midwives whose roles in the family and community, and the way they navigated the Valley in search of plants and medicines, served to claim these places as Métis spaces.[18] His stories tell of Métis values, community practices, protocols, and responsibilities to one another, while demonstrating the persistence of cultural values and kinship responsibilities in sharing resources.

The relationship between kinship and place is significant. In our first interview, I asked Bob a question regarding his genealogy—what were his parents' names? He gave them and with no further prompting from me went on to use kinship relationships to identify individuals according to where they lived in relation to his household. He would remember stories and events; for instance, in describing where he grew up, Bob began this way: "Down in Katepwa. . . . Down in the Valley, in the Valley that is where I lived. Grandpa Charlie Racette and Grandma Maross used to live across the bridge from us, we lived on the north side of the Valley, and they lived on the south side of the Valley. Grandpa Norbert, they lived a little further down the Valley, and his family, they were all pretty well born there. But Grandpa Charlie Racette and them, there's a few of them older ones that were probably born in the reserve."[19] Where people lived in relation to Bob and his kinship relationship with them featured prominently in his stories. Through mapping and naming, Bob recalled places, events, and kinship relationships that defined the bounds of his family and community across physical space.

Bob used kinship and place to explain how the Métis used and occupied the Valley landscape. Here's a story Bob shared about his grandmother picking medicine:

> My old grandfather and grandmother lived on top of the hill, and she used to go up on the hill there, and I thought once in a while she was out there digging wild turnip, but it wasn't wild turnip she was after, she was after medicines. She would walk all over them hills and in the coulees looking for medicines. She used to walk, and she was fairly old already. . . . That was Koohkoom Maross, we called her. That was Grandpa Charlie Racette's wife. Grandpa Norbert Racette was Charlie's brother, you see Koohkoom Maross was a Bellegarde from File Hills, Little Black Bear.[20]

This simple story of how Bob's grandmother collected medicine in the Valley conveys a sense of place and relatedness, and grounds the storyteller in their local landscape.

This story also provides insight into cultural practices of naming older community members as grandparents, aunts, and uncles, regardless of whether they were in fact immediate relations. "Grandpa Norbert" and "Grandpa Charlie" were brothers of Bob's paternal grandfather, Louis Racette. This naming of kinship relationships helps to define the bounds of this community and demonstrates connections to other communities. In this instance, it draws a kinship relationship between the Katepwa road allowance to individuals from Little Black Bear Reserve in the nearby File Hills north of the Valley.

Recognizing the significance of kinship in Bob's stories, I pieced together a genealogy of families and individuals based on the names he had mentioned during his interviews. The sheer number of relatives he discussed and the complexity with which he described these kinship patterns demonstrated that "who one is related to" was important to how Bob understood himself. His stories recognize the importance of kinship relationships and the roles and responsibilities of community members in looking after one another. As kinship relationships were central to Métis values, individuals acted in the spirit of family to ensure the well-being of the entire community.

Although I had two very rich sources—Bob's stories and his map—I knew that one was incomplete without the other. Relationships to the land take many forms; as I recreated a family genealogy to determine kinship relationships, I sought to trace this community's relationship to the land. Stories and historical and archival documents provide evidence of this relationship. By deep mapping, I can plot out these overlapping spatial and familial relationships. Bob's stories provide layers of meaning about the Valley landscape, the people who lived there, and the ways they used and occupied the space. The map's layered meaning provides an idea of the spatial and social organization of this community. Locating some of the places described in Bob's stories required knowing more about land use in this environment in order to accurately reproduce the map and verify its contents. When Bob passed away, I worked with others to enhance his map.

Working with other community members to incorporate additional maps allowed us to make a composite rendering of Bob's map to corroborate its contents, pinpoint locations, and expand the scope of stories and land-use activities. Using large maps drawn on paper and a handheld Global Positioning Systems (GPS) technology, I documented and verified individual, family, and community land-use activities and mapped kinship relationships and patterns of community formation. GPS technology uses satellites to identify precise locations according to geographical coordinates and my handheld device allowed pinpoint accuracy of

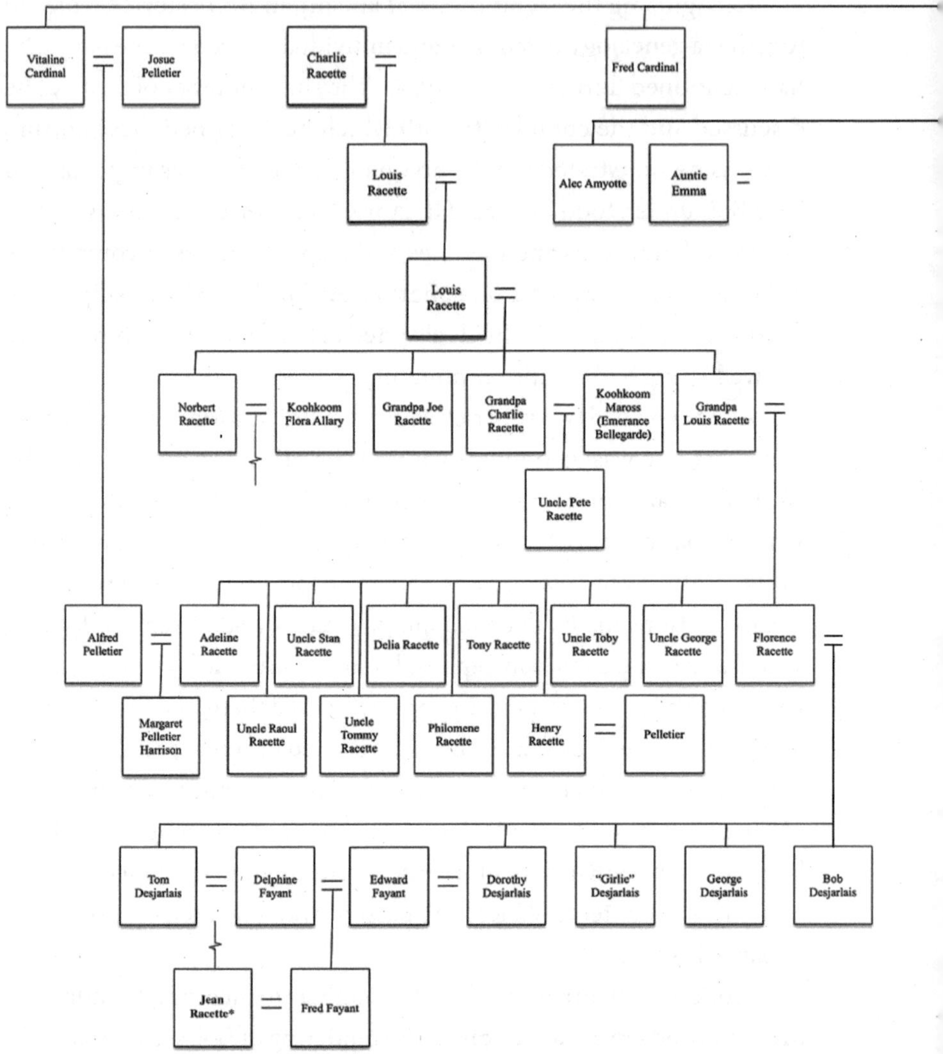

*Jean Racette is the child of Norbert Racette and Koohkoom Flora Allary

Figure 6. Bob Desjarlais's Genealogy (as mentioned in his interview). Courtesy of Cheryl Troupe.

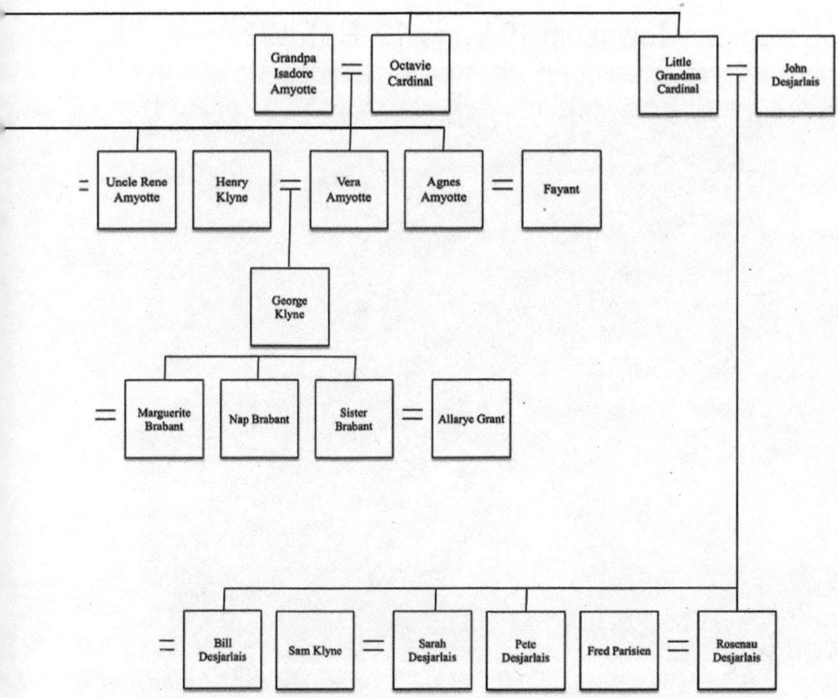
Grandpa Isadore Amyotte
Octavie Cardinal
Little Grandma Cardinal
John Desjarlais
Uncle Rene Amyotte
Henry Klyne
Vera Amyotte
Agnes Amyotte
Fayant
George Klyne
Marguerite Brabant
Nap Brabant
Sister Brabant
Allarye Grant
Bill Desjarlais
Sam Klyne
Sarah Desjarlais
Pete Desjarlais
Fred Parisien
Rosenau Desjarlais

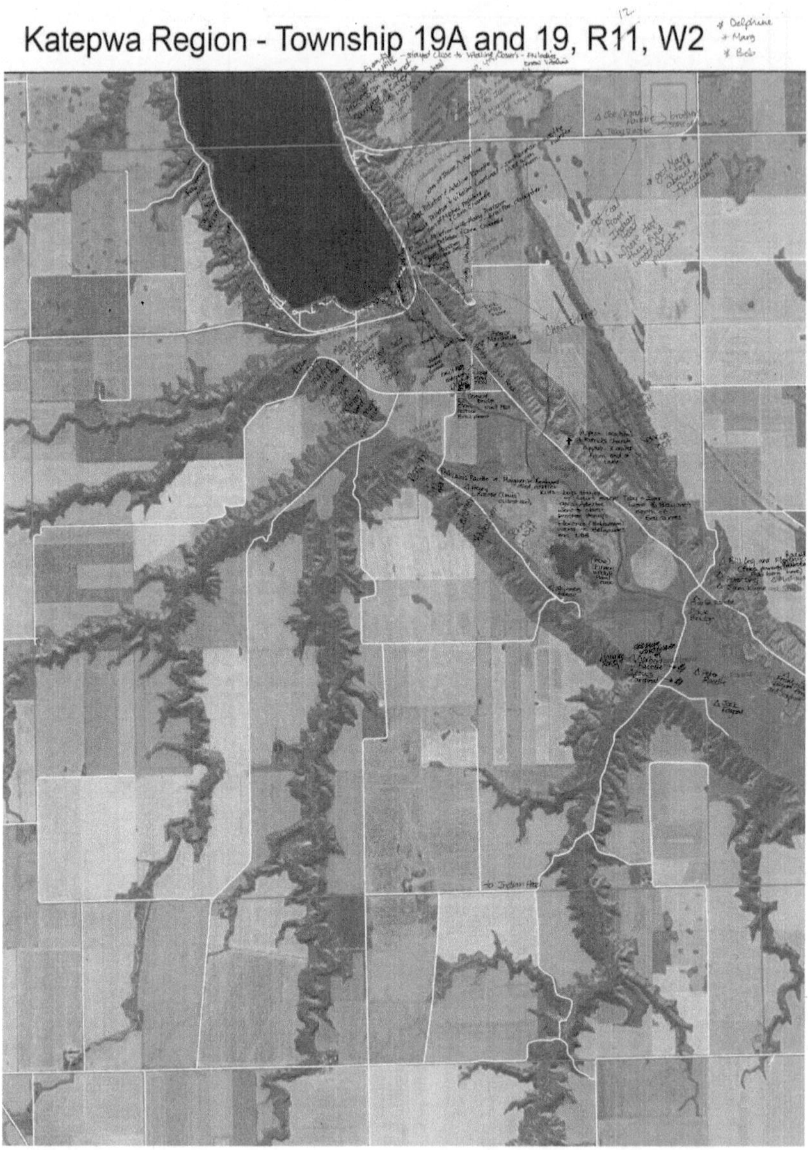

Figure 7. Bob, Margaret, and Delphine's Map. Courtesy of Cheryl Troupe.

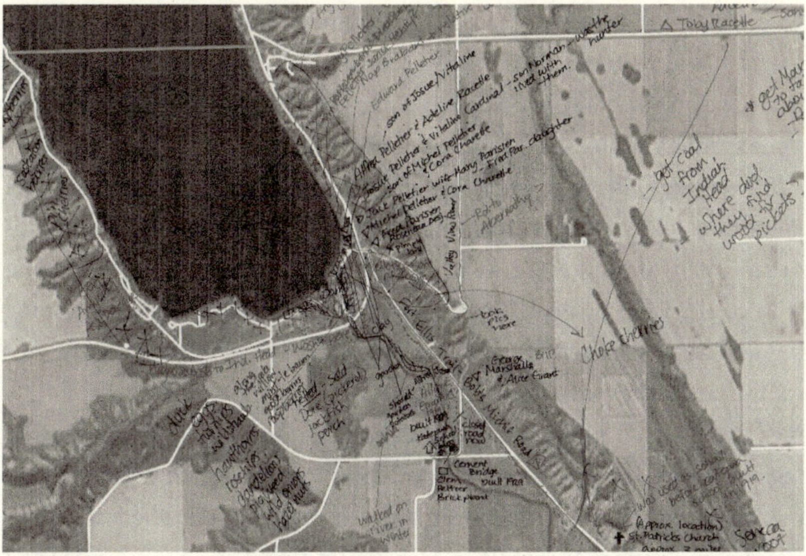

Figure 8. Detail of Bob, Margaret, and Delphine's Map. Courtesy of Cheryl Troupe.

specific places or points according to their longitudinal and latitudinal coordinates. Interviews with Katepwa community members and Bob's relatives Margaret Harrison and Delphine Fayant Desjarlais were crucial in confirming and adding further layers of stories to Bob's map.

As Bob's stories had served as place-based narratives, both Delphine and Margaret also used place to organize their stories. Delphine grew up towards the east end of the Valley and married Tom Desjarlais, Bob's brother.[21] Her maternal grandparents were Florence Allary and Norbert Racette. Florence is the grandmother that Bob refers to as Koohkoom Flora. Norbert was brother of Bob's maternal grandfather Louis Pelletier dit Racette. Unlike my first interview with Bob, Delphine's interview took place not on the land but at her home. Margaret and I visited Delphine who, now with impaired vision, recited from memory the spatial organization of the road allowance community where her family lived. Together we mapped stories related to extended family and community land-use activities, wherein families gathered food, picked berries, fished, and where men laboured for farmers. Delphine described the work of her grandmother Florence similarly to how Bob described Koohkoom Maross, as a respected medicine woman and midwife who traversed the Valley and its coulees picking medicines.

Margaret Harrison grew up living in a cluster of homes along the lakeshore. I have spent much time listening to and recording her stories of family history and of growing up in the Valley.[22] She was someone who could not only walk (and drive) the land to help verify Bob's map but add her own layers of meaning. Margaret spoke at length about her mother and aunt's work producing hooked rugs. The women in her family made rugs that her father and uncle would sell across the Valley, bringing additional income into the home. She told how each sister covered one side of the Valley as sales territory to keep peace in the family and avoid competition. Margaret and I spatially represented these extended family and community formation practices within the cluster of houses along the lake, but also between clusters further down the Valley. We also mapped long-lost physical and built spaces, including the Katepwa School, church, bridges, and roads, and documented stories associated with each of these places. We also spent many hours talking about and mapping stories related to berry picking, gardening, fishing, and food preparation, preservation, and consumption. What Bob started, Margaret and Delphine verified, collaboratively creating a detailed map of the Katepwa Lake road allowance community, and demonstrating a rich cultural, social, and economic landscape of Métis experience.

Reading Margaret's Map

A few months after Margaret and I physically walked the land, she gifted me a handmade hooked rug depicting her Katepwa road allowance home. Her artistic rug making is both a historical practice that ties her to this place and a contemporary mnemonic device that allows her to remember and share. Her gift acts as both a mental and a geographic map that she created to share stories about growing up in the Valley, the places

Figure 9. Vitaline Cardinal and Josue Pelletier. Photograph courtesy of Margaret Harrison.

she knew, the work that women did, and the foods they grew, harvested, and prepared.

The scene in her rug depicts her family home, describing where they lived "snugged in close along the lakeshore" at the east end of Katepwa Lake.[23] A tight-knit community where all the families were directly related, they often shared resources and spent time working and socializing together. Although the only home represented in the rug is her own, she shared many stories about her paternal grandparents Josue Pelletier and Vitaline Cardinal, who lived next to Margaret and her parents. She also shared stories of aunts, uncles, and cousins who also lived along the lake.

Margaret spoke about her own home and that of her grandparents. Both faced south, overlooking the lake, while on the north side was the road. Between the road and the house, they had a large garden. On the east side of the house there were a few large trees that she believes someone must have planted. She has included one of these trees in the foreground of the rug and thinks it may have been a black poplar. Next to the house, she has included a small outbuilding, an outdoor toilet. However, they also had a barn, located behind the house, where they kept their two horses, wagon, and sleigh. She recounted that it was difficult to keep enough hay to feed the horses and so her father pastured and moved them around to ensure they had enough feed. They regularly relied on her uncle Raoul, who worked for a local farmer, to supply them with hay.

Margaret also shared stories about her grandfather's smokehouse and her grandmother's summer kitchen. The smokehouse stored food and was where fish were hung and smoked. It also served as a shed where her grandfather kept his tools and horse tack. The summer kitchen was a small outdoor space shaded by trees where her grandmother and mother did their cooking, food preservation, and domestic work. Each summer, her grandmother had a cookstove hauled outside so that its use did not heat up the house. She recalled that separate buildings were commonly used as summer kitchens by many families in the area. Her grandmother, however, preferred cooking outdoors. Margaret recalled that there was also a table where she made bread when it was too hot inside. Margaret also remembered regularly eating outdoors in the summer. There was a large rose bush beside the house, which brought her fond memories and prompted stories of her mother, Adeline. Roses were Adeline's favourite and one of the main floral designs she used to decorate her hooked rugs.

Margaret's parents kept lake water in a steel barrel on the porch to be used for washing and hauled drinking water from a well. Her grandmother always had a big washstand, pail, and basin ready for washing, and a dipper hung on a nail on the wall. There was always hot water in a kettle on the stove and in a boiler on the side of her mother's cookstove. Her mother worked hard to maintain the woodpile close to the house. As kids, Margaret and her siblings helped haul wood as well as water from the lake for laundry, which they always did on Mondays. They heated water on the stove and then cleaned clothes using a scrub board in a washtub. On Tuesday, her mother and grandmother did the ironing, using the stove to heat up the irons. They ironed tablecloths, pillowcases, and all types of clothing, including men's white shirts that were worn to the Catholic church on Sunday. On Saturday, women did the baking, making pies, bread, and bannock. Margaret recalled that they rarely had more than two or three bread tins and would also use large jam pails, or whatever kind of pail they had, that could fit into the oven. Margaret's rug depicts a clothesline with freshly washed clothes hanging on it, also representative of women's work. A patchwork quilt in the scene prompts Margaret to share about how women in her family saved all the rags and old clothes to repurpose into blankets and rugs.

Vegetable gardens and equipment used to work the land are also depicted. Margaret described large gardens on the north side of their house between it and the road, where they predominantly grew root vegetables such as potatoes, turnips, and carrots. These vegetables were important in Métis diets because they could be stored easily and for long periods of time, usually through the winter. They also had a smaller garden where they grew vegetables like radishes, beans, and lettuce. As kids, it was their job to do the weeding and haul water for watering. They didn't have many tools for working the land, but she remembers her dad breaking the ground with a team of horses, trying to churn the hard dirt to prepare it for planting. In the rug's background, Margaret has depicted the Valley hillside and coulees, conveying stories about the wheres, whens, and hows of harvesting plants, berries, and medicines. Trees represent the various types of berries, such as saskatoons and chokecherries, that they picked.

This map reflects Margaret's identity, family, and community history. She uses this rug to spatially document her family home, outbuildings, and gardens in relation to the lake and Valley resources. She has also included symbolic aspects of her history. Four flowers on the border represent the floral pattern that she and female kin used on their hooked rugs, while the crosses in the upper corners reflect the significance of the Catholic Church in Margaret's life and community more broadly. To the right of the house, she has included an infinity symbol, a contemporary symbol of Métis nationalism and cultural pride. And so, just as Bob's hand-drawn map depicted his understanding of family and community, so does Margaret's rug. This is her map of the Valley and with it she articulates her understanding of who she is and where she comes from.

Bringing together her rug, Bob's hand-drawn map, the large paper maps, and the place-based stories shared in oral history interviews, I have attempted to layer these resources to create new digital maps. First, I mapped the spatial organization of families identifying several family-based clusters. Close family connections within each cluster, but also kinship connections between clusters, are evident—as first demonstrated in Bob's map and explained more fully through his stories. Once mapped, there appeared to be a large empty space between family clusters. This space fell in the middle of the Valley in what is now a marshy area. But in the early to mid-twentieth century, this was prime agricultural land farmed by the Skinner family. English settlers, Thomas Skinner and his family had come to the Qu'Appelle Valley in 1882. He and his sons, as they came of age, took up homestead land and by the early twentieth century, the family was considered one of the region's largest landowners.[24] Throughout this period the Skinners were known to regularly employ Métis labour. The practice continued as Bob related that Thomas's sons Ernest "Ernie" and Frederick regularly hired Métis men as a seasonal labour force well into the 1940s.[25] By mapping Skinner's land alongside Métis residences, a pattern emerged that placed Métis residences on the periphery of settler land. This also explains the two residences seemingly removed from the family clusters in the Valley. These were individuals who worked for the Skinner family, and thus lived close to their job, but who remained within their extended family network in the Valley. What the map does not reflect, however, are the temporary camps of families of farm labourers who moved closer to the fields during harvest season, sometimes for days, weeks, or months at a time, living in tents. For those living in these temporary camps, work was a communal activity where all members had roles to fill. Men's and women's roles were complementary and supportive of one another. Men worked in the fields, picking rocks, potatoes, or stooking wheat, women often worked alongside them, while the grandparents and older children stayed in the camps to watch the younger children and prepare food.[26]

When mapping land use, a clearer picture of the Valley environment emerges. Métis harvested all kinds of berries and hazelnuts from the bushes that lined the lakes, river, and the Valley coulees. Bob, Margaret, and many other Métis shared stories of entire families going berry picking, hoping to collect enough to store for the winter. Once fruit was gathered, children helped the women to crush and dry the chokecherries into little patties. Margaret pointed out places where berries were found and suggested that there was some recognition and respect for berry patches as being within the territories of certain aunties and old ladies in Margaret's family. The locations of these good berry patches were often, in jest, kept secret from others. Interviews with Métis throughout the larger Valley region support the idea that certain berry patches were the special territories of aunties and older ladies. However, it is likely that memories of these places became associated with specific women who considered these places their favourite spots and not because it was their exclusive harvesting territory.[27]

Men hunted deer and small game on the Valley hillsides and in the coulees. Delphine recalled that on the top of a hill her father would set snares for partridges and prairie chickens. Bob described his first hunting experiences where he learned the ethics and protocols of hunting, particularly about making tobacco offerings, when not to hunt certain animals, and around respecting mating season and pregnant animals and their young. By following these guidelines, he understood that he was acting within a Métis worldview that privileged relationships to human kin but also relationships with animals, the landscape, and the Valley environment.

The coulees were also where families picked Seneca root that was then dried and sold, as well as where the old ladies harvested medicines and other wild plants. Bob recalled his Koohkoom Maross often walked the coulees picking medicines while Delphine shared that she and her siblings accompanied their mother and grandmother, helping to dig for plants and medicines and learning about the Valley environment. These women shared their knowledge and skills across families and the larger Métis community. These families, in turn, shared food with Maross in exchange for her services.

When asked about the use of the Qu'Appelle Lakes and river, Bob and Margaret both spoke about the plenitude of fish caught and how families relied on fish for the winter. Men and women fished year-round, but during the fall, they netted fish in large quantities and hung them on drying racks before packing them in gunnysacks for future use. Speaking fondly about the tasty fresh fish of their youths, both Bob and Margaret said they no longer trusted that the fish in the Qu'Appelle Lakes or the river were good to eat. When asked about where on the lake people fished, Margaret noted that the dam where Katepwa Lake entered the Qu'Appelle River had always been a particularly lucky spot to fish.[28] This was also a good spot for men to hunt ducks and for children to gather duck eggs.

When mapping land use around the lake and river, Delphine and Margaret talked about the distance that had to be covered to fetch water. Stories suggest that up to a quarter mile was a terribly long distance for Delphine's young, short legs. Margaret also spoke about picking plants along the shore, like wild mint for a tea they called *la baum,* and she also talked about a large spot at the east end of the lake where clay was gathered. Margaret was not exactly sure what the clay was used for but recalled that her grandparents gathered it. Likely this clay, when mixed with grasses, served as chinking in log houses. This was an annual activity, done each spring. Although Bob did not speak about the clay bed, he talked at length about his uncle, Clem Peltier, who had a brick plant not far from the Katepwa School. Peltier made bricks there and distributed them throughout the Valley and the region. It is possible that Peltier accessed raw materials from the same or a similar clay bed.

This brick plant was one of the physical built spaces that we mapped and that held Métis stories. Others included the Katepwa School, attended by many of the community's children, and the trails and bridges used when walking to and from their relatives.[29] We also mapped and named roads built by Métis as part of relief projects in the 1930s. Bob shared a great deal about the work that his father, uncles, and cousins did in building these roads. I renamed the Fort Ellice Trail the Michif Road, according to the name Bob used for this road.

Geographically rooting these stories in the landscape explains Métis social, cultural, and economic activities as well as their values, community practices, protocols, and mutual responsibilities to one another. Mapping these stories grounds these families in their territory and makes the Qu'Appelle Valley a Métis place. The families who made up the Katepwa Lake road allowance community lived according to a worldview defined by their extended family networks, the responsibility individuals had to their immediate and extended family, and their relation to the geography and landscape.

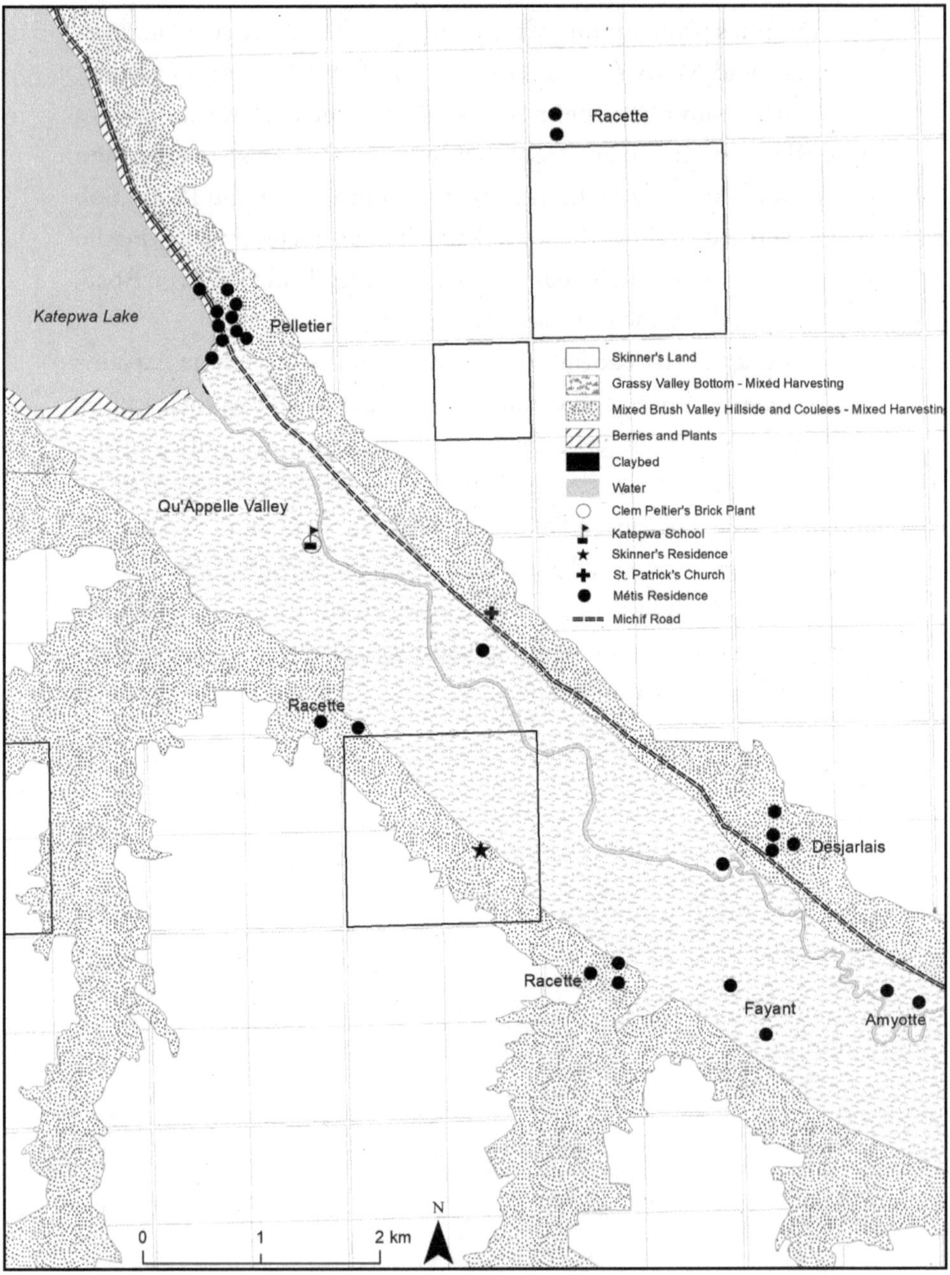

Figure 10. Katepwa Lake Road Allowance Residency Patterns and Land Use, 1930s–1950. Map courtesy of Cheryl Troupe and Matthew Kunkel.

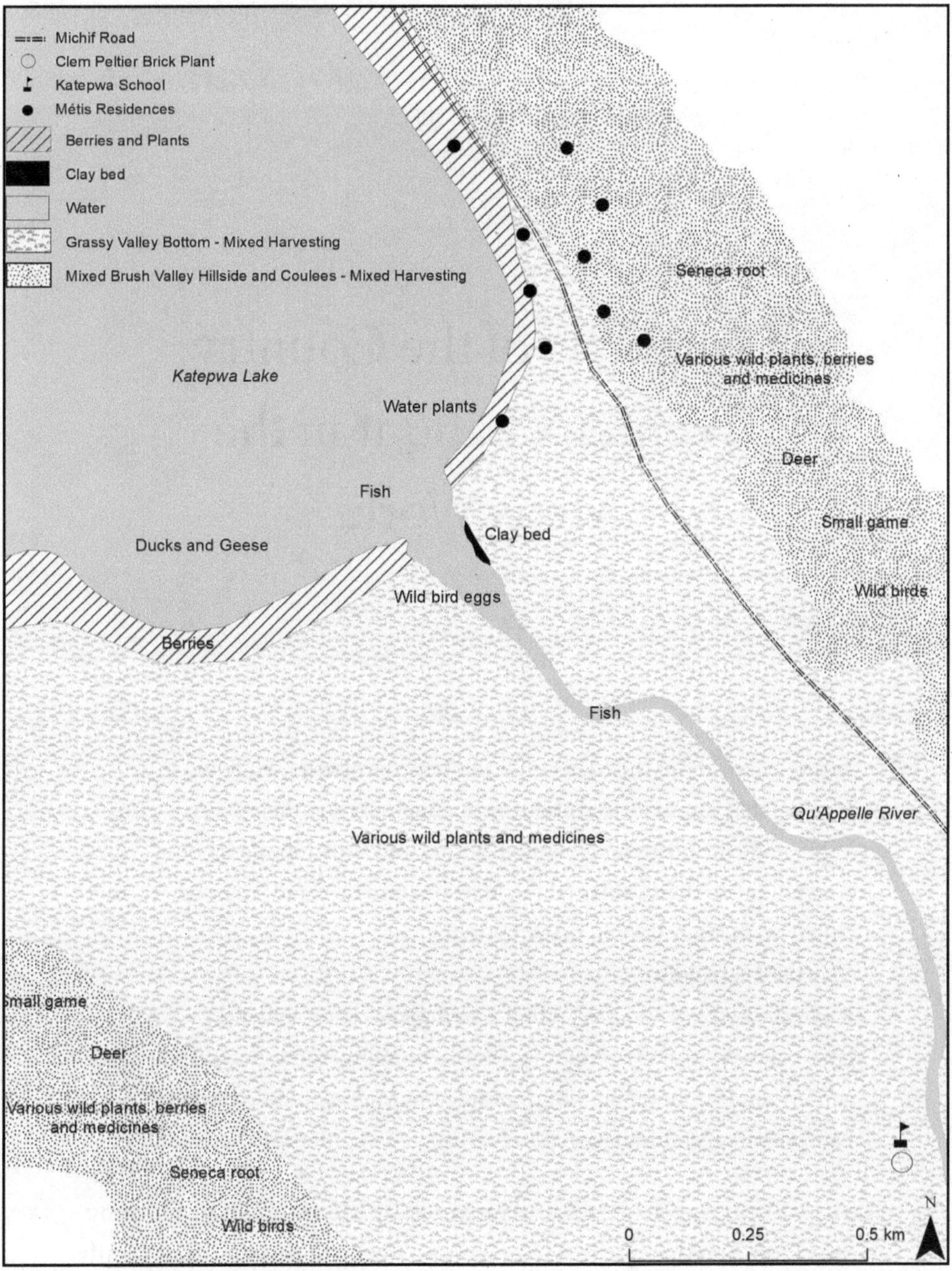

Figure 11. Detail, Katepwa Lake Road Allowance Residency Patterns and Land Use, 1930s–1950. Map courtesy of Cheryl Troupe and Matthew Kunkel.

Chapter 2

Daughters of the Country: Women's Labour in the Métis World

> You've heard about the Métis men and how they lived their lives
> It's time that someone told about their daughters and their wives
> Who made the meals and mended clothes and kept a spotless home
> And tended to their babies while their sons and husbands roamed
> And who did they have to thank for that?
> May I tell you bluntly?
> It was those shawl-wearing, rabbit-snaring, moccasin-making,
> bannock-baking, floor-mopping, wood-chopping, snowshoe-mending,
> garden-tending, berry-finding, pemmican-grinding, hide-cleaning,
> hair-preening, child-rearing, persevering... Daughters of The Country![1]

THESE LYRICS, WRITTEN and recorded by Métis musician and songwriter Don Freed, capture Métis women's critical roles in their family economy, and social and political networks in the nineteenth century. They also provide a glimpse into women's gendered responsibilities during the journey across the plains for the seasonal buffalo hunt. Women's labour and expertise in food production and preservation were crucial for the success in the buffalo hunt and trade. Women processed vast amounts of buffalo meat and hides, for both personal consumption and trade. They contributed necessary skill and labour to the Hudson's Bay Company (HBC) posts that employed their husbands and to the social, economic, and political networks within which they operated. As the buffalo herds declined and Métis economies changed, women's influence increased as their importance in food production and family maintenance grew.

By the early nineteenth century, the fur trade increasingly relied on pemmican as its main food supply.[2] It was an energy-dense food—containing between 3,200 and 3,500 calories per pound—that fed an extensive network of fur traders and voyageurs across the west, and the fur trading society that developed around its trade, use, and distribution.[3] Although pemmican was made from meat of various large game, and even fish, it was pemmican made from buffalo that fuelled the fur trade. Pemmican involved drying the meat until it was brittle enough to pound into flakes, which were then mixed with melted fat or tallow to form a paste. Berries were added for flavour and extra nutrients. The hot mixture was poured into airtight leather bags and sewn up to prevent spoilage.[4] Each bag could hold close to 100 pounds of pemmican. Called a bull, or taureau, these bags of pemmican stored easily, lasted a long time, and were highly portable, making them well suited for transport and trade.

Buffalo robes and hides were the main object of Indigenous hunters on the southern Great Plains, but pemmican was the commodity sought by Indigenous hunters on the northern plains, including the Métis.[5] The pemmican trade informed Indigenous decision-making and ultimately shaped hunting strategies. As the pemmican and robe market expanded, prices rose, encouraging increased hunting and different hunting strategies. The Métis adapted their hunts to meet market demands, integrating themselves into the system as producers, traders, and consumers, and made decisions based on market changes.

Following the 1821 merger of the HBC and the North West Company, the HBC restructured, cut costs, reassessed its purchasing policies, reduced its labour force, and closed posts. The HBC's ensuing monopoly reformed the provisions trade and drove prices down, limiting Indigenous peoples' economic opportunities. A steady and increasing local market for buffalo in Red River and the Métis' growing reliance on European goods such as guns and ammunition encouraged them to hunt more. The subsequent failure of agriculture and famine in the Red River Settlement from 1825 to 1827 were also factors that encouraged Métis hunting, increasing the size of their annual hunts to produce more pemmican.[6] In the decades following the merger, markets continued to change, shifting towards trade in tallow, buffalo tongues, and robe production, motivating the Métis to expand beyond pemmican production and into the American robe trade in the 1830s.[7]

Increased market demand encouraged the Métis production of buffalo robes and pemmican. By the 1840s, Métis buffalo hunts were huge and highly organized, including over 1,000 Red River carts, 1,500 people, 1,000 horses (both buffalo runners and cart horses), and 500 draught oxen.[8] They generally engaged in two large hunts per year: in summer and late fall or early winter. The summer hunt was oriented towards the market and producing pemmican for trade, while the fall or early winter hunt was for robe production and meat for Métis subsistence. As the size and scale of the robe trade increased, the Métis began engaging in a third smaller fall hunt to specifically secure for themselves winter food supplies.[9]

The Métis were increasingly being drawn into the world of European mercantile capitalism with the buffalo hunt and robe production, which relied heavily on women's labour.[10] By the 1850s, they had carved out an economic niche for themselves supplying pemmican and robes to the HBC and American fur posts further south. Métis traders not in the employ of the HBC acted as "freemen" or "free traders," trading outside the Company's monopoly and asserting their independence.

For the Métis, buffalo hunting was a subsistence activity, a socio-economic endeavour, and demonstration of political autonomy. Hunt organization reflected their understandings of the landscape and its resources and dictated how families arranged themselves to best strategically utilize environmental assets. During the summer and early fall, buffalo herds were large as they moved out from parkland areas onto the plains to feed. During the winter, they broke off into smaller herds, moving back into parkland areas to find food, water, and shelter.[11] Grasslands could support larger herds compared to the parklands. So, as the buffalo herds shifted in size and scale when moving across the plains, so too did the brigades of Métis buffalo hunters who pursued them.

Métis social and family structures, and by extension communities, were instrumental to their economic success. Like other band societies, Métis families lived in extended family groupings and hunted along kinship lines created largely through intermarriage. These Métis hunting "brigades" allowed for flexibility in coming together in response to labour demands when resources were plentiful during the hunts. This way, the Métis worked together to make their livelihoods, create and strengthen kinship relationships, and solidify their social, economic, and political bonds. Brigades varied in size but could number up to about twenty-five interrelated nuclear families.[12] In many instances, kinship relationships between women bound these brigades together.[13] Hunting as a group, they moved in a seasonal rotation from places such as White Horse Plains, Red River, and Pembina on to the western plains following the herds.[14] Hunting together was of economic necessity dictated by the size of the herds and because pemmican and robe production was labour intensive. Living, travelling, and hunting together also created opportunity to reinforce bonds of friendship and strengthen kinship ties; this was an economic lifestyle, grounded in Métis social structures. Indeed, reliance on kinship relationships and reliance on mobility are markers of Métis identity.[15]

Hunts were significant social, economic, and political undertakings, with elected leadership, strict rules of governance, and gendered roles and responsibilities. A high degree of organization was necessary due to the number of people involved and because of the threat of attack by competing Indigenous hunters. Men hunted, protected the camp, and filled leadership roles, while women processed the meat and hides, prepared food, and cared for the family. Although gendered, men's and women's work was complementary, equally valued, and conducted to best meet the family's needs.

Individual experience, skill, and ability determined roles and responsibilities. Appointed by consensus with authority understood and respected, formal leadership usually lasted only for the duration of a specific hunt. Despite this transience, the influence and respect leaders garnered ensured that they acted as buffalo hunt chiefs or captains in successive annual hunts. The chief's reputation in supplying robes and provisions to the HBC was also a significant factor. After 1821, the HBC sought out hunters like Cuthbert Grant and others from White Horse Plains, who were seen as reputable and reliable, giving them preferential treatment and generous credit.[16] Consequently, it was not only their skill and experience but also their standing with the HBC, connections, and market access that afforded buffalo hunt chiefs their positions.

Hunt organization reinforced shared responsibility for governing, leading, guiding, and protecting the camp. In addition to the hunt chiefs or captains, guides or mounted scouts located the herds and led the party to them. They served on a rotating basis, selected for their experience and knowledge of the plains landscape.[17] The captain and other men organized the nightly camp, ensuring that all carts and individual encampments were in the proper place with guards taking turns protecting the horses and camp each evening.[18] At night, the Métis placed their carts in a large circle for protection, with wheel hubs side by side and trams pointing outward. These were important defensive measures to protect the Métis in their long-standing dispute with the Dakota.

Prior to embarking, parties agreed to formal and practical laws to govern the hunt. These laws reveal the social and moral codes used to ensure safety, harmony, respect, and order while travelling and hunting together. The laws regulated individual and group behaviour so as not to jeopardize the success of the collective and included strict consequences for disobedience. The laws governing the 1840 hunt prohibited hunting on Sunday, demonstrating the importance of continued religious observance for the devoutly Roman Catholic Métis while on the hunt. A Catholic priest often accompanied the hunters to conduct regular mass, bless the hunters before embarking on the hunt, and perform a daily recitation of the Lord's Prayer. In the priest's absence, the hunt chief ensured prayers were conducted each evening and before the hunt.[19]

Hunt laws also outlined rules of conduct and consequences for insubordination. For instance, no party was to leave the group without permission or engage in the hunt before a general order was given. It was important that no individual or party broke off from the collective hunting party, which could potentially scare and scatter the herd. If an individual broke these rules, the consequences were significant. For a first offence, the offender might have his saddle and bridle cut up. For a second offence, his coat might be cut up and for a third offence, the offender could be flogged. Finally, any person convicted of theft could be brought to the middle of the camp and publicly humiliated by being called a thief three times in front of the assembly.[20] Destruction of the hunter's bridle, saddle, and coat seriously impacted their ability to work and brought shame to their family, particularly to the women who produced these items. Métis interpreter, hunter, and guide Peter Erasmus describes an 1875 incident in his memoirs where buffalo hunt chief Gabriel Dumont fined a man named Alexander Fisher several skins as punishment for scattering the herd, which forced the hunting party to travel much further to make their kill.[21] Dumont dispersed the forfeited property to the guards and those in need; while bringing dishonour to himself and his family, Fisher's punishment would also have redistributed wealth across the hunting party.

Buffalo hunting was labour-intensive and relied on the efforts of both men and women. By far, the most labour-intensive work women did was to process the meat and hide into robes, pemmican, and dried meat for trade and their own use and consumption. The exhaustive process of skinning and butchering the animals began following the hunt. Then the proceeds were transported back to the camp wherein women continued their work, drying meat and making pemmican, dressing the skins, and separating the tendons, bones, horns, and fat. One such example of buffalo processing was described by Father Georges-Antoine Belcourt, recounting an 1845 hunt.[22] Women began by removing the small hump above the buffalo's neck called the *petite bosse* before making an incision along the back to remove the hide. They would next remove meat and fat from the carcass in various cuts, including the tongue and stomach, both considered delicacies. The HBC purchased tongues for their own consumption and for export to American markets.[23] Women cut the meat into long narrow strips, which they worked by hand, rolling it between their palms until it was about a quarter inch thick. Then it was hung on makeshift wooden stages to dry in the sun or over a small fire. Once dried, the meat was ground down into flakes and made into pemmican. The last task for women was to render the fat or tallow into oil for cooking and making pemmican and to break and boil the bones to extract marrow, which they stored in cleaned and dried buffalo bladders.[24] Processing also required the help of young children to gather fuel for the fires and older girls to keep the fires going, turn the meat, and keep the dogs away.[25]

The HBC purchased two types of pemmican graded as "ordinary" or "fine," depending on the coarseness of the meat flake and whether berries were added.[26] Regardless of quality, there was no denying the importance of pemmican to the Métis diet and economy. Pemmican preserved fresh meat from spoiling and lasted for months, allowing for long-distance trade and stockpiling for the winter months. When hunting was poor and few other foods were available, it was often all that stood between the Métis and starvation.[27] For all its durability it was also versatile; Métis consumed pemmican straight from the bag, roasted, boiled, or fried in grease.[28]

The process of tanning hides and robes was also labour-intensive, with women contributing the bulk of time and effort. Men assisted with the initial processing after which the women prepared the meat for drying, and then cut, stretched, scraped, and tanned the hides. Women were experts at such processing, with skill developed over years of practice.

Hide preparation depended on its intended use. Women began by stretching the skin on a frame and drying it in the sun until hard. If they were making a robe, the flesh was scraped off the inside, leaving just the thick coat of fur on the outside. The inside would be treated with a mixture made from animal brains, which tanned the skin and made it soft and pliable. Robes were generally made for trade, but the Métis also used them as blankets, coverings, and in making coats, hats, and saddle blankets. If making a hide, they scraped and tanned both sides of the hide, removing both the flesh and hair. The women would next remove the hide from the frame, wash and wring it out, and then dry and smoke it over the fire, darkening its colour and making it water resistant.[29] The preparation of a single hide often required the labour of more than one individual, particularly when wringing it out and stretching it over the fire. Women would use the prepared hides to make and decorate all types of garments including moccasins, saddles, and hunting equipment not just for their families but also for sale and trade.

In addition to the meat and hides, Métis women processed sinew for sewing and trade and made shaganappi useful for rope, animal harnesses, and protecting the wheels of their Red River carts.[30] They also made gunpowder horns, coat hangers, and ornaments of various kind from buffalo horns.[31] Women's labour was essential to the processing of the buffalo and the production of robes, hides, pemmican, dried meat, and other smaller items used to trade at the fur posts and bring income into the family.

Despite the thoroughness with which the Métis extracted resources from the buffalo, some observers accused them of being wasteful and leaving great amounts of meat to spoil on the plains. Eager to kill a large quantity of fat buffalo during the summer hunts of the 1850s and 1860s, Métis could be selective about which of their kill they butchered. They may have abandoned their initial kills if they later found a larger herd or a herd of fatter animals.[32] In an 1861 fall hunt, the early Red River newspaper the *Nor'Wester* reported that Métis hunters, under the leadership of William Hallett, had disparagingly abandoned a large kill of buffalo bulls in favour of 600 "fine cows" they subsequently killed.[33] Focused on the market, Métis hunters often harvested only the most easily accessible and valuable cuts of meat and fat, leaving the remainder. Under the hot summer sun, it was necessary to work as quickly as possible to curb spoilage. Métis had to discriminate what they took, casting off animal carcasses they deemed too skinny, sometimes taking only the petite bosse or the tongue they considered delicacies. They also regularly discarded hairless summer buffalo skins that made poor robes and were deemed of little value.[34]

Waste was often unavoidable, but Métis stories of the hunt suggest that they often took care in preventing waste and spoilage. Hunter Patrice Fleury countered the allegations he had heard about the wanton buffalo slaughter by his fellow Métis, arguing that they did indeed take care to avoid excess waste and spoilage. In his experience in the 1860s and 1870s "no waste was permitted."[35] Hunting parties generally killed no more than the women in the brigade could timely process, which often meant killing no more than five or six buffalo per week.[36] Given the small number of animals taken at one time, this likely describes a smaller hunt by a single hunting brigade and not the large annual collective hunts. Regardless, his reminiscences reveal that the Métis considered ways to avoid excessive waste.

Echoing Fleury's perspective, fellow buffalo hunters Louis Goulet and Norbert Welsh remember attempts to reduce and minimize waste by being selective in their kills. Buffalo fat was highly sought after and hunters aimed to kill buffalo with the largest amount of body fat, having a clear preference for buffalo cows over bulls.[37] Cow meat was generally more tender, which was good for making pemmican and dried meat in the summer, while bull meat tended to be tough, particularly in spring and summer. In the winter, both cows and bulls were at their fattest and their hides thick and of the best quality.[38] Métis hunters were also selective about the age of the animals they hunted, preferring the meat and hides of buffalo up to two years old. As buffalo aged their hair became coarse, which reduced the quality of the hide.[39] However enticing a herd might be, Goulet contended that they never killed more than the women could quickly dress and credited women's skills in minimizing wastage and making poor-quality meat more edible.[40]

Women also took care to minimize waste. Welsh recalls killing a cow and harvesting only the hide and a piece of the fattest part of the animal. Returning to camp, he presented his wife Cecilia Boyer with the hide expecting her to process it. Boyer only smiled and kicked the hide away in refusal; she had previously warned him against taking hides only for sport, insisting that she would not dress any hide without the accompanying carcass. In the end, Welsh passed it on to his mother-in-law so it would not go to waste.[41] Boyer's refusal to process the hide was a way of admonishing her husband and holding him to be more judicious and less wasteful. While Welsh's account of this episode contradicts his insistence that the Métis avoided waste, it shows how his wife's authority over her own labour was not to be trifled with. He also noted that he never again killed only for the hide, but always returned home with both the hide and the carcass.[42] This example is indicative of women's roles in the hunt and authority over their labour. Boyer's confident refusal to comply with her husband's request is not surprising given Welsh's description of her as a hard-working and independent woman, who even hunted buffalo herself.[43] Although it was uncommon for women to hunt buffalo, Boyer's case indicates that Métis women could assume roles and responsibilities outside of prescribed gender roles when required.

It was also women's responsibility to set up camp, organize and prepare meals, maintain the cooking fires, and make sure everyone had something to eat. Women had a significant degree of authority regarding the distribution of food at camp, including sharing fresh meat across the extended family, so that everyone, particularly the Old People, had enough to eat. HBC trader Isaac Cowie noted that the Métis hunting in the 1860s and1870s always allowed old and widowed men and women

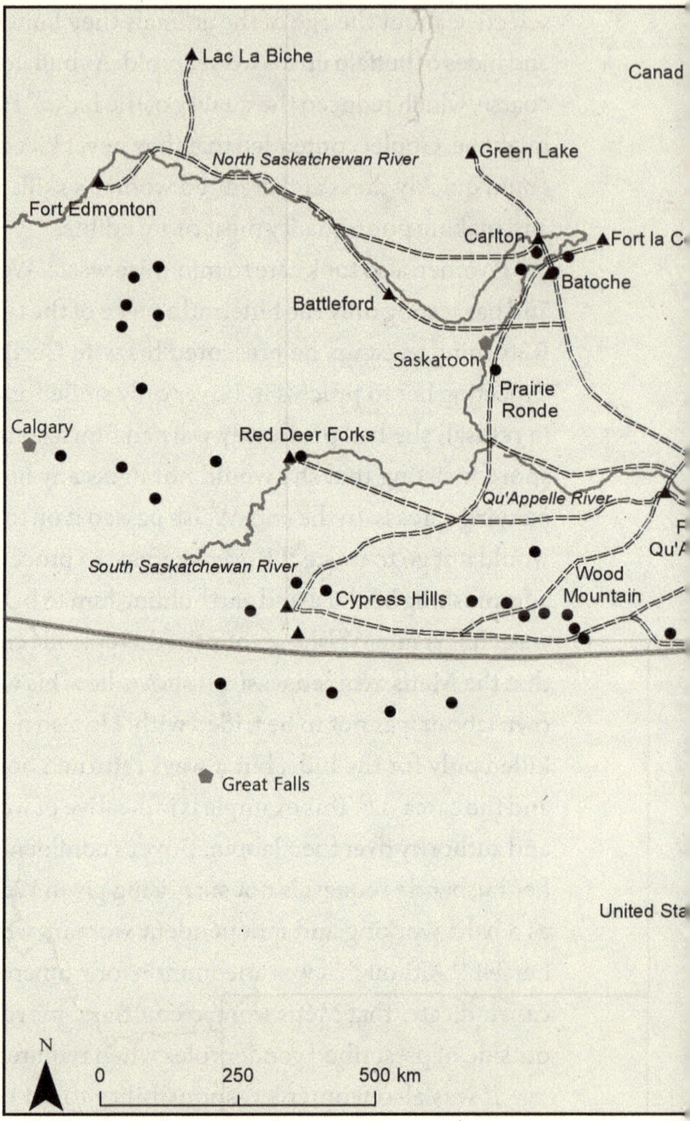

Figure 12. Red River Cart Trails and Métis Wintering Sites c. 1850–1860s. Map courtesy of Cheryl Troupe and Matthew Kunkel.

to help themselves to the best carcasses in the field.[44] The Métis, however, did not perceive their elderly to be helpless; rather it was out of respect

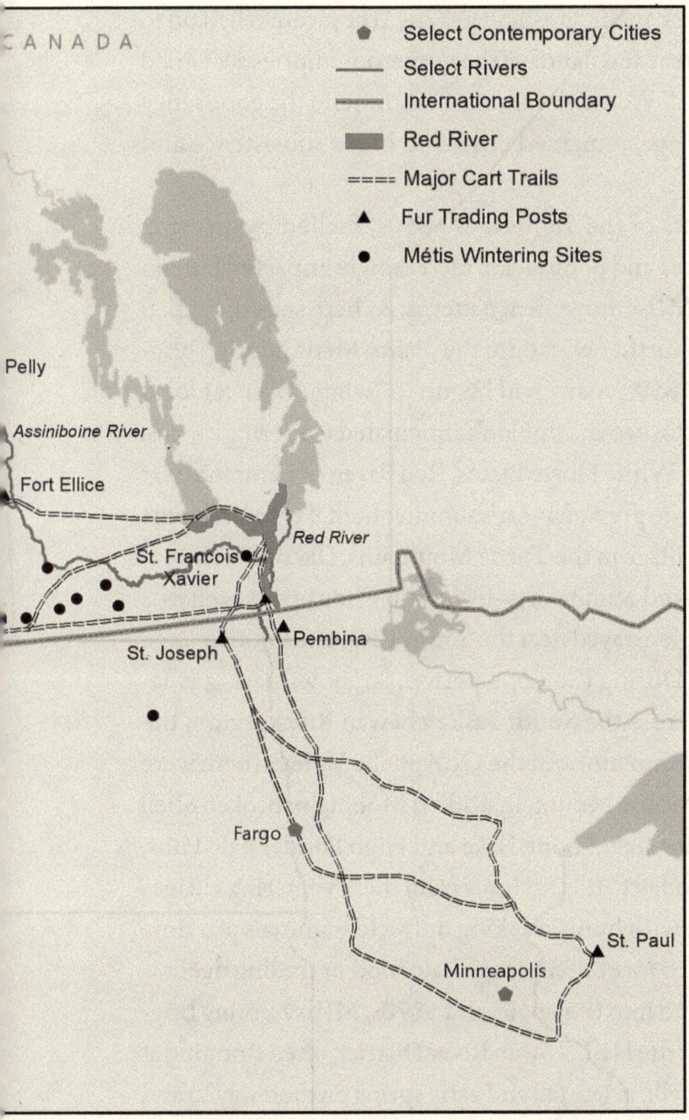

for their age and experience that younger Métis offered them such care. As Cowie noted, it was older, often widowed women who produced the finest marrow fat, tallow, and meat for the traders.[45] The respect older women earned was not just for their buffalo-processing abilities but also their knowledge of plants, medicines, and healing. They were relied on to set broken bones and treat and bandage the numerous injuries sustained during the buffalo hunt.[46] Women's expertise, labour, and the goods they produced, at whatever age, remained crucial to Métis subsistence and economic livelihoods.

The intensive hunts of the 1840s and 1850s, fuelled by growing demand for buffalo robes and pemmican, increasingly impacted buffalo numbers and changed Métis movement patterns. As herd sizes dwindled and moved further and further west onto the plains, Métis hunting brigades followed. By the 1850s, many had begun to "winter over" at locations across the plains close to the buffalo's anticipated wintering ranges. This meant returning to White Horse Plains, Red River, or Pembina next spring rather than after the previous year's summer hunt. Father Belcourt described a wintering village in the Turtle Mountains, Dakota Territory, in 1853, which numbered about forty-five to fifty houses, as well as a camp of about 400 people arrayed near the Souris River and another large camp at Long River.[47] During the same period, larger wintering villages were popping up across the South Saskatchewan River region, the Cypress Hills, Wood Mountain, and the Qu'Appelle Valley. There were also smaller villages at Moose Mountain, Riding Mountain, Broken Shell Creek, Moose Jaw Bone Creek, Long Lake and High Pond, Eagle Hills, Old Wives Lake, and the Dirt Hills.[48] Hunts from these wintering villages were generally limited, with hunters taking only a few animals at a time and usually only those to meet their immediate food or trading needs.

By the late 1850s and into the 1860s and 1870s, Métis hunting brigades moved throughout the HBC's Swan River District, often stopping at Forts Ellice and Qu'Appelle in late fall and early spring on their way to and from their wintering grounds. Fort Ellice was located on Beaver Creek near the confluence of the Assiniboine and Qu'Appelle Rivers, while Fort Qu'Appelle was situated further west in the heart of the Qu'Appelle Valley on the Fishing Lakes. These strategic spots, located within an extensive network of cart trails that moved goods and people, became significant stopping places and sites of commerce for Métis as they moved to and

Figure 13. Red River Cart Trail, Qu'Appelle Valley, CU 1107976. Photograph courtesy of Digital Collections, University of Calgary.

from the western plains. Stretching from St. Paul, Minnesota, across the northern plains, these trails broadly defined the geography of the Métis world, connecting families, communities, and economies.

Visits by Métis hunting parties to Forts Ellice and Qu'Appelle reveal a regular regional movement pattern.[49] In October 1856, close to thirty Métis moved through Fort Ellice on their way to wintering sites at the Qu'Appelle Lakes, Broken Shell Creek, and High Pond.[50] Many came from White Horse Plains and the Red River region while others came north from Pembina. The following year, people in upwards of eighty tents camped at Fort Qu'Appelle on their way to their wintering grounds.[51] In the spring, several of these Métis returned east to the Red River and White Horse Plains regions.[52] Many, including Daniel and Alexander Geroux McGillis, George Fisher, Paul Desnomie, and George Racette junior and senior, travelled with male relatives, demonstrating the continued and widespread practice of travelling, living, and hunting along extended family networks.

Forts such as Ellice and Qu'Appelle remained important economic spots as the wintering villages increasingly became sites of production, commerce, and trade. In the wintering camps, Métis women continued their animal processing work, although at a less intense pace. They spent little time making pemmican but continued to dry meat and tan hides. They also took advantage of cold weather to preserve fresh meat either by hanging it in strips on makeshift scaffolds in their small winter cabins or, more often, by freezing it. Women remained responsible for feeding their families and rationing dried meat and pemmican resources stored during the spring and summer. As well they spent time making all types of clothes, moccasins, bags, and saddles which they decorated with elaborate floral beadwork, silk, and quill embroidery, to be used within the family or sold to the HBC.[53]

In these camps, Métis acted as independent traders, supplying extended family members with a variety of goods, generally in exchange for buffalo hides and furs hunted during the winter. Eager to attract Métis trade and neutralize this competition, the HBC responded by establishing semi-permanent seasonal outposts or "flying posts" in or near Métis encampments.[54] Throughout the 1860s and into the early 1870s, HBC employees of Fort Ellice and Qu'Appelle regularly travelled to the camps on both short trading excursions or for the season, spending the winter acquiring furs and provisions, particularly when supplies were low at the forts. The HBC also sent traders to the larger wintering camps at Moose Mountain and Wood Mountain, as well as to smaller camps at Long Creek and Pipestone Creek, in present-day southern Saskatchewan. Employees were selected for their experience, employment history, and kinship relationships that may have extended into the camps themselves and therefore would benefit the HBC trade. In the late 1850s, William McKay, chief trader at Fort Ellice, sent "Old Antoine Desjarlais" to Moose Mountain for the winter trading season. An experienced Métis trader, Desjarlais was an interpreter and trader for the HBC at Lesser Slave Lake in the 1810s before moving east into the Swan River and Souris River regions where he established two independent trading posts in defiance of the HBC monopoly. From 1836 to 1840, he operated Fort Desjarlais on the Souris River near present-day Brandon, Manitoba, with his brother Marcel, his son Baptiste, and sons-in-law Charles DeMontigny, Eusebe Ledoux, and Simon Blondeau, before rejoining the HBC in the 1850s.[55]

Desjarlais's time at Moose Mountain was quite profitable for the HBC and demonstrates the flexibility and independence that some Métis possessed when acting as either HBC employees or as freemen according to the situation. In November 1858, Fort Ellice employees twice travelled to the village to retrieve furs Desjarlais acquired from the Métis, returning to the post with furs from ninety-nine foxes, 153 kit foxes, 318 skunks, 116 badgers, nine wolves, and two buffalo robes.[56] Later the same winter, the post sent five men led by Jean Baptiste Bourassa, an experienced and long-term employee of the HBC, to Moose Mountain seeking any fresh meat provisions Desjarlais had to spare. Acquiring no meat, each of the five-member party returned with a dog sled loaded with buffalo robes and furs Desjarlais had accumulated.[57] Bourassa's trading prowess speaks to his skill and experience, to the size of the wintering village, the relationships Desjarlais had there, and the hunting success of those wintering there. Métis in these encampments appreciated and came to expect this pattern of trade in their winter villages, as noted by Chief Trader McKay.[58]

Trade in the Métis winter camps was profitable for the HBC and important when food at the forts ran low. In February 1858, the chief trader at the Qu'Appelle Lake post spent three days at Wood Mountain, returning with four bags of pemmican, one buffalo shoulder, one buffalo bosse and some tongues, as well as six robes, ten red fox pelts, and eight skunks.[59] He repeated the trip again a month later, returning with his sleds loaded with supplies and furs.[60] In early 1863, HBC traders again visited the wintering village at Moose Mountain, securing nearly 600 pounds of assorted provisions where only a month earlier, Joseph Parisien, a Métis HBC employee, had already acquired nearly 600 pounds of pemmican, sixty pounds of dried meat, and some provisions.[61] The large quantity of this trade demonstrates the significant capacity and importance of these wintering villages, particularly Moose Mountain and Wood Mountain, as sites of production and commerce.

As Métis began wintering over, they also increasingly became employed by the HBC posts at Forts Ellice and Qu'Appelle, working as skilled and unskilled labourers in both formal and informal capacities. Some were formally employed on contracts of varying lengths, others on a temporary basis according to the job or trip. Working in a temporary and ad-hoc fashion provided flexibility and a measure of independence while ensuring access to resources and employment when necessary. Employed for a day, week, month, or longer, the Métis often moved between posts as required. As early as the 1851–52 trading year, men such as Simon Blondeau, who had previously worked with his father-in-law Antoine Desjarlais at Fort Desjarlais, along with William Daniel, John and François Desmarais, John Fisher, Bonaventure Guardapuis, Louis and Pierre Levellier, Alexis Peltier, and others, were employed as servants at Fort Ellice.[62] Some of these men remained long-term HBC employees, engaged in the Swan River District into the late 1870s while others chose to leave the Company and act as independent freighters, traders, and buffalo hunters.[63] As freemen, they could intermittently provide general labour to the forts in exchange for rations or work off debts. For such Métis men, these labour arrangements provided economic options beyond the annual buffalo hunts and offered a measure of economic independence and distance from the HBC.

Métis worked for the HBC in a variety of positions. As servants, men carried out essential routine tasks such as hauling and chopping wood, working in the gardens and hayfields, and taking care of the post's horses. Those with carpentry and blacksmith skills would build and repair the vehicles for transporting goods and provisions. They also built, repaired, and maintained HBC buildings and fences. Their hunting and fishing abilities were utilized to provide fresh meat. Hunting, fishing, building canoes and carts, and making dog sleighs and snowshoes depended on Métis' traditional skills and expertise developed through the mastery of the plains environment. Many also worked the canoe or York boat brigades, moving goods and provisions back and forth on the region's river systems.[64] By the 1860s, however, the method of moving goods shifted from water to overland freighting along the matrix of cart trails the Métis knew well.

Métis expertise, particularly their knowledge of the physical environment and the extensive cart trails, made them ideal candidates to freight goods and guide trading parties. Their understanding of the region's social and political dynamics also made them indispensable as interpreters. In the Swan River District, trusted and reliable men such as Antoine Desjarlais, William Daniel, William Birston, and Pierre LaPierre were depended on as guides and interpreters. They led hunting and trading expeditions across the North-West, into First Nations camps, and Métis wintering villages where they acted as interpreters and helped the HBC facilitate trade. Possessing specialized local and regional knowledge, the Métis created a niche for themselves, useful to the HBC but also as guides, interpreters, and hunters for the exploratory expeditions of Captain John Palliser, Henry Youle Hind, the Earl of Southesk, William Francis Butler, Walter Cheadle, and others.[65] However, skill and experience were not all that was required to obtain these positions. Personal relationships also mattered; according to Isaac Cowie, it was the influence of Chief Trader Henry Munro Fisher that secured his sons Alexander and John their positions. For a time, John worked as an interpreter at Fort Ellice and Alexander as horse guard at Fort Qu'Appelle.[66]

While Métis men were engaged with the HBC in varying positions, their First Nations or Métis wives also contributed labour and expertise to running households and to the operation of the forts. Women's general and domestic labour and specialized expertise was rarely under formal contractual arrangement but it was ever present. They well understood their economic role in food production but also the social and political functions food could facilitate.

Women cleaned the chief factor's home, the fort's buildings and yard, and shovelled snow.[67] In some instances, women worked alongside men to mud and thatch various Fort buildings.[68] They processed hides and robes of animals hunted by their husbands and other employees and made all types of clothing, moccasins, and snowshoes that they sold to the post and its employees. Women planted, maintained, and harvested the Fort's large vegetable gardens, they made pemmican and dried meat, and hunted, fished, and snared small game for the post's consumption. Consequently, Métis employees and their wives often found themselves both securing and producing rations for the HBC and providing for their own family's food supply.

HBC employees received lodging, allowances, and rations according to what was available at the post, the work they performed, and their position in the Company. Employees and their families generally lived in proximity to, or within the confines of, the Fort but would continue to provide food for themselves and their families, while also receiving rations and allowances. European employees, including the commissioned officers, clerk, and postmaster, received the largest supply of rations followed by the post interpreter, servants, and labourers and last, by the Métis and First Nations employees.[69] Women generally received half of men's ration allocation, while children received one quarter.

Rations regularly included pemmican, fresh or dried meat, as well as seasonal vegetable produce from the Fort's gardens. In an effort to conserve pemmican stores for trade, the HBC also gave fresh meat such as rabbits, prairie chickens, ducks, and fish.[70] They considered flour a luxury item and rationed it sparingly, which encouraged women to save it for special occasions and times of sickness or emergency.[71] Families received a weekly allowance of tallow or fat and occasionally milk for the children, dried berries, and rough barley.[72] Employees also had access to a variety of foods and supplies in exchange for their earned allowances and regularly took at least part of their allowance in foods such as butter, grease, tea, sugar, and rum. If women received allowances for their labour, they tended to exchange it for items such as tea or sugar.

Employees usually received additional rations at Christmas and New Year's including tea, sugar, and tobacco as well as rice, raisins, chocolate,

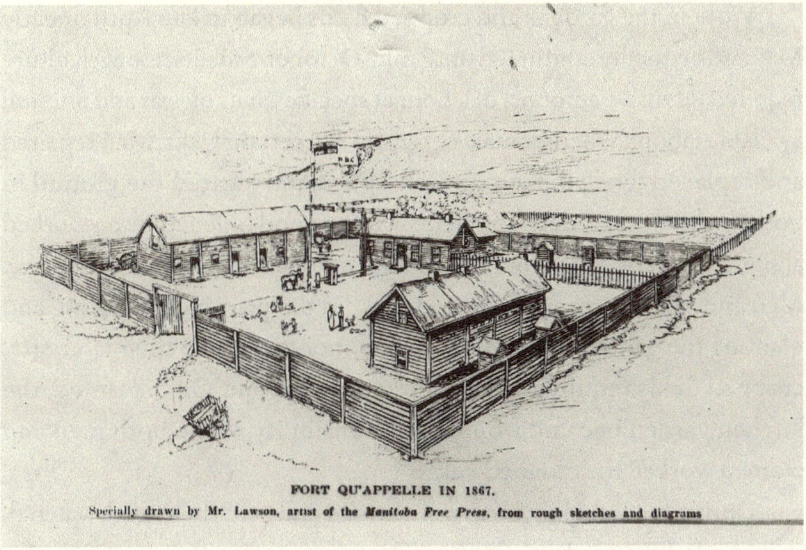

Figure 14. Fort Qu'Appelle c. 1867, R-A38. Provincial Archives of Saskatchewan.

flour, and clay pipes.[73] During Isaac Cowie's time at Fort Qu'Appelle, employees and their families feasted on a New Year's dinner of roast buffalo tongue and bosse, cakes, plum pudding, chocolate, and tea.[74] Employees also received gifts of tobacco and clay pipes, which some of the older women insisted they also receive, demonstrating that they understood the value and contribution of their labour.

From the late 1850s to the 1870s, there were at least two gardens each at Fort Ellice and Fort Qu'Appelle. Both had a kitchen garden within the Fort walls as well as cropland outside for growing potatoes and barley as well as hay for the horses and oxen. Fort Qu'Appelle's kitchen garden covered as much ground as the Fort itself, measuring approximately 22,500 square feet or about half an acre, and was protected by a ten-foot-high picket fence. Picket fences around the kitchen gardens kept out the post's dogs, and rail fences around the cropped fields helped deter game such as deer from entering the fields to feed. The cropland was a short distance from the Fort and about ten acres in size.[75]

Work in the gardens and cropped fields began in late April or early May and generally continued until mid-October. Small-scale agriculture required intensive amounts of labour at specific times of year and often all available labour, whether male or female, for certain tasks. Men repaired and replaced fence pickets and ploughed and cleared the ground in both the kitchen gardens and fields. Women and older children worked alongside, clearing the ground, digging for stones, and spreading manure. Men and women readied the seed and did the planting. Preparing and planting the gardens could take up to a month. Due to their large size, cropped fields required significantly more labour. Once planted, the kitchen garden became women's responsibility, while both men and women worked the cropped fields.[76]

During June and July, men, women, and older children hoed, watered, and weeded the gardens. Crop maintenance during the short summer growing season often fell to women whose husbands were often trading and freighting away from the Fort.[77] By late August and into September and October, plants were ready to harvest, requiring substantial labour over a short period of time. There were potatoes to dig, barley and hay to cut and stack, and it all required hauling back to the Fort. Different activities required varying amounts of labour resulting in more women than men in the fields during harvest. For instance, in September 1867, six men worked cutting barley and hay, alongside forty-five women who gathered and stacked it.[78] Consequently, the Forts fundamentally relied on women's labour in planting and harvesting their gardens and crops.

Women's labour and expertise was particularly important when rations at the posts were low. In the 1850s and 1860s, Mary Cook's skills in snaring small game proved essential in feeding her family and HBC employees. The wife of Fort Ellice's Chief Trader William McKay, Cook regularly accompanied her husband hunting and trapping, and would embark on her own excursions. Such independence of action illustrates her own, and her husband's, confidence in her ability to support the family through hunting. In March 1859, Cook set out on three separate occasions, once with her husband and his interpreter, bringing in over

Figure 15. Mary Cook (Mrs. William McKay) family, c.1870, CU174765. Photograph courtesy of Digital Collections, University of Calgary. Front row—left to right: unknown sister of Mary Cook; Mary Cook; unknown sister of Mary Cook. Back row: James McKay, later judge on Saskatchewan Court of Appeal; Gilbert McKay; Angus McKay, Hudson's Bay Company employee; and Joseph McKay.

fifty rabbits, and twice on her own.[79] Family members, other women, or sometimes a male post employee would accompany Cook on these trips.[80] She was not the only woman known to have hunted for the Fort when food supplies were low. Over four days in March 1863, women were recorded to have snared forty-five rabbits for the Fort's food provisions.[81] But it was a period of scarcity and these efforts were not enough to sustain the Fort; a short time later several Indigenous employees and their families were "turned out" to fend for themselves to reduce the consumptive pressure on available post rations.[82] Directed to leave the Fort, these families were forced to hunt and fish on their own until Fort supplies improved. "Turning out" employees and their families was a common practice intended to keep costs down and protect valuable stores of pemmican from being consumed as rations. The situation at Fort Ellice must have been dire in 1859, as immediately following these families' departures, Mary Cook herself and her children also left the Fort, striking off to hunt.

While her leaving the Fort demonstrated the importance of Cook's hunting expertise, she also understood the social and political value her food labour brought to her husband's trade. For the Métis, food and the act of dining maintained and strengthened social, economic, and political relationships. Cook embodied this understanding when she and her husband, Chief Trader McKay, hosted HBC clerk from Fort Qu'Appelle Isaac Cowie in 1867. Feasting on Cook's extravagant and skilfully prepared meal of wild game, fish, preserved wild fruit, and garden vegetables, Cowie proclaimed that the McKays personified hospitality.[83] On another occasion, Cowie recalled dining with Peter LaPierre, interpreter at the Touchwood Hills post, north of the Qu'Appelle Valley. Cowie found the lodge floor covered in buffalo robes and a showy display of brightly coloured blankets, down pillows, and a brightly painted table. For dinner Madeleine Bourassa, Métis wife of Jean Baptiste Bourassa, LaPierre's second in command, had prepared a sumptuous meal of buffalo meat, fried donuts, and tea with sugar—a luxury.[84] LaPierre spared little expense for the occasion as dining with

Cowie could politically strengthen trade relationships between his large extended family and the HBC clerk. Similarly, Norbert Welsh described a special meal of elaborate Métis dishes prepared by his wife Cecilia Boyer for Nêhiyawak Chief Starblanket in the 1880s, acknowledging the importance of Boyer's cooking in inspiring a prosperous trade with Starblanket and his party. Boyer cooked meatballs or boulettes, fried bannock called beignes or croxegnols, and a savoury pudding called pouchine dans le sac, all of which the Chief enjoyed. Boulettes were made from chopped, seasoned meat formed into small balls. Rolled in flour, they were cooked with potatoes or other vegetables as a simple stew or soup. Like doughnuts, beignes or croxegnols were made from a dough of flour, fine tallow, and water that was rolled out, cut into squares, and fried in boiling fat. The maker cut four or five slits on the edge of each square before cooking, so that when cooked beignes looked like fingers twisted into "fancy shapes, all criss-crossed."[85] These were a treat reserved for special occasions and celebrations and sometimes tossed in a mixture of cinnamon and sugar. Pouchine dans le sac is a suet pudding made with flour, tallow, raisins, and spices boiled or steamed in a cloth bag and served with a sauce made from brandy.[86]

Meals in Métis homes were not usually this extravagant. Most relied on buffalo, supplemented with fish, deer, and small game, prairie chickens, ducks, geese, eggs, and other harvested wild foods. Meat was generally served roasted, boiled in a stew, or consumed as dried meat or pemmican. The Métis also regularly consumed the fat, bone marrow, and other parts of the animal, including the offal, so there was generally little waste.[87] On special occasions, they may have served boulettes or tourtière, a pie made with chopped, seasoned meat filling in a pastry crust. Harvested wild fruits and vegetables were eaten fresh, dry, or added to soup, stews, and pemmican. Saskatoon berries, strawberries, raspberries, pin cherries, and chokecherries were common. In addition, wild vegetables such as wild onions and prairie turnips (*psoralea esculenta*) were enjoyed. Métis preserved these foods by spreading them on a large cloth or hide to dry in the sun. Drying chokecherries was especially labour-intensive work for women, children, and Old People who crushed the berries between two rocks as a type of mortar and pestle. They mashed only a small handful of berries at a time ensuring that the pits were broken open. Then they formed the crushed pulp into small patties and laid them out on large sheets or pieces of canvas to dry in the sun. Sometimes, these berry-laden sheets were placed on the roof of the porch, shed, or house to dry undisturbed, except by birds.[88] After two or three days, the dried berry patties were stored in gunnysacks or canvas bags. Once dried, chokecherries could be stored for a long time. When ready to be prepared, they would be fried with flour, lard, and sugar into a thick paste that was served with meat and eaten as part of regular meals. Called grens in Michif, the fried berries had a sweet taste and a gritty texture and, like other berries, provided necessary vitamins to the Métis diet.

Produce from the seasonal vegetable gardens was also important, particularly as families began remaining year-round in their wintering villages. By the 1860s, there was a growing settlement along the Qu'Appelle Lakes, near the newly erected Roman Catholic Mission where Métis took up small plots of land along the lakes and river. The Valley environment was rich with resources, increasingly crucial as the buffalo herds declined.

Meals were cooked outside in warmer weather, over a fire or a small wood stove. As families moved into their winter cabins however, cooking moved inside, done over the clay hearth of the fireplace or, if fortunate, over a wood-burning stove. Cooking and eating utensils made of metal were acquired from the HBC, while Métis would themselves fashion bowls, plates, and spoons out of wood or bone.

Food and goods acquired directly from the HBC or from other Métis traders supplemented diets and provided necessary food preparation and consumption accouterments. These traders, who lived and travelled intermittently with the Métis hunting brigades, provided a store of trade goods easily accessed by families.[89] Flour, sugar, and tea were staple items carried by most traders, but spices, cheese, jams, and jellies, preserves, bacon and canned meat, chocolate, coffee, currants, mustard, oatmeal, black pepper, pimento, raisins, and rice were also available from the posts. Flour was the main ingredient in bannock or la galette, an unleavened bread important to the Métis diet, particularly when game was scarce.[90] Most of the foods obtained through trade were not part of everyday Métis diets but they did enjoy foods such as chocolate, raisins, currants, and coffee on special occasions or holidays such as Christmas and New Year's.[91] Traders also carried items such as tobacco, kettles, cooking pots, utensils, blankets, cloth, axes, knives, guns, gun powder, alcohol, chinaware bowls, plates, cups, and saucers that the Métis readily purchased. An English company, W.T. Copeland and Sons, produced a range of transfer-printed, patterned earthenware available to Métis at HBC posts from the 1820s.[92] Chinaware teacups were particularly popular by the 1860s and 1870s and while Métis families may not have owned many of these pieces, most had a few in their possession.[93]

Cultural convention dictated that Métis share food amongst extended family and with visitors to their homes. Sharing food ensured that all members of the extended family were provided for and that kinship relationships remained strong. When visitors arrived, a meal or reception became an excuse for a celebration that might last for days. Sharing food accompanied all social occasions, celebrations, dances, and visiting during the cold winter months. Winter gatherings occurred also when the Métis celebrated marriages, told stories of the old days, and prepared special foods. Evening celebrations began with a big meal, followed by singing contests and dancing late into the night. Very competitive, the Métis often vied with one another to see who prepared the best meal, who best played fiddle, sang, or danced, and even who would be the first to wear through their moccasins or develop muscle cramps from dancing.[94]

Between 1868 and 1869, hunters, politicians, and leaders among the Métis, Pascal Breland and Solomon Hamelin wintered north of the Qu'Appelle Valley between the Touchwood Hills and Last Mountain Lake posts. Breland and Hamelin were familiar with the region, having wintered in the Qu'Appelle in the 1850s.[95] Breland regularly opened his home to extended family and community members, in social celebration and to maintain kinship and political relationships. On one occasion, Breland's wife Marie Grant, daughter of Cuthbert Grant, prepared a lavish meal of buffalo meat, rice and raisins, cakes, and rum punch for Isaac Cowie and members of the winter camp, which, Cowie noted, "befitted persons of their importance."[96] Festivities of singing, fiddling, dancing, and sharing exciting stories of buffalo hunting and Métis life on the plains followed the meal.[97] Such festivities were common in Métis wintering camps and could last for days, particularly around the New Year. Celebrated more than Christmas, the New Year was a time to socialize and reaffirm family bonds, as well as an opportunity to break the monotony of the winter cold. New Year's celebrations often lasted from New Year's Day until Epiphany or All Kings' Day, on 6 January.

Food, as we have seen, was not always plentiful and Métis occasionally faced periods of want. Women toiled for their families constantly planning how they would feed them in the coming days, weeks, and months. In her memoirs, Marie Rose Smith recalled her mother Marie Delorme's determination and practicality in approaching her familial responsibility. Marie Rose's mother was a resourceful provider who regularly rationed their flour, sugar, tea, and tobacco, making sure the family had enough to eat, and conserved their supplies while they travelled.[98] Métis women used these opportunities to teach their children about the prairie environment, passing on intimate knowledge of the land and ecosystems related to the seasonal cycles of plants and animals, as well as the vital skills of food harvesting and preparation, which became increasingly crucial as the buffalo herds declined.

After the buffalo hunts in 1870 and 1871 failed, families increasingly settled in the Qu'Appelle Valley on a year-round basis, looking to live off the Valley's resources and HBC provisions.[99] The herds were followed far from home in the spring of 1871 and when the Métis hunting brigades returned to the Qu'Appelle post later that summer, they recounted tales of starvation and famine on the plains. Some lamented going without food for at least three days at a time, being forced to eat gophers, buffalo sinews women had saved for sewing, and "any wolf which they had the good luck to poison."[100] Away from homes and unable to harvest the local game, fish, and plants, they had few options but to ask for the HBC's support. Unfortunately, provisions at the Fort were also in short supply, having shipped out what meagre pemmican they had managed to accumulate throughout the winter. While little pemmican had been prepared due to a shortage of buffalo tallow, the HBC did have a supply of pounded meat not yet processed into pemmican, which they were eager to trade to their hungry customers. Some Métis had little more than their horses to trade and reluctantly sought HBC credit. Credit was, of course, determined in consideration of the conduct and loyalty individuals had displayed to the Company.[101] For most, the only abundant food source available were the sucker fish that swarmed the creeks. Métis ate the fish, disliked but eaten as a last resort, served with milk, barley, and potatoes.[102] The following year, there were upwards of 400 to 500 people living around the Roman Catholic Mission at Qu'Appelle who had little to eat but dried fish.[103] It was in times of scarcity such as these that the wild foods harvested and preserved by women became increasingly important and, likewise, reinforced a reliance on vegetable gardens.

As Don Freed's song lyrics that begin this chapter convey, Métis women filled critical roles in mid- and late nineteenth-century family economies and social networks. They contributed essential skills and labour, rendering buffalo both consumable and economically profitable. They contributed indispensable knowledge and labour in their homes and to the successful operation of the HBC posts where their husbands were formally engaged. Métis women understood their economic roles in food production, and the social and political functions that food could facilitate. Food was central to all Métis social gatherings and celebrations. On these occasions, Métis spared no expense as they knew well the impact that serving a fine and memorable meal could have in strengthening social, economic, and political relationships. Women were flexible and decisive in how they conducted themselves and in their contribution to their family's food production.

The decline of the buffalo changed the way in which Métis families lived. Hunting brigades chose to winter over on the plains before taking up land on a year-round basis. By the 1860s, there was a visible Métis presence in the Qu'Appelle Valley where they increasingly participated in a mixed economy supplementing their subsistence hunting and gathering activity with small-scale agricultural production to varying degrees. With this shift, women continued to fill complementary and central economic roles in relation to food production, ensuring the survival of their families.

Chapter 3

Petitioning for Rights and Taking Up Agriculture

Your Excellency,

The half-breeds of the Lakes Qu'Appelle and environs offer you today their homage, and submit to you the following petitions, which they present in their name and in the name of all their brethren scattered over the prairies, and beseech you to give them a favorable hearing, and to remember them in the various arrangements that the Government may make with the Indians.

They ask you—That the government allow to the half-breeds the right of keeping the lands which they have taken or which they may take along the River Qu'Appelle. The right of fishing in all the lakes of the above mentioned river. The right of hunting freely in the prairies west and south-west of the Lakes Qu'Appelle, without being arbitrarily hindered by the Indians, but only in virtue of the regulations that the Indians in concert with the half-breeds and the Government shall

> establish hereafter for the good of all. The right of trading at the Lakes and environs of the Lakes Qu'Appelle.
>
> Signed the Half-Breeds of the Qu'Appelle Valley
> Lake Qu'Appelle, 11th September 1874.[1]

THE HALF-BREEDS OF the Qu'Appelle, as they referred to themselves in this 1874 petition to the Dominion Government, recognized the necessity of collective action to safeguard their economic livelihood, land tenure practices, and way of life in the face of competition over environmental resources, oncoming treaty negotiations, and encroaching settlement. A year-round settlement was quickly growing around the Qu'Appelle Lakes as families began spending longer periods of time in their wintering camps hunting buffalo and working as traders and freighters. By the 1870s, as many as twenty-five Métis families lived on the Qu'Appelle Lakes, and approximately 1,000 more regularly and seasonally moved through the region.[2] The shift from wintering to permanent settlement was the result of complex political, economic, and social factors. The most significant was access to the diminishing buffalo herds and the necessary shift towards small-scale agricultural production. The political climate in the Red River region leading up to and following the 1869–70 Red River Resistance and subsequent creation of the province of Manitoba also influenced these families' decision to make the Qu'Appelle Valley a year-round home.[3]

Settlement in the Valley provided reliable access to a steady supply of resources and placed the Métis in better reach of the diminishing buffalo herds. From this location, many continued hunting further west onto the plains and wintering in the Cypress Hills, Wood Mountain, Moose Jaw Bone Creek, and the Souris River before returning to their homes along the Qu'Appelle Lakes. Proximity to the HBC posts at Forts Qu'Appelle and Ellice also ensured that the Métis were able to maintain relationships with the fur company. Rather than trading at Fort Garry nearly 500 kilometres to the east, Métis increasingly relied upon the posts in the Valley region for a steady supply of trade goods. These posts also provided independent traders like Norbert Welsh, Antoine Larocque, St. Pierre Poitras, Augustin Brabant, and others ready access to goods traded by First Nations and Métis along the network.[4] For Métis in general, proximity to Forts Qu'Appelle and Ellice provided temporary labouring or freighting opportunities and an emergency source of food or supplies during times of scarcity.

Like the HBC posts, the St. Florent Mission, established in 1866, was a natural stopping place for the buffalo brigades and a significant factor in drawing families to the Valley. Devoutly Catholic, the Métis looked to the mission for solemnizing marriages and performing baptisms and funeral rights. Norbert Welsh noted that he alone transported at least sixty bodies to the mission for burial.[5] These were individuals who had died in Métis winter camps and settlements far removed from St. Florent and even further from Red River. Consequently, the Qu'Appelle Lakes region—with the HBC post at Fort Qu'Appelle and the St. Florent Mission—became a hub of social and economic activity. It superseded Red River in importance for Métis who settled nearby but also for those wintering and living year-round at Willow Bunch, the Cypress Hills, and Wood Mountain.[6]

This shift towards permanent settlement along the familiar Qu'Appelle Lakes allowed the Métis to maintain a worldview that privileged kinship relationships and a mixed subsistence lifestyle. Métis found support from their familial relations already in the region but also protection, fuel, and access to the Valley's environmental resources. These families intimately understood the territory and the resources it provided, relying on the buffalo hunt and supplementing their diet with trade and harvested foods from the natural environment and their small gardens.

By the 1860s, there was a burgeoning Métis population in the region that was quickly growing. By 1874, there were at least thirty-one families, represented by their heads, who signed a petition to Alexander Morris, lieutenant governor of the North-West Territories, seeking protection of their land rights and rights to hunt, fish, and trade in the region.[7] A

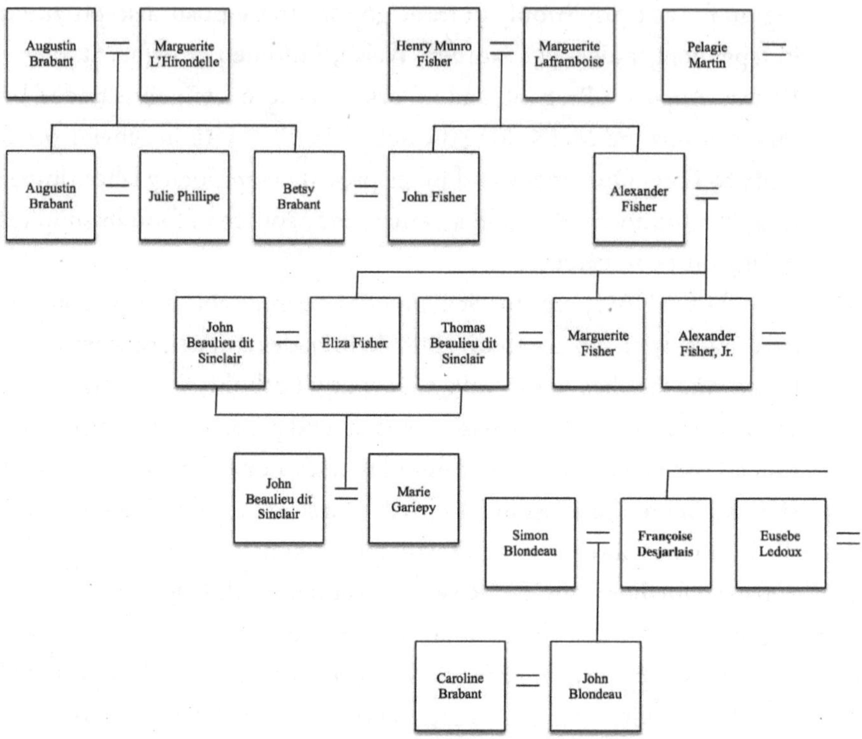

Figure 16. Antoine Desjarlais and Susanne Allary Genealogy. Courtesy of Cheryl Troupe and Neil Soiseth.

similar petition in 1881 indicates a significant population increase.[8] The same year, the federal census enumerated at least eighty-seven Métis households, comprised of roughly 500 individuals.[9] Arguably, by the late 1870s and into the early 1880s, there was already a considerable, and increasing, Métis presence in the Valley environs.

It was not a single extended family hunting brigade that came to the Valley but an intricate web of interrelated and extended families, many of whom had already hunted and travelled together by the time they took up year-round occupancy. The families of Antoine Desjarlais and his second wife Susanne Catherine Allary, Charles Pelletier and Suzanne Bercier, Antoine Larocque and Françoise Laliberte, and others

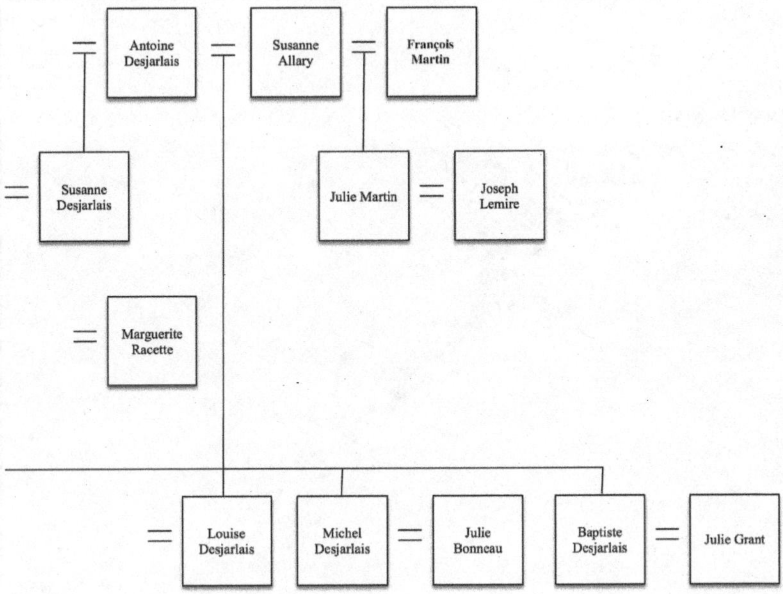

had been part of a hunting brigade under the leadership of Jean Baptiste Wilkie, hunting together as early as 1850.[10] The brigade, comprised of families from St. François Xavier as well as those from Dakota Territory settlements at Pembina and St. Joseph, wintered together across the west at Turtle Mountain, Wood Mountain, Cypress Hills, and Milk River.[11] By the late 1870s, many of these families moved north into the Qu'Appelle while others moved west towards Spring Creek, Montana.[12] Consequently, at the time the Métis committed to year-round settlement in the Valley, their already-strong kinship connections were becoming even more complex.

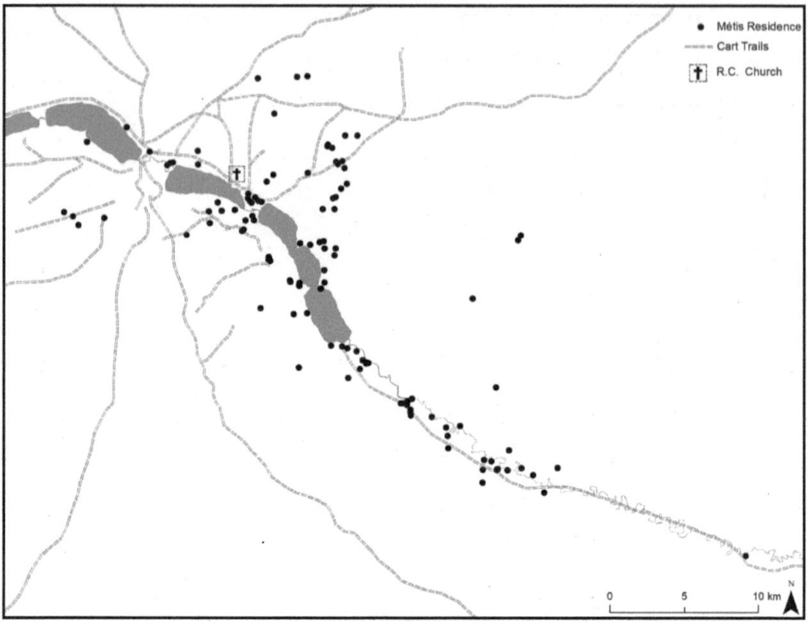

Figure 17. Métis Occupancy in Qu'Appelle Valley Prior to Survey, 1881–1882. Map courtesy of Cheryl Troupe and Matthew Kunkel.

By the 1860s Antoine Desjarlais's extended family included the Fishers, Blondeaus, Bonneaus, Grants, Racettes, and others. His extended family demonstrates the complex organizational structure typical of Métis families and settlements of the period.[13] Desjarlais was married at least twice: first, to Pelagie Martin and later to Susanne Catherine Allary. The latter union was also the second marriage for Allary, having first been married to François Martin. The familial relationship between Pelagie and François Martin is unknown, but they were likely closely related. Desjarlais and Allary remarrying within their extended kinship network after the deaths of their respective spouses solidified relationships across family lines.

Desjarlais and Pelagie Martin's daughter Susanne and her husband Alexander Fisher lived in the region by the 1860s. Alexander, the son of Henry Munro Fisher and Marguerite Laframboise, worked for the

HBC. His brother John and his wife Betsy Brabant were also nearby,[14] as were Allary and François Martin's daughter Julie and her husband Joseph Lemire who entered into treaty in 1874 and resided north of the Valley on Muskowequan reserve.[15] Alongside these families were at least four of Desjarlais and Allary's children, Françoise, Louise, Baptiste, and Michel.[16] Françoise married Simon Blondeau in 1850 and by 1865 they were established with their eleven children, some of whom were already married and living with their own families.[17] Louise was married to Eusebe Ledoux; Baptiste married Julie Grant, daughter of Cuthbert Grant and Marie McGillis; and Michel was married to Julie Bonneau, daughter of François Bonneau and Marie Favel. By 1870, Baptiste and Julie had at least five young children, and Michel and his wife Julie Bonneau at least six. Enlarging the extended family, Julie Grant's brother James and his wife Josephte Helene Gariepy and their children also lived close by.[18] So did Eusebe Ledoux and first wife Susanne Bonneau's daughter, Marie. She was married to Antoine Fayant, son of Antoine Fayant and Josephte Pelletier.[19]

This family system became more complicated with each successive generation, and quickly included the children of John Beaulieau, Augustin Brabant, George Racette, and others. Two of Alexander Fisher and Suzanne Desjarlais's daughters, Eliza and Marguerite, had married brothers John and Thomas Beaulieau; while their son Alexander Jr. was married to Marguerite Racette, daughter of George Racette and Isabel Vandal. John Blondeau, son of Simon Blondeau and Françoise Desjarlais, was married to Caroline Brabant, daughter of Augustin Brabant and Julie Phillipe. Brabant's sister Betsy was married to John Fisher, brother of Alexander Sr.

Female kinship relationships were at the centre of these large extended Métis families. It was a structure carried over from the buffalo hunt and paralleled other Métis settlements of the period, including those along the South Saskatchewan River at Batoche, St. Laurent, and La Prairie Ronde, as well as in the Spring Creek and Lewistown areas in Montana.[20]

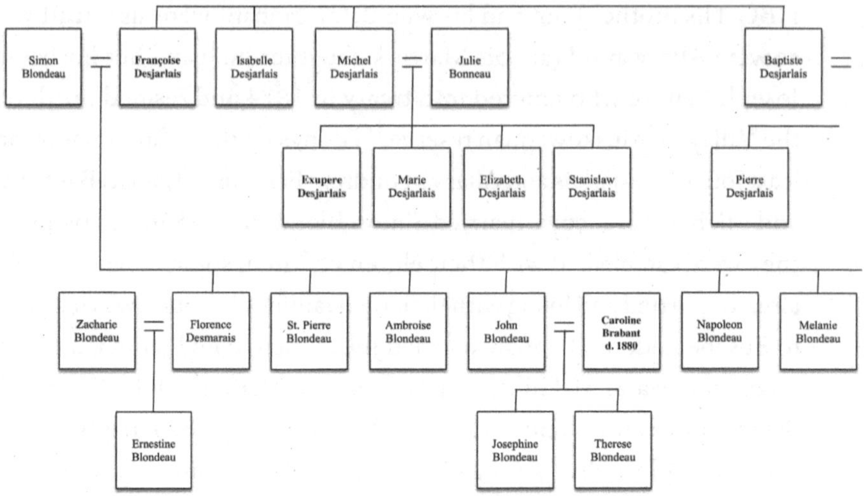

Figure 18. Simon Blondeau and Françoise Desjarlais Genealogy. Courtesy of Cheryl Troupe and Neil Soiseth.

By 1881, Simon Blondeau and his wife Françoise Desjarlais, aged sixty-five and sixty, had unmarried adult children Napoleon and Caroline living with them, as well as their daughter Melanie, son Joseph, and twins St. Pierre and Ambroise.[21] Close by, but in their own homes, were Simon and Françoise's adult children: Simon Jr., John, Zacharie, and Louison.[22] Simon Jr. and John were both widowed, raising their young children. In 1873, Simon and Françoise's son Simon Jr. married Julie Hamelin, daughter of Gaspard Hamelin and Louise Landry, and their son John married Caroline Brabant, daughter of Augustin Brabant Jr. and Julie Phillipe. Both Julie and Caroline died in 1880. Simon and Françoise's son Zacharie, his wife Florence Desmarais, and their young daughter, as well as Zacharie's brother Louison and wife Marie Antoinette Robillard were living close by. Marie Antoinette's parents, Jean Baptiste Robillard and Isabelle Comtois, were also residents in the region.[23] Jean Baptiste and

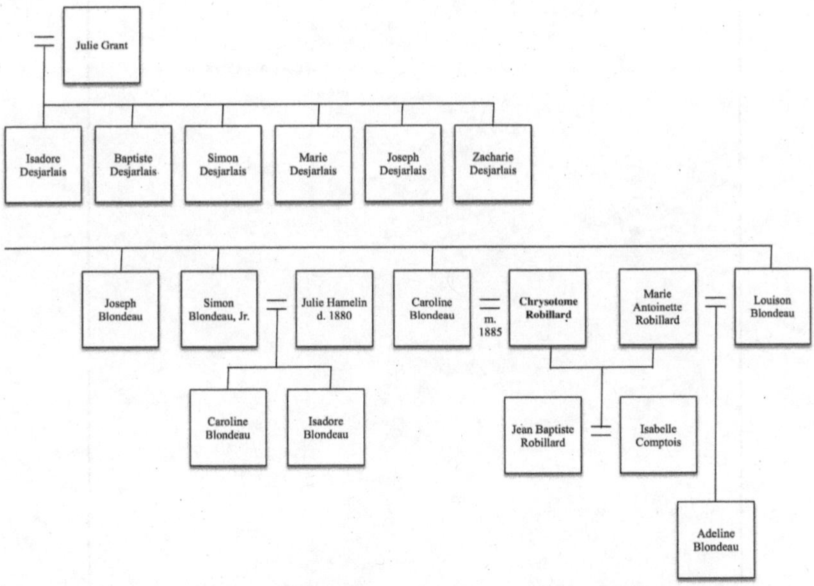

Isabelle's son Chrysotome later married Simon and Françoise's daughter Caroline in 1885, thus strengthening the kinship relationship between the Robillard and Desjarlais families.

The presence of siblings, aunts, uncles, and cousins further complicated the extended family. Living within the Blondeau/Desjarlais extended family network were several of Desjarlais's siblings, including Baptiste, Michel, Isabelle, and Julie. Françoise's brother Baptiste, his wife Julie Grant, and their seven children lived next to Simon and Françoise.[24] Michel Desjarlais and his wife Julie Bonneau and their four children were also nearby.[25] Three of their four children, Elizabeth, Marie, and Exupere, were over the age of eighteen, unmarried, and living with their elderly parents. By 1886, Desjarlais's unmarried sister Isabelle Desjarlais and half-sister Julie Martin also resided here.[26] Blind and living alone, Martin lived close to John Blondeau. Considering Françoise Desjarlais's

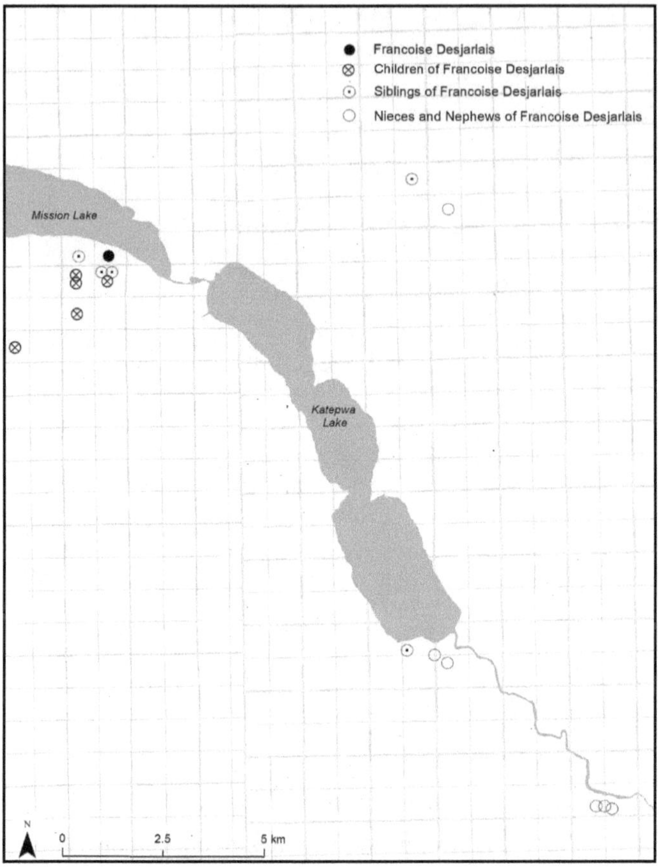

Figure 19. Simon Blondeau and Françoise Desjarlais Extended Family Residences, 1880s–1890s. Map courtesy of Cheryl Troupe and Matthew Kunkel.

elderly siblings lived within the cluster of her immediate family suggests the complexity of intergenerational kinship relationships, the significance of female kinship, and the obligations that existed across extended family lines.

Just as Françoise Desjarlais was central to her extended family network, so too was Madeleine Beauchemin Klyne to hers. As the Klyne family settled into the Valley, their large extended family included the Desjarlais, Desnomme, Bellegarde, Davis, Poitras, Landry, Gosselin,

Figure 20. Madeleine Klyne family, Lebret, c. 1890s, R-A8823. Photograph courtesy of Provincial Archives of Saskatchewan. Front: Madeleine Beauchemin Klyne and daughter Madeleine Klyne Desjarlais. Back: granddaughters Marie Rosine and Justine Desjarlais. They appear to be holding prayer cards.

and Vallee families. Madeleine and her husband Michel Klyne had moved throughout the territory hunting buffalo on both sides of the Canada/United States border. In 1871, they came to the Valley from the Devil's Lake area of Dakota Territory in the United States with all but two of their adult children and their respective families. In the same period, Madeleine's mother Charlotte Pelletier and Charlotte's siblings, Josephte, and Charles, came to the Valley with their respective spouses and children. They had been part of the large brigade hunting under the

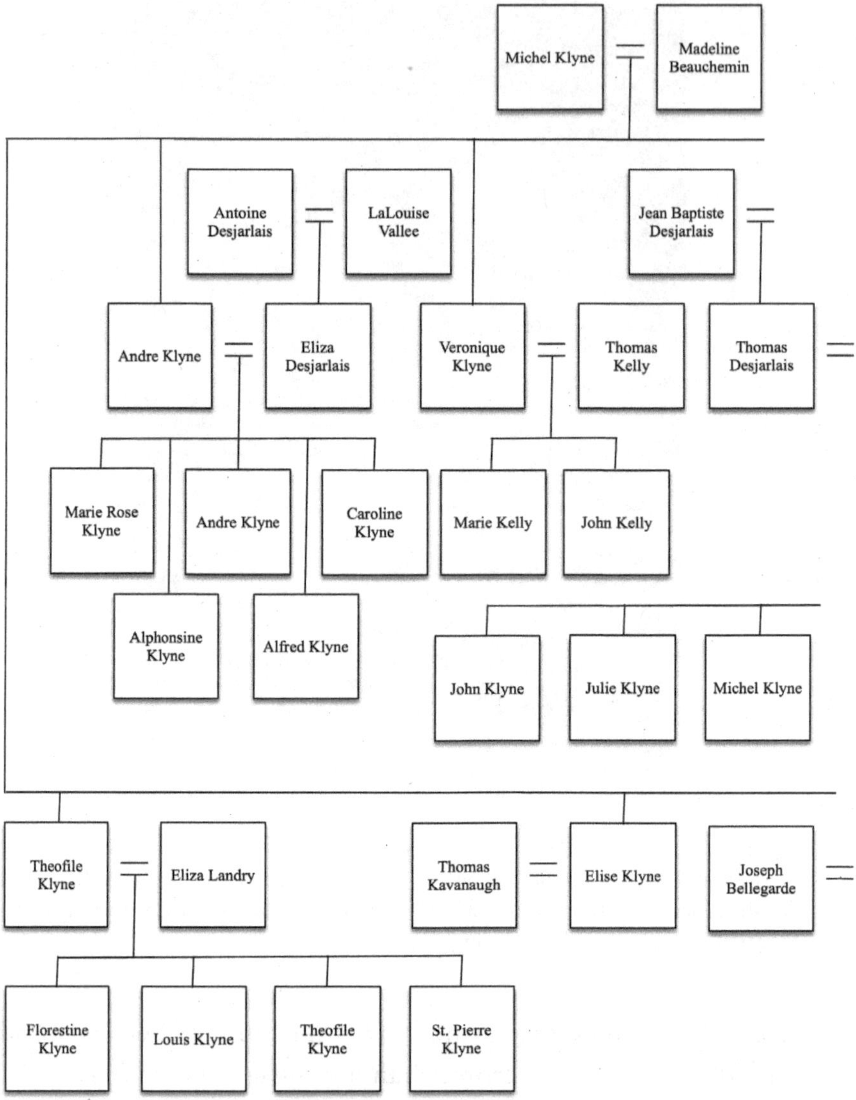

Figure 21. Michel Klyne and Madeleine Beauchemin Genealogy (select). Courtesy of Cheryl Troupe and Neil Soiseth.

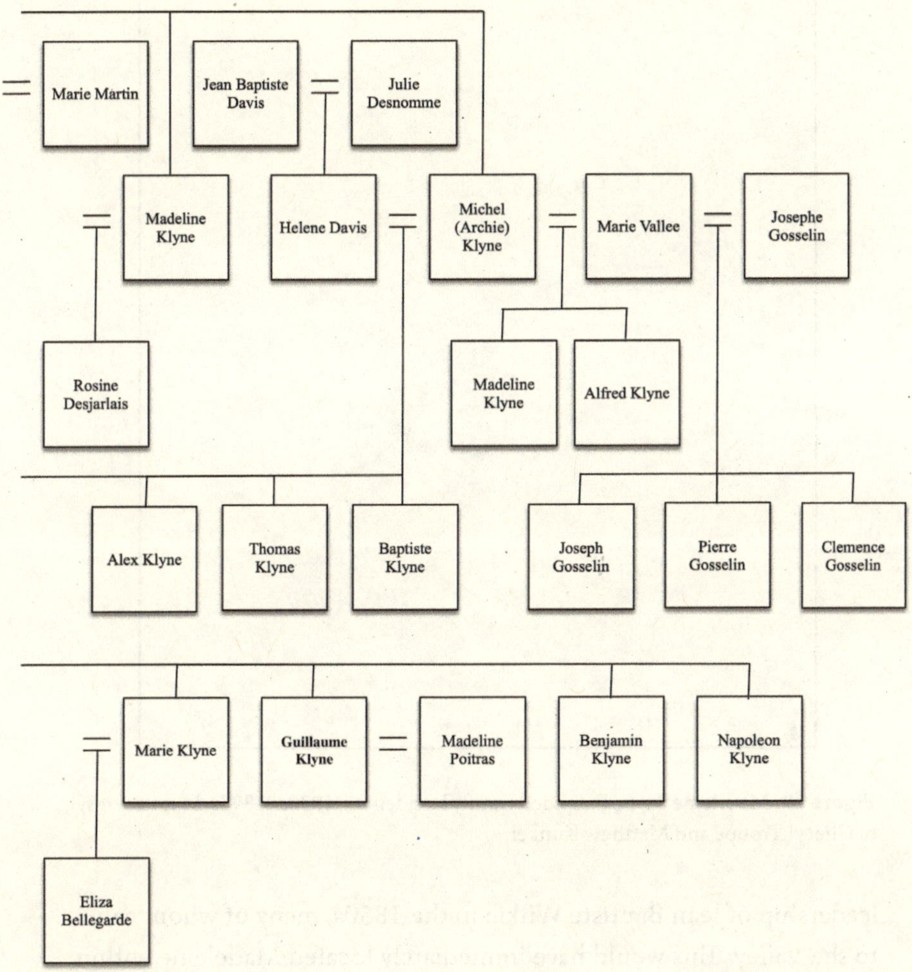
Marie Martin
Jean Baptiste Davis
Julie Desnomme
Madeline Klyne
Helene Davis
Michel (Archie) Klyne
Marie Vallee
Josephe Gosselin
Rosine Desjarlais
Madeline Klyne
Alfred Klyne
Alex Klyne
Thomas Klyne
Baptiste Klyne
Joseph Gosselin
Pierre Gosselin
Clemence Gosselin
Marie Klyne
Guillaume Klyne
Madeline Poitras
Benjamin Klyne
Napoleon Klyne
Eliza Bellegarde

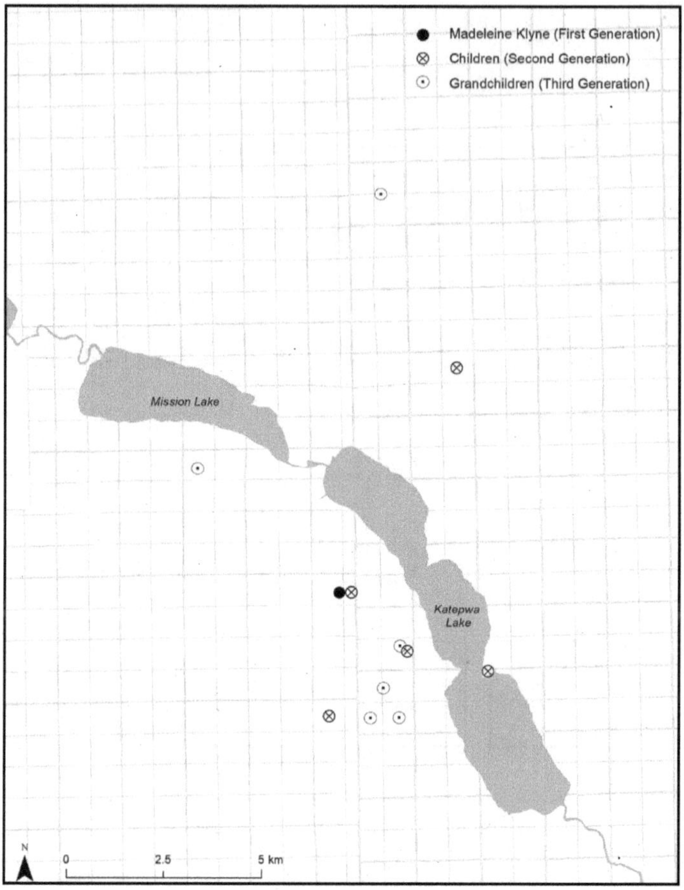

Figure 22. Madeleine Klyne Extended Family Residences, 1880s–1890s. Map courtesy of Cheryl Troupe and Matthew Kunkel.

leadership of Jean Baptiste Wilkie in the 1850s, many of whom came to the Valley. This would have immediately located Madeleine within a complex interconnected network of extended family relationships in the Valley while also recognizing how kinship relations spanned broad territories and even crossed international borders. Despite relocating and settling in the Valley, Madeleine, her mother Charlotte, and her mother's siblings remained connected to Métis in the United States as the Pelletiers lived, hunted, and intermarried with the Azures, Bergers, and Wilkies that settled in Spring Creek, Montana. For instance, Madeleine's mother Charlotte had first married Antoine Azure and then André Millet dit Beauchemin, Madeleine's father. In addition, Madeleine's son Ben Klyne remained within the Montana community and wintered at Milk River, Dakota Territory, while son Guillaume remained at Wood Mountain.[27]

Taking up land along the Qu'Appelle Lakes, the Madeleine and Michel Klyne family spent time, at least seasonally, at Wood Mountain and the Cypress Hills to hunt and renew family relationships. When Michel Klyne died in 1875 Madeleine remained in their home, living with her teenage son, Napoleon, and surrounded by her children.[28] Three of Michel and Madeleine's sons, André, Theophile, and Michel, and four of their daughters, Elise, Veronique, Madeline, and Marie, lived close by with their respective spouses and children.[29] Collectively, Madeleine's immediate family in the Qu'Appelle Valley comprised at least forty individuals.

Taking Up Agriculture: Métis Land Holding Patterns

When settling into the Valley, Métis families emulated the land tenure customs at Red River and in other Métis communities across the west, selecting lands in long narrow plots that fronted the water to ensure access to multiple resources. Other Métis settlements of the period, such as St. Paul des Métis, Batoche, St. Laurent, and Isbister's Settlement in Prince Albert, also employed these recognizable land tenure practices when establishing themselves away from Red River.[30] They built homes close to lakes or rivers for easy access to potable water, water for cleaning and washing, and water as a transportation corridor. Lots included areas for vegetable gardens, land for growing hay, grazing areas for cattle and horses, as well as access to firewood. The long, narrow structure of river lots ensured that residences remained close to one another. This land holding pattern allowed for support across extended families and helped maintain cultural and family traditions, including food practices

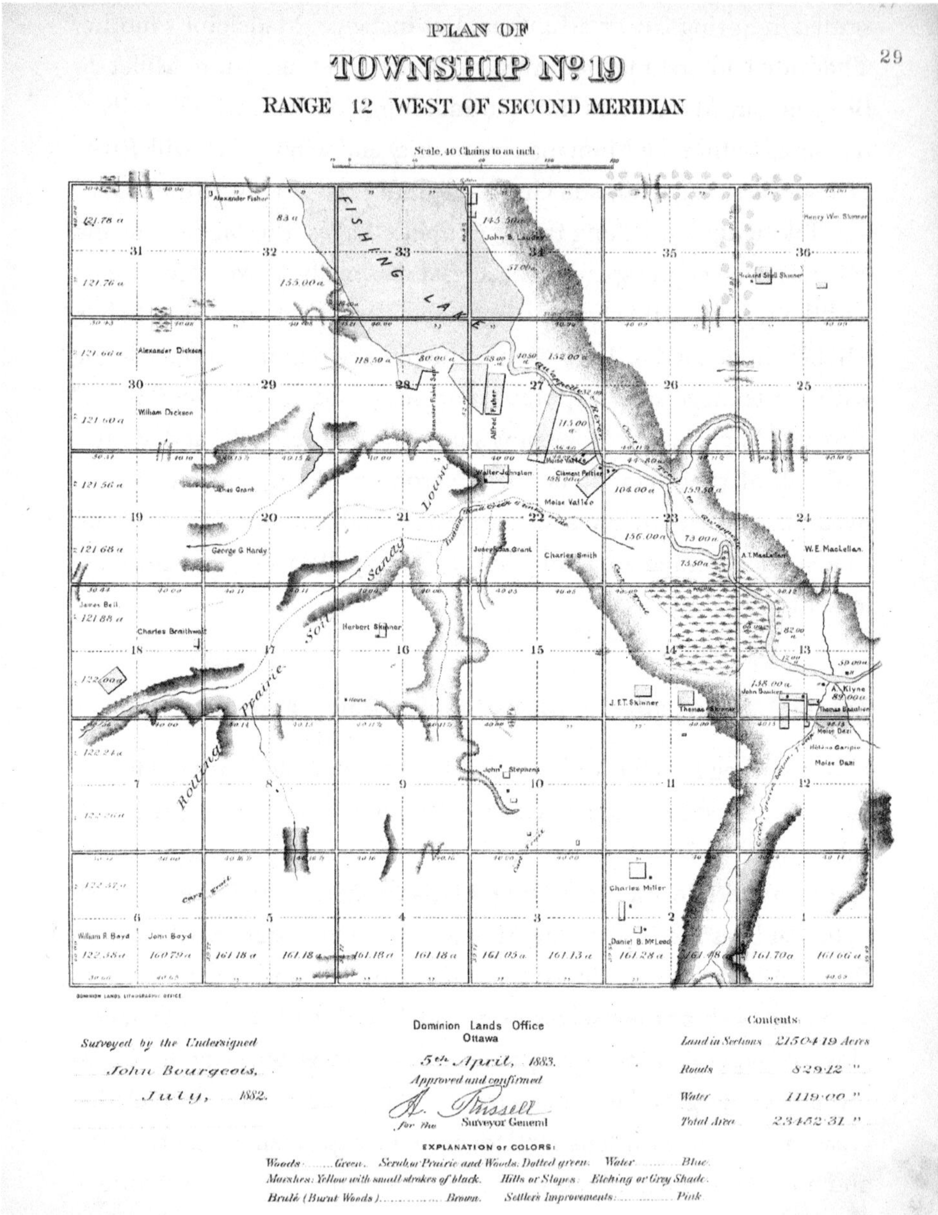

Figure 23. Dominion Land Survey (Township 19–Range 12–West of Second Meridian), Qu'Appelle Valley, c. 1883. Map courtesy of Provincial Archives of Saskatchewan.

that merged economic and social activity with cultural knowledge and understandings.

This settlement pattern was not unique to the Qu'Appelle Valley. However, when compared to the organized survey of river lots in other similar Métis settlements, river lots in the Qu'Appelle Valley were less systematic. Father DeCorby, a Catholic priest at the St. Florent Mission, described Métis land holdings along the Qu'Appelle Lakes as almost haphazard where "each cut his piece after his own fashion. This one took a little point. That one a stream, where there was a little wood and good lands; another marked for himself a good length on the little piece of woods which covers the southern declivity of the Valley."[31] The way Qu'Appelle Métis took up land, however, was not indiscriminate but followed social customs, particularly those that privileged extended family kinship relationships. For the Métis, living close to one's family members was paramount.

Upon selecting their plots, families quickly planted large vegetable gardens, a practice carried over from Red River and their experiences with HBC.[32] They had been practising small-scale agriculture in the Red River region since the mid-1820s to supplement the buffalo hunt and seasonal labour opportunities with the Company.[33] This practice fit well with the seasonal nature of Métis life by allowing them to be away for the hunts. They simply planted their gardens prior to embarking onto the plains, leaving them unattended throughout the growing season and harvesting them upon their return. While this practice suited the Métis, it caused concern amongst Red River settlers who viewed the Métis as poor farmers, insincere in their agricultural efforts. As Red River politician, administrator, and writer Alexander Ross disparaged, the Métis, being hunters, farmers, and fishermen "as whim and circumstances may dictate," choose to "farm to-day, hunt to-morrow, and fish the next, without anything like a system," resulting in untended and ultimately failing crops because of their absence.[34]

By the 1870s, HBC Clerk Isaac Cowie noted that while most Métis continued buffalo hunting when they could, they supplemented their economy with other food harvesting practices, including vegetable gardening. A few, he suggested, had even begun to move away from the hunt and farm on a larger scale, but it was the Métis' enduring reliance on the hunt, and not the quality of the land or their agricultural skills, that impeded their success. Gardening, he argued, "[had] been tried with varying success; crops of wheat, barley, Indian corn, potatoes, and common kitchen vegetables, in good seasons, turning out fair returns. Abundant water, pasture and hay and an open country make stock-raising profitable and easy."[35]

The promise of good land and agricultural success was clear. Visiting the region in August 1881 with Governor General Lord Lorne, Reverend Doctor James MacGregor and W.H. Williams, special correspondent for the *Toronto Globe* newspaper, echoed views about the quality and fertility of the land and its potential. MacGregor recounted a settlement of Métis farmers "cutting down splendid crops of wheat and barley" as well as Catholic mission priests with well-tended gardens of "potatoes of marvelous size, water-melons, musk-melons, tomatoes, French beans, and cabbages."[36] Visiting a small Métis claim with a flourishing garden of corn, potatoes, wheat, oats, barley, and various root crops convinced the governor general's party of the region's agricultural potential.[37] While not explicit as to whose property they described, it was likely Antoine Larocque's claim. A retired buffalo hunter and trader, Larocque and his wife Rosalie Laplante settled in the Qu'Appelle Valley to a life of farming and trading by the early 1870s.[38] Lorne's party had visited Larocque, noting he possessed a "remarkably pretty and promising claim" with "all sorts of ordinary vegetables flourishing luxuriantly and in a fairly advanced state for the time of year."[39] Inspecting Larocque's fields, Williams was particularly impressed with the wheat fields that he noted were within days of being ready to harvest and looked to be "absolute perfection in quantity, size, weight, texture and colour."[40]

By the early 1880s, Métis families were spread throughout the Valley region, most working small claims of one to eight acres with just enough land under cultivation for a vegetable garden and small hay and barley fields. There were also some, like Larocque, that were increasingly clearing larger plots of land.[41] Despite the small size of many of these farms, when examined within the context of the extended family, some families had sizable farming operations. For instance, Madeleine Klyne and her children farmed over seventy acres of land.[42] Although they did not farm collectively, kinship obligations and responsibilities would have ensured they shared resources and helped one another out when required.

Regardless of the size of their farms, the Métis overwhelmingly remained intent on maintaining a mixed subsistence of hunting, fishing, and gathering wild foods, supplemented with small-scale agricultural production. This economy allowed families to continue the complementary gender roles practised during the buffalo hunt, where everyone contributed necessary labour. Families and communities spatially organized themselves as they had when hunting buffalo, in large extended groupings and along hunt kinship lines. Living in proximity to one another, these families recognized themselves as having shared rights, responsibilities, and territory, and a sense of unity. They demonstrated this in the petitions they forwarded to government seeking recognition of their occupancies.

Conflicting Land Tenure—The Transfer of Rupert's Land, the Red River Resistance 1869–70, and Scrip

Qu'Appelle Métis recognized the necessity of protecting their land and way of life and began petitioning the Dominion Government in the early 1870s. They were concerned about the future of the buffalo hunt and changes in their social and political environment, including issues of incoming settlement and encroachment. They were also anxious over the events of the 1869–70 Red River Resistance that led to the entrance of Manitoba into Confederation.

With Confederation in 1867, Canada's first prime minister, John A. Macdonald, and the new Dominion Government quickly recognized the value of acquiring Rupert's Land for Canada and the British Empire's future prosperity.[43] The Métis did not oppose the transfer of Rupert's Land but were concerned about what a new order of government would mean for their way of life and were angry about the government's lack of consultation on the transfer.[44] Ottawa made no assurances they would respect Métis occupancy rights, and people feared the loss of their river-lot farms. This only increased anxiety amongst the predominately Roman Catholic Métis as they faced growing pressure from Protestant settlers from eastern Canada moving into the Red River region.

The Métis acted to protect their interests and Louis Riel emerged as their leader. They thwarted the federal government's initial survey of the settlement and seized Upper Fort Garry, the main HBC trading post at the forks of the Red and Assiniboine Rivers, before declaring themselves a provisional government. These were political and mainly peaceful acts symbolic of Métis determination to stand up for their rights, at least until the 1870 execution of Thomas Scott, a Protestant, Canada Party supporter opposed to Métis action.[45] Before Scott's execution, the Métis believed themselves politically justified and not disloyal to the new Canadian government. They felt they were merely defending rights that the existing government was ineffective in ensuring.[46] The Métis held Fort Garry until government agreed to negotiate the terms by which Red River and Manitoba would enter Confederation. For the Métis, foremost in their minds as a condition for entry was the protection of their land rights.

The Manitoba Act was passed on 15 July 1870. Section 31 of the Act set aside 1.4 million acres of public lands for the Métis, meant to extinguish their existing title to land in the new province.[47] This title was based on their occupancy of the region prior to the imposition of Canadian authority over the territory. Under the Act, Métis heads of families were to receive 160 acres of land while their children were to receive 240 acres. Not spelled out in the Act but through orders-in-council, the "provision of scrip" was the administrative process of extinguishing Métis title to land. Individual claimants appeared before a scrip commissioner, completed an application, and swore an affidavit. If approved, they received a paper certificate redeemable for land or money scrip that when presented at a Dominion Lands Office could be applied to surveyed land. A land scrip certificate (as opposed to tangible land) represented an entitlement to either 160 or 240 acres, while a money scrip certificate entitled the bearer to $160 or $240 worth of land, which the government valued at one dollar per acre. Considered real property, land scrip had certain limitations on its sale, whereas money scrip, considered personal property, was much easier to dispose of. Scrip coupons did not include an individual's name, making them easily exchangeable by the bearer. The ease of scrip exchange resulted in most of it ending up in the hands of speculators who used it to gain title to large blocks of land that they could sell for a profit.[48]

Further administrative challenges created frustrations for Métis claimants.[49] Not only were there language and literacy barriers in completing applications and affidavits, but misinformation and misunderstanding plagued the process. There was also no shortage of fraud. Having to appear before the scrip commissioner and the Dominion Lands agent interfered with the Métis seasonal cycle, and land speculators were consistently present, eager to buy up any, and all, available Métis scrip for a fraction of its value. The most considerable challenge, however, was the slow pace of implementation. Distribution of the scrip certificates did not begin until 1876 and by this time many Métis were already permanently living outside Manitoba, making it difficult for them to receive their scrip.

Whether the Canadian government acted in good faith when negotiating or fulfilling the promises outlined in the Manitoba Act or if the government deliberately designed the scrip process to keep land out of Métis hands continues to be debated.[50] The Canadian government undermined Métis land rights by passing legislation that made it easier to dispossess the Métis of their land through the scrip process and all levels of government and private individuals were duplicitous in this. Through legislation, delay, and administrative shuffle, Government failed to honour Métis land tenure and the promises made in the Manitoba Act.[51] The scrip process became a pragmatic solution to the problem of

Métis rights. It supported individual land ownership and had the potential to transform the Métis into modern agricultural settlers; alternatively, they would sell the land to white settlers. Either way, Canada would achieve its desired goal of acquiring Métis land for agricultural settlement.[52]

The Métis did not flourish in Manitoba after 1870. Although they had won concession on major objectives, including a distinct province with guaranteed land and cultural rights, their victory was hollow. Scrip failed to secure a Métis land base, and they soon found themselves with little choice but to permanently relocate further west to former buffalo-hunting wintering places, joining relatives already in the North-West. This diaspora after 1870 accelerated and made permanent the seasonal pattern of wintering on the plains that Métis hunters had followed since the 1840s.

For Qu'Appelle Métis, this experience in Manitoba remained fresh in their minds. Despite living in the Valley, most remained connected through extended family to the Red River parishes and some had applied for scrip. Others had not participated in the scrip process, having been living outside of Manitoba on 15 July 1870, the date the Manitoba Act came into effect. The fact that Qu'Appelle Métis believed themselves to possess unextinguished land rights loomed large.

The Qu'Appelle Petition, May 1873

In early May 1873, John Fisher and ten other Qu'Appelle Métis petitioned North-West Territories Lieutenant Governor Alexander Morris intent on having their land rights recognized.[53] This was the first in a series of petitions. Pledging their support for government, they made it clear that they understood their political milieu. They had the support of all the Métis of the North-West and the friendship of the Nêyihawak, Nakota, and Nahkawinniwak. Peace existed amongst the Métis in the North-West and they affirmed their intent to continue encouraging peace and respect for the government amongst their neighbouring First Nations. Without doubt, these assurances were included to convince the government that there would not be a repeat of political unrest in the North-West as in Manitoba in 1869–70.

The petition spoke to pressing issues for Qu'Appelle Métis but also to larger political issues impacting all Métis across the North-West. Foremost, they sought protection over the land they occupied. They recognized the transfer of Rupert's Land had annexed the North-West to the Canadian government and, like in Manitoba, the Métis in the North-West did not have clear title to the land they occupied. They wanted protection of their land holdings because they were aware the government intended to and was already giving incoming settlers preference in distribution of land. They argued that the government had not adequately managed Métis land rights in Manitoba and had treated the Métis poorly. Three years had gone by since the Manitoba Act was passed and promises made to the Métis through scrip remained unfulfilled. Qu'Appelle Métis wanted confirmation that they would not be treated like their relations in Manitoba, asking for guarantees that land rights would be dealt with in a timely and fair manner.

The petitioners also drew attention to larger political concerns for Métis across the west. Connections between the Qu'Appelle families and those in Red River remained strong, and the Qu'Appelle Métis remained socially, politically, and economically loyal to their relations, despite their relocation to the Valley. They expressed their belief that in 1869–70 Governor William McDougall had acted without the queen's instruction in "declaring war" on the Métis in Red River and asked for a general pardon for Louis Riel and his principal supporters. They were also frustrated that following the resistance, the government gave political appointments to Dr. John Christian Schultz and Colonel John Stoughton Dennis, who were both highly unsympathetic to the Métis. A surveyor, Dennis came to the Red River colony prior to the insurrection intending to survey the land for settlement and was leader of the survey party halted by the Métis, while Schultz, an influential member of the Canadian party, was actively engaged in overthrowing Riel's provisional government in

1869–70.[54] The Métis saw these political appointments as the Dominion government's attempt to fuel further tensions.

The petition initially fell on deaf ears. A month later, Morris replied, ignoring the Métis' requests, instead chastising them for styling themselves a "Council."[55] Undoubtedly cautious from the Manitoba experience where the Métis formed a provisional government in absence of existing authority, Morris reminded the petitioners that the laws of England were in effect in the North-West. The North-West Council, not the petitioners' "Council," was responsible. Morris also disregarded the request for Riel's pardon, replying that only the queen of England possessed the authority to grant such a request. Despite these setbacks, the government's inaction and dismissal of the Métis' requests did not deter them but strengthened their resolve in having their voices heard.

Treaty Four Petition, September 1874

Just over a year later, the Métis again petitioned the Canadian Government, this time presenting themselves to Morris as a larger collective, calling themselves "the half-breeds of the Lake Qu'Appelle and environs . . . in their name and in the name of all their brethren scattered over the prairies."[56] This petition was prepared immediately before Treaty Four negotiations were held in the Qu'Appelle Valley. This was a significant event for the Métis who were eager to protect their land holdings at a time when First Nations were entering into negotiations with the Canadian government to ensure their own economic future. Calling for the recognition of their rights and guarantees to the land they already occupied in the Valley, thirty-one heads of Métis families signed the 11 September 1874 petition.

The Métis used what influence they could muster by calling upon one of their own, Pascal Breland, to deliver the petition to the lieutenant governor. They believed that Breland, an old buffalo hunter turned political statesmen, could and would champion their cause. A prominent trader and farmer from White Horse Plains, Breland was a magistrate for

St. François Xavier in the early 1850s and by 1857 was serving on the North-West Council. In 1872, the Government of Canada sent Breland to the Qu'Appelle region in advance of treaty negotiations to counsel Nêhiyawak and Nahkawinniwak Chiefs, distribute gifts, and make assurances of what was to be promised in treaty. Most importantly, he was to report back to the government on the existing conditions.[57] Familiar to First Nations and Métis in the region, Breland was a trusted and fitting candidate for this position. He and his wife Marie Grant had wintered in the Valley in 1868–69 and had kinship connections to many of the petition's signatories.

Like Fisher's earlier petition, the 1874 petition asked the government to protect Métis lands and livelihoods.[58] The Métis made three requests. First, they asked for protections over their way of life and recognition of their rights to the lands they occupied and those that they may take (as their children came of age) along the Qu'Appelle River. They called for recognition of fishing rights in the Qu'Appelle Lakes, rights to hunt freely west and southwest of the lakes, as well as the right to trade in the Qu'Appelle region. Understanding the ongoing treaty negotiations, they requested the right to hunt without interference from First Nations and agreed that they would uphold any arrangements that First Nations might make with the Métis or Canadian government. While not explicitly referring to the treaty process, their petition demonstrates recognition and understanding of shared rights and access to the territory. Second, petitioners asked that the Roman Catholic Church have its land rights recognized and that the same rights and privileges extended to the Métis also be given to the Church. These requests were indicative of the Métis' devout nature and the important role the Church played in their lives. Third, they asked for laws protecting the buffalo hunt. With ongoing worry about the declining herds moving further from the Valley region, they requested a law preventing hunters from wintering too far out in the prairies, which could increase access and invite the possibility of overhunting. Once a strategy to ensure continuous access, wintering was now understood to be detrimental to the diminishing herds. As an additional protection, the petitioners asked the government to compel hunters to hunt collectively. As a distinctive and codified practice of the Métis, hunting in a group ensured order, regulated behaviour, and encouraged collective success. Requesting the government to regulate directives so integral to the Métis hunt reveals the considerable impact the thinning herds had on their social and economic structures.

The Métis did not want their petitioning to derogate from the treaty process that their First Nations relatives were negotiating. They were eager to have the treaty concluded and simply wanted their voices heard and rights recognized. The inclusion of diplomatic language regarding the extension of kinship relationships to First Nations also exposes Métis apprehension of their place in a three-way race where parties competed for the same land and resources. Several petitioners signed the treaty as witnesses to its negotiation and used their presence and existing relationships with First Nations chiefs and others present to leverage political support.[59] There were probably many more non-signing Métis petitioners present throughout the negotiations, making a political statement, if by presence alone. Government made no promises to Métis during the treaty process, despite First Nations chiefs asking the government to treat their Métis brothers fairly and justly, voicing support for continual Métis hunt in the west.[60]

Although the government refused Qu'Appelle Métis to collectively enter Treaty Four in 1874, there were many instances throughout the 1870s where Métis were in fact included in the numbered treaties.[61] By the time treaty negotiations began, there was no enumeration of Métis communities nor had Métis rights in the North-West been extinguished. As a result, the government allowed Métis who wished to be included in the treaty as "Indians" to do so, prompting several groups of Métis who met the definition of Indian under the Indian Act (1868) to enter Treaties Four, Five, and Six.[62]

The decision to allow Métis to enter treaty was complicated. This was largely due to the government's ambiguous and changing definitions of who was and who was not an "Indian." The Indian Act (1868) defined Indians in a way that included many Métis:

> Firstly. All persons of Indian blood, reputed to belong to the particular tribe, band or body of Indians interested in such lands or immoveable property, and their descendants;
>
> Secondly. All persons residing among such Indians, whose parents were or are, or either of them was or is, descended on either side from Indians or an Indian reputed to belong to the particular tribe, band or body of Indians interested in such lands or immoveable property, and the descendants of all such persons; And,
>
> Thirdly. All women lawfully married to any of the persons included in the several classes hereinbefore designated; the children issue of such marriages, and their descendants.[63]

By this definition, Métis women who married treaty men gained treaty status, along with any children they might have. In addition, Métis with extensive kin connections who lived among First Nations or had at least one parent considered an Indian or living as an Indian, would have qualified to take treaty.

Just as complicated was the definition of who was, or was not, considered Métis. At the time of treaty negotiation, Alexander Morris, acting as Indian Commissioner, classified Métis into three categories. The first class, like Métis at St. Laurent, Qu'Appelle, and Edmonton, he recognized as farmers and property owners because they made their living by farming and trading. The second class, he viewed as Indians because they lived with and like Indians. However, he had more difficulty defining the third class. This group, he observed, did not farm but lived "a wandering life" with no permanent homes, following the buffalo in "the habits of the Indians."[64] He recognized the impact of the collapsing buffalo herds on the Métis and their perceived economic similarity to First Nations livelihoods, but did not see this as reason enough to allow their entrance into treaty. Rather, he suggested land be set aside for them, when and if they were to settle into an agricultural lifestyle, as well as assistance be provided to help them adjust to an agricultural economy.[65] Morris did not recognize the Métis as having rights equal to First Nations but understood the complexity of discerning where the Métis fit.

Kinship relationships between First Nations and Métis families and communities were complex and boundaries or distinctions between them were, in practice, often blurred. As a result, many did enter treaty with bands across Treaty Four territory. For example, Cowessess band membership was historically flexible and inclusive of not only Nêhiyawak but also Nahkawinniwak, Nakota, and Métis, which permitted several Métis families to enter Treaty Four.[66] Similarly, many Métis also took treaty with George Gordon First Nation in the Touchwood Hills area because their lifestyle was indistinguishable from their First Nations relatives.[67] However, despite the same legal classification, once under treaty, officials attempted to find distinctions between First Nations and Métis for decades afterwards, suggesting that such differences mattered more to Indian Agents and government officials than to Indigenous peoples themselves.[68]

In the Qu'Appelle Valley, First Nations and Métis families intermarried and family networks extended into and across First Nations communities. Studying the large extended Desjarlais family, Métis historian Heather Devine demonstrates the complexity of cultural identity that existed for many families and how this undoubtedly influenced their decision to take treaty.[69] By the 1860s, brothers Antoine and Baptiste "Nishecabo" Desjarlais were living in the Qu'Appelle Valley with their grown children and grandchildren. Despite both men dying before the negotiation of Treaty Four, the choices their children made whether to enter treaty reveals much about their cultural identification. HBC clerk at Fort Qu'Appelle Isaac Cowie recounted his impression of Nishecabo, stating that Desjarlais identified more as Nahkawinniwak than Métis, and that he followed Indigenous spirituality and knew and practised medicine.[70] These cultural worldviews and spiritual leanings undoubtedly influenced his children's decision to take treaty with Muskowequan's Nahkawinniwak band north of the Qu'Appelle Valley.[71] Although some but not all of Antoine's children took treaty, they did ask in their petitions for similar privileges. They were well aware they were competing for fewer resources at a time when treaties restricted First Nations land occupancy and government policy opened land for incoming settlers.

Lieutenant Governor Morris's response to the 1874 petition, like the previous one, disregarded any rights-based Métis claim.[72] He did, however, agree to present the petition to the Privy Council of Canada, communicate the Métis' wishes to the Minister of the Interior, and submit their request for laws regarding the buffalo hunt to the North-West Council, but there was no assurance of Métis lands rights. Having just completed treaty negotiations, the government's priority was to only deal with those under treaty and relocate First Nations to reserve lands so that the remaining unoccupied land could be opened for settlement. The message was clear: Canada would not deal with the special claims of Qu'Appelle Métis and would continue to treat them as any other settler. As promised, Morris apprised the Privy Council Office and Minister of the Interior David Laird of the Métis position in October that year. While Morris stressed that the Métis' request for protection of lands they and the Church occupied was not unreasonable, he was confident that the Métis were now "happily allayed" as he had reassured them of their property rights as landowners.[73]

Morris, however, misjudged his settlement of Métis claims. That same October, Father DeCorby at the Qu'Appelle Mission wrote to Laird on behalf of the Métis describing their increasing anxiety and affirming his belief that the Métis had specific rights based on their occupancy and sovereignty over the territory.[74] The Métis, he asserted, had made a "type of conquest" over the territory by encouraging and maintaining peace with local First Nations. He pressed the minister, asking that the government treat the Métis with justice and generosity in honouring their claims and that they not be held to the strict lines imposed by a looming grid survey. This was a reasonable request, DeCorby argued, given the nature of the Valley environment. If the Métis were to be bound to the incoming township grid survey system, he cautioned, families would not have access to necessary resources currently found on the irregularly shaped plots they occupied. Two months later, DeCorby received notice that the Minister of the Interior's Office had received his letter, but they took no action.

The Qu'Appelle petitions were important for demanding the recognition of Métis rights in the Valley region and part of a larger political movement of Métis resistance. During this period, Métis from settlements across the west petitioned government, seeking recognition of their rights and protections for their way of life, as requested by Qu'Appelle Métis.[75] In early September 1876, thirty Métis at Fort Walsh, including some who signed the earlier Qu'Appelle petitions, submitted a petition to North-West Mounted Police Inspector James Morrow Walsh requesting admission to Treaty Four.[76] They recognized Walsh as an agent of the Canadian government, acting on behalf of the superintendent general of Indian Affairs, David Laird.[77] They identified as half-breeds of the Nêhiyawak and Nahkawinniwak, arguing they had lived on the plains all their lives and "adopted the customs of the Indians." They asked government to relinquish their as-yet unfulfilled Manitoba scrip claims and admit them into treaty. They requested the same annuities as treaty bands and recognition of their own kinship relationships and rights as Métis and asked to elect their own chief. This petition should not have surprised Walsh as only days earlier, Nêhiyawak chiefs assembled at Fort Walsh—to receive their treaty annuities—requested Walsh's presence at their encampment. The chiefs showed support for the Métis' petition, demanding they be admitted into treaty and provided with benefits equal to what they had themselves received. Walsh responded sympathetically but reasoned that the government would not allow Métis to enter treaty without the approval of the superintendent of Indian Affairs. He explained that the Métis had received a land grant in Manitoba and cautioned that if the Métis were allowed to enter treaty, they might receive both treaty annuity and scrip. In conciliation Walsh conveyed that if there were Métis who wished to give up their scrip claims he would forward their individual requests to Indian Affairs for consideration. Walsh forwarded the petition to the Minister of the Interior, David Laird, and reported his meeting with the Nêhiyawak chiefs who, he noted, regarded the Métis "as their brothers of the plains and were not inclined to part company with them now."[78]

Less than a month later, a large group of Métis presented themselves to government representatives at Fort Qu'Appelle.[79] Many were individuals who had earlier petitioned Lieutenant Governor Morris during Treaty Four signing in 1874. Questioned if they belonged to a specific band or recognized a particular chief, the Métis replied as they had at Fort Walsh: they wished to enter treaty as their own band, distinct from other bands, with a chief they elected. They prioritized recognition of their rights as Métis, sought inclusion in treaty on their own terms, and were pragmatic in their need to secure the means to support themselves and their families. Finding that the Department of the Interior's representative, M.G. Dickieson, would not accede to their demands, some pivoted to present themselves as members of the First Nations bands present. Dickieson refused to pay annuities to those not already on the treaty paylists unless they willingly took an oath that their fathers were or had been First Nations. The Métis refused to do so. They held steadfast to their rights when petitioning both Walsh and Dickieson. Although they were requesting entry into treaty, they would not be forced to give up their rights as Métis.

Dickieson made a risky decision presenting this caveat to the Métis as treaty paylists could have grown substantially had they accepted. He also ran the risk of angering the First Nations chiefs. Unlike those at Fort Walsh, the chiefs gathered at Qu'Appelle did not want the Métis admitted into their bands.[80] They were so anxious about the possibility that they implored Archibald McDonald, HBC officer in charge of the Swan River District, to act on their behalf and convince Dickieson to restrict the Métis' entry. McDonald refused to interfere and ignored their request. He did however, work to persuade the Métis not to press the issue further.[81]

In their petitions, Qu'Appelle Métis saw it necessary to reaffirm kinship relationships with local First Nations, using the language of brotherhood to liken themselves to their First Nations relatives. At the same time, First Nations leaders acknowledged familial relationships to the Métis in their treaty speeches and meetings with government. In some instances, their desires aligned with the Métis, and they asked that the government not forget about their relatives; in other instances, they eagerly wanted the Métis excluded from treaty benefits. Using the language of kinship demonstrated that First Nations and Métis recognized a bond between them. Yet, there were clear distinctions between First Nations and Métis from the government's viewpoint in acknowledging and negotiating land rights. As a result, access to land and resources was complicated and even hotly contested between First Nations, Métis, and incoming Anglo-Canadian settlers.

For the Qu'Appelle Métis, admittance into Treaty Four could have provided some economic security and recognized their rights as Métis. Furthermore, entering treaty as their own band would have allowed families to maintain kinship relationships and obligations to one another. The request to join treaty, however, was just one potential solution to the situation and its refusal only strengthened Métis resolve to protect their economic livelihoods and way of life.

In other parts of the North-West, Métis took similar political action, submitting petitions to the government to redress grievances and protect their rights. In 1877, Métis at Blackfoot Crossing on the Bow River petitioned for assistance in transitioning to an agricultural economy and for relaxation in game laws so that they might continue to hunt during the transition period.[82] The following year, approximately 280 Métis, including those in the Qu'Appelle Valley and Cypress Hills region and from La Prairie Ronde, Wood Mountain, Willow Bunch, and Montana, petitioned for protection and regulation of the hunt.[83] This was a claim of sovereignty over a large hunting territory that encompassed most of the western plains, including the Qu'Appelle Valley. Concerned about their economic future, signatories were families that had regularly wintered together in the Cypress Hills and saw themselves as a collective, with an ever-increasing sense of nationhood. Petitioners asked for a grant of land, about 150 miles long and fifty miles wide along the U.S.-Canada border, beginning where the Pembina River crossed the border. They also requested that the buffalo hunt be re-opened in the winter between 14 November and 15 February of each year.

The North-West Council had passed an Ordinance for the Protection of the Buffalo in 1877 that First Nations and Métis hunters saw as an affront to their economic livelihoods.[84] The ordinance set out what, how, and when animals could be hunted. It regulated a closed season for hunting female buffalo from mid-November to mid-August each year, and specifically allowed First Nations, excluding the Métis, to hunt from 15 November until 14 February.

Governor General Lorne Petition, 1881

In 1881, seven years after the last Qu'Appelle petition, families began petitioning once again, taking advantage of the Governor General Marquis of Lorne's cross-country tour of the new dominion. According to Norbert Welsh, a party of nearly 100 Métis, mounted on horseback in their finest display of horsemanship and collective identity, welcomed Lorne's party when it reached the Valley in August. Positioning themselves at the top of the south side of the Valley, they lined the trail in an honour guard as the governor general's party approached and fired a salute in the air when the party halted. The governor general, moved by the display of hospitality, shook hands with each rider. The Métis mounted again, fired another salute, and then, on prancing and galloping horses, escorted the party into Lebret.[85]

Following on the heels of this visit, 113 heads of Métis families submitted a petition to Lorne seeking recognition of their rights and land protections.[86] They argued that the government had treated them unjustly in denying them scrip for being temporarily absent when Manitoba entered Confederation in 1870. Similar to what had been offered in Manitoba, they requested scrip for heads of families and grants of land to their children. No longer arguing that Manitoba Métis had been poorly treated, as in previous petitions, they now wanted compensation equal to what their Manitoba relatives had received. They reminded the governor general of the government's promise during Treaty Four negotiations to recognize and respect Métis land rights. They requested a survey of their existing river lots rather than a plan in the grid township system the Dominion Land Survey was set to impose. Last, they drew attention to their desperate economic conditions because of declining buffalo numbers and herd movement across the international boundary and asked for assistance with farm implements and seed grain to support an economic shift towards agriculture.

Thoughts of the future were never far from the minds of the Qu'Appelle Métis. An economic shift towards small-scale agriculture required they maintain the lands they already occupied but also that they secure more lands for their growing families. Of the petition signatories, fifty-nine were landholding heads of families. The remainder were their adult and minor male children, some as young as nine or ten. The young age of these signatories reveals that the Métis were not only advocating for their own rights but also thinking strategically about their children's futures and their own families. While only adult men and male children signed the petitions, this did not mean that women's or girls' rights went unrecognized by their families. Women and girls were afforded the same protections alongside their husbands and fathers. For instance, both Elise and Veronique Klyne were married to non-Métis, Thomas Kavanaugh and Thomas Kelly, respectively. Both Kavanaugh and Kelly indicated they signed on behalf of their wives, asserting recognition and protection over their wives' rights, even if they themselves did not possess any.

Although unsuccessful in petitioning the governor general, the request for agricultural assistance indicated a considerable change in the Métis position from seven years earlier. Qu'Appelle Métis were no longer asking for broad access to hunting grounds west and southwest of the Valley but for assistance in adjusting to the new agricultural order that would soon be ubiquitous across the prairies. The new position, more in line with the language of treaties and potentially closer to what the government seemed to support, was perhaps a compromise made in recognition of changing times and the end of the buffalo hunt. Despite this, the Métis request was denied and only a month later, the Dominion Land Survey began in the Valley. The survey used the grid township system, ignoring Métis river lot land tenure practices. Métis landowners soon found their properties arbitrarily divided up by invisible survey lines and themselves increasingly entangled in a foreign administrative and bureaucratic process that challenged their rights and conflicted with their landholding practices.

In the 1870s and into the 1880s, Métis in the Qu'Appelle Valley and across the west made attempts to have their voices heard and rights recognized. Petitioning was not only a means of community action but also a public and political demonstration of Métis occupancy of the Qu'Appelle Valley as their homeland. They understood the context in which they lived and the changes coming with the decline of the buffalo, treaty negotiations, impending survey, and incoming settlement. Faced with economic changes, they were motivated by government inaction and refusal to recognize Métis rights and grievances. Aware of the treatment and experience of Métis in Manitoba, they demanded their rights be recognized and sought protections over private property and collective hunting territory that would allow them to maintain their way of life. Astutely, they petitioned multiple agents within the Dominion Government and took advantage of opportunities presented to them, eager to have their petitions forwarded to those in positions of authority. Government ignored the Qu'Appelle petitions, like they did those from other Métis, until forced by Louis Riel and his supporters to pay attention to the Métis' claims.

CHAPTER 4

Asserting Sovereignty to Secure Land

> All these settlements were always close to a lot of water. They made sure that if they were going to make a settlement, they made a settlement where they weren't going to run out of water. Because they knew all along that there were plenty of animals around here, lots of deer, rabbits. So, this is a real ideal place, you have got lots of water, lots of animals, you got lots of wood to burn, you know. Everything was here and then they get out into these hills here, this is where they found all the medicine.[1]

WHEN THE DOMINION Land Survey of the Qu'Appelle Valley began in 1881, surveyor T.R. Hewson found Métis families settled on small plots of land primarily along the lakes and river. The Métis took up land in ways that worked with the natural contours of the Valley environment and close enough to one another that social and familial bonds could be maintained. They recognized the importance of being close to water and having access to multiple sources of food and fuel. As Bob Desjarlais describes above, the Qu'Appelle Valley was the ideal place. These understandings of land tenure were central to the Métis but conflicted with those of the Canadian government, eager to open the prairies to colonization.

The opening of the prairie west for agricultural settlement in the late nineteenth century has been a key feature of the Canadian national narrative. By the late nineteenth century, the North-West was increasingly perceived as a frontier of great agricultural importance, a fertile garden to be settled.[2] To achieve this end, it was necessary to convert the region's potential as an agricultural "garden of Eden" into a reality. The Dominion Lands Act (1872) affirmed Canadian sovereignty in the west and opened land up for orderly and rapid settlement.[3] The Act set out a codified process for granting land to individual settlers, land colonization companies, railways, and the HBC.[4] It also set aside land for First Nations reserves and, in later amendments, the distribution of Métis scrip. A key feature was to lay out the foundation for homestead policy, serving as a blueprint to entrench individual land ownership and settlement processes, including eligibility criteria and homesteader responsibility. The policies of land survey and homestead, in addition to the provision of Métis scrip, provided little benefit to the Métis.

Scholars have long recognized the influence of the United States' Homestead Act (1862) on Canadian land and homestead policy.[5] Chester Martin argues that in creating a land policy to open the west for settlement, the Canadian government looked to the American example because they dealt with similar issues of expansion, transportation, and settlement.[6] Based on Thomas Jefferson's 1795 Northwest Ordinance, the Homestead Act legislated Jefferson's ideal of democracy as stemming from individual land ownership, free homesteads, and family farms.[7] The American grid system appealed to both countries because it "expedited the mapping, absorption, and individual ownership of the terrain. It permitted the land to be sold, bought, and owned in the most uncomplicated and timely fashion" and created real estate developers out of both nations.[8]

According to the Dominion Lands Act (1872) land survey followed a square township survey system.[9] Each township measured thirty-six square miles, divided into thirty-six sections. Each section measured one square mile or 640 acres. Each section was numbered one to thirty-six and further divided into four quarter sections of 160 acres each.[10] Even-numbered sections in each township were available for homestead, while the railway reserved the odd-numbered sections. The Canadian Pacific Railway (CPR) received these sections as partial payment for building the railway. In each township, the HBC reserved one and three-quarter sections, and local municipalities reserved two sections for local schools. The HBC retained a portion of land with the transfer of Rupert's Land to Canada.[11] Once land was surveyed, the HBC could dispose of it as they wished. The lands reserved by the CPR and the HBC were available for purchase and in some instances, were available for leasing.

The Dominion Land Survey was theoretically precise.[12] It cut across the landscape with disregard to the topography or vegetation. In the same way it bisected the landscape, it also cut through Qu'Appelle Métis' individual land holdings where land tenure practices privileged access to all available resources and proximity of households to one another for the maintenance of cultural and economic practices. Indeed, the square township grid system ignored existing use and accumulated knowledge of the landscape, in preparation for new incoming settlement, creating frustration, resentment, and anger for those already living there.[13]

Once the area was surveyed, the Department of the Interior offered free homesteads of a quarter section, or 160 acres, provided the homesteader pay a ten-dollar administrative fee. In the Dominion Lands Act (1872) any person (male or female) who was the head of a family or over age twenty-one could take up a homestead.[14] By 1876, the criteria changed, lowering the age of taking a homestead from twenty-one to eighteen, and restricted it to men; the only way women could establish a homestead under the revised provisions was as the sole head of their family.[15] Persons classified under the Indian Act (1876) were also ineligible for a homestead.[16] Upon payment of the filing fee to the land agent, prospective homesteaders could make entry on a quarter section. Land agents and homestead inspectors housed in Dominion Lands Offices, located in western towns, administered the process. These offices were governed by the Dominion Lands Branch, created within the Department of the Interior. After filing, homesteaders had to prove they were a bona fide settler before they received a "patent" or formal ownership of the land. Although there is no clear definition of "bona fide" in the Act, it meant individuals who, in good faith, intended to take up agriculture and farm the land and excluded land speculators and absentee landowners. Homesteaders had to make several necessary improvements and remain in continual residence on the property for at least six months a year during the first three years.[17] Improvements included building a home and fences and demonstrating annual progress in clearing and farming the land. If successful after the three-year mark, they applied to the local land agent or homestead inspector for patent. The application process included a detailed declaration providing individual and familial information, the amount of land broken, cropped, and fenced, and details about livestock and buildings. The process also required that two witnesses known to the homesteader attest to the truth of their application. If approved, a patent would be issued and the homesteader became the formal landowner. With patent to the original homestead, the owner became eligible to obtain a second adjacent quarter section to expand their farm. If unsatisfied with the completion of improvements, the homestead inspector could deny patent, forcing the homesteader to forfeit his claim. The land was then available for re-entry by someone else.[18]

A significant aspect of the Dominion Land Survey for the Métis was the plotting of roads around each township grid. Prior to 1881, road allowances between each township and section measured ninety feet. However, that year, the Dominion Lands Branch reduced the width of the road allowance to one chain, or sixty-six feet, which eliminated two of the roads crossing each township from east to west. Together with the cart trails that existed prior to survey, these lands were set aside for public roads, which the Dominion Government transferred to the responsible territorial or provincial authority.[19]

The Dominion Lands Act and Qu'Appelle Valley Survey

When the Dominion Land Survey of the Qu'Appelle Valley began in 1881, surveyor T.R. Hewson found Métis settled in family clusters primarily along the lakes and river, recording nineteen claims in just two townships on the north side of the Qu'Appelle Lakes.[20] Each claimant had made improvements and was farming small plots. Finding many Métis away, presumably hunting, fishing, or freighting, Hewson was unable to take claimant declarations and instead listed their names, claim size, and the nature and value of any improvements. While there were several that had larger claims of more than ten acres broken, most had claims of one to eight acres. In many cases, such claims were comprised of more than one small plot of land. For instance, George Fisher, Peter LaPierre, Joseph LaPierre, Antoine Larocque, Alexander Petit Didier, and Norbert Welsh each had two parcels of land, and John Simpson had six small plots. Having more than one parcel of land, however, did not guarantee that the claimant had a large acreage broken. For instance, four claimants with more than one parcel of land had fewer than two acres broken and even John Simpson, who had six small plots, had less than eight acres broken.

Table 1. Broken Acres, Hewson Survey

Acres Broken	No. of Individuals
>2	4
2 to 4	5
5 to 9	4
10 to 20	2
20+	4

In the following two years, Dominion Land surveyors assessed the remainder of the Valley region. They recorded the claims of thirty-six Métis in six separate townships, including eleven claims in the townships surveyed by Hewson.[21] With few exceptions, families concentrated in Township 19–Ranges 11 and 12, Township 20–Ranges 12 and 13, and Township 21–Ranges 13 and 14.[22] Surveyors documented a total of 128 separate claims, thirty-six of which were Métis. Comparison of these claims with improvements documented on township survey maps reveals that more Métis claims existed than surveyors initially recorded. This may be because the surveyor general sometimes used a single surveyor's record to create each township map. For instance, the map for Township 19–Range 11 replicated the field notes and draft maps of surveyor John Bourgeois in the summer of 1882.[23] In other instances, they used multiple surveyors' records over a period of a few years' time. This was the case with the map of Township 21–Range 13. It is a composite created from the records of surveyors Clementi and Hewson in 1881, W.T. Thompson in 1881, J.F. Garden in 1881, C.C. DuBerger in 1885, J. Lestock Reid in 1886, and Samuel Brodie in 1886.[24] These maps indicated existing claims and improvements, often accompanied by the claimant's name. Comparing these maps with the claims reported by surveyors reveals a different picture from that initially recorded. In four townships—Township 19–Range 11, Township 19–Range 12, Township 20–Range 12, and Township 20–Range 13—surveyors sketched and labelled thirty-three claims as belonging to Métis individuals. This was five more than the twenty-seven they recorded in their 1881 report. In the remaining two townships, Township 21–Range 13 and Township 21–Range 14, we must rely on Hewson's reported nineteen Métis claims. Available township survey maps sketch the size and location of claims, but do not label them. There is no way to decipher between Métis and non-Métis claims. Using the number reported by Hewson and those identified on the four other survey maps reveals that the number of Métis claims was at least fifty-two, many more than the thirty-six reported. Reasons for the discrepancy are unknown but other versions of these township survey maps do exist. Following the survey, Dominion lands policy required that claimants register their pre-existing claims so that they received patent to their lands. When Métis registered their claims, the number of claimants far exceeded fifty-two.

Table 2. Métis claims documented by Dominion Land Surveyors, 1881–1882

Year of Survey	Twp	Total Claimants	Métis Claims reported	Métis Claims Documented by Hewson	Métis Claims Documented on Twp Survey Maps
1882	Twp 19 R 11	34	2		3
1882	Twp 19 R 12	31	11		14
1882	Twp 20 R 12	33	7		6
1882	Twp 20 R 13	19	7		10
1881/1882	Twp 21 R 13	9	7	15	0
1881	Twp 21 R 14	2	2	4	0
		128	**36**	**19**	**33**

The survey of the Qu'Appelle Valley in 1882 and 1883 prompted a rush of British immigrant Ontario settlers into the region, eager to take up newly available land and encouraged by the building of the railway and expectations of rail line access. Historian Lyle Dick notes the intensity of the land rush, suggesting that land in Township 19–Range 11 in the Abernethy region, immediately north of the Qu'Appelle Valley, was quickly taken up in a matter of days.[25] These were farmers taking up individual homesteads as well as a few seeking to farm on a much larger and corporate scale, including William Robert Bell on the south side of the Valley and William Richard Motherwell in the Abernethy area, who both took up land in 1882.[26] Immigration into the region continued at a heady pace and by 1885, there were nearly 7000 people living in the District of Assiniboia, including 5147 farm operators occupying 1.6 million acres of land and cultivating 160,000 acres.[27] By 1886–1887 numbers were quickly stagnating because of poor crop yields and intermittent harvests resulting from prairie fires, drought, grasshopper and gopher infestation, and early frost.[28] By 1891 the number of farmers had marginally increased to 5694, but the acreage occupied and farmed dropped to 1.59 million acres and 151,000 acres, respectively.[29]

In the summer of 1882, a Dominion Lands Office opened in Fort Qu'Appelle to deal with the distribution of homestead lands. It was staffed with a lands agent responsible for recording and adjusting homestead claims and notifying those with pre-existing claims to enter their holdings. At the direction of the Dominion Lands Office, surveyors were to document all improvements and gather evidence of any existing claims they encountered during their work.[30] As an encouragement, they received an additional fifty cents pay for each claim affidavit or declaration they took.[31] Although they had the responsibility of recording pre-existing claims, they had no authority to settle the many disputes that arose during the survey.[32]

When documenting existing occupancy, surveyors frequently encountered claimants challenged by the imposition of the survey. In some instances, surveyors were apathetic towards taking declarations because they doubted Métis intentions in taking up farming and thought little of their attempts to improve the land. Skeptical of whether the Métis were intent on becoming bona fide settlers and farmers, Dominion Land Surveyor C.C. DuBerger noted that the Métis residing in small little encampments of one or two tents or a "kind of small shanty" with very little land under cultivation "looked more like men remaining there for speculation than with the intention of cultivating."[33] This was a legitimate concern, given the rampant land speculation this system engendered.[34] Annoyed at the task of having to stop his survey work to take claim declarations, DuBerger complained about the number of Métis he met when surveying Township 18–Range 12. These claimants all required declarations and caused him to lose valuable time each workday. As a compromise, and reasoning that he did not have a pen or paper to record their declarations, DuBerger deferred any claimants until the end of each day, requesting they visit his camp in the evening.[35]

Petitioning for Rights Amidst Survey, August 1882

In August 1882, the Qu'Appelle Métis again petitioned government asking for protection over the lands they occupied.[36] Addressing their petition to Lieutenant Governor Edgar Dewdney, they requested he forward their petition to Minister of the Interior John A. Macdonald, who they believed would treat them fairly. With the recently completed and ongoing surveys, the Métis' fears of encroaching settlement were increasingly realized. They anxiously awaited recognition of their land rights, and because of the grid survey system, many found themselves not only living on parcels that crossed survey lines but also on lands allocated to land colonization companies and the CPR. The Ontario and Qu'Appelle Land Company had purchased land in the Qu'Appelle Valley in 1882 and began enforcing the survey lines, selling off lands occupied by the Métis and seeking to dispossess them of their claims.[37] Refusing the company's demands to either purchase the plots they occupied or to abandon their properties, the Métis instead sought patent to their lands, arguing that they were "justly and legally entitled to the same" because of their prior occupancy. They had taken up land as early as 1860 and had complied with government requirements by building homes and outbuildings, cultivating the soil, and living in continuous residence. They had even built a church and a school and opened roads and bridges, which they argued would be an important advantage for any new settler. In all, forty-four individuals signed this petition, representing approximately twenty-five families.

Land colonization companies were a mechanism used by the Canadian government and the CPR to facilitate land sales and promote settlement. These companies purchased large blocks of land at a reduced rate on agreement that they would encourage and secure homesteaders. In 1882, twenty-six companies received charters to buy odd-numbered sections outside the railway belt. The railway belt was the strip of land, twenty-four miles wide, on either side of the main railway line. The odd-numbered sections of the railway belt were set aside for the CPR as part of their payment for constructing the railway. Colonization companies purchased this land at two dollars per acre. If they were successful in securing homesteaders on the adjacent even-numbered sections within five years of purchase, they received a rebate of one dollar per acre on the odd-numbered sections. Once homesteaders occupied the even-numbered sections, the odd-numbered sections increased in value and were sold by the companies at higher prices. Part of the role of these colonization companies was also to accelerate construction of roads and bridges between settled and unsettled areas. Numerous colonization companies bought land in southern Saskatchewan and in the Qu'Appelle Valley region, including the Qu'Appelle and Long Lake Land Company and the Ontario and Qu'Appelle Land Company. Often these colonization companies, like in the case of those in the Qu'Appelle Valley, were owned and operated by eastern bankers, lawyers, politicians, and by land and scrip speculators who acted as sales agents.[38]

Dewdney responded to the Métis petition with a sense of urgency because he viewed the Métis as equivalent to Euro-Canadian settlers in function and in rights—petitioning as farmers, eager to convert the prairie into farmland and to protect their private property. He immediately telegrammed the Minister of the Interior informing him that the Ontario and Qu'Appelle Land Company had begun "warning off" the Métis and claiming their lands.[39] He recommended to the minister that the land company be notified not to interfere with the Métis holding existing claims in the region.[40] He followed up the telegram with a letter to the minister the same day, enclosing the petition and personally advising him of the situation.[41] The Métis, he stressed, were "very uneasy about their holdings" but as "the pioneers of the district" deserved fair consideration.[42] He implored the minister to send either Commissioner Aquila Walsh or Inspector William Pearce to the region to examine and equitably adjust conflicting claims.

When the Métis heard no response from their 1881 petition to the governor general or the 1882 petition to Lieutenant Governor Edgar Dewdney, they enlisted the support of Thomas Wesley Jackson to advocate on their behalf. A local businessman and politician, Jackson was part owner in the Qu'Appelle and Long Lake Land Company. His investment in the company likely influenced his decision to advocate for the Métis in their grievances with the competing Ontario and Qu'Appelle Colonization Company. Jackson was also a justice of the peace and elected to the Council of the North-West Territories from 1883 to 1886, stepping down because of his involvement with the railway companies.[43]

Communicating with Dominion Lands Agent at Qu'Appelle J. Gordon, Jackson spoke specifically of the property occupied by the Roman Catholic Mission, St. Pierre Poitras, Norbert Welsh, and Louis Flammand. According to the recent survey, all four parties occupied the same section.[44] Each individual recognized their neighbour's claims and that of the mission, but their allotments did not conform to the legal subdivision imposed by survey. Jackson looked to solve problems created when more than one party occupied and had made improvements on the same section. Posing several questions to the lands agent regarding the nature of Métis claims, Jackson asked how individual claims would be determined if they did not conform to the legal survey subdivision. What were the rights of an individual making entry when their buildings or plot of land was spread over more than one section? What were the rights of individuals, if after being surveyed their plot of land was determined to be on HBC or school lands? To what extent would the government recognize any transfer of land made and acknowledged by the Métis? Further, if recognized, to what extent was possession of land evidence of such transfer? Last, in cases where plots of land had been sold, what rights succeeded to the purchaser? Seeking to untangle these claims, Jackson suggested that either the Dominion Land agent answer his questions and deal with these claims, or that he refer them to some other inexpensive mode of arbitration. Jackson also requested that the rules governing land patents be varied and that the Métis be treated with "liberal considerations" not only because of their prior occupancy but also because the plots of lands they occupied along the Qu'Appelle Lakes and River had very little land suitable for cultivation. Which, he argued, they cultivated "without even the commonest agricultural implements."[45]

As Jackson advocated to the local land agent, Dewdney continued pressing the Minister of the Interior. Dewdney reminded him of the Métis' previous petition and their conflicting claims with the Ontario and Qu'Appelle Land Company and implored him to act on the Métis claims.[46] "The sooner their claims are dealt with, the better," he argued. Many of the petitioners deserved consideration because he viewed them as bona fide settlers. "There are a number of half-breeds in this district who have settled in the Qu'Appelle Valley for many years," Dewdney wrote. "[They] went on their usual hunt for buffalo, returning to their homes at different times during the year. [While] others have settled since 1879 and have remained pretty constantly on their land."[47]

The necessity of settling Métis claims was clear but complicated by the very nature of Métis land holding practices. Métis plots of land were irregular in size and shape and did not conform to the square township system laid out by the Dominion Land Survey. Holdings often straddled survey lines and in many instances, multiple families occupied an individual survey section, particularly those that fronted the Qu'Appelle Lakes or River. Most, Dewdney noted, had not claimed long, narrow river lots like Métis in other parts of the North-West, but that the bulk of the claimants had taken up irregular-sized and -shaped homesteads close to one another and near to the water so that they could catch fish. Indeed,

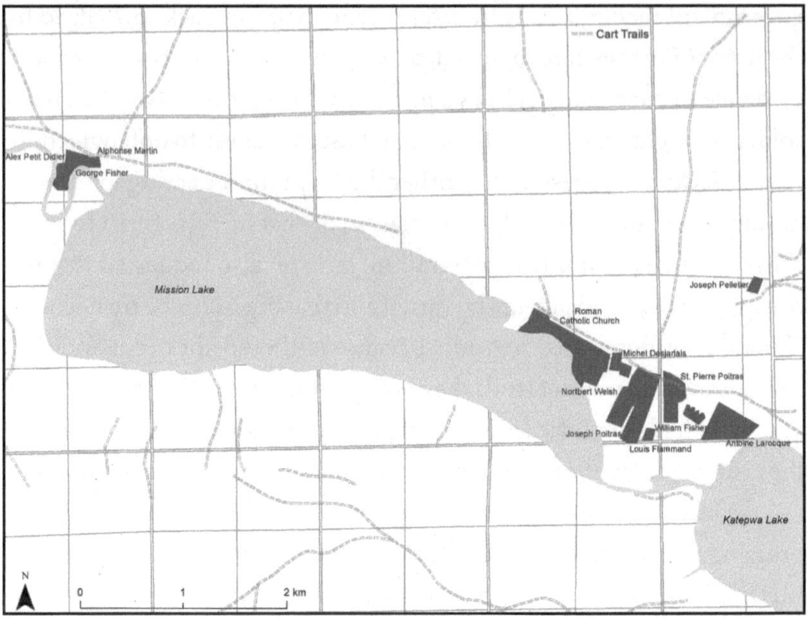

Figure 24. Métis improvements (Township 21–Range 13–West of Second Meridian), T.R. Hewson Survey, June 1881. Map courtesy of Cheryl Troupe and Matthew Kunkel.

the Métis followed a land holding practice that privileged their way of life and experience of the natural landscape. Although more haphazard than elsewhere in the North-West, Métis in the Qu'Appelle Valley did indeed occupy the land according to a river lot system. For those who fronted the water, their plots were generally long and narrow, whereas others occupied plots of land of irregular shape and size, and were removed from the waterfront but within reasonable access. This ensured that the Métis could utilize different landscapes and access a variety of resources.

Regardless of the size, shape, or location of the lots the Métis occupied, the fact that they overlapped within individual sections of the survey caused concern amongst the Métis and government.[48] Lands held by the Métis were becoming increasingly valuable to Euro-Canadian settlers and even causing land scrambles by land speculators eager to acquire as much land as possible. If the parties were unable to agree amongst themselves to a fair division of the property, the easiest solution to settling these disputes, Dewdney suggested, might be to sell the claims and divide the proceeds amongst the parties. Claimants would then have the privilege of selecting homestead on any unoccupied government land with an immediate issue of patent, provided they had occupied their old claim for some time. He further advised the Minister of the Interior that the best course would be to enlist an independent third party in no way connected to the land speculators in the Qu'Appelle Valley.

Upon receipt of Dewdney's March 1883 letter, the minister referred the matter to Dominion Lands Commissioner Aquila Walsh in July, asking him to investigate and report on Métis claims.[49] However, due to more pressing business, Walsh did not immediately visit the Qu'Appelle Valley.[50] Instead, Dominion Lands Inspector William Pearce visited the following month to inspect and adjust existing claims.[51] He took evidence of eleven cases, seven that he settled immediately and four that required further investigation. He held two over for investigation and decision until the Commissioner of Dominion Lands Walsh could visit the following April. At the time of Pearce's inspection, two or three additional claimants had also come forward presenting new claims, asking he investigate. These new claims, appearing three years following survey, perplexed Dominion Lands officials. They rationalized the delay on the economic lifestyle and mobility of the Métis who continued to make a living from hunting and freighting, which sometimes necessitated being away from home for months at a time, and they believed that the Métis were not seriously interested in taking up the land for farming.[52]

A few months later, Jackson contacted Minister of the Interior Senator David Lewis Macpherson requesting further settlement of the Métis claims. Appointed to the Senate upon Confederation in 1867, Macpherson was a successful businessman, railway supporter, and politician. He was also a close associate of John A. Macdonald and loyal member of the Conservative Party. In 1881 he became Minister of the Interior on a temporary basis and in October 1883 was formally appointed to the position with Macdonald retaining responsibility for Indian Affairs and the North-West Mounted Police (NWMP).[53] Addressing Macpherson privately on behalf of several Métis, Jackson reminded the minister that the Métis had repeatedly informed government of their grievances. There would be few claims to deal with and most would not be troublesome, he argued. Most were Métis "who have never received anything from the Government, and who, it has been admitted, are entitled to some consideration."[54] The following spring, the minister responded that he was very anxious to settle Métis claims and had, the previous September, instructed Walsh to investigate.[55] No mention was made of Pearce's inspection or adjustment of claims and Jackson heard nothing more on the matter.

Registering Pre-Existing Claims

As Qu'Appelle Métis had demonstrated in their petitioning leading up to survey, they were eager to have their pre-existing claims recognized. Having lived and worked the land prior to survey, most had built homes and outbuildings and had lands broken, cropped, and fenced. They recognized the necessity of protecting their investments in the land but were reluctant to conform to the square township system. The Dominion Lands Act required that they register their existing parcels of land with the nearest Dominion Lands agent. Their prior occupancy and improvements allowed them to make direct applications for patents, rather than apply for homesteads, which would have required they make similar improvements demanded of new homesteaders. If unable to make application at the time of survey, pre-existing occupants were to enter their claim as soon as possible with the nearest Dominion Lands agent. Applying for patent to their land as a homestead was the only possible means for pre-existing occupants to maintain and protect their occupancy. If they did not enter their claim, it was forfeited and became available for incoming settlers. The Dominion Lands Act and homestead policy treated Métis entering their pre-existing claims as settlers, recognizing their lands as homesteads based on their prior occupancy, rather than on any pre-existing Métis rights to the land.

For the Métis, converting existing claims into the square township system was problematic. Métis land tenure and economic practices conflicted with the square township survey system and homestead policy. The requirement that homesteaders maintain continual residency may have been a means to encourage long-term agriculture and deter land speculators, but it also conflicted with Métis lifestyles that necessitated individuals be away from their homes hunting or working for extended periods of time.

Recognizing the need to adjust to the new agricultural order, as Métis began registering their existing claims, they also began to identify as farmers.[56] By 1881 as many as sixty-eight Métis households labelled themselves as farmers, rather than strictly as hunters.[57] This was likely due to the necessity of meeting homestead regulations, requiring individuals' resolve to take up agriculture. Despite their declaration as farmers, most continued to rely on hunting, fishing, and freighting work and were regularly away from their properties for months at a time, engaged in such activities.[58] This type of outside employment and time away from home was common for Euro-Canadian homesteaders as well.[59] However, not all Métis chose to declare themselves farmers to meet the new requirements. Twenty-three households, including those of Xavier Desnomme and Alexander Fisher Jr., professed their occupation as hunters despite their mixed economic practice. Both Desnomme and Fisher did also engage in farming activity and registered their existing land claims with the Dominion Lands Branch. Based on their prior occupancy and cultivation of the land they received patent as farmers, demonstrating that Métis individuals could be both hunters and farmers.

When Métis began registering their pre-existing claims they did so as settlers with claims based on prior occupancy and improvements, not on any outstanding issue of Métis rights that may have existed. The issue of Métis rights or land allocations based on the Manitoba Act remained unsettled in the North-West. In total, there were at least 104

Métis individuals occupying plots of land in the immediate Qu'Appelle Lakes region before they began registering claims. Each had lived on their property prior to survey or prior to 1883 and so applied directly for patent rather than for homestead entry. For the most part, the Métis lived clustered around the Qu'Appelle Lakes and the Roman Catholic Mission at Lebret.

The size and scope of Métis claims varied but generally pertained to relatively small plots of land. A sample of ninety-one existing claims reveals that fifty were less than ten acres in size. Twenty-eight were between ten and nineteen acres; nine were twenty to twenty-nine acres; and four were more than thirty acres.[60] Sixty-two of these claimants declared that they had fenced at least part of their property. Fencing was not only necessary for those with livestock but also physically demonstrated occupation. Thirteen had less than ten acres fenced; sixteen had between ten and nineteen acres fenced; twenty-three had between twenty and twenty-nine acres fenced; and ten had more than thirty acres fenced. Of these ten, five had thirty to forty acres fenced; four had fenced sixty to eighty acres; and one, Xavier Desnomme, had 140 acres fenced. Desnomme lived on the southeast section 34 of Township 20–Range 14–West of the second meridian with his wife and three children. By 1881, he built a house, two stables, and a storehouse and by 1886 had eighteen acres of land broken, most of which he farmed. He also owned at least seven horses.[61] Desnomme had a growing farm and by government criteria would have been determined a bona fide settler. That Desnomme had fenced such a large amount of land suggests his intention to farm more land, acquire more horses, and even raise cattle. However, his declaration as a hunter, rather than a farmer, in the 1881 census reveals his insistence on maintaining a mixed subsistence economy and that he was not yet ready to rely solely on agricultural production.

Desnomme may have been reluctant to commit entirely to agriculture but some Métis in both the Qu'Appelle Valley and what became the area of Ste. Delphine had some success in farming and ranching. Following the provision of scrip in 1885, several Métis moved north of

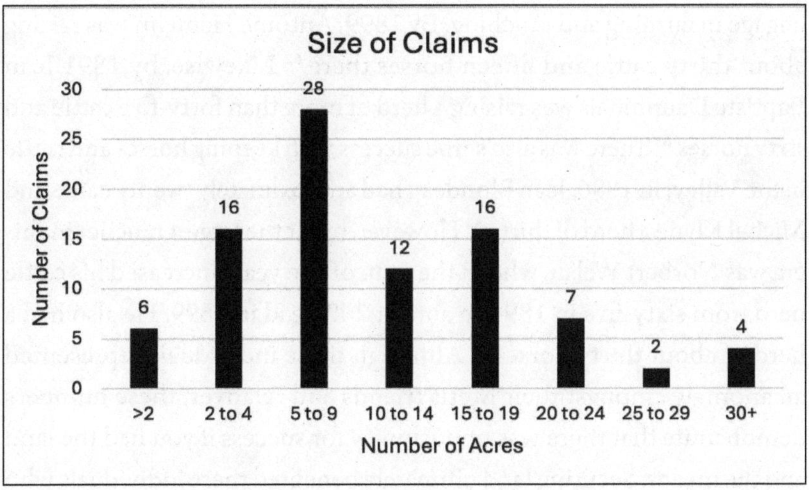

Figure 25. Size of Pre-existing Métis Claims. Source: Qu'Appelle Valley Homestead records, Provincial Archives of Saskatchewan.

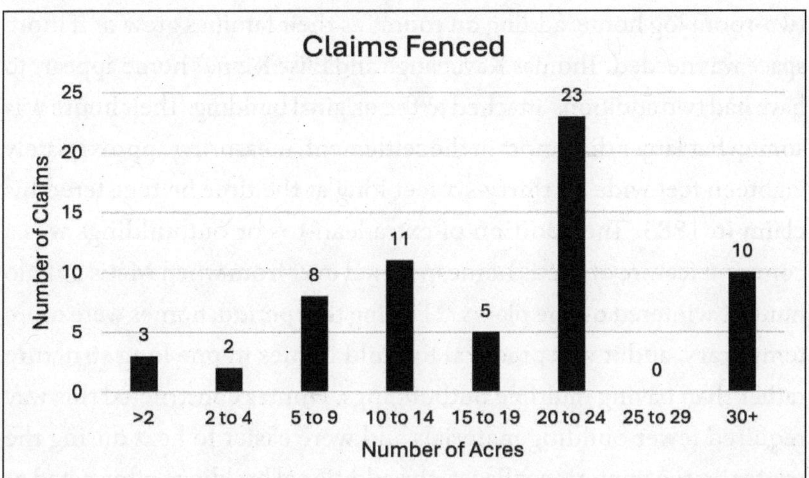

Figure 26. Acres Fenced. Source: Qu'Appelle Valley Homestead records, Provincial Archives of Saskatchewan.

the Valley to Ste. Delphine, located close to the File Hills reserves, which increasingly became home to Métis families looking to secure land and engage in farming and ranching. By 1899, Antoine Hamelin was raising about thirty cattle and fifteen horses there.[62] Likewise, by 1891 Jean Baptiste Dauphinais was raising a herd of more than forty-five cattle and sixty horses.[63] There was also some success with keeping horses and cattle in the Valley; in 1886, Jean Blondeau had approximately twenty cattle and Michel Klyne a herd of thirty.[64] However, by far the largest rancher in this era was Norbert Welsh, who in the span of five years increased his cattle herd from sixty-five in 1894 to almost 200 head in 1899. He also had a herd of about thirty horses.[65] Although these individuals represented an anomaly amongst their Métis friends and relatives, these numbers demonstrate that there was opportunity for success if you had the land and the means. Securing land ultimately benefited these individuals who operated considerable ranching operations.

Métis claims generally consisted of a small log home, stable, and a few other outbuildings. Often families started by building a small one- or two-room log home, adding on rooms as their families grew or if more space was needed. Thomas Kavanaugh and Elise Klyne's home appears to have had two additions attached to the original building. Their house was somewhat larger than most in the settlement, measuring approximately eighteen feet wide by thirty-six feet long at the time he registered his claim in 1883. The addition of extra lean-tos or outbuildings was a common feature of Métis homes, carried over from when Métis buffalo hunters wintered on the plains.[66] During that period, homes were more temporary, and it was practical to build homes in one long structure rather than having multiple outbuildings. Homes constructed this way required fewer building materials and were easier to heat during the winter. In the wintering villages, the additional buildings often acted as storehouses for supplies and stables for horses or livestock.[67]

In the Qu'Appelle settlement, while most homes were less than 400 square feet, there were a few that were significantly larger. Thirteen homes were smaller than 200 square feet, sixty-one were between 200 and 400 square feet, and twenty-one were larger than 400 square feet. Of those larger than 400 square feet, eight were between 400 and 500 square feet, and thirteen larger than 500. Three of these were considerably larger. For instance, both Antoine Larocque's and St. Pierre Poitras's measured 800 square feet and Antoine Fayant's home was an impressive 1,125 square feet. Most claimants had at least one outbuilding, most often a stable. Stables housed livestock as most Métis maintained at least a small herd of horses, two being the natural minimum required for field work. Some, however, had more than two, and many also raised cattle and pigs. Barns and granaries were common as barns were necessary for storing livestock feed and granaries any grain produced for market sale. Twelve individuals recorded having a granary, indicating that they may have been producing enough hay or barley for storage or sale. Common outbuildings included storehouses, a shed, and in some cases, a separate kitchen. Thirty-five had at least one storehouse or shed, generally used for storing farm implements. Five individuals had separate kitchens or cooking spaces that they used during the summer months when it was too hot to cook and prepare foods inside. A significant amount of food preparation and preservation took place in the summers, and so the Métis welcomed the extra cooking and preparation space. In addition, two claimants also had hen or "milk houses," revealing that they maintained at least a small number of these animals for subsistence. Four claims also had wells.

As the imposition of the Dominion Lands Act (1872) and homestead policy artificially divided up Métis landholdings and located multiple claims on individual township sections, Métis occupied a tenuous position often challenged by distant and unsympathetic authorities. They were anxious about maintaining their lands in this new political order and had questions that needed answering lest they be vulnerable to the imposition of colonial land policies and incoming settlement.

Qu'Appelle Métis continued petitioning for recognition of rights to the lands they already occupied but also Métis rights based on their prior occupancy in the North-West Territories and fulfillment of promises

Figure 27. Thomas Kavanaugh and Elise Klyne home, c. 1880, R-A 7483, Provincial Archives of Saskatchewan.

Figure 28. Métis Settlement, Wood Mountain, 22 miles North of Boundary and 416 miles West of Red River, Manitoba, June–August 1873. Library and Archives Canada/ George M. Dawson fonds/e011156508.

made under the Manitoba Act. They found themselves in a shared contest with First Nations and the new national government for access to land. Under the treaty system the government recognized the distinction between First Nations and Métis and held true to those differences in how they responded to and acknowledged First Nations and Métis rights.

The Dominion Land Survey reorganized Métis land holdings as settler spaces and required they conform to the standardized square township system. The Métis continued advocating to have their land disputes heard and resolved, with petitioning being their preferred political strategy. They saw themselves as part of a larger community, connected to Métis in Manitoba and across the West. Qu'Appelle Valley Métis continued to voice their concerns and demand recognition of their rights.

Registering their existing claims as settlers and using the homestead policy was the only way the Métis could maintain their land holdings. In doing so, they demonstrated to the government that they already practised small-scale agriculture in addition to maintaining a subsistence lifestyle. They shifted to the new system of land holding by occupying their lands as settlers and securing land title in a way recognized by the Canadian government. Tensions over land tenure, however, remained high and were complicated by the fact that Ottawa was willing to deal with the Métis only as settlers, recognizing their rights as prior occupants of specific parcels of land. The government remained unwilling to recognize, let alone address, any unextinguished land rights Métis possessed from their occupancies within the North-West Territories prior to the imposition of Canadian authority.

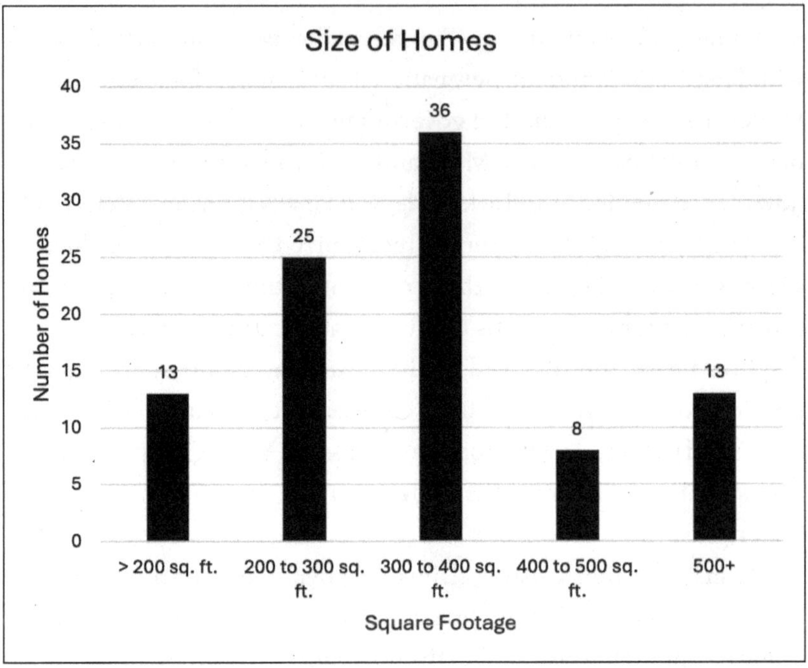

Figure 29. Home Size.Source: Qu'Appelle Valley Homestead records, Provincial Archives of Saskatchewan.

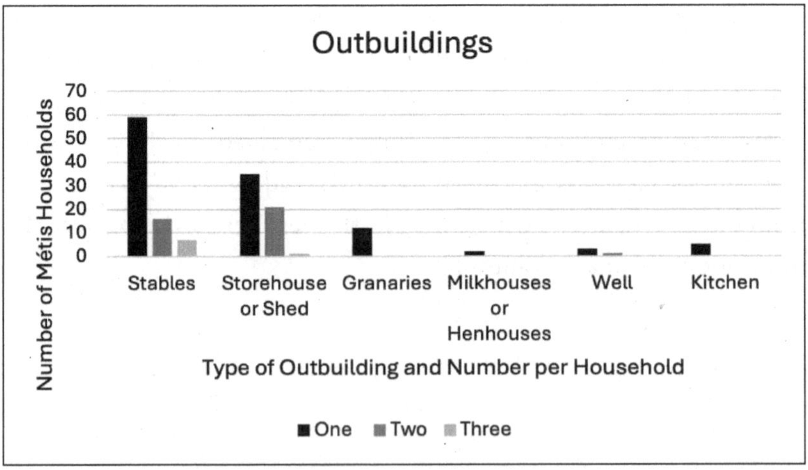

Figure 30. Outbuildings. Source: Qu'Appelle Valley Homestead records, Provincial Archives of Saskatchewan.

Chapter 5

Securing Land Tenure: North-West Half-Breed Scrip and Homesteading

BY 1885, QU'APPELLE Métis, like other Métis across the North-West, were still waiting for the Canadian government to deal with their rights. These were rights to territory collectively held by Métis in the North-West Territories and those that Qu'Appelle Métis and others had petitioned be recognized throughout the 1870s. It had been fifteen years since the Manitoba Act (1870) had established a process to extinguish Métis title in Manitoba and six years since amendments were made to the Dominion Lands Act (1879), affirming that the government would deal with Métis rights in the North-West.[1] Métis, however, would not remain patient much longer. Tensions were rising as Ottawa continued to impose the land survey, dividing up the landscape according to a square grid system. The Métis were increasingly anxious about having their rights recognized, especially the right to their familiar land tenure practices within the new order. As Métis found themselves further immersed in a foreign bureaucratic and administrative system, they continued to press their claims, expecting the government to act.

Frustrated, Métis in the South Saskatchewan River region sought out Louis Riel to champion their cause. Returning from exile in the United States, at Batoche Riel quickly began gathering support and peacefully advocating for government action on Métis rights. Ignored, he and his supporters moved towards organized and armed resistance, forcing Ottawa to deal with Métis concerns. With the threat of uprising, the federal authorities finally acted on Métis claims.[2]

The North-West Half-Breed Claims Commission

In late January 1885, the Minister of the Interior David Macpherson recommended to the Privy Council that the time had come to settle outstanding Métis claims in the North-West Territories. Amendments to the Dominion Lands Act in 1879 were intended to accommodate the extinguishment of existing Métis title in the North-West, but action had yet to occur.[3] The minister now advised that the process must begin with an enumeration of the Métis conducted by a three-person commission.[4] A 28 January 1885 Order-in-Council confirmed its creation and appointed three commissioners to the North-West Half-Breed Claims Commission: Ontario lawyer William Purvis Street as chairman; Roger Goulet, a Dominion Land surveyor from St. Boniface, Manitoba; and lawyer and clerk of the North-West Council Amédeé Emmanuel Forget of Regina. Narcisse Omer Cote, secretary for the Department of the Interior, was appointed commission secretary. More importantly, the order outlined the commission's mandate to conduct an enumeration and did not include any commitment to extinguish Métis rights or to distribute scrip.[5]

Preliminary plans began taking shape but it was not until 30 March 1885, four days after the military defeat of Major Crozier and a party of North-West Mounted Police by Métis forces in the Battle of Duck Lake in the South Saskatchewan River region, that an order-in-council gave the commission the authority to do more than enumerate the Métis, but to begin satisfying existing claims of Métis resident in the North-West and outside of Manitoba as of 15 July 1870.[6] Through this action, the government hoped to convince the Métis that they were acting in good faith and potentially defuse growing tension among the Métis.[7] The commission was to provide scrip to the Métis in the North-West as it had in Manitoba a decade earlier. In Manitoba, the scrip process had been a pragmatic government solution for extinguishing Métis title to land, removing the Métis from the land unless they were committed to becoming bona fide settler farmers. In the North-West, scrip would not only quickly extinguish Métis land title once and for all but clear the way for unencumbered settlement. Indeed, the scrip system would help the Dominion Government transform prairie land use and tenure, facilitate western settlement, and promote the privatization and sale of public homestead lands to the benefit of farmers, ranchers, bankers, and land speculators.[8]

The commission's authority stemmed from the order-in-council and the Dominion Lands Act (1883).[9] Amendments in 1879 included claims for Métis resident in the North-West Territories, outside of Manitoba, but did not outline policy or procedure for extinguishing claims.[10] This was different from how Ottawa had dealt with Manitoba Métis, where the Manitoba Act specifically set aside land for the extinguishment of Métis rights. Instead, in the North-West Territories, a series of twelve orders-in-council throughout the 1880s and 1890s laid out and then clarified policy for extinguishing Métis rights.[11]

Initial dates were set for the commission to visit Fort Qu'Appelle, Touchwood Hills, Regina, Maple Creek, Calgary, and Fort McLeod, with future dates for St. Albert, Edmonton, Fort Saskatchewan, Victoria, Fort Pitt, Battleford, St. Laurent, St. Louis De Langevin, Duck Lake, St. Antoine de Padoue, and Prince Albert. Dominion Lands Offices distributed public notices and the Minister's Office communicated its plans to the Department of Indian Affairs, the CPR, and the NWMP.[12] The Minister's Office requested the CPR and the NWMP help distribute notices of upcoming sittings and invited Indian Affairs to have local Indian agents attend, anticipating that many Treaty First Nations would appear before the commission to be enumerated as Métis.[13] It was hoped that the presence of the agents able to identify treaty individuals who claimed both a treaty annuity and the right to participate in scrip would alleviate confusion or tension that arose.[14] The Indian agents would help explain that those under treaty were ineligible for enumeration unless they applied for enfranchisement under the Indian Act, under which conditions the government would deal with them in an equitable and liberal way.[15]

Before embarking on their work, Commissioner Street requested a meeting with Prime Minister John A. Macdonald asking that the commission's powers be increased, and they be allowed to offer scrip to eligible Métis.[16] Macdonald agreed and authorized the additional powers, including to take evidence and settle claims on the spot. Their instruction was to report the names of Métis heads of families and children living in the North-West Territories prior to the creation of Manitoba on 15 July 1870, as well as the names of those deceased and their heirs. They were to report on any Métis grievances, either against the government or amongst themselves in connection to surveys of their lots, and to hear evidence and take declarations from Métis.[17] Claimants were to come before the commission, complete a declaration providing evidence about residence, occupation, family genealogy, names, and birthdates of children. Applications were reviewed against ledger books listing previous claimants from Manitoba and then, in most cases, if their application was approved, they received a scrip certificate for land or money scrip.[18]

In the North-West Territories, like Manitoba, the Dominion Government allocated both land and money scrip.[19] Land scrip certificates, made out for a specific number of acres, required the grantee to present the certificate at a Dominion Lands Office in exchange for unoccupied surveyed land. Once exchanged, patent for the parcel of land would immediately be issued. Land scrip was transferable to another individual prior to the issue of patent. Money scrip was a coupon for a specific dollar amount, payable to the bearer and exchangeable at the Dominion Lands Office for unoccupied surveyed land, initially at a rate of one dollar per acre. To be eligible for scrip, Métis had to have been resident in the North-West Territories (outside of the province of Manitoba) at the time of effective Canadian authority over the region on 15 July 1870. North-West Half-Breed Scrip policy initially authorized Métis heads of families, if they already occupied a parcel of land, to receive that land to the extent of 160 acres. If less than 160 acres, commissioners were to issue a scrip certificate for the difference. If Métis heads of families did not already occupy a parcel of land, they received scrip for $160 dollars, redeemable in land at one dollar per acre. Children of Métis heads of families, if they already occupied a parcel of land, were to receive that land to the extent of 240 acres. If less than 240 acres, they received scrip for the difference, redeemable at one dollar per acre. Children not already occupying land were to receive $240 scrip, redeemable in land.

The Scrip Commission's first sittings were planned to take place in Fort Qu'Appelle on 7–8 April 1885. Deputy Minister of the Interior A.M. Burgess notified a member of the North-West Council at Fort Qu'Appelle, Thomas Wesley Jackson, of the commission's visit, who then relayed information to the Métis.[20] Challenges plagued the commission even before it began sitting. Only days into their work, Commissioner Street had concerns. On their way to Fort Qu'Appelle, he wrote to Minister of the Interior David Macpherson requesting the power to provide both scrip and land title to the Métis if they already occupied but did not hold title to land.[21] These individuals, he argued, had property rights based on their occupancy in addition to their unextinguished Indian title, as described in the Manitoba Act, which made them eligible for scrip. If desired by claimants, he reasoned, "would it not be advisable to grant scrip, 160 or 240 dollars, permitting them to acquire title to land in occupation through possession. Otherwise, Government really gives nothing for Indian title."[22] The next day, Street pleaded his case on another matter, requesting the authority to settle supplementary Manitoba scrip claims by allowing Métis eligible for Manitoba scrip the same terms as those in the North-West Territories.[23] However, his real concern remained the provision of scrip to those Métis already occupying land. Street argued for the distinction between property rights based on occupancy and Métis rights based on Indian title, recognizing that the Métis would conceivably be discontented if treated as settlers with no compensation for extinguishment of Indian title based on their presence in the North-West prior to the assertion of Canadian authority over the region. For many in the Qu'Appelle Valley, they had already received patent to their land holdings through the Dominion Lands Act, and so eagerly awaited the opportunity for the government to deal with their existing Indian title. The minister responded to Street's requests with no objections to giving scrip and allowed occupants to acquire title to land already occupied through possession.[24] With this issue dealt with, the commission prepared for its first sitting.

The NWHB Claims Commission Meets the Qu'Appelle Métis

The commission arrived in Fort Qu'Appelle on 8 April 1885, later than planned, and immediately met with a group of Métis in Jackson's office. The Métis were ambivalent and suspicious of whether the commission really had the power to take evidence and grant scrip on the spot.[25] This attitude, Commissioner Street argued, was natural, considering the government had long acknowledged but not acted on Métis rights. The Métis were critical of the government, and even combative, stressing that their rights had been ignored for fifteen years. It would not be "until the war is over," the Métis proclaimed, that they would be ready to discuss their claims.[26] The war they spoke of was the Métis resistance brewing in the South Saskatchewan River region. Qu'Appelle Métis saw themselves as part of a larger Métis collective that spanned the North-West. Waiting on settling their claims was a risky position, but Qu'Appelle Métis supported Riel and Métis at Batoche and believed they had similar rights and grievances.[27] Taking such a risk demonstrates that the Qu'Appelle Métis firmly believed in the larger Métis cause and suggests their belief that the Métis at Batoche would be victorious in securing Métis land rights.

Long-standing government inaction had created significant tensions amongst the Métis, not only in Qu'Appelle, but across the North-West. Government officials, including Jackson, were aware of the threat of armed resistance. Months earlier, in September 1884, Jackson cautioned Sir Hector Langevin, Secretary of State for the provinces, of the anxiety and frustration amongst Qu'Appelle Métis. If their demands were not met, he assured, there was "great danger of the Half-breeds of Qu'Appelle going into rebellion as well."[28] Attempting to defuse these tensions during the commission's visits, Jackson, along with one of the Métis, referenced only as "Mr. Fisher," tried to persuade the rest to accept the same scrip concessions as those in Manitoba had received.[29] This, Jackson argued, along with the request for the immediate settlement of Métis occupancy claims, had been the recommendation approved by the North-West Council, on the advice of Archbishop Alexandre-Antonin Taché and Bishop Vital Grandin.[30] Archbishop Taché and Bishop Grandin were well versed on the Métis cause, having been missionaries amongst the Métis since the 1840s and 1850s.

The Métis voiced their concerns and conditions at this meeting.[31] To Qu'Appelle Métis, it was unacceptable that in the initial North-West Half-Breed Scrip provisions, Métis heads of families and their children were to receive money scrip if they did not already occupy land. Instead, the Métis asked for land and not money scrip for both children and heads of families, reasoning that Manitoba children of Métis heads of families had received land, rather than money scrip.[32] The commissioners agreed to put the issue of children's scrip before the government, but refused to do so for heads of families, maintaining that in Manitoba heads of families received only money scrip and not land scrip. The commission offered heads of families in the North-West Territories equal to what Métis in Manitoba had received. The Métis acquiesced and did not press the issue further. They did, however, make additional demands that the commission grant scrip to Métis fighting alongside Riel. They spoke with common purpose and strong sympathy, arguing they were unwilling to accept any settlement unless those fighting with Riel receive the same scrip concessions.[33] The commission ardently refused their ultimatum, asserting that the Métis taking arms against government had forfeited any rights they possessed.

After the 8 April meeting, Street apprised Minister Macpherson of the Métis' outstanding concerns. Referencing the recommendations made in Jackson's letter to Langevin, and given the commission's timing in relation to the fight at Duck Lake, Street stressed the necessity of meeting the Métis' conditions if the commission were to succeed.[34] Consequently, all children, he argued, would refuse money scrip and instead demand scrip for 240 acres of land, the same option as provided under the Manitoba Act. Second, he suggested that Métis occupying waterfront lots be allowed the opportunity to purchase their water frontages at one dollar per acre and select 160 acres of available homestead land.[35] This arrangement was based on the condition that the Métis make full payment of their waterfront properties within two years, after which they would receive full patent to the 160-acre parcel. Street's plan was a change from the original provision that allowed those who already occupied their property to receive title for it if not more than 160 or 240 acres, dependent upon whether the individual was a head of a family or child of a head of a family. If less than the appropriate 160 or 240, they were to receive the difference in scrip. This proposal, Street argued, would apply to only a few cases, and in each case, the acreage was small.[36] It obtained approval on the condition that the area of these parcels not exceed forty acres.[37] Street's offer was satisfactory to the Métis as it represented a reasonable accommodation that allowed them to keep their waterfront parcels and access the full amount of their scrip entitlement.

Table 3. Manitoba Scrip and North-West Half-Breed Scrip

	Manitoba Act	North-West Half-Breed Scrip (original provision)	NWHB Scrip Revision
Half-breed Heads of Families	Land grant of 160 acres or an issue of scrip in the amount of $160 1876 revision by Order-in-Council: only scrip in the amount of $160, receivable in payment for the purpose of Dominion Lands, should be issued to Métis heads of families.	If occupying land—grant of the lot or portion of land occupied to the extent of 160 acres. If the plot of land is less than 160 acres, scrip issued for the difference. Scrip redeemable in land at the rate of one dollar per acre, For those not occupying land —scrip issued $160, redeemable in land.	$160 Scrip in addition to land occupied. Purchase of small water frontages at one dollar per acre not to exceed 40 acres. Payment to be made within two years. In addition, they be allowed to select 160 acres, the patent for which would be offered after payment received for waterfront parcel.
Children of Half-breed Heads of Families	Land grant of 240 acres	If occupying land—grant of the lot or portion of land occupied to the extent of 240 acres. If the lot is less then 240 acres, scrip issued for the difference, redeemable in land, at a rate of one dollar per acre, or if not occupying land, scrip to be issued for $240	240 acres of land scrip instead of $240 money scrip

The First Sitting of the NWHB Claims Commission, Fort Qu'Appelle

With local Métis concerns seemingly initially alleviated, the commission resumed in Fort Qu'Appelle on the morning of 9 April. They had been invited to hold their sitting at the Qu'Appelle Industrial School by Father Hugonard, the Roman Catholic priest at the Lebret Mission and principal of the school. They eagerly agreed, recognizing that Hugonard's close relationship with the Métis would be beneficial to their work.[38] Métis from across the region, including those who had met with the commission the day before, arrived at the school, many anxious and uncertain to appear before the commissioners. Father Hugonard spoke with the Métis, eager to relieve their apprehension, and in late morning appeared before the commission with an elderly woman. Street recalled that Hugonard had to almost push her into the room, telling the commission she wanted to claim her scrip.[39] The woman, Madeline Hamelin, presented herself to the commissioners with trepidation, providing the necessary details for her claim.[40] Born at St. Boniface in 1840, she was the daughter of Bonhomme Hamelin and Marie Allary. She married Joseph Amyot at St. Josephs, Dakota Territory, in 1861 and by 1865, they were living at Wood Mountain.[41] By 1870, they lived in the Qu'Appelle Valley region on a year-round basis. Amyot died only days before Hamelin appeared before them. When she finished her declaration, two witnesses, Baptiste Dauphinais and Antoine Hamelin, took an oath verifying the details of her claim, including the death of her husband.[42] Completing her application, she received $160 scrip as head of her family. When she left the room, a small crowd gathered around her, seemingly anxious and even unhappy that she had participated in the process. Charles Alloway, an agent for a Winnipeg banker, approached Hamelin eager to purchase her scrip, which she sold for eighty dollars. Undoubtedly, selling her scrip to Alloway provided a desirable cash infusion for the elderly woman whose husband had just passed away. According to Street, the news quickly spread that the commission was handing out certificates readily converted into cash and from that point, they were "besieged from morning till night by applicants."[43]

The North-West Half-Breed Claims Commission approved over 238 applications at this sitting. Of these, 183 were to heads of families and their children and fifty-five to deceased heads of families and their children. Only twenty-six of these claimants asked specifically for land scrip and in the short time between their request and the approval of their claim, many changed their minds, asking for money instead. In the days that followed, additional Métis followed suit. To the surprise of government officials, of the 168 children who were entitled to take land scrip, all but three took money scrip.[44] Deputy Minister Burgess was particularly surprised to learn this, particularly after the Qu'Appelle Métis had initially refused to deal with the commission unless they were authorized to grant scrip certificates for land.[45]

It is unclear why these individuals changed their minds after community leaders so vehemently advocated for land scrip. Present at the sitting, Thomas Jackson professed to have counselled the Métis on the importance of land and encouraged 70 percent of them to take land rather than money scrip. However, hearing rumours that Riel and the Métis along the South Saskatchewan were to be victorious, Jackson reasoned, encouraged Qu'Appelle Métis to change their minds and ask for money scrip so they might purchase what they needed as "the land would ultimately belong to them."[46] The timing and the collective nature of the decision to take money over land scrip speaks to the fierce nationalism maintained by these families in support of their friends and relatives fighting in the Batoche Resistance and their confidence of a Métis victory.[47] Métis success at Batoche would have guaranteed Métis land rights, and would have eliminated the necessity of land scrip to secure individual lands.

The decision to cash out their scrip quickly, hoping to hold on to land by means of victory at Batoche, was a risky gamble that played into the hands of land speculators eager to purchase these scrip certificates at a discount. Likely, the decision to take money scrip was also a response to the economic situations families were in. Selling their scrip provided immediate cash families could use to pay off debts to local merchants or to purchase necessary food and supplies. Many required immediate and practical solutions to their circumstances, which selling their scrip could provide. Even though Métis leaders may have first advocated for land scrip to secure long-term gain, many simply and practically could not see further than their immediate future.

Lands Patented Prior to Scrip—Dealing with Waterfront Properties

Given that many of the Qu'Appelle Métis already held patent to their lands under homestead policy, the original scrip provision guaranteed that claimants with patented land would receive less for the extinguishment of their rights than that received by those who didn't currently hold patented land. Métis leaders advocated for changes to this provision, which Street conveyed to the minister. The minister approved, believing there were to be only a few cases where this would be an issue.[48] Those who held patented waterfront properties were given the option of paying one dollar per acre for land they held under patent, and then receive scrip equivalent to 160 acres, which they could use to select from lands open for homestead. Conditions were limited to waterfront properties of less than forty acres and required payment within two years. Once paid in full, the claimant received patent for the additional scrip land. In total, there were at least fourteen such cases, including those of John Simpson, Antoine Hamelin, and Simon Blondeau.[49]

In the spring of 1875, after living in the region since at least 1869, John Simpson and his wife Catherine Robillard took up year-round residence on a narrow lakefront plot of land on the south side of the Qu'Appelle Lakes.[50] The son of Thomas Simpson and Jane Sutherland, Simpson was born in Red River in 1833 and lived in the North-West Territories since childhood. He entered the service of the HBC in 1849 as a boatbuilder and carpenter at Cumberland House, then at Norway House, Fort Garry, and Fort Pelly. In 1871–72, he was engaged as a

Table 4. Scrip issued to holders of waterfront claims

Claim Number	Claimant	Scrip Amount
50	Marie Klyne	$34.00
148	Simon Blondeau Jr.	$59.60
150	Napoleon Hamelin	$132.00
172	Antoine Hamelin	$40.00
177	Norbert Welsh	$116.00
178	Alex Fisher	$80.00
179	François St. Denis	$110.00
180	Alphonse Martin	$29.69
1487	Louis Flammand	$152.00
1527	John Fisher	$48.00
1554	Antoine Larocque	$80.00
1559	Gabriel Fisher	$64.41
1560	Baptiste Desjarlais	$20.58
1561	John Simpson	$147.46

carpenter at Fort Qu'Appelle.[51] Simpson's property, when surveyed in 1881, was comprised of six small plots measuring less than eight acres in total but located in six separate quarter sections. In 1884 he registered his existing claim on the southwest Section 23–Township 12–Range 14 where his home and outbuildings were located. He took up residence on the lakeshore thinking he "would be allowed to keep [his] narrow lake front and have [his] land given [him] behind for agricultural purposes as was allowed in the province of Manitoba."[52] By the time he received patent, Simpson and his family had made significant improvements including to their home, measuring less than 500 square feet, and a stable. He also fenced his property and broke and farmed at least two acres. When surveyed, his land location became the fractional Quarter Section 23–Township 21–Range 14, a plot of land equivalent to 12.54 acres. When applying for scrip, he agreed to pay one dollar per acre for the 12.54 acres within two years and requested scrip of $160, which he could redeem for 160 acres. Rather than paying the $12.54 within two years, he asked that the $12.54 be deducted from his $160 scrip, reducing it to $147.46.[53]

Table 5. John Simpson existing claims, surveyed in 1881

Location	**Size**
NE 10-21-14	0.28 acres
NW 14-21-14	0.64 acres
SE 15-21-14	2.85 acres
NE 15-21-14	0.31 acres
SE 22-21-14	2.79 acres
SW 23-21-14	0.77
Total	**7.64 acres**

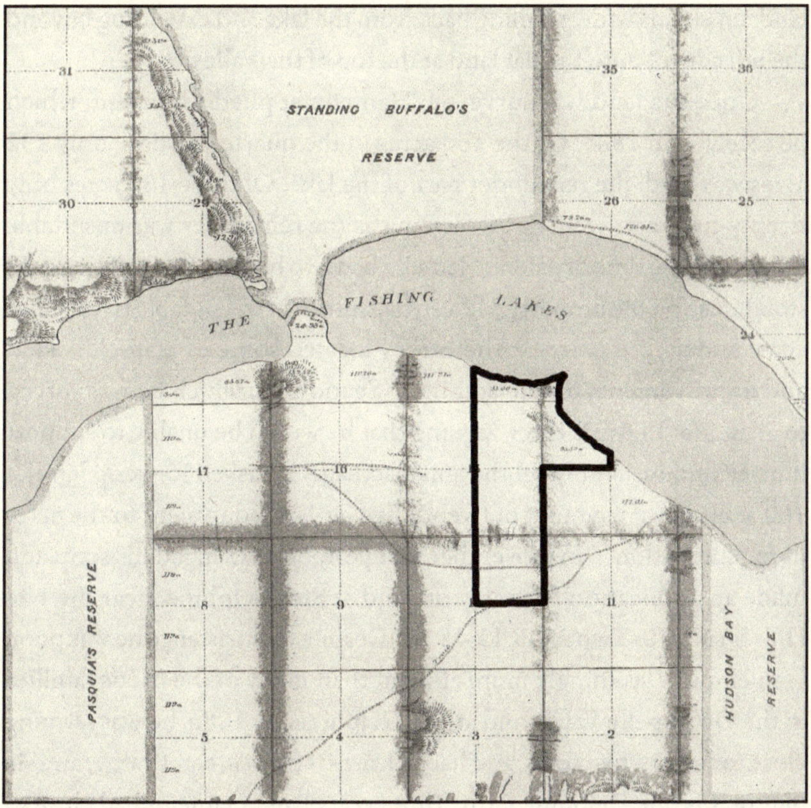

Figure 31. John Simpson waterfront claim crossing six quarter sections (Township 21–Range 14–West of Second Meridian). Map courtesy of Cheryl Troupe and Matthew Kunkel and Provincial Archives of Saskatchewan.

Like Simpson, Antoine Hamelin also agreed to purchase his waterfront claim with the understanding that he would receive $160 scrip that could be used to make a claim for a homestead of 160 acres once he had paid in full for his original claim.[54] His claim was a small flat piece of land in what became the northeast Quarter Section 17–Twp 21–R 12–W 2. He had purchased the property in 1880 from another occupant for $575. He purchased the land believing it was a claim like the waterfront parcels allowed in Manitoba and, when surveyed, expected to receive patent to land ten chains wide, running back from the lake and extending beyond the hillside up onto the flat land at the top of the Valley.[55]

Once the land was surveyed, Hamelin applied for patent, which he received in 1884. Of the 160 acres in the quarter section, only 132 acres was land, the remainder part of the lake. Of these 132 acres only twenty-five acres were fit for farming as the remainder was unsuitable hillside. At the time of patent, Hamelin had two houses, two stables, and a storehouse on the property. He also had fifteen of the suitable twenty-five acres under cultivation.[56] The survey located some of Hamelin's land and improvements on the adjoining Section 20, which he was forced to abandon. In April 1885, arguing that he would be unable to support himself and his family off the small acreage, he asked for scrip land of 160 acres upon payment of twenty-five dollars, equivalent to the acres fit for cultivation.[57] In November that year, he exchanged his scrip and made an application for entry on land at Ste. Delphine, near the File Hills on NE 10–Twp 25–R 12–W 2.[58] Despite his insistence he was poor, Hamelin was seemingly more affluent than many of the Métis families in the Qu'Appelle Valley and at Ste. Delphine. By 1886, he was farming close to twenty-five acres, and had at least six horses, eight cattle, and six pigs on his Ste. Delphine farm. Three years later, Hamelin had close to thirty head of cattle.[59]

In 1884, Simon Blondeau and his wife Françoise Desjarlais received patent for a fractional quarter section on Section 3–Twp 21–R 13–W 2 that fronted the water. By this time, they had been living on the property for nearly twenty years and had built a 400-square-foot house, a stable measuring close to the same, and a 12 x 12-foot storehouse. Blondeau's land measured 100.40 acres, of which he was farming fifteen.[60] A year later, scrip provisions entitled him to receive $160 scrip, redeemable for land. He requested scrip in the amount of $59.60 as compensation for the difference between the amount of his patented land and 160 acres.[61] He offered to pay one dollar per acre for the 100.40 acres within the two-year time frame so that he might obtain an additional free grant of 160 acres of land as a homestead in addition to his $160 scrip entitlement.

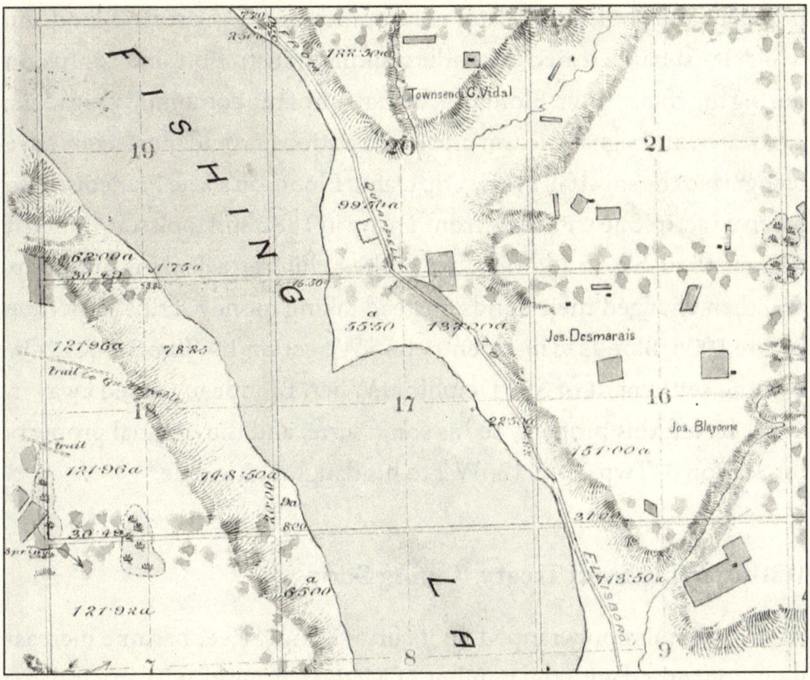

Figure 32. Antoine Hamelin's waterfront claim (Northeast Quarter–Section 17–Township 20–Range 12–West of Second Meridian). Provincial Archives of Saskatchewan.

He also asked for this land to be as near his current residence as possible. Blondeau's request was more than the allowable forty-acre waterfront criteria, so the commissioners did not have the authority to grant his request. Rather, they only had the authority to give him $59.60 scrip, which he could redeem for land. When explained to him that he would receive patent to this land without payment, the Scrip Commission secretary Cote recorded Blondeau's satisfaction with the agreement. For his scrip, he received only $59.40 redeemable for land, not his $160 entitlement. Considering he already had patent to his fractional quarter section of 100.40 acres, his scrip amount topped him up to 160 acres, equivalent to a homestead quarter section. To that end, Blondeau did not benefit from scrip to the extent that he should have, and yet, the commissioners noted his approval. A translator communicated the matter to Blondeau, which must have created misunderstanding, frustration, and confusion during the transaction. Blondeau, being one of the community's leaders, advocates, and signatories on previous petitions, would most likely have recognized the shortfall in his scrip claim. Blondeau's wife Françoise also received scrip. She withdrew from Treaty in 1882 and took scrip when it became available. In addition, five of their children asked for land scrip, and then changed their minds, instead taking money scrip. Sometime before 1906, Blondeau made entry on SW Section 14–Twp 25–R 12–W 2 in the settlement of Ste. Delphine. When Blondeau passed away in 1906, he left this property to his son, Pierre, and the original property on Section 3–Twp 21–R 13–W 2 to his daughter Melanie.[62]

Withdrawing from Treaty, Taking Scrip

As the commission wrapped up its first sitting, Street became increasingly concerned with the number of Métis registered as Treaty Indians appearing before them asking to withdraw from treaty and take scrip. For many Métis, taking treaty when Indian Act definitions allowed, offered a modicum of security rather than having to wait and risk the possibility of receiving scrip in the future.[63] Once scrip extended into the North-West, however, Métis on the treaty paylists eagerly looked to withdraw and access their long-awaited scrip entitlements. Scrip was the recognition and compensation for title that the Métis had passionately advocated for and as well as a financial benefit.[64] However, like their entry into treaty, withdrawal proved complicated. Realizing the absence of policy to deal with such withdrawal requests, the commissioners sought the minister's guidance.[65] Receiving little support, Street decided to accept scrip applications from women who wished to withdraw from treaty, which he forwarded to the minister with specific questions. Deputy Minister Burgess responded, with no answers, but requested an investigation into the Indian Act for clarification.[66]

Indian Act definitions of who was or was not an "Indian" had become more explicit in 1876, which helped to clarify where Métis fit within treaty, if at all. According to the Act, the term Indian referred to "First, any male person of Indian blood reputed to belong to a particular band; Second, any child of such person; Third, any woman who is or was lawfully married to such person."[67] It also defined who qualified as a "Half-breed," and thus ineligible for treaty. Accordingly, the Act declared that Métis admittance into treaty was reserved for those who were not heads of Métis families and had not received scrip in Manitoba. Heads of families, could, under very special circumstances, be accepted into treaty but only on an individual case-by-case basis, adjudicated by the Superintendent-General of Indian Affairs.[68] While this amendment helped clarify where Métis fit within treaty, it did not outline a process by which they could be removed or could remove themselves, and by 1878 Lieutenant Governor and Superintendent of Indian Affairs David Laird remained challenged in "distinguishing certain half-breeds, who have adopted Indian habits, from full-blooded Indians."[69]

Further revisions to the Act in 1879 reveal policy makers' desire to remove Métis from treaty, and a process for doing so.[70] Removal required that the individual refund all annuity monies received and if they could not do so, they could repay this debt through a reduction in the quantity of land or money scrip received.[71] Five years later, Indian Act amendments eliminated the repayment clause, signalling a clear commitment on behalf of the government to encourage Métis to withdraw from treaty in favour of taking scrip. Under this revision, discharge from treaty became as easy as signifying in writing one's desire to do so, accompanied by two witnesses who swore an oath.[72] These amendments coupled with the decision to issue scrip in 1885 resulted in a flood of applicants requesting removal.[73]

From an economic perspective, allowing Métis off the treaty rolls reduced the size of reserve populations and the cost of ongoing annuity payments in exchange for a one-time grant of land, which the government had in abundance. In the File Hills reserves alone, withdrawal under these circumstances reduced reserve population by 15 percent.[74] Undeniably, the option to withdraw affected reserve numbers and proved to be a cost-saving measure for Indian Affairs.[75]

For the Métis, opting out of treaty to receive scrip meant the possibility of acquiring their own land and being free from the restrictive measures of reserve life under the Indian Act.[76] It also meant forfeiture of their homes and rights to any improvements, including cattle and implements, which belonged to the band.[77] For some, this decision may have implied a refusal of reserve life and the bureaucratically constructed category of Indian but for most the exchange of security was more often theoretical than real as life off reserve was only marginally better.[78]

During sittings across the North-West Territories in 1885–1886, the Scrip Commission allowed 1,164 applications for scrip, over half of which were those who withdrew from treaty the previous summer.[79] In Fort Qu'Appelle alone they approved 100 claims for Métis who had left treaty. Thirty-four of these were heads of families and sixty-six of their children.[80] Most left treaty with little or no personal property, living with, and relying on, relatives and integrating themselves into extended kinship networks. For example, when Julie Martin along with seven of her children and three grandchildren discharged themselves from the Muskowequan Band in the Touchwood Hills, they looked to her extended family in the Qu'Appelle Valley for support. She applied for and received discharge from treaty in late April 1886, but did not receive her scrip for six months.[81] A widow with few options, she relocated to live within the cluster of residences along the Fishing Lakes close to her brother, Baptiste Desjarlais, and sisters, Isabelle Desjarlais and Françoise Desjarlais Blondeau and their families.[82] Living in these intimate family groupings ensured a network of kinship relationships for Métis, like Martin, to rely on as they adjusted to life outside the bounds of the Indian Act. It also allowed them to adopt or maintain a lifestyle of itinerant farm labour, supplemented by subsistence activity as they attempted to eke out a marginal economic existence.

Many left treaties thinking they would immediately receive scrip, but for most, like Martin, it was not the case. By late 1886, many in the Qu'Appelle Valley area had still not received their scrip and were increasingly vulnerable to merchants and scrip speculators willing to advance credit and goods. Those leaving treaty had few options and at first sold their scrip to speculators at low prices so they could support themselves and their families. This sale and purchase of scrip represents one of the breakdowns of the scrip system. By making scrip transferable, the government opened Métis land up to speculation by extremely eager and successful land buyers, bankers, and businessmen. In many instances, they were able to acquire a power of attorney for individuals and convince them to sell their scrip even before withdrawing from treaty.[83]

By October 1886, many like Martin were in desperate economic circumstances. Determined to receive their certificates, Qu'Appelle Métis petitioned Thomas White, Minister of the Interior.[84] They demanded immediate action on their scrip claims and that their children, if not eligible for scrip, receive a fifty-dollar gratuity in lieu of future treaty annuities they would have received. The petition was signed by thirty-four heads of families formerly belonging to the Muskowequan, Pasqua, Muscowpetung, Cowessess, and O'Soup bands as well as other reserves in the area.[85] Included amongst the signatories were all but one of Julie Martin's seven children, along with three of her grandchildren.[86] Thomas Jackson described the Métis' poor economic situation, part of which resulted from scrip delay, and stressed the urgency in dealing with their concerns because winter was quickly approaching.[87] As encouragement to promptly settle scrip claims, he also reminded the minister of the benefit and long-term cost savings of these individuals no longer being on the treaty rolls.

Before responding, White sought the opinion of the deputy minister of the Interior who rejoined that, upon consulting the Indian Act and the acting deputy superintendent general of Indian Affairs, there was no foundation for the claim that these children receive such gratuity. White informed Jackson, and the local Qu'Appelle newspaper reported on the results, helping to clarify the situation.[88] The Minister of the Interior followed the letter of the law but showed little, if any, empathy for the Métis position. The law was clear. There were no provisions in the Act to comply with the petitioner's request but if the claimants could show a precedent, the government might be willing to reconsider the issue.[89] As a result, many Métis remained in destitute circumstances, anxiously awaiting their scrip claims and vulnerable to merchants and bankers, eager to buy up Métis scrip.

Scrip Speculation

Scrip may have provided a short-term benefit to the Métis, but it did little to safeguard their long-term security. Most had few options but to sell because it was the most practical response to their pressing economic situations.[90] They needed to feed their families or pay off debts to merchants and businesses who had given them credit or money in advance of scrip. Although speculators offered to purchase scrip certificates at lower than face value, it was cash, and it was immediate. There were no administrative delays, making it a tempting, if temporary, solution to Métis' economic circumstances.

Scrip was well-suited to the quick transfer of land title from one person to another. Its classification as either land or money, and the regulations around its dispersal and exchange encouraged, and even invited, speculation.[91] Land scrip regulations made it difficult for Métis to take advantage of it, which in turn pushed them to sell. Redeeming scrip required a visit to the Dominion Lands Office often far from where the individual lived, or economically unfeasible to travel to.[92] Land scrip certificates were made out in the individual's name and only they could exchange it for land. It could not legally be assigned to anyone else until it had been issued to the bearer at the Dominion Lands Office. Once presented, land scrip could only be redeemed for unoccupied surveyed land, which might also be far from where the bearer already lived. Moving to such a location was generally not an option because it would require financial resources and mean disruption of extended family groupings and kinship networks. Farming was also risky and required capital that many Métis did not have. Additionally, taking up land for agriculture on a scale larger than what they already practised with their gardens was not always an attractive option for Métis who preferred a seasonal semi-migrant economy or wished to continue a subsistence-based lifestyle of hunting, fishing, and harvesting the natural environment.[93]

Unlike land scrip, money scrip certificates were not made out to the individual and could be redeemed at the Dominion Lands Office by anyone in possession of one, making them desirable to speculators. This was a critical policy error that quickly placed scrip in the hand of speculators. Considered "personal property," money scrip certificates could be easily bought and sold with no restriction, unlike land scrip, which was considered "real property" or "real estate." Title to the land could only be transferred and this required administrative registration.

Money scrip was easy to acquire in comparison to land scrip, which was time-consuming and often difficult, but not unattainable. The ease with which money scrip was bought and sold encouraged a preference amongst both Métis and speculators who became motivated to offer higher prices for them.[94] Lax regulation also emboldened speculators to commit forgery, fraud, and impersonation.[95] Speculators manoeuvred around regulatory issues by acquiring power of attorney and acting as an agent for the claimants. In some instances, negotiations were done prior to the individual even applying for scrip. At other times, speculators paid local Indigenous people to visit the Dominion Lands Office and fraudulently redeem others' scrip certificates.

While the government and its representatives may not have known the extent of scrip speculation, they were fully aware of its existence, and even accepted and assisted speculators in the process.[96] Hearing schedules were made public, and speculators, like Charles Alloway, followed the commission, carrying large amounts of cash ready to purchase scrip at each sitting. Speculators even commonly travelled with the commission itself. Speculation became such common practice that the Department of the Interior created a banking arrangement through the Dominion Lands Office where speculators could deposit scrip until they required it for payment of lands, thereby making their future land transactions both convenient and efficient.[97] Scrip speculation contributed to the creation of a wealthy regional elite and enabled the purchase of large amounts of land by a relative few.[98]

There is no dispute that the government opened the field to speculation when they created the difference between land and money scrip regulations. However, scholars disagree on whether it was acting with benevolence towards Métis interests or with intent to dispossess them of their lands. Scholars such as D.N. Sprague, Ken Hatt, and Joe Sawchuk argue that scrip policy was poorly conceived and administered.[99] Regulations aimed at discouraging speculation applied only to land scrip but the trade in money scrip was "wide open." Money scrip, then, was devised to enable speculation, ensuring that Métis would quickly sell. The presence of speculators and the ease with which they bought scrip ensured the removal and ultimate dispersal of Métis from their lands. Others, such as Thomas Flanagan, contend that the government was well intentioned and attempted in good faith to protect Métis lands.[100] In their opinion, Métis made the rational choice to sell their scrip. However, the decision to sell or not was complicated.

In implementing the scrip system, the government treated Métis according to their different interests. Those who were already property owners with farming investments, those who left treaty to access scrip, and those very poor families all acted and benefited or lost out in different ways. Early in the commission, there were efforts to accommodate Qu'Appelle Métis, revising policy to better suit those who owned their properties outright, and those who wished to maintain their small waterfront properties. The government also found ways to implement policy for Métis to withdraw from treaty to take advantage of scrip, albeit to their own ultimate benefit by reducing reserve populations and the financial responsibility of Indian Affairs. Ultimately, there were very real weaknesses and failures in scrip policy mainly due to its implementation and the carte blanche speculators had in buying up land. For those who were not already property owners, once they sold their scrip, they had few options but to relocate themselves to any available land in a region quickly filling up with settler farmers taking up homesteads. For many, this meant a move to the road allowance or to land that lined the Qu'Appelle Lakes.

The 1885 Scrip Commission ran its course and because of its limited schedule missed numerous individuals and entire communities. In 1886, a second commission was formed, this time with Roger Goulet as the sole commissioner. The intent was to visit communities, including again at Fort Qu'Appelle, to hear from individuals previously missed. A year later, the government initiated a third commission with Goulet and Narcisse Omer Cote acting as commissioners. Cote had been secretary for the two previous commissions. These were only three commissions in a series of many that operated over the course of twenty-one years to deal with and extinguish Métis claims in the North-West Territories.[101] Into the early twentieth century, there remained Métis in the Qu'Appelle Valley who still had not applied for or received scrip.

Post–1885 Scrip

Not quite a year after the first Scrip Commission hearing at Qu'Appelle, Lieutenant Governor Edgar Dewdney visited the community and inquired about Métis widows and orphans that had relocated from the South Saskatchewan River Valley to the Qu'Appelle following the Battle of Batoche. Finding these women and children with very little, Dewdney arranged to give them food and provisions and for the community's men to receive work freighting 600 bags of flour to Batoche. The Métis eagerly accepted the offer, responding by formally welcoming the lieutenant governor to the Valley and expressing their loyalty and confidence in him and his administration.[102] Four months later, in June 1886, Norbert Welsh wrote Dewdney citing the Métis's continued inability to find work and requested the federal government to again provide freighting work.[103]

Dewdney did not immediately respond to their appeal, instead forwarding the request to the Minister of the Interior asking he conduct a study of the Métis' economic situation before approving any form of assistance. In early December, W.A. Clark, a local Justice of the Peace, began surveying Métis settlements along the Qu'Appelle Lakes and at File Hills. Accompanied by Welsh, Clark visited families in the region, finding them "happy, healthy and contented, although in poor circumstances, and not very bright prospects for the future."[104] Most had horses, Clark noted, but were unable to find freighting work with their teams, and consequently had little or no potential for supporting themselves and their families besides selling wood, hunting, or fishing. The Métis, he maintained, remained able and willing to work, should it be available. Concerned that government intervention amongst the Métis might create discontent amongst the growing settler population, Clark warned that if support was to be provided, the Métis should not receive charity but be made to work for any assistance received.[105]

Dewdney refused to help the Métis, interpreting Clark's report to mean that although there might be a few cases of individual distress, there was no general destitution amongst the Métis. The Métis, he reasoned, were not impoverished enough that they required government intervention in the form of employment. In fact, some, such as Welsh, were even in "fairly comfortable circumstances."[106] With no reprieve available from the lieutenant governor or the Department of the Interior, the Métis continued to do what they could to support themselves and their families, taking work when and where it was available.

Despite Dewdney's opinion, Clark's report painted a grim but seemingly accurate portrayal of the economic situation of the Métis. He identified 123 Métis households in the Qu'Appelle Region: eighty-five in the Qu'Appelle Valley and thirty-eight near the File Hills reserves, in the settlement of Ste. Delphine. The movement to Ste. Delphine was in many ways a response to the dispossession of Métis from their lands in the Qu'Appelle Valley following scrip.[107] There was already a small population of Métis near the File Hills by the mid-1880s, but by the turn of the century the population had grown significantly as families moved out of the Qu'Appelle Valley.[108] The growth of settlement in this region was also due to the establishment of a rail line at the southern end of the File Hills reserves in 1905.[109] Rail transport made the movement of grain out of the region less expensive, making agriculture potentially more profitable.

Métis relocation to Ste. Delphine reflected how the scrip system and homestead policies did in fact benefit some Métis, at least initially. Some were able to use scrip and homestead policies to relocate their families, yet remain within extended family groupings, within familiar territory, and in doing so, continue to access necessary environmental resources. By 1886, more than forty Métis families from the Qu'Appelle Valley had taken up land and were living in the Ste. Delphine area. Some of these families had received scrip in the 1870s under the Manitoba Act, but most received money scrip in 1885. A few exchanged their scrip for homestead land, and many more eventually applied for homestead as settlers. Despite being separated by a distance of about sixty kilometres, connections remained between the Qu'Appelle and Ste. Delphine families. Often it was a son or a daughter of those in Qu'Appelle who struck out for Ste. Delphine. For instance, in the early 1880s, Suzanne Bercier Pelletier's son Edouard and grandson François lived with her in a home along the south side of the Qu'Appelle River. Once they received scrip, Edward and François both took up land separately at Ste. Delphine, along with Suzanne's sons Joseph, Alphonse, and Alexander. Suzanne remained in her home in the Qu'Appelle with her son Cuthbert and daughter Suzanne Ross nearby.

Intent on farming, the Perreault and Hamelin families were some of the first to take up land at Ste. Delphine. In 1886, Antoine Hamelin traded his scrip for land and he and his wife, Philomene Perreault, left the Qu'Appelle Lakes region for Ste. Delphine. Other family members followed, including their son Albert and daughter-in-law Marie Suzanne Beaulieau dit Sinclair. Marie Suzanne, whose parents also lived in the region, had received 240 acres of land scrip which she exchanged for land at Ste. Delphine.[110] Albert and Marie Suzanne held this land for only a short time, selling it to Joseph Brunet two years later. By the late 1880s, there were also four generations of Isabelle Perreault's family living in the region, some of whom had taken scrip in Manitoba.[111] By the turn of the century, the Amyotte, Beaulieau, Blondeau, Cardinal, Dauphinais, Desjarlais, Desmarais, Klyne, Laliberte, Larocque, Malbeuf, Pelletier, Poitras, Robillard, Ross, St. Denis, and Vallee families among others could also be found in the Ste. Delphine area. It was clear for the Métis that relocating to Ste. Delphine was an opportunity for families to take up land within familiar territory and continue to live close to one another in extended family groupings.

While some, such as Marie Suzanne and her father-in-law Antoine Hamelin, used their scrip to secure land at Ste. Delphine, most did not. Instead, many applied for homesteads as settlers, which made them vulnerable to the provisions requiring homestead improvements. From the time of survey in 1882–83 until 1899, close to twenty Métis made homestead entries in the Ste. Delphine and File Hills area. Between 1900 and 1910, the number increased to more than 110. At the same time, Métis in the Qu'Appelle Valley were also applying for homestead. From 1882 to 1899, more than forty Métis made homestead entries; between 1900 and 1910, over 140 more. After 1910 however, the number of new entries significantly dropped with fewer than ten Métis families applying in the 1910s.

By 1912, there were close to 100 Métis families living in the immediate Ste. Delphine area. Many attempted to farm but were challenged by a lack of capital and thwarted by complications and penalties in navigating homestead policy and interacting with land agents. By the end of the decade most no longer owned land or farmed at Ste. Delphine.[112] Rather, many had given up and were forced by poverty to sell, returning to the Qu'Appelle Valley where they took up residence on the road allowances along the lakes.

Applying for Homestead

Homestead policy required applicants to demonstrate their intent to become bona fide farmers. This included paying the required fees, making necessary improvements to their lands, and maintaining a continual residency on the property for six months a year. Even if the Métis could pay the necessary fees, they lacked capital to invest in farm improvements and, for many, the continual residency requirement came into conflict with family responsibilities, the necessity of being away from home working, and the nature of Métis economic practices that required being away for periods of time to hunt or fish.

Whether the Métis met these criteria was often at the discretion of the homestead inspector and the local land agent. Homestead inspectors questioned the intention of Métis such as Joseph Gosselin, John Klyne, and Charles Racette to become bona fide settlers because they lived off their homestead, regularly leaving their homes to find work but also to hunt and fish. Many others frequently lived with parents or children for short periods of time, helping when elderly parents were sick or providing extra support in maintaining their small farms. In August 1885, a homestead inspector challenged Joseph Gosselin's continual residency on his homestead. Gosselin argued that it was family responsibility that kept him away. At the time of inspection, Gosselin had a log "shanty" and stable built and about seven acres cropped. Despite this evidence of occupation, the inspector noted Gosselin was "a half-breed and didn't reside on the property" but instead lived "most of the time on his brother's homestead." Gosselin justified his absence on his own homestead explaining that he had been residing with his father and helping him farm. Gosselin also indicated he worked for other farmers to earn enough money to finish building his own home and one for his widowed sister and her family.[113]

Similarly, homestead inspectors questioned John Klyne's residency and therefore his suitability as a settler. By August 1885, Klyne had built a small log cabin and had a few acres cropped and ten acres freshly broken.

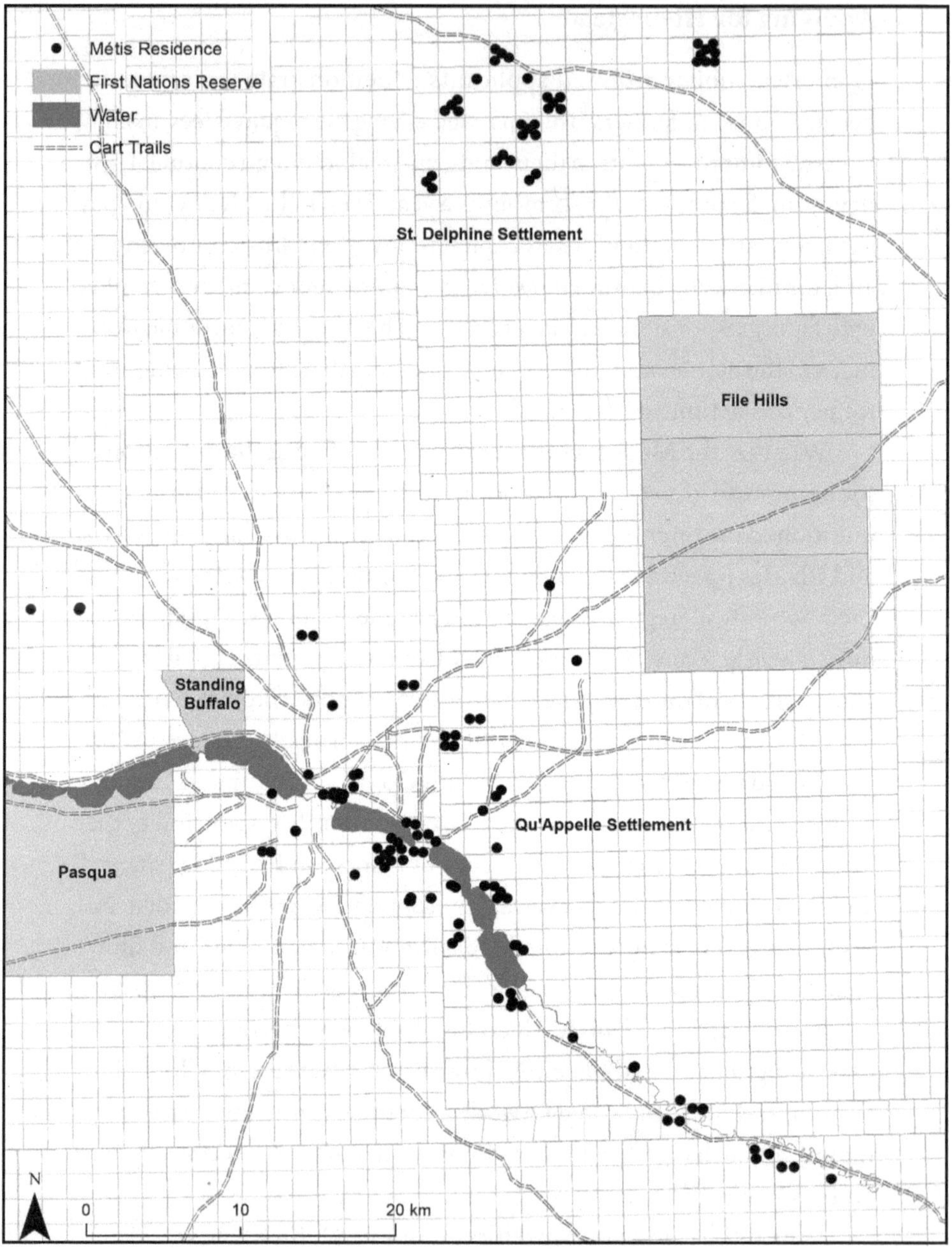

Figure 33. Métis identified in W.A. Clark Survey, 1886. Map courtesy of Cheryl Troupe and Matthew Kunkel.

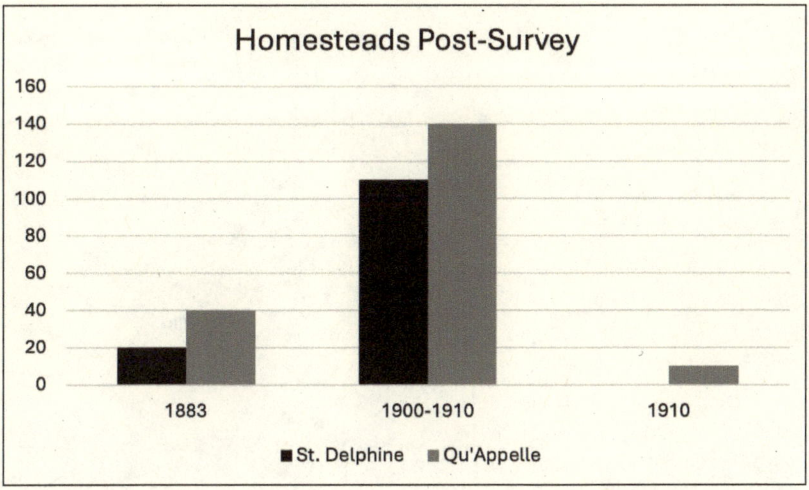

Figure 34. Homesteads at Ste. Delphine/File Hills and Qu'Appelle Valley, 1883–1910. Source: Qu'Appelle Valley Homestead records, Provincial Archives of Saskatchewan.

Despite this, the inspector declared Klyne, "a half-breed, was . . . a very poor, undesirable settler" because he was frequently absent from his residence, living with his father.[114] The following April, the Dominion Lands Branch notified Klyne that he must be in permanent residence by 1 May 1886 to comply with the residency clause. The local agent forwarded Klyne's application for patent to the Dominion Lands Branch in Winnipeg, but it was not until August 1888 that the land agent ordered another homestead inspection. This second inspection did not go well. The Office of the Dominion lands commissioner informed Klyne that they had refused his application for patent because of the inspector's "very unfavourable report." The inspector had visited Klyne's claim in late August and found improvements consisting of about nine acres cropped and six acres of broken ground overgrown in weeds. There was also "a small mud and log dwelling worth about $10 and a stable of about the same materials but of no value" on the property. Finding no one in residence, the Commissioner's Office challenged Klyne on the accuracy of his homestead application, questioning if he continually resided on his homestead from April 1884 to 25 July 1888, as indicated on his

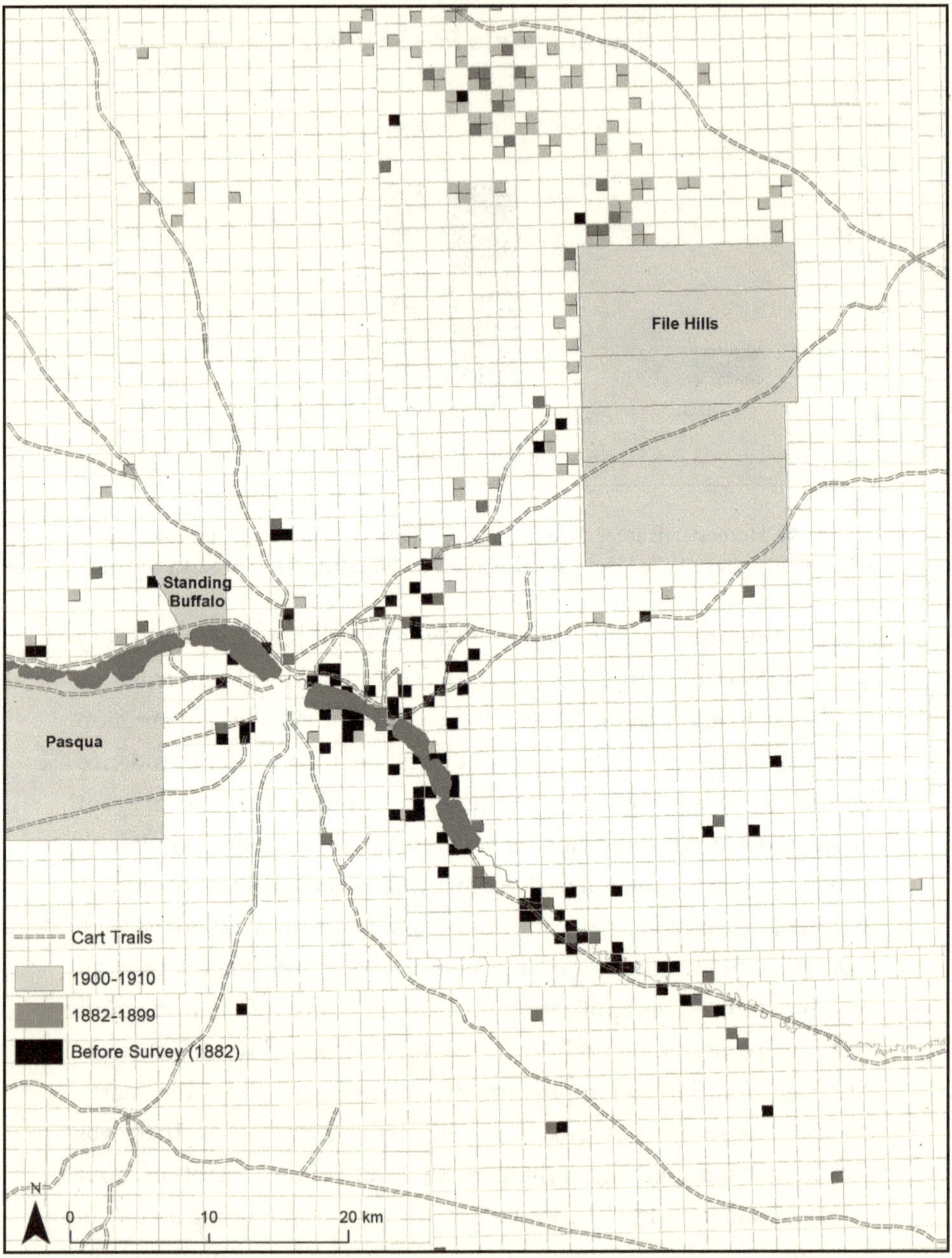

Figure 35. Métis Homesteads at Ste. Delphine/File Hills and Qu'Appelle Valley, 1883–1910. Map courtesy of Cheryl Troupe and Matthew Kunkel.

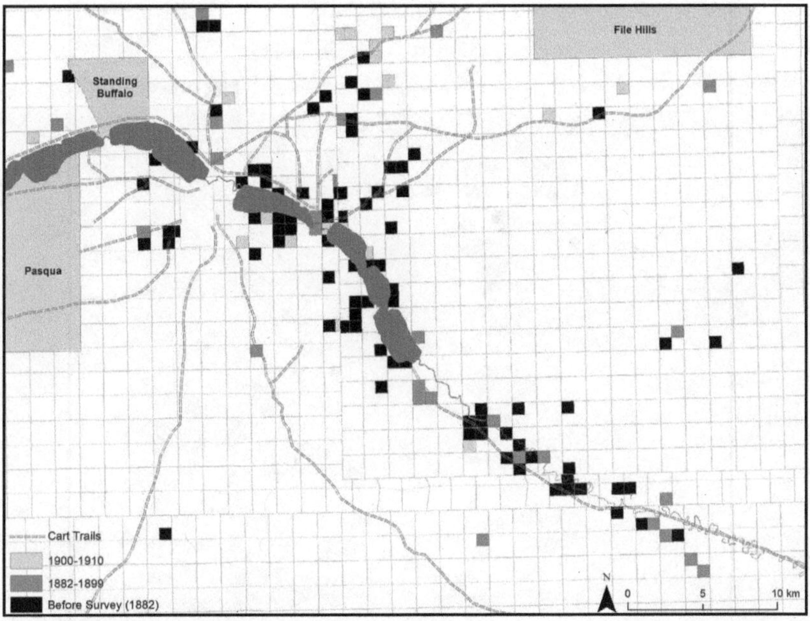

Figure 36. Detail, Métis Homesteads, Qu'Appelle Valley, 1883–1910. Map courtesy of Cheryl Troupe and Matthew Kunkel.

declaration, or if he lived with his father on another section. Under these circumstances, Klyne would have to make another application for patent when, or if, he could show that he had performed the necessary settlement duties. By this report, Klyne was not a bona fide settler, despite his claims or any improvements he had made.

Homestead inspectors and lands agents were critical of the intent and ability of Métis to become farmers, often characterizing them as "unlikely to succeed" or as not bona fide settlers.[115] In the case of the Blondeau brothers, Napoleon, John, and Zacharie, it was merely because they were Métis that homestead inspectors believed they would not or could not become serious farmers. Upon inspection, Napoleon had about one acre broken, and no house built. The lack of permanent housing, the inspectors claimed, encouraged Blondeau to be frequently absent, and because he was Métis, was "not likely to follow agricultural pursuits

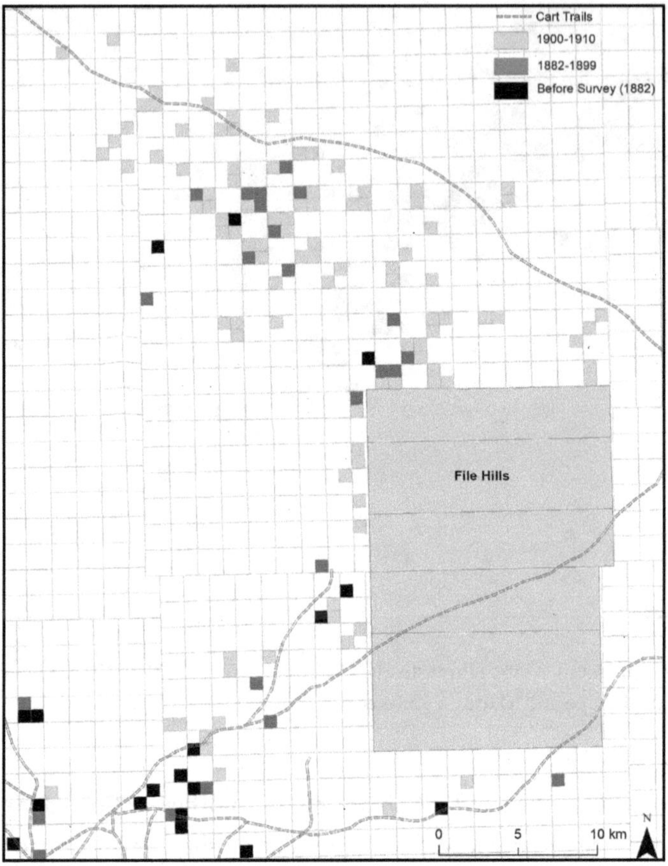

Figure 37. Detail, Métis Homesteads, Ste. Delphine/File Hills, 1883–1910. Map courtesy of Cheryl Troupe and Matthew Kunkel.

to any extent."[116] Blondeau rebutted that he had frequently been living close by with his father, Simon, due to his own ill health.[117] Regardless, the inspector cancelled his entry, noting he was not a desirable settler or serious farmer because he was not endeavouring to improve his homestead.[118] In 1885, Blondeau made a second but unsuccessful attempt to re-enter his homestead on the same quarter section. The following spring, the land was entered on by Chrysotome Robillard, Blondeau's brother-in-law. Robillard received patent for the land in 1899 after the inspector reported that Blondeau had been away from the region for some years and had abandoned the property.[119] In 1909, Blondeau made another attempt to establish a homestead, making an entry not far from his original parcel. He built a home and two stables, and within the first year, had fifteen acres broken and two acres fenced. Throughout this time, he continued to support himself hunting, fishing, gardening, and freighting. He received patent for this land in 1912.[120]

The homestead inspector treated Napoleon's brothers Jean and Zacharie in a similar fashion. Jean took up land before the 1882 Dominion Land Survey and attempted to register his claim in 1884, making little progress. The reason for this is unclear, but in 1889, he made another application. The local land agent took Jean's application and forwarded it to the Dominion Lands Office in Winnipeg for approval. A week later, the Lands Office returned Jean's file requesting the local agent conduct an inspection. Hearing nothing by the following spring, the Winnipeg Dominion Lands Office requested a status update prompting the local agent to order an inspection. The inspection took place four months later. There is no indication or reason given for such delay. At the time of entry, Jean had two log homes and stable built on the property, had fifteen acres broken and a herd of approximately twenty horses. Despite these improvements and the farm's "neat appearance," the homestead inspector still did not believe Jean to be serious about farming the land.[121] He did, however, finally approve the patent in late October 1890.

Zacharie Blondeau began the process of registering his claim in July 1883 expecting patent to be granted quickly; it took close to two decades. At the time of applying for patent he had about six acres under cultivation and had planted a garden with at least a half an acre of onions and potatoes each year since taking up occupation. He had built a small log house and stable and had purchased a wagon, plough, and two horses. Despite these improvements, the Lands Office requested an inspection. In October, fearing cancellation, Thomas Jackson inquired about the status of the claim on Blondeau's behalf. The land agent gave no indication about when the inspection would take place, but reassured Jackson that at present, they would not cancel the claim. The claim was inspected nine months later. No further action was taken on the file by either the Dominion Lands Branch or Zacharie for nearly a decade, until land agents again in September 1893 required him to prove his case. This required another inspection, and in November he made a statutory declaration and provided affidavits from his brother Simon Blondeau and Pierre Desjarlais swearing to his improvements. The land agent was still not convinced by this testimony, and notified Zacharie that it would be necessary he increase the amount of land under cultivation before reapplying for patent. In July 1895, the homestead inspector again inspected his claim, taking affidavits from two witnesses and looking to ensure that Zacharie had made the necessary improvements. Finally satisfied, the inspector reported that he must pay an inspection fee before patent approval. Zacharie did not receive patent for another six years, until May 1901.

There is no indication in Zacharie's file why it moved so slowly through the Dominion Lands bureaucracy, or why he did not pursue the matter in a timelier fashion. The delay may have resulted from government apathy when dealing with the Métis, who, they perceived, were not, and would not be, serious farmers. With Zacharie's initial inspection in 1884 however, the inspector recognized that he did in fact continually reside on his claim and that he had made some improvements. Despite this evidence, the inspector noted that Zacharie, like his brothers, appeared to not be doing much "to advance the interests of agriculture."[122] Zacharie's inaction in pursuing his claim may also have resulted from his inability to make a living farming this particular plot of land, which, he lamented in his declaration, was of poor quality for farming.[123] The complications and bureaucratic delays Zacharie Blondeau and his brothers Napoleon and John experienced as well as those faced by Joseph Gosselin, John Klyne, and others were not unique. Despite these men's improvements and demonstrated commitment to farming, homestead inspectors continually questioned Métis residency, their commitment and ability to farm, their mobile nature, and the necessity to be off their property.

The extent to which Métis were willing to become farmers, and be successful, was a common concern for homestead inspectors. Most Métis did not take up land exclusively for farming, but maintained a mixed economy of small-scale agriculture, hunting, and fishing, supplemented by freighting and seasonal employment when available. Even for those who wished to take up farming, their poverty limited their success. For many there was a very practical reason for delays in receiving patent or for the loss of homestead lands. Being poor, many could ill afford the required fees. In July 1884, Thomas Jackson noted in a letter to the commissioner of the lands branch that there were numerous Métis in the region requesting extensions in paying the required entry fees.[124] Jackson pleaded for leniency, arguing that many Métis were "so poorly off this season," it was feared that, without the extension, by spring many would lose their properties to incoming settlers. Many lost their lands this way while others sold when they could no longer afford to farm.[125] By the time scrip was distributed in 1885, it was already too late for many Métis on the verge of losing their property. By the 1910s, many had moved off their homesteads in the Qu'Appelle Valley or away from Ste. Delphine and returned to the Valley. Whether through the failure of the scrip system or the regulation and administrative process of the homestead policy, at the end of the nineteenth century, Métis who remained in or returned to the Qu'Appelle Valley had few options. Displaced and dispossessed, for many their only choice was to move to unoccupied Crown land at the edges of each township, or for some, to the road allowances along the Qu'Appelle Lakes.

By 1885, many Métis in the Qu'Appelle Valley had already secured their land holdings, registering their pre-existing claims as settlers through the homestead process. Others anticipated securing land through government recognition of their unextinguished rights in the North-West Territories, as had happened in Manitoba. By March 1885,

Ottawa was finally ready to deal with the Métis in what they considered to be a fair and equitable way. Scrip policy dealt with Qu'Appelle Métis in different ways, depending upon their needs and sometimes to their benefit. As the government amended scrip policy to recognize pre-existing ownership under homestead policy, Métis made demands about the policy direction and type of scrip—land or money—that would best meet their pressing needs. They urged the government to deal with their small waterfront claims to their benefit and insisted on accommodations for Métis who wished to withdraw from First Nations treaties and take scrip.

There were, however, significant challenges in the scrip system. Government was often slow to distribute scrip, and its very nature encouraged speculation. The flaws in the system allowed scrip speculators to buy up any available scrip certificates quickly and easily, which merchants and bankers purchased as quickly as they could. Those Métis most destitute were also the most vulnerable and had few options but to sell, paying off local merchants or purchasing supplies to meet their immediate needs. Even those who already held patent to the land they lived on found themselves in a precarious situation as money from scrip might help in the near future but would not sustain families long term. Some were able to use their scrip, along with homestead policy, to secure land in the Qu'Appelle Valley and near File Hills, re-establishing themselves along extended family lines. Even though these policies intended to secure Métis land tenure, it was difficult for individuals to maintain land ownership and they frequently faced discrimination and racism from unsympathetic Dominion Lands agents. The 1885 implementation of the North-West Half-Breed Claims Commission increasingly immersed Métis in a complicated bureaucracy, yet they continued advocating for their interests, finding ways to position themselves in a system beleaguered with challenges. They attempted to secure land tenure so they might continue to live in familiar territory and according to culturally recognizable ways. Some acted practically to alleviate their immediate poverty whereas others found ways to secure more long-term benefit.

In effect, scrip did little to change the Métis' economic situation. The North-West Half-Breed Scrip policy of the late 1880s, or the subsequent scrip commissions into the early 1900s, ultimately failed the majority of Métis. Most lost or sold their scrip to speculators for a fraction of its value. The implementation of scrip policy did not consider Métis ways of life or how to make the economic transition to agriculture succeed. Instead, most ended up landless. Scrip did not provide the guarantee of land rights that the Qu'Appelle Métis had so vigorously championed, but that was never its intent. The way the government implemented scrip through the Dominion Lands Act and in tandem with homestead policy only complicated Métis efforts. As a result, scrip simultaneously displaced and dispossessed the Métis, opening the land for orderly agricultural settlement of the North-West and pushing them to the road allowance.

Chapter 6

"We Got Our House Built by Seneca Roots": Life on the Road Allowance

In the summertime we used to go out and dig Seneca root. It was really something to go out there and dig that Seneca root and we would get out there and Dad would kill a deer and Mother would can it and Grandma was with us again, and most of the time we traveled in groups, hey. Like, my Uncle Sam and Auntie Sarah and their family and Uncle Joe and his wife, my Aunt Clara, they used to come and so we kind of traveled in groups. Same thing in Lebret, those guys in Lebret they traveled in groups, they went all over and dug Seneca root, they used to go all the way down south to a place they called Strawberry Lake and they used to go all the way down there and dig Seneca root, these people from Lebret. We used to go up into the reserve, north and we used to go south of the reserve and dig Seneca root there. We would take the tent and go and stay out there for a month or so.[1]

IN MANY PRAIRIE communities Métis had cultivated their own plots of land prior to the advance of Euro-Canadian settlement, and by the late nineteenth and early twentieth centuries some had achieved a degree of success as farmers, ranchers, and merchants.[2] Yet, amidst a growing settler society, most struggled to hold on to their land while also maintaining control over their economic livelihoods. Métis were increasingly displaced, removed from the plots of land they called home, pushed to the margins of Canada's growing economy, and physically displaced to the road allowances, the periphery within Canada's land tenure system. Métis struggled in these marginalized spaces to adapt to new economic realities and sought out any available labour opportunities: picking buffalo bones, selling or trading resources, such as cordwood, berries, fish, or Seneca root they had harvested from the environment they knew well, or providing a temporary and itinerant labour force in the developing settler economy. As Bob Desjarlais describes above, digging Seneca root was often a collective activity where families moved across the land together, much like they had when hunting buffalo only decades prior. Digging Seneca root this way allowed the Métis to maintain important social systems and cultural practices while also entering the cash economy. Seneca Snakeroot (*Polygala senega*) is a perennial plant commonly found in open woods and prairies, from southern Alberta to western New Brunswick. When chewed and swallowed it provides pain relief, soothing a sore throat, or when made into a poultice and applied to cuts can relieve pain and prevent infection.[3]

Some men found work with local merchants as labourers, freighters, gathering and delivering hay, and cutting fence poles and pickets.[4] Generally, these employers paid in goods and merchandise from their stores rather than in cash. Others found work as guides, interpreters, and carpenters, suppliers of wood, hay, oats, barley, and beef to the NWMP, or as labourers, cutting and transporting railway ties for the CPR. Working for the CPR was a short-term but significant source of income for many. By the mid-1870s, a market for buffalo bones had emerged in American cities such as Detroit, Chicago, and St. Louis, requiring vast quantities of bones for fertilizer-processing plants and in sugar refineries.[5] Growing demand combined with the 1885 completion of the CPR across western Canada ensured economical and efficient shipping of the bones to eastern centres. Buffalo bone picking created economic opportunity for the Métis, albeit in the short term. As a result, well into the twentieth century, many relied mostly on cutting cordwood, freighting, selling fish, collecting and selling Seneca roots, picking rocks and clearing farm fields to bring a modest income into the family.[6] This work provided a meagre and often sporadic income, as work was generally seasonal and not very profitable.

The Métis lived within a complex barter economy where, as compensation for their labour, they relied upon and received necessary food or supplies that they did not produce themselves. Employment opportunities were welcomed but brought only a very modest income into the family. Women and older children regularly laboured beside men in the fields, recognizing that some work required everyone's labour.[7] As men found work with local farmers, women worked as domestics: cooking and cleaning in the homes of their husband's employers, or in the barns, milking cows and tending livestock. Often young women took work as domestics to support the family and remained working in these roles even after they married.[8] Women also sometimes found work as domestics in nearby convents and schools.[9] In some instances, women sought to maximize their income by selling or trading Seneca root, garden produce, and the products of their own barnyard animals, such as butter and eggs, to their neighbours and local merchants. They also sold beaded, embroidered, and other handmade products, helping contribute to the family economy and ensuring families were fed.

Buffalo Bone Picking

The creation of a market and growing demand for buffalo bones brought economic opportunity to prairie Métis, but it was surely heartbreaking knowing that this would be the last time they ventured onto the plains in search of buffalo. This time however, they were not following the herds, but instead harvesting the bleached white bone carcasses left behind over previous decades.

When picking buffalo bones, Métis families worked together in the same extended family groupings they had in the hunting days. In these "bone-picking outfits," men, women, and children gathered as many bones as possible, loading them into their Red River carts and freighting them to the nearest merchant or to one of several collection depots that had sprung up along the expanding rail lines. Each cart, when packed carefully, held between 800 and 1,200 pounds of bones and earned approximately three dollars per load.[10] Not necessarily gendered, the division of labour in picking buffalo bones reflected familiar strategies where all members of the family contributed their labour, ensuring they met necessary labour demands.

The trade in buffalo bones provided a transitional, short-lived but essential economic opportunity for the Métis. Although prices fluctuated, buffalo bone pickers generally earned anywhere between five dollars and $8.50 dollars per tonne.[11] In 1882 and 1888, Métis trader and merchant Jean-Louis Legare at Willow Bunch, North-West Territories, paid collectors six dollars to $6.50 per tonne for the approximately 30,000 tonnes he purchased, whereas in 1889, bone pickers from the Qu'Appelle Valley received upwards of seven dollars per tonne.[12] In 1892, Saskatoon merchants increased their rate from $5.50 to seven dollars per tonne to six to eight dollars in order to attract business and remain competitive, but also to compensate bone pickers for the increasing distance required to gather bones further afield from the merchants and the rail depots.[13] A year later, they again increased their prices, from $6.50 to $8.50 per tonne.[14]

By 1890, as rail lines extended from Regina north towards Saskatoon, bone pickers quickly gathered the remnants of the herds in areas close to the rail lines. By August that year, bone pickers gathered more than $7,000 worth of bones throughout the Qu'Appelle region and transported them to the side of the rail line close to Lumsden, north of Regina.[15] The same year, bone pickers, including Métis from north central Saskatchewan and the South Saskatchewan River region, delivered as many as 50,000 buffalo skulls to Saskatoon together with as many of the other bones they could find.[16] In 1890 and 1891, the quantity of bones shipped out of Saskatoon was equivalent to over 200,000 buffalo. In 1894 and 1897, the total weight of buffalo bones shipped out of western Canada was over 22,000 tonnes.

Unmistakably, the trade in buffalo bones was lucrative, at least for a short duration. The volume of bones delivered to merchants, however, quickly outpaced the railroad's shipping capacity, forcing merchants and railways to stockpile their investments along the rail lines awaiting shipment east. Often, merchants and rail line workers stacked the buffalo bones in the shape and size of the railcars, as seen below.

Figure 38. Buffalo bones at Saskatoon, Saskatchewan, 1890s. Image courtesy of Saskatoon Public Library.

For their labour, local merchants paid buffalo bone pickers with goods or cash. Joe Blondeau recollected stories of his grandfather picking buffalo bones throughout the Qu'Appelle Valley region and hauling them to Regina to be traded for beef to feed his family.[17] Similarly, Saskatoon merchant W.H. Duncan regularly offered goods in trade for bones, which the Métis, familiar with this type of exchange, readily accepted.[18] Acting as a middleman between producer and purchaser, merchants handled the bones and transported them to the rail line or local depot for sale, financially benefiting from Métis labour. Buffalo bone picking provided an invaluable but short-lived economic opportunity for both the Métis and local merchants. By the end of the 1890s buffalo bone picking came to an end as the last remnants of the great buffalo herds, their bones, had once more disappeared from the western plains.

Itinerant Temporary and Seasonal Labour

As buffalo bone picking ended and settlement in the Qu'Appelle Valley increased, so too did the opportunity for Métis men and women to engage in agricultural labour. For many Métis families living on the road allowances, working as farm labourers was how they survived.[19] Men worked for farmers on a seasonal or short-term temporary basis, finding work by the job or by the day, week, month, or season. They picked rocks and cleared fields, planted and harvested crops, gathered hay, tended livestock, fenced and cut cordwood and fence pickets, often with women and children at their side, contributing along the way.

Early twentieth-century British farmer and homesteader Georgina Binnie-Clark recalled that local Métis men regularly hired themselves out by the job, often building fences for neighbours and farmers in the Qu'Appelle Valley region. She often took advantage of the labour force Métis men provided, on one occasion hiring for the job of building three miles of wire and picket fence. The entire job, including pickets provided by Tom Klyne, and labour cost Binnie-Clark $160.[20] Similarly, John Joe Larocque, a member of one of the very few more affluent Métis farm families in the Qu'Appelle region, remembered his father hiring several Métis men on a temporary or short-term basis when large amounts of labour was necessary.[21] They cut cordwood and at harvest time they stooked and threshed the grain.[22] Often, Larocque recalled, there was "a whole Métis outfit" of men working for his father.[23] Consequently, Métis men served as a temporary and ready labour force, particularly important at certain points in the season, such as planting and harvest, which required large amounts of labour.

Large amounts of labour were also required to prepare fields for spring planting. Fields needed to be picked clear of rocks, roots, and weeds. Caroline Henry recalled that her father often "worked out" for farmers, as did her mother, who was a very hard-working woman.[24] Families spent days together in the fields, picking rocks they loaded onto a wooden sled they hauled behind a team of horses called a stone boat. Margaret Harrison also describes times during the 1940s when her mother, aunts, and older cousins worked alongside her father and uncles picking rocks and weeds.[25] Once, in the field, she recalls the farmer lining everyone up, giving instructions, and handing out big sacks or buckets to hold the weeds they picked. They spent all day in the field picking weeds, emptying their bags or buckets when they were full.[26] As one of the older children, it was Margaret's role and the role of grandparents to remain close to the wagons or where they camped to look after the younger children and prepare meals while the adults worked the fields. The complementary and flexible nature of Métis family economic structures, where women and older children contributed labour, benefited farmers and encouraged entire families to engage in wage-labour activities.

While not only working alongside men in the fields, women and older girls also worked as domestics in settler homes, providing housekeeping, sewing, and cleaning services. In many instances they also helped with vegetable gardening, cleaning the barns, milking cows, tending to chickens and livestock, and helping with butchering. By the late 1940s, some women more formally and frequently gained wage employment of their own. In some instances, women found work cleaning cottages in the spring and fall or in the summer resorts that were developing around the Qu'Appelle Lakes.[27]

Despite women working with men in the fields, there was an increasingly pronounced gendered division of labour within this growing agricultural economy where men and boys were responsible for farm work and seasonal labouring jobs that could bring in goods or wages, and women and girls were responsible for housekeeping or domestic responsibilities such as preparing food, cleaning house, making soap, washing, baking, and sewing as well as for cultivating vegetable gardens, milking cows, and feeding chickens. Women's labour remained crucial as they maintained these and the customary responsibilities of caring for the children and Old People and harvesting, preparing, and preserving food and medicines.

Children's labour also continued to contribute significantly to the Métis family economy. Older children often began working in their early teen years, supporting the family reserves. Josephine Tarr told how she and her brother often gathered and sold small loads of wood they hauled from the bush, earning about two dollars per load. They gave the money to their mother to purchase essential food items for the family.[28] Likewise, Norma Welsh recalled that in the 1940s she and her siblings worked eight to ten hours a day picking potatoes at the Roman Catholic Church's farm near Katepwa, earning about a dollar a day which they used to help the family. This was a considerable amount of money, which could buy a full bag of groceries.[29] Both Bob Desjarlais and George Klyne worked for farmers when they were as young as twelve to fourteen years old.[30] The work was not easy, nor did it pay that well. Klyne herded sheep for twelve dollars per month while Desjarlais tended "about thirty-five head of cattle, about sixty pigs and a chicken house full of chickens" during the winter with additional responsibilities added in the spring when they began to work the land.[31] For this work he received room and board and a nominal wage.

Like young men, women also took on work at an early age.[32] In the 1930s, Agnes Poitras Pelletier, then only eleven, worked for a bachelor, cleaning house and washing clothes. At age fifteen, she started working for other settler families, providing the same types of services, earning twenty-five cents a day, or five dollars per month, plus room and board.[33] Caroline Henry and sisters Agnes Amyotte Fisher and Celina Amyotte Poitras also began working for farm families at a young age.[34] Henry recalled quitting school to work outside the home during the summer and winter months for fifteen dollars a month, performing housework, milking cows, cleaning, and sewing.[35] At thirteen, Poitras worked as a domestic for a family in Lebret earning seven dollars per month.[36] Like her mother and sister Agnes, Poitras washed and sewed for other farm families before she got married.[37] Learning these skills from their mothers and grandmothers, domestic work prepared young Métis women for life as mothers and homemakers. The work of young men and women was done to support the family, even if only for room and board.[38] Working outside their homes helped free up food, resources, and space, thus alleviating the pressure parents felt in supporting the family.

The itinerant, temporary, and seasonal nature of agricultural work sometimes required families to move within the Valley region, relocating to be closer to their employer's fields. This allowed women and children to provide their labour within a customary family-based economic structure and remain within familiar territory and close to relatives. Living in proximity to their employers, however, did not necessarily guarantee work but it would have made it easier to secure work as it arose. This sometimes meant living in tents, old buildings, or granaries close to farms during the growing season, or in some instances, if they were fortunate, moving into houses owned by an employer.

By the early twentieth century, Thomas Skinner and his family were well established farmers in the Qu'Appelle region. Like other settlers, the Skinner family relied on Métis labour on a seasonal basis, often employing the same men in consecutive years, hiring their wives as domestics, and allowing families to live in homes on their property. Bob Desjarlais's maternal grandfather Louis Racette worked for Thomas

Skinner as early as 1916 and lived in a house on their property.[39] By the 1930s, Ernie and Frederick Skinner, like their father, Thomas, also employed Métis labourers in both short-term and seasonal arrangements.[40] Desjarlais recalled that his dad, uncles, and many other men in the region worked for Ernie Skinner well into the 1950s.[41] Like his father, Ernie often allowed seasonal labourers, like Racette, André Klyne, and others, to live in old buildings and shacks on his property while they worked for him.[42] Likely many others camped in tents on Skinner's property during planting and harvest when farm activity required large amounts of labour. For some, like Racette and Klyne, what began as temporary or seasonal opportunities turned into long-term employment over consecutive generations and many seasons.

Employing many Métis men, the Skinner family also hired wives and older daughters of some employees, engaging them as domestics and for certain farm chores, in effect, employing the next generation of these families as they entered the workforce. In the case of the Skinner family, they regularly employed two and sometimes three generations of the Racette and Desjarlais families, demonstrating a pattern of employment based on close-knit, long-term, and intergenerational working relationships between families.

Working for local farmers on a seasonal basis provided the Métis with a more stable income than as daily or temporary workers who depended on random jobs that needed completion. However, it was still a very meagre income, compensated in room and board or paid in food or meat in exchange for labour. Ernie Skinner, for instance, regularly compensated his employees with food rations from his personal supply.[43] George Klyne recalled his family receiving food and supplies such as lard, sugar, flour, and porridge at the end of each month in exchange for work. Skinner kept a large supply of such necessities on hand to pay his employees, but also in case families ran short and required extra.[44] Although payment in food rations was the principal means of compensation, he occasionally paid his employees with small amounts of cash when requested.[45] Bob Desjarlais recalled that Ernie "had his own little ways" of making sure that his employees were cared for and that no one went hungry.[46] Each fall, he regularly bought pails of dried saskatoon berries from Métis women to distribute to hungry families in the winter. He often provided winter clothing to employees' children and gave the women and children small Christmas presents each year. He also let former employees such as Louis Racette, Henry Poitras, and Joe Cardinal live on his land long after they were too old to continue working for him.[47] In this way, Skinner acted with benevolence and kindness towards his former employees in exchange for years of their loyal service. When Ernie Skinner died, he bequeathed a quarter section of land (SE 8–Twp 19–R 11–W 2) in the Qu'Appelle Valley to the provincial government for the exclusive use of "retired Métis."[48] The lands adjacent were also owned by the Skinner family and were occupied by two or three Métis families that continued to work for the family into the 1960s.[49]

Whether physically working alongside one another, or in increasingly gendered ways, the complementary nature in which men, women, and children engaged in farm labour activity reinforced their Métis family and community roles, as practised for generations. The communal way in which they conducted economic activity ensured that all members of the family continued to fill complementary economic and social roles as had occurred when hunting buffalo years earlier and when engaging in wage labour for HBC posts in the late nineteenth century. The balanced, yet often gendered, nature of these roles also continued as families engaged in the settler economy in ways beyond farm labour.

Cordwood, Berries, and Seneca Root: Harvesting and Selling Products of the Environment

In addition to agricultural labour, Métis cut wood, caught fish, and harvested wild foods such as berries and Seneca root for trade or sale to local merchants, farm families they worked for, or others in the Valley region. Selling or trading these items brought much-needed goods, supplies, and even cash into the household. They traded these goods for meat, butter, and other items the family required but did not produce themselves.[50]

During the summer months, Métis families picked wild saskatoon berries, pin cherries, and chokecherries that lined the shores of the Qu'Appelle Lakes and filled the Valley coulees. While they picked these for their own consumption, they also picked for sale or trade. Families also spent the summer digging Seneca root that they dried and sold to local merchants and the HBC. For women, this harvesting activity enabled them to enter a cash economy and for many it became "a good way of making money."[51] Selling berries and making and selling hooked and braided rugs helped Mrs. Rene Amyotte support her family, and even to purchase a milk cow.[52] Selling Seneca root also helped Caroline Henry's mother support her family. Henry recalled accompanying her mother and siblings on short excursions from home, walking the coulees from morning until night looking for the plant, at the same time as gathering other plants such as berries or hazelnuts and medicines.[53] Her mother saved all that she earned from digging, drying, and selling the plant so that she was able to purchase the logs for their home. It was such an important economic contribution that Henry remarked, "we got our house built by Seneca roots."[54]

Indigenous peoples and settlers intensively gathered Seneca root throughout southern Saskatchewan in the late nineteenth century.[55] One of few ways that First Nations women could earn income, Seneca root was a valuable resource. The scale at which it was harvested was noted in 1894 when Crooked Lakes Indian Agent Allan MacDonald noted the root as being the chief article produced for sale on the southern Saskatchewan reserve, while Indian Agent J.B. Lash at Muskowpetung, north of the Qu'Appelle Valley, reported that gathering Seneca root provided those on reserve with a large amount of money. This should have been welcome news, particularly during a period of crop failure, but Lash worried that harvesting Seneca root kept First Nations people off reserve for a too extended period.[56]

Figure 39. Family picking stones at Davidson, Saskatchewan, early 1900s, S-B1860, Provincial Archives of Saskatchewan. The family in the photograph were not identified.

Figure 40. Women with buckets, Crooked Lake, Saskatchewan, 1940s. Image courtesy of the Gabriel Dumont Institute Archives. The women in the photograph were not identified.

Figure 41. Louis Racette and team of horses. Photograph courtesy of Margaret Harrison.

Selling Seneca root continued well into the twentieth century.[57] For Métis, excursions to pick berries or dig Seneca roots were generally family affairs enjoyed by all members, even children. Some dug for Seneca root in the immediate vicinity of their homes while others travelled farther into the Valley region to harvest. Desjarlais recalls his entire family, including his grandmother, parents, and siblings, loading up in the wagons and travelling within the Valley, setting up camp in different places where they could find Seneca root, but also where they were close to the farms where the men found work; women and children, he noted, dug while men worked the fields. After setting up camp, they spent the day moving through the valley hills and coulees searching for the plant. His father would join them in camp at night, and then return to the fields in the morning. When they finished digging in the immediate area or had to walk too far from camp to find the plant, they would hook up the horses and wagon, break camp, and move two or three miles down the Valley. Again, they would set up camp and the process continued.[58] While harvesting Seneca root, they would also have been on the lookout for other wild plants and medicines. Families harvested berries in the same manner, in movable camps close to farm fields but within reach of sought-after plants. Harvesting plants in this fashion allowed Métis families to engage in more than one economic practice at a time: men in the fields, women, and children in the natural environment.

The Métis used a special tool made from wood or the metal springs of an old wagon, with a small pick attached to the end to dig the root. The tool was inserted next to the plant and used to loosen the ground around its base, and to lift the plant with the root intact. Pickers were careful not to break the plant from its root before removing it from the ground, and to not to dig so much that they left a large hole in the ground. This way, Desjarlais noted, when "you pull your digger out, a lotta times you, you hardly leave any marks where you were. That's the way my dad taught us."[59]

Once they harvested the plants, they separated the root from the top of the plant, leaving the flowers behind so the plant could re-seed itself.[60] Then they cleaned and hung it to dry in preparation for sale. The Métis sometimes sold the root when it was still green but obtained a better price when sold dry. It took a considerable amount of time to dry, up to three or four months. They packaged the dry roots in large bags or burlap sacks and sold them by the pound to local merchants in exchange for cash, food, or goods. They also shipped the roots directly to merchants in large centres such as Winnipeg.[61] Joe Blondeau recalled that in the 1930s, his family picked Seneca root that his parents and grandparents traded to local merchants, receiving about twenty-five cents per pound.[62]

Women's Sewing and Handicraft Production

Women were engaged in the settler economy not only at work in the fields alongside men, as domestics in settler homes, and selling prized berries or roots. They also regularly made and sold decorative household objects and clothing they produced using their time-honoured skills in sewing, beading, embroidery, and other decorative arts taught by their mothers and grandmothers. Norbert Welsh recalled that in the late 1880s he commonly bought products, particularly moccasins, made by local Métis and First Nations women to sell in his store at File Hills.[63] This economic practice has a long history, dating to the early years of the fur trade, when Indigenous women produced clothing and goods, which they traded to the fur company posts in exchange for trade goods.[64]

From the early fur trade period continuing well into the twentieth century, Métis women provided clothing and material goods to fur traders, settlers, and newcomers. They made a concerted effort to adapt their work during the fur trade to emerging rural economies, producing and selling hand-crafted and often decorative items for new markets.[65] These skills in sewing and handiwork were essential to supporting Métis families and a critical component of their economy.

In the late nineteenth century, Melanie Blondeau supported herself and her family through her sewing skills. Born in 1866, Melanie was the daughter of Françoise Desjarlais and Simon Blondeau and sister, aunt, or cousin to many of the Blondeaus resident in the Valley. She was forty years old when her father died in 1906, leaving her the title to the homestead on which she, her mother, Françoise, and aunt Isabelle lived.[66] In 1913, Amelia Paget, a member of the Canadian Handicraft Guild, travelled to the Qu'Appelle Valley, seeking out the work of Métis women, particularly those of the Blondeau family. At the time, Paget and the guild were working with the Department of Indian Affairs to market traditional arts unique to Canada.[67] Paget had spent her childhood in the Qu'Appelle Valley and was familiar with the reputation of First Nations and Métis women in the region for their fine handiwork.[68] She remembered the Blondeau women for their "fancy work they did in quill, silk and beadwork, as well as for moccasin making."[69] Arriving at the Qu'Appelle Lakes, Paget found Melanie, Françoise, and elderly Isabelle living in a small cottage along the lakeshore across from the Qu'Appelle Industrial School. Melanie was their sole support, earning a living off the very important handiwork skills taught to her by the older women.[70] Impressed by Blondeau's skill, Paget left materials and instruction for her to produce several decorative items for the guild, and arranged for her to become an instructor in these handicrafts at the industrial school. Blondeau worked at the school from 1914 to at least 1931, earning on average $225 annually.[71] This income supported Blondeau, and her mother and aunt, and in addition to her ownership of the land on which they lived, such skilled work provided extra economic security for her family, particularly as they aged.

As the twentieth century progressed, there were fewer Métis women in the Qu'Appelle Valley like Blondeau able to produce decorative items; nevertheless, women's sewing and handicraft production continued. Access to supplies such as fine silk embroidery threads, beads, fine wool cloth, and hides was likely a challenge for women with meagre means. However, they continued to practise their handiwork, often shifting production from embroidered and beaded items to creating items such as hooked and braided rag rugs, made with readily available and less expensive materials such as old clothes and blankets.

Many Valley women, including Margaret Harrison's mother and aunts, used the sewing and other decorative arts skills passed on by their mothers and grandmothers to make and sell items of clothing and decorative household objects into the 1940s.[72] The economic support from women's sewing labour was a critical and stable component of the family economy, particularly during the road allowance period. Celina Amyotte Poitras recalled that such skills were instrumental in supporting their family, particularly during the 1930s when, she recalled, "there wasn't a speck of work for men"—it was women's skills and sewing labour that brought food and supplies into the home.[73] Poitras did a lot of sewing for farm families as it was one skill that she could rely on. She generally sewed in the evenings by the light of a coal oil lamp, after the children were asleep, and her daily household chores were complete. Sewing was generally done by hand, as few had access to sewing machines until after the Second World War.

Margaret's mother, Adeline Pelletier dit Racette, also worked and sewed for several farm families. Sometimes the work came through her brother Raoul, who worked for farmers on the north side of the Valley around Abernathy.[74] When stooking or harvest time came, Margaret's family and grandparents would join Raoul in the fields. Margaret remembers her mother and grandmother helping with butchering pigs and cattle, bringing home the leftover meat and offal to clean, cook, and make blood sausage. Margaret also recalled Raoul often putting in a good word with farmers and their wives about Adeline's work ethic and sewing skills, encouraging them to hire her. In return for her sewing work, Adeline often received food and supplies, as well as boxes of old clothes and fabric that she would disassemble to remake into clothing and blankets for the family. She would also save fabric for making hooked rugs.

Adeline and her sisters Florence, Agnes, and Louise were not only well known in the Valley for their sewing work, but also for their hooked rugs sold throughout the Valley.[75] Agnes lived in nearby Indian Head and worked mending uniforms for the RCMP, Louise lived south of the Qu'Appelle Lakes and worked at the Fort Qu'Appelle hospital as a seamstress and in the laundry, while Florence, like Adeline, sewed for neighbouring farm families. Florence's son, Bob Desjarlais, recalled his mother sitting at her sewing machine from the time she got up in the morning until well after dark, sewing for settler families but also making her own family's clothing and blankets. The goods these women's labour provided significantly helped to support their families and reduced dependence on hunting, fishing, or purchasing food and goods, which was important because working for farmers often took them away from their own food harvesting activities.

Women recycled almost every piece of clothing they could. They got old clothes from farmers they worked for and remade the materials into new pieces. They mended, darned, and patched still usable clothing, and when a piece could no longer be worn, they took it apart, sorted, saved, and cut them into strips for rug making. Hooked and braided rugs, made and sold by Métis women, were popular décor in Métis and settler homes in the Qu'Appelle Valley during the early twentieth century.[76] Scraps of old clothes would be dyed different colours in preparation for turning them into rugs. They often earned as much as three or four dollars for a single rug—generally enough to feed a family of four for about a week—or they traded the rugs for food items like butter, eggs, or meat that they did not produce for themselves.[77]

Sewing and rug-making skills were practised and passed on across the Pelletier, Cardinal, and Racette extended family. Hooked rugs displaying a floral pattern were common amongst rug makers in the Qu'Appelle Valley. Margaret's paternal grandmother, Vitaline Cardinal Pelletier, made hooked rugs as did Vitaline's sisters La Rose Cardinal Desjarlais and Octavie Cardinal Amyotte. Octavie's daughter-in-law Emma also provided for her family by selling hooked and braided rugs as well as by picking and selling berries. Through these activities, she was even able to save enough money to purchase a milk cow.[78]

Joseph Moran remembered his mother sold handmade rugs to bring some income into the family, often its sole support.[79] For many years she took the train from Lebret to Regina where she marketed her rugs in exchange for clothes or money. She conducted a prosperous trade, attracting the attention of the local police, perhaps because she was selling her goods without any type of required licence or formal business establishment but more likely simply because she was Indigenous. The attention she received forced her to be discreet when selling to her customers, conducting her business, and avoiding the authorities' watchful eyes.[80] Clear in this story is the drive of women like Mrs. Moran to support their families despite challenges they faced, even potential confrontation with the law. Mrs. Moran was simply acting out of necessity, filling an economic role not filled by her blind husband. As the sole or main breadwinner in their families, women like her exemplify the effort that Métis women would exert in devising strategies to do whatever necessary to support their families.

The extended family nature in which rugs were made also translated into how they were sold, as families recognized informal sales territories. Vitaline Cardinal's rugs were sold by Margaret's paternal grandfather, Josue Pelletier, who, she noted, was a fish peddler, selling fish, berries, and rugs throughout the Valley. He spoke little English, mostly Nêhiyawêwin and Michif, but he knew which farm families were likely to purchase his wares. He would peddle Vitaline's rugs from the Katepwa road allowance community to the south side of the Valley and then on to Indian Head, where he and Vitaline most often did their business. The family considered this his territory, while the north side of the Valley towards Abernathy was where Margaret's parents, Alfred and Adeline, and her uncle Michel and Aunt Cora did their business selling Adeline's rugs. Being on opposite sides of the Valley ensured that the family could cover a large territory without overlapping their sales. Similarly, Adeline's sister Florence sold her own rugs starting at the top of the hill on the north side and moving down into the Valley, being careful not to cover the same territory as Adeline. This strategy dispersed Métis hooked rugs across the Qu'Appelle Valley region "so their patterns, or their rugs never met," while also helping to reduce potential for competition between craftswomen and maintain family cohesion.[81]

From the late nineteenth and into the mid-twentieth century, Métis across the prairies increasingly integrated into the settler economy. Often living on the road allowance, their integration was not as landowners but as temporary and seasonal farm labourers, and peddlers of products harvested from the natural environment. Engaging in wage labour provided some economic stability and allowed Métis to continue to live within familiar territory that they intimately understood. Gathering buffalo bones, moving rocks, cutting wood, harvesting Seneca root and berries, and selling fish and the handmade products of women's labour helped families maintain their economic independence and their connection to the land even when it was increasingly occupied by outsiders. Most often, compensation for these economic activities was food or supplies the Métis did not produce themselves. As a result, the Métis lived within a complicated barter economy where they traded their labour for the goods, supplies, and many of the foods they relied upon.

Families did what they could to survive, and often continued to work within an integrated family economy, where all members of the family, including children, had valuable skills, abilities, and labour to contribute. Women's labour, however, made a decisive contribution to the family economy as they worked alongside men in sometimes gendered, yet flexible, complementary, and diverse ways. Often, labour demands required that all members of the family contribute regardless of gender distinctions. Women found opportunity to engage in a cash economy outside of the home, working as domestics or selling the products of their labour, all the while remaining the centres of domestic activity within the family. In many instances, women successfully marketed their traditional artistic and sewing skills, taught to them by their mothers and grandmothers, to bring additional income and necessary food and supplies into the home. Together, Métis families took advantage of the economic opportunities that presented themselves, and in doing so, adapted to the western prairie's growing settler agrarian economy in ways that were often familiar and not merely the complete adaptation to a foreign way of life.

Chapter 7

Going Hunting Rabbits: Women's Labour in Feeding the Family

An old trapper lived during a time when food was scarce, and people were poor. The old man needed to feed his family and was intent on going out trapping. Being poor, however, he had very little snare wire, and even less to bait the snares. Using his last piece of bannock as bait, the old trapper went out into the Valley and set the snare. Returning the next morning, he found the snare untouched, and the bannock gone. Frustrated but determined that the mischievous rabbit would not outsmart him, the old trapper came up with a new plan. Being resourceful, he decided to use pieces of the long thin laces of his high-top moccasins to bait the snare. The next morning, he returned to check his snare. Again, the snare was untouched, and the bait was gone. The rabbit had eaten the laces. Now, even more determined to outmanoeuvre the rabbit, the old trapper came up with a new plan. He would use the pepper from his wife's kitchen! Taking the pepper,

> he went out in search of a big flat rock on which to set his new trap. Finding one, he placed a small pile of pepper on the rock and then sat in wait. When the rabbit appeared he sniffed the pepper, and instantly started to sneeze. The rabbit sneezed so hard that he hit his head on the rock and killed himself. And so, the poor old trapper was finally able to feed his family.[1]

OVER THE YEARS, George Klyne shared multiple versions of this humorous story with me.[2] It is a story that his father, Andrew, shared with him as a child in the 1930s. The story recognizes the real-world value of inventiveness and creativity during difficult economic times. It speaks to how the Métis adapted their hunting practices, using whatever means available to ensure their success. It also acknowledges the continued complementarity of gender roles in food harvesting, for in George's story, it was the wife's property, the pepper from her kitchen, that ultimately made the old trapper successful.

In 1886, when local magistrate W.A. Clark surveyed the Métis' economic situation in the Qu'Appelle and File Hills (Ste. Delphine) Métis settlements, he painted a bleak picture.[3] His survey provides a window into a moment of time for Qu'Appelle Métis as they reorganized themselves spatially and economically following their receipt of scrip. Most families were poor and had very little food stored for the winter. This was quite common. Yet, despite their poverty, Clark considered few of these families destitute enough that they required government intervention. This was principally because subsistence hunting and fishing remained a viable means of support. For many, it was their only means of support. These practices remained vital to Métis diets well into the mid-twentieth century as families continued to harvest, grow, and preserve most of the foods they required, and to trade for additional staple items, using the goods they produced or their labour as currency.

Métis families lived according to a seasonal cycle, harvesting resources when available and preserving food for the winter months. Fish, deer, rabbit, prairie chicken, ducks, and geese, as well as a wide variety of wild plants, berries, and seasonal garden vegetables, were available. Families grew or collected most of what they ate. What they did purchase included items such as flour, sugar, tea, and salt and pepper.[4] They also regularly traded their labour for goods they did not produce themselves, including beef, pork, or chicken, milk, butter, eggs, cream, and other staples.[5] Acquisition of food, whether hunted, trapped, caught, grown, or picked, required a significant investment of labour and time; food preservation and preparation were equally as labour- and time-intensive.

Despite the wealth of environmental resources, the possibility of a lean year and scarcity was ever present. For some, the money they received from selling their scrip helped financially, at least for their immediate future. Many supplemented their income by freighting, selling wood, or taking day labour with the Roman Catholic Mission or neighbouring farmers when available. However, to ensure they were able to do this work, it was necessary to maintain at least one or two horses, which demanded additional financial, labour, and time commitments. For the Métis, keeping horses fed and in "good order" was important because their livelihood depended upon it. A team of two horses was necessary for the types of work available—farm labour, freighting, hauling wood, etc. Considering many families described in Clark's survey maintained at least one or two horses speaks to their importance. In addition to horses, Clark found that some also maintained other livestock, mainly a few cattle and pigs and likely a few chickens. Over half of the households had at least one cow, thirty-five had more than one, and twenty-seven had at least two pigs. Antoine Larocque was one of the community's largest livestock owners with four horses, four pigs, and a herd of fifteen cattle.

While keeping livestock would have helped feed Métis families, they also relied on what they could store for the winter. Most, however, had very little, if any, potatoes, flour, meat, or grain in storage and despite growing vegetable gardens, there is no indication that families had any other root vegetables stored. Of the 123 families surveyed, 114 had no potatoes, 119 had no meat, and 110 had no fish laid aside for the future. Of the nine households with a surplus of potatoes, it was only the families of Augustin Brabant and James Grant who had enough to last the winter or share amongst their extended family. Of the four households with meat stored, Moise Vallee and Michel Klyne had enough to feed their families for the winter.[6] While food stores were low for most households, the majority did have at least a small quantity of flour on hand and one resident, Hilaire Boucher, had a significant surplus. While he was fortunate to have ten sacks of flour on hand, he had no meat or potatoes.[7] Similarly, Vallee and Klyne, who had significant meat stores, had very little flour. Clearly there was a notable difference across households as to what families had available to them for the winter months. Excess of one type of food did not necessarily guarantee stores of other types of food. In most instances, families had one type of food stored and in no household did families have all three basic staples of meat, potatoes, and flour. Even in the five households Clark identified as more financially secure, or "well-fixed," stores of meat, potatoes, and flour were lacking.

Just as there were notable variations across families, there were also differences between the two settlements. Those in Qu'Appelle had less flour but more meat and fish, while no households in Ste. Delphine had fish stores, likely because they were located almost sixty kilometres north of the Qu'Appelle Lakes. This suggests that Ste. Delphine families may have relied less on fishing and more on hunting, trapping, and other subsistence activities. Clark also frames fishing, and to a lesser degree hunting, as a last resort, particularly for the elderly in both locations, if not relying on their children. While these elderly individuals did likely fish to help support themselves, they were central to their large extended families, which would have ensured they had more than just fish to eat.

Women in the Survey

While Clark describes the economic situation for elderly Métis as dire—forced to rely solely on hunting, fishing, or their adult children—so too is the economic situation of Métis women. Clark noted a total of fifteen households headed by women, twelve of whom were widows. In five instances the women lived alone, whereas others had children living with them. Most female-headed households had little food stored for the winter, few horses or cattle, and little prospect of supporting themselves; therefore, according to Clark, they had few options. A widow with two young boys, Mrs. William Beaulieau, he noted, was going to have to kill her only cow to support herself and her children, while Suzanne Bercier Pelletier, aged seventy-five, lived alone and was solely dependent upon family members.[8] Similarly, Madeleine Pelletier Bourassa, aged sixty, and Madeleine Klyne, seventy-nine, were both supporting their households by fishing or hunting small game and with their garden produce.[9] Indeed, women's economic situations seemed grim but they were not destitute. Clark misunderstood the ethic of sharing that existed amongst Métis families. They lived within an economy that privileged extended family and kinship relationships with all members of the family contributing their labour and sharing in the provisions.

Kinship responsibilities allowed women, despite their old age, to maintain their own households. It was as common for elderly men and women to live alone as it was for them to reside with younger generations. Often, Old People had unmarried adult children or sometimes grandchildren living with them. It was the role of younger generations to look after the elderly and help take care of tasks such as hauling water or chopping wood. In return, older generations cared for young children, acted as cultural teachers and mentors, shared food, and contributed their labour to the extended family. Older women were valued for their specialized knowledge around food production, medicines, midwifery, and funeral protocols, and were the custodians and transmitters of traditions and religious beliefs. They also often played a significant role in family governance, working to ensure the maintenance of harmonious relationships across the extended family. Consequently, older women remained respected and vital members of their family networks. Their position and food harvesting, preparation, and production abilities ensured that they maintained their independence and autonomy, keeping their own households and residing separate from but still close to relatives.

Clark's recording of Suzanne Bercier Pelletier as an old widow entirely dependent on son-in-law Roderick Ross overlooks the important matriarchal role she played in her family.[10] The widow of Charles Pelletier, she lived in the Qu'Appelle Valley surrounded by son Cuthbert and daughter Suzanne, wife of Roderick Ross, and their respective families.[11] Living close to her adult children and grandchildren, Pelletier would have taken an active role in helping care for her grandchildren, as well as contributing her labour to harvesting, gardening, and food preservation and preparation. For a time, her son Edouard and his five children lived with her, but by 1886 Pelletier lived alone, maintaining her own household after Edouard relocated to the Ste. Delphine or File Hills area.[12] Pelletier's sons Joseph, Alphonse, and Alexander had already taken up land and were living in the File Hills area by the time Edouard moved.[13]

Suzanne was not entirely dependent upon her son-in-law as Clark assumed. Rather, she was central to the Pelletier extended family. Likewise, through her deceased husband Charles, she was also part of a much larger extended family network across the Valley region, stretching north to File Hills that included, among others, the St. Denis, Ross, Desjarlais, and Lemire families. Pelletier's kinship relationships then extended into the large Fayant and Klyne families as her sister-in-law Josephte was married to Antoine Fayant and her niece was Madeleine Beauchemin Klyne.[14] In addition, two of Pelletier's children, Alphonse and Josephte, were married to the children of Jean Baptiste Desjarlais and Marie Martin. Another of Desjarlais and Martin's children, Thomas Desjarlais, was married to Madeline Klyne, daughter of Madeleine Beauchemin Klyne and granddaughter of Charlotte Pelletier. Each of these families would have respected the familial relationship and fictive kinship to Pelletier and recognized her as one of their aunties or grandmothers, following the cultural practice of naming older relatives as grandparents, aunts, and uncles regardless of whether they were, in fact, immediate relations. She would have been well taken care of in her old age.

Madeleine Pelletier Bourassa's situation was similar. She was the widow of Jean Baptiste Bourassa, who had died in 1882 after working many years for the HBC at Shoal Lake and Forts Pelly and Ellice.[15] Jean Baptiste had been under the employ of Pierre LaPierre in the late 1860s when Madeleine prepared a sumptuous feast for LaPierre and HBC clerk Isaac Cowie, described earlier. Together, Madeleine and Jean Baptiste had nine children, many of whom entered Treaty Four in 1874. Madeleine and Jean Baptiste along with adopted daughter Bella took treaty with the Nahkawinniwak—Nêhiyaw at Pasqua First Nation, while daughters LaRose and Madeleine took treaty with the Nêhiyaw at George Gordon First Nation, and son Baptiste took treaty with the Nahkawinniwak at Cote First Nation.[16] In 1886, four years after Jean Baptiste had died, Madeleine and her children discharged themselves from treaty to apply for scrip.[17] As Clark noted in 1886, not only was Bourassa widowed, but she had received her $160 scrip and was going to support herself by hunting rabbits.[18] Leaving treaty, Bourassa moved to the Qu'Appelle Lakes, living temporarily on Section 8–Twp 21–R 13–W 2, close to the Roman Catholic Mission at Lebret at the west end of Mission Lake, where there were already several Métis families living on the same township section.[19] Arguably, some of these families may have been trying to eke out a living close to the mission rather than in the family-based communities that lined the Qu'Appelle Lakes, as there were few evident kinship relationships between the families residing on this section.

For Madeleine, however, her children LaRose, Madeleine, and Patrice were living nearby and her son Pierre and two grandsons, David and Isadore Camille, lived with her. These grandsons went on to attend the nearby Lebret Industrial School in 1885, when their father Baptiste moved from the Qu'Appelle Valley to Fort Pelly with his second wife.[20] LaRose married Pierre Flammand the year they entered treaty and daughter Madeleine married Norbert Pelletier in 1881.[21] Both Bourassa's daughters were living in the region with their husbands and families, as were son Patrice and wife, Catherine Daniel, who lived at File Hills.[22] Sharing her household with her adult son Pierre and two grandchildren,

Bourassa would have maintained her traditional role in the household, contributing her domestic labour including looking after her grandchildren, while her son and grandchildren would have fulfilled their own gendered and generational roles in the household. Bourassa had a network of adult children and their families in the region, which would have allowed her to contribute to the large extended family economy. This spatial organization influenced and supported women's abilities to maintain their positions in the family economy and contributed to the ability of women like Suzanne Bercier Pelletier and Madeleine Pelletier Bourassa to support themselves well into old age. Living within these large networks provided mutual support, social inclusion, and opportunity for older women to exercise their traditional roles in the family, including fishing and hunting small game to support themselves and their families. This pattern remained consistent in Qu'Appelle Métis communities into the mid-twentieth century.

While Clark's survey provides important insight into the pantries and storerooms of Qu'Appelle and Ste. Delphine Métis families, it also raises questions about whether Clark was merely recording what he observed and concluded there were few food stores, or if those he visited were free to speak about their realities. Clark notes that at least one individual, Baptiste Desjarlais, refused to give any information, suggesting not all were open to sharing information with the government agent. Most likely Clark recorded a combination of what he saw and what was shared with him but did so misunderstanding or simply underestimating the centrality of resource sharing and daily and seasonal food gathering in Métis life.

Fishing for a Living

Métis men and women regularly fished as required to feed their families. Madeleine Klyne and her three daughters, Elise Kavanaugh, Marie Bellegarde, and Madeleine Desjarlais, maintained a robust fishing practice on Katepwa Lake well into the late nineteenth century.[23] While fishing may have been a primary means for the Klyne women to feed their families, the matriarch Madeleine, with the help of her youngest son, Napoleon, also farmed a small parcel of land. When Madeleine applied for homestead patent to her land in 1883, she had lived on the property since 1873 and had a home, stable, and storehouse built. She had also had eight acres under cultivation for the previous two years.[24] At almost eighty years of age, Madeleine not only included her land in the family economy but also her labour in working with her daughters to maintain their fishery. Her experience demonstrates that women, and in this instance, older women, contributed their skills, expertise, and labour to the family food supply.

Fishing remained an important food source for Qu'Appelle Métis families well into the twentieth century. Perch, whitefish, northern pike, and walleye were generally plentiful in the Qu'Appelle Lakes.[25] Families close to the lakes depended on fish during the winter, during times of need, and when other foods were unavailable. Fishing was a year-round activity, but fishing technology was seasonal in nature, with different tools, resources, and labour requirements at different times of the year. When the lake water was open, fishermen used boats, barbed hooks, spears, and nets. In winter, they used handheld augers to break the ice, nets to fish, and dog sleds to move their catch and nets to and from shore. A small sled pulled by one dog could easily haul a fisherman's equipment and catch, and so they remained a popular mode of transportation for fishing well into the 1940s.[26]

When the water was open, Métis used nets for fishing the lakes or hooks and spears to fish at the Katepwa Lake dam, in the Qu'Appelle River, or in the Valley's many creeks. Children learned to fish at a young age, starting in the river and creeks, rather than in the lakes. Spring fishing at the Katepwa dam was particularly rewarding and consistent because fish were spawning and plentiful. Fish were often so plentiful that fishermen easily caught them using rudimentary fishing equipment, such as a simple "stick with a piece of rope on it and a hook in the end," by using a pitchfork, or even just by dipping in a pail.[27]

Many preferred using nets because once set they could leave them unattended, and most importantly, nets yielded a larger catch than fishing by other means.[28] Generally, Métis used two types of net: gill and seine nets. Both types were vertically deployed nets with weights along the bottom and buoys at the top to hold the net at the water's surface. Gill nets were generally set in a straight line, fixing one end to an immobile object at shore and using a boat that they most often built themselves to extend the net into the water where it was attached to another immobile object such as an anchor, the boat itself, or in the case of a narrow water body, the opposite shore. Seine nets were similar and set in different ways. For instance, two people might wade through the water dragging the net between them forming a U-shape, or they might set the net by attaching one end to an immobile object and wading or boating through the water, dragging the net in a semi-circle formation.[29]

Larger yields guaranteed that the Métis would have fresh fish, preserve for the future, and share across the family. Most spent a considerable amount of time in the late summer and early fall preparing their catch; cleaning, smoking, drying, and sometimes canning. However, it was not only preparing and preserving that required large amounts of labour. Setting the nets and bringing in the catch also required significant labour and necessitated that they often, but not always, fished in groups. Margaret Harrison recounted that the men in her family generally worked together when fishing, each labouring to set the nets and bring in their catch "because they would need every hand."[30]

Hunting and Snaring

Like fishing, hunting, and snaring of wild game had long been central to the Métis diet. In the Qu'Appelle Valley, game was often abundant, and hunters did not have to travel very far from home to be successful. Delphine Desjarlais recalled that in the 1940s, her "Dad would go and hang snares at the top of the hill and in the coulees. Mostly for rabbits and prairie chickens," and that they "were never short of meat."[31] Deer, rabbits, ducks, prairie chickens, and even gophers fed hungry families.[32] When hunting and snaring, some followed protocols respecting the relationship between humans and animals, and most followed cultural traditions of food sharing among the larger extended family. When hunting ducks or large game like deer, men used guns and ammunition and often worked in small groups, much like when fishing. However, when hunting and snaring smaller game like rabbits or prairie chickens, women, and occasionally older children, commonly contributed their skills and labour.[33]

It was common practice for women, particularly older women, to hunt and snare wild game to feed themselves and their families. It was also the role of older women to pass on their knowledge and cultural protocols about hunting to younger generations. Young people in return helped the elderly and were not just recipients of care.[34] Assisting grandparents with daily tasks such as hauling water, chopping wood, or working in the gardens taught young people their familial responsibilities, about growing and harvesting cycles of wild foods and vegetable gardens, and knowledge related to plants and medicines. The relationship between young and Old People was crucial for passing on necessary economic skills and specialized knowledge.

Boys and girls prepared for adulthood by learning to set snares for rabbits and other small game. Delphine Desjarlais recalled the boys in her family hunting rabbits in the early 1940s.[35] In the Welsh family, Norma Welsh and her sisters Pauline Anderson and Billie Robison remembered both boys and girls learning to set snares, something they grew up doing.[36] As children aged, boys received ongoing instruction and education from their male relatives to hunt larger game. Bob Desjarlais recalled his first hunting experience with his father Bill and uncles, where his responsibility was to chase the deer out of the bush and into the open.[37] When a hunt was successful, it was also his job to build a fire while his dad and uncles skinned and quartered their catch. Bob then cooked the first few pieces of fresh meat and shared it amongst the hunting party. Knowing this was always his responsibility when learning to hunt, he even carried small shakers of salt and pepper in his pocket to flavour the meat.[38]

Desjarlais acknowledged that when hunting, his father and those his father hunted with often followed Indigenous protocols passed down by their parents and grandparents. They made small offerings of tobacco to the Creator before the hunt and were careful to respect mating season, pregnant animals, and their young.[39] Most were also cautious to take only what was necessary to feed their families.[40] When duck hunting, Métis hunters were prudent in taking only what was necessary despite the large number of ducks migrating through the region in the fall.[41] By following these protocols, Desjarlais's father and his hunting party were engaging in a small spiritual ceremony asking for the Creator's guidance and showing respect, gratitude, and humility. They were also respectfully acknowledging and honouring relationships beyond just their human kin to include animals, the landscape, and the Valley environment.

The Métis' economic position often limited their hunting success. People were poor and had little money to purchase ammunition or necessary hunting supplies but adapted hunting techniques and did what they could with available materials. Desjarlais recalled that when his grandmother had no shells for her gun, she would use snare wire or even hair from a horse's mane or tail to catch prairie chickens.[42] Unmistakably, the Métis could be resourceful in securing necessary materials to continue their subsistence food harvesting practices, like George Klyne's story about using pepper to catch a rabbit suggests.

Scarcity, in terms of purchasing power to acquire hunting equipment, necessary food supplies, and even in wild foods, was always present. There were seasons when wild foods failed to appear and when animals and fish populations were in flux, making them unavailable for harvest. Consequently, the Métis were used to living with little and compensated by sharing what they had. Sharing, especially food, helped to ensure the good of the collective during times of scarcity. Not sharing was seen as disrespectful and violated strongly held cultural values.[43] Even when people had very little, they made efforts to ensure there was enough, even a small amount of bannock and tea, to feed any potential visitors.

The way the Métis continued to share food in times of scarcity was a cultural practice carried over from the buffalo hunts decades prior, where families distributed meat throughout the extended family, including providing the choicest cuts to the elderly. This ensured that no one went hungry. This practice continued well into the twentieth century. Desjarlais recalled that his father and uncles often tried to kill more than one deer, so that meat could be shared across the family. Despite the large quantity of meat necessary to keep families fed, rarely was deer meat preserved and stored; fresh meat was given away, only what was needed was kept, sometimes only enough for two or three meals.[44]

Consuming meat fresh was not only out of concern for its spoilage or that meat preservation was labour-intensive and time-consuming but rather was in response to increasing government surveillance and regulation of Métis hunting and fishing activities. Unlike First Nations, Métis did not have protected hunting or fishing rights guaranteed in treaties. Instead, federal and provincial government conservation policy regulated such Métis activities, as it continues to do today. Into the early twentieth century, Métis hunters frequently came into conflict with government hunting regulations that prohibited hunting deer out of season or without a licence.[45] Due to their poverty, and the necessity of feeding their families, Métis hunters had few options but to hunt without a licence and to disregard seasonal restrictions on their traditional means of support. The illegality of hunting necessitated immediate consumption of killed game and prompt sharing around the family rather than preserving it and running the risk of discovery and prosecution by the game wardens.[46] Consequently, this may have been a factor why Clark reported in his 1886 survey that few families had meat stored for the winter.

Métis families were leery of keeping stores of wild meat on hand because provincial game wardens and police officers were known to enter people's homes looking for such contraband.[47] In Roy Poitras's home, they were always scared of the police, and his mother, Celina Parisien, was afraid of having any deer meat on hand. First Nations friends and relatives often visited their home, bringing wild meat as a gift. Celina hesitated to accept these gifts and had to balance this fear with the prospect of insulting her guests by refusing, which could impact kinship relationships.[48] It was legal for Treaty First Nations to possess wild meat, but the same laws did not apply to the Métis. Regardless, they were friends and relatives, and so gifts of food were regularly exchanged during visits. Although afraid, Roy's mother would never turn down the gift because according to Roy, "you never turned nothing down because you're insulting the people. That's giving. That's the way they were raised. You don't ever insult."[49]

Consequences for hunting big game, waterfowl, or smaller fur-bearing animals without a licence or for the illegal possession of wild meat could be harsh. On one occasion in the mid-1930s, while on patrol in the Lebret area, a field officer or "game guardian" with the provincial Department of Natural Resources, Joseph Zépherin (J.Z.) Larocque, came across William Fisher trapping muskrats without a licence. Deeming Fisher to be in violation of wildlife protection regulations, Larocque notified the local RCMP officer at Fort Qu'Appelle, who laid charges. Fisher appeared before a Justice of the Peace and pleaded guilty. He received a fine of ten dollars plus court costs of three dollars. Unable to pay his fine, he served fifteen days in the Regina jail.[50] While severe, these punishments were exacerbated by the seizure of guns, ammunition, and any catch that the game guardians might have confiscated. While this meant less for families to eat in the immediate future it also brought a great deal of shame for families when one of their members was caught and punished for illegally hunting.

Game guardians worked with local RCMP to apprehend and punish those who hunted or trapped illegally. However, guardians, including Larocque, were on occasion sympathetic to the Métis and would turn a blind eye when it came to hunting and trapping infractions.[51] J.Z was the son of Antoine Larocque and Rosalie Laplante and born and raised in the Valley. Farmers and traders, the Larocques were more affluent than their Métis kin, largely due to Antoine's business acumen, his successful farming efforts, and ability to hold on to their land during difficult years. J.Z. received an education in Winnipeg and, upon returning home to the Valley, he held several influential positions within the community. From 1914 to 1921 he served as an officer of the Saskatchewan Provincial Police, training that likely served him well when in 1924 he was appointed game guardian for the Qu'Appelle region. J.Z., like his father, Antoine, was a lifelong Liberal party supporter and a friend of Saskatchewan premier James G. Gardiner. This undoubtedly influenced J.Z.'s career appointments, providing him with steady employment throughout his career.

Counter to the above account, as game guardian, Larocque was often compassionate towards his fellow Métis and regularly visited their homes while he was on patrol. If they had little to eat but wild meat, he rarely confiscated their food. He sometimes ignored illegal hunting and on occasion even encouraged it.[52] He urged some Métis, such as Bob Desjarlais's father, Bill, to hunt particularly when the Old People in the community had little to eat.[53] Larocque was well aware that Desjarlais did not possess a hunting licence, yet encouraged him to hunt because as Métis, Larocque understood the importance of making sure that family and community had enough to eat and that the Old People were taken care of. Likely, he also understood that hunting restrictions, seasonal limits, and not being able to afford the required licences were not going to keep the Métis from hunting. Out of necessity and compassion, Larocque allowed the Métis to circumvent the law, and in exchange, Bob acknowledged that his father never took more than they needed.

In practice, Larocque often acted with benevolence towards his fellow Métis, but as in the case of William Fisher, he was also a provincial government employee tasked with enforcing game regulations. Larocque's records reflect these efforts and confirm oral history recollections. In July 1937, Larocque reported to his superiors that he had received a complaint that two Métis, Maurice and Fred Parisien, were trapping without a licence. Upon investigation, Larocque found they had been trapping without the required licence but were doing so out

Figure 42. J.Z. Larocque, n.d. Image courtesy of the Gabriel Dumont Institute Archives.

of necessity as both were on municipal relief with large families to feed. Recognizing their dire economic situation, Larocque decided not to prosecute.[54] Just as Métis families made decisions about whether to comply with game laws, Larocque made decisions about the law's application, balancing the need for enforcement with the maintenance of kinship networks and relationships. For Larocque, people's hunger often trumped the need to enforce game laws. Unfortunately for the Métis, Larocque was but one such game guardian. Others frequently patrolled the area, as did the police, eager to apprehend those breaking game laws or in possession of illegally obtained meat.[55]

Game law enforcement not only affected food supply but acted as a form of cultural repression as fear of government intervention stymied Métis' cultural etiquette of food reciprocity. Celina Parisien's fear of being caught with wild meat was real and shared by others across the community. In many Métis communities, it was generally the women who instructed hunters on the types of food needed and who determined the distribution of meat across the extended family.[56] The tradition of sharing fresh meat avoided risk of spoilage and ensured quick consumption, which was increasingly important with intensified government regulation and surveillance. While sharing food fulfilled kinship responsibilities and allowed individual families to quickly rid themselves of evidence they were hunting out of season or without licences, the gifting or sharing of wild meat put families at risk.[57] To minimize risk, women worked quickly and efficiently to use the meat and bones, removing the evidence from plain sight and then burning the remains.[58]

Gathering

Métis families relied upon wild plants like berries, rose hips, hazelnuts, and wild parsnips as well as duck, geese, and mud hen eggs collected in Valley marshes to complement their diet of fish and game. They also gathered plants for medicinal purposes and some, such as Seneca root, specifically for sale. Gathering and harvesting wild plants was generally a women's activity, with the help of children and Old People. However, men also contributed when necessary, working with their families as an economic unit particularly when picking berries or digging Seneca root. These activities required additional concentrated labour as the environment provided a wealth of berries, ripe during a short period of time. When in season, all family members worked diligently to harvest as many berries and wild foods as they could to eat fresh, preserve, and store. Similarly, digging Seneca root required additional labour to harvest a large enough quantity for profitable sale.

Plant harvesting was ongoing according to the seasonal cycle. In the spring, some women tapped maple trees for sap to make syrup.[59] In 1946, J.Z. Larocque described the practice in the *Regina Leader Post,* recalling that every spring, Mrs. Françoise Blondeau Robillard would "punch a little hole in the trunk of the tree and eventually go home with a pail of sap which she will boil down into maple sugar."[60] Taught by her mother, Françoise Desjarlais Blondeau, Robillard had been making this syrup since she was young and was now passing these skills on to her grandchildren. Robillard's niece and Blondeau's granddaughter, Lucy Desjarlais Whiteman, recounted that she and her sister Bertha helped their grandmother tap up to 200 maple trees one early spring.[61] The sheer number of maple trees tapped made additional labour necessary. Children's labour was significant in all types of food harvesting activities, including making maple syrup and picking berries.

During the summer months, berries lined the lakes, river, and the coulees and families often went out in large family groupings, sometimes for days at a time, picking berries throughout within the Valley region.[62] Lawrence Welsh described the familial nature of these berry-picking excursions and their yearly movement through the Valley region picking berries and camping at spots along Mission Lake, Katepwa Lake, and at Pasqua and Standing Buffalo reserves.[63] Similar collective family activities were recalled by Bob Desjarlais and many others who also described berry picking and digging Seneca root on a continuum from the old buffalo hunts carried out along extended family lines.[64]

Berry picking was cyclical as different species ripened at different times: first, saskatoon berries, followed by gooseberries, strawberries, and raspberries, and finally chokecherries that ripened by mid-August. Owing to their abundance, berries were easy to pick. All that was required was to "pull the branch down and tie it, then pluck the berries. We tied pails onto our body with a rope or a belt."[65] Children were also involved in picking, crushing, and drying berries for winter storage.

While families were picking berries, they might also have been harvesting any number of plants and medicines that grew throughout the region. Berry picking may have spurred the movement through the Valley, but those with specialized plant knowledge were always looking out for certain plants and medicines that grew only in specific places. It was generally the older women who held this knowledge, but some men also possessed it. Harvesting medicinal plants was not only specific to these berry-picking or Seneca digging excursions. Rather, Métis picked medicines on an ongoing basis, according to cultural and specialized knowledge of the plant's use. Old People who knew medicines had a very intimate and expert knowledge of their environment, knowing when, where, and how to harvest specific plants.

Bob Desjarlais told how his Koohkoom Maross often went out alone "walking all over the Valley coulees" to gather medicines.[66] While Koohkoom Maross tended to gather medicines independently, such activity was not always solitary. Delphine Fayant Desjarlais recalled she and her siblings accompanying their grandmother when she picked medicines.[67] Her grandmother used these excursions to share stories, teach about plants, and pass on important life lessons. Regardless of whether medicines were gathered alone or with family, those who knew medicines felt a responsibility to share their knowledge and skills, and in return, food and other resources were shared in exchange for such knowledge.[68]

Just as it was the responsibility of those with medicinal knowledge to share their services, it was also custom for Old People to use collective harvesting activities as opportunities to share their knowledge. These activities were places where teaching and mentoring opportunities enabled children to learn important practical knowledge, cultural values, and protocols around picking medicines, in much the same way hunting would be learned. Joe Welsh recalled the importance of berry patches as sites where children learned valuable lessons, heard old stories, and learned about traditional protocols. A lesson he learned in the berry patch was about patience—patience in steadily picking berries, and not eating what you picked.[69] As the bags filled up with berries, the Old People shared stories and lessons on Métis history, culture, value systems, and ethics, including the relationship between humans and the natural and spiritual worlds.

Many recount how the Old People made offerings before picking berries and harvesting plants and medicines.[70] Welsh noted that his Aunt Margaret always made an offering of small candies or sweets when picking berries that she would leave on the ground near a wild crocus. This offering, he noted, was for the "Little People" or the Memeguayiwahk (Ma-ma-kwa-se-sak), supernatural beings in Nêhiyaw and Michif folklore who take form as very tiny humans. Sightings of Little People are reported north of the Qu'Appelle Valley at nearby George Gordon reserve.[71] Nêhiyawak and Nahkawinniwak author and storyteller Eleanor Brass from Peepeeksis reserve in the File Hills observed that Little People were understood to live underground in sand hills, caves, or under rocks along bodies of water.[72] They were considered stone workers able to make arrowheads, flint knives, and stone heads for hammers, which they traded with Nêhiyawak for items such as buffalo meat, hides, and porcupine quills. Although small, they had mysterious powers and, while harmless, were known to play tricks on people. Consequently, they were often blamed when anything peculiar happened.

Little People were frequently blamed when objects went missing. As a child, Joe Welsh's sister Norma recalled how the Little People played innocent pranks such as untying your shoelaces when walking in tall grass.[73] To keep the Little People from mischief, Métis made offerings of sugar, candies, or tobacco in special places, such as in berry patches, which the Little People were known to frequent.[74] Like their Aunt Margaret, Joe and Norma's sister Billie Robison would offer the first few berries she picked, dropping them on the ground so that Little People could reach them. The Little People liked and deserved gifts of shiny objects, sweets, or berries, as one of the many things people believed they could do, Welsh noted, was to "keep away any ticks when you are picking berries."[75]

Berry picking was also a time and place where older girls learned important lessons about womanhood, and their roles in the family and community. These spaces were deeply significant as teaching spaces, with Welsh describing them as the place "where our culture is, in the berry patch."[76] Such spaces were multi-layered in meaning and in use, sites not only for harvesting foods but for teaching and mentoring.

Concepts of specific individual or family territory did not define these places. Rather, multiple families used and assigned their own names and meanings to them. Often, they were named for stories or events that happened there, or for the individuals who considered specific places their favourite berry-picking or gathering spots. In some families there was a degree of recognition and respect for places, such as berry patches, as the private places of certain individuals. Joe and Norma Welsh remember certain berry patches as being the private places of an auntie or old lady, named for a woman's "favourite spot" though not considered their exclusive territory. Indeed, their Aunt Margaret tried to keep her berry patch a secret, never telling anyone exactly where she picked.[77]

Growing

Families predominantly grew vegetables that kept well and stored for a long period of time, including potatoes and other root vegetables such as onions, carrots, beets, and turnips. They also grew vegetables such as lettuce, cabbage, peas, beans, corn, and squash.

Living on the road allowances or on land that the Métis did not own did not keep them from using all available space. Here they cleared and worked any available patches of land for their gardens. It was not uncommon for families to have more than one garden with some as large as one to two acres.[78] Desjarlais recalled that in the 1940s, his grandmother Koohkoom Maross had a large and bountiful garden of at least two acres. She grew all variety of vegetables, even watermelon and squash, and regularly planted at least an acre of potatoes.[79] He noted that this quantity of potatoes was common, and necessary because families were big. That his grandmother grew such a large garden, and quantity of potatoes, suggests she likely shared produce with her extended family.

Métis attempts at gardening continued to be complicated by the short growing season, weather, and their poverty. Gardens often produced poor harvests, forcing families to go without.[80] Growing conditions were vulnerable to the weather, despite being in proximity to a reliable water sources. During the 1930s, drought impacted gardening activity and forced families to rely on what they could harvest from the natural environment or seek out rations from the municipal government.[81] In times like these it was even more important that families preserve and stockpile food for the future. For most road allowance Métis in the Qu'Appelle, the municipal authority governing decisions about Métis relief was the Rural Municipality of North Qu'Appelle No. 187.[82]

Métis poverty was intensified by their initial relocation to the road allowance and undermined their ability to acquire seed, tools, or gardening implements. Consequently, gardeners bought only a few seeds, and were careful to collect their own seeds for the following year.[83] For the most part, families had few gardening tools or implements.[84] In general, men worked the land using a team of horses when available and the entire family shared in the planting.[85] Women tended the gardens and children pulled weeds and hauled water. Working as a family unit, those with horses, tools, and farm implements also aided their extended family in getting their gardens prepared for seeding. Despite not owning the land on which they lived, Métis gardening on the road allowance was a demonstration of continuity to past land use practices and connections to the Valley landscape.

Preserving for the Future

Just as food harvesting was cyclical, so too was food preparation and preservation. Because families were large, sizable stores of food were necessary to feed family members throughout the year. Métis women consistently harvested, prepared, and preserved food, spending a great deal of their time this way. Hunted, caught, gathered, or grown, if it wasn't eaten fresh, food needed preservation, salting, smoking, drying, or canning, to span the winter months. Margaret Harrison recalled that her mother, Adeline Pelletier dit Racette, was always preparing for winter.[86]

Women preserved whatever food they could, drying and canning all kinds of berries, fruit, and vegetables for later use. Saskatoon berries and most others, except for chokecherries, required little preparation before drying. Crushing chokecherries was often an activity where women and children worked together. Norma Welsh described how her grandmother and others in the family would come together, each bringing their favourite stones used for crushing the berries. This was also a social occasion, where women would gather, drink tea, and visit while working.[87] Working together broke the monotony of repetitive tasks, offered an opportunity for women to socialize, and helped to maintain and reinforce kinship relationships.

If glass jars called "sealers" were available, women canned a large quantity of berries, sometimes stewed with sugar. Margaret Harrison recalled that her mother canned up to 100 jars of saskatoon berries each year.[88] Each sealer usually held about two quarts (approximately 1.8 litres). If smaller jars or tins were available, women also processed berries into jam, jelly, or syrup. Smaller, less abundant berries like strawberries or pin cherries were often considered more precious than the plentiful saskatoon berries or chokecherries and so families saved the jam or jelly made from them for special occasions such as Christmas or New Year's.[89]

While most families consumed meat when it was fresh to avoid punishment from government wildlife and fisheries agents, they sometimes also smoked, dried, and canned meat, including small game such as rabbits. As before, meat was cut into long thin strips and hung outside on stages to dry in the sun or smoked over a fire. This practice, carried into the twentieth century, was similar to how buffalo meat was prepared a century earlier. They ate the meat once it dried or pounded it into flakes and fried it with lard and berries when making pemmican. Women also canned meat if glass jars or used tin cans were available. Bob Desjarlais remembered his mother saving large tin cans for storing meat and that feeding their large family for the winter could require up to 300 large jars of meat.[90] Deer meat was not included in such preparation practices, for fear of the game wardens or police catching them with illegally hunted meat. Most likely the meat Métis women canned was beef, pork, or poultry they may have received from settler farmers in exchange for their labour.

Women prepared fish fresh and preserved it by smoking, drying, and canning. For drying and smoking, fish were cut open and hung flat to dry on ropes or wire or on stages built outside or in a small outbuilding. Fish either dried in the sun or were dried and smoked over a low fire. Delphine Desjarlais noted that they often dried their fish outside on ropes and wire, strung up like a clothesline.[91] Margaret Harrison recalled that her grandfather had an outbuilding, which he called a hanger, where her grandparents dried and smoked fish.[92] The building had rows of poles and wire strung up high across the shed to hang the fish. It also served as a tool shed and a place to store other dried foods. Once dry, fish was stored in canvas or burlap bags. Women also preserved fish by canning it in sealed jars in a brine made of salt and vinegar. Many remember their mothers canning fish eggs and preserving whitefish and suckers with vinegar and ketchup to alter the taste and turn the fish pink, resembling salmon.[93]

Women used salt to preserve fish and meat such as pork, beef, and chicken that families may have received from their farmer employers. They also used sugar to preserve fruit, and vinegar and salt to make a brine for pickling vegetables and preserving fish. They used wax to seal jars of fish eggs, jam, jelly, or syrup and to cover root vegetables such as turnips, which helped prolong their shelf life. They also used lard to seal food in jars or tins.[94] Most of these items, including salt, sugar, vinegar, and wax, were purchased from local merchants with cash or from their employers, in exchange for their labour.

Storing fresh food for any length of time meant it needed to remain cold. Many families used underground root cellars to store garden produce, meat, and dried or canned goods. They also may have used a well to keep butter, cream, and milk cold. Joseph Blondeau recalled a cellar dug into the ground under the house used to store vegetables.[95] Dark, damp, and below ground, root cellars stayed cold using ice cut from the Qu'Appelle Lakes.[96] Root cellars lined with ice and covered and packed in sawdust were cold enough to store meat for quite a few months.[97] However, not all families were fortunate enough to have a root cellar or a well for cold storage. Having no cold storage available significantly limited the quantity of food stored and could put families in a precarious position.

The amount of meat and fish families were able to store fluctuated over time. While Bob and Margaret both recall their families having meat and fish stores available in the 1940s, this was clearly not always the case, as Clark's 1886 survey demonstrates. Métis families in the Qu'Appelle endured periods of want and sometimes even excess, allowing them to preserve for the future. Despite such fluctuation, the ways these families gathered, preserved, and prepared these foods remained consistent.

Feeding the Family

For Métis families, everyday meals were simple and basic. This simplicity was not because Métis families did not enjoy cooking or could not cook more extravagant meals but due to their limited means. Despite sometimes having very little, people were generous with what they did have. Most Métis women also had little space in which to work. Houses were small and cramped because of large families, and designed with collective living, working, and sleeping spaces in mind, rather than with separate spaces or rooms.[98] This left little room for a kitchen, or for preparing meals. As a result, kitchen space was small and not well equipped. Most had a simple wood stove, woodbox, water pail, handmade table and chairs or benches, and a humble cupboard for limited food storage and cooking and eating utensils. In the heat of the summer, much of the food preparation and cooking took place outside, using a wood stove moved outside specifically for that purpose, over an open fire or in a summer kitchen.[99]

Soups and stews were common because they were economical and could be made with simple and often limited ingredients. They also constituted a hearty meal, generally made from available meat and vegetables in a bone broth, with a handful or two of dried berries added for flavour. The addition of a few extra vegetables or pieces of meat could always feed a few more mouths. Métis cooks kept soups and stews on the stove so that they would be readily available when people were hungry or when visitors arrived. In many Métis homes, "the soup was always on," reinforcing the cultural convention of hospitality and sharing.[100]

Rubabou was a popular stew made from rabbit, prairie chicken, or dried meat, boiled in a thick broth with onions, carrots, potatoes, and other vegetables.[101] Soup made with duck, fish, or dried meat was popular, as were boulettes. This meal of boulettes served with fried bannock or beignes (loosely translates as "the bullets and the bang") was similar to the meal described by Norbert Welsh in the late 1880s, demonstrating its popularity across time and generations.[102] It remains a favourite dish served in Métis homes on holidays and special occasions today. Contemporary Métis make beignes with yeast in a bread dough that is made like a deep-fried doughnut, an English fritter or the French pastry beignets, which is where the Métis derived the Michif name. When making beignes, the dough is rolled out until it is about a half inch thick and then cut into squares, making one or two cuts down the centre of each square so that it cooks evenly. Sometimes the dough is twisted before immersing it in hot oil. French beignets are generally covered in powdered sugar while the Métis version is generally not. In his memoirs, Welsh referred to these pastries as croxegnols or *croquignoles.*

Métis families ate meat that had been prepared by boiling, roasting, or frying. Norma Welsh and her sisters Pauline Anderson and Billie Robison recalled a dish their mother made called *tarreaux*. Made with dried meat, fat and berries, tarreaux was a variation of pemmican.[103] Their mother would mix dried meat with lard and either fry it on the stove or cook it in the oven until crispy before adding dried berries to form a paste.[104] Agnes Pelletier remembered her mother making a similar dish and sometimes adding raisins.[105] Families also ate rabbit, seasoned with salt and pepper and boiled, fried, or as a tourtière, or minced pie. They also roasted duck and prairie chicken, often serving it with bread stuffing. Some recall that during hard times they even ate gophers.[106] These they roasted whole, outside on a stick over an open fire or in the oven, after first singeing off the hair.

Fish was prepared in a multitude of ways, often dependent upon its type. Métis cooks prepared larger whitefish fried, baked, or in soup, and smaller fish, like perch, they baked whole.[107] When frying fish, they left the skin and fins intact so that the fins would be crisp. Prepared this way, fish was a favourite of many.[108] Fish was also baked with the skin left on. This worked well for small fish like perch because there was little waste, and it saved the time and effort of cleaning and filleting. Billie Robison remembered whole perch being baked this way, and when cooked they peeled the skin and ate the meat and eggs if present.[109] Many considered fish eggs a delicacy. Margaret Harrison recalled gathering and eating eggs from the burbot fish, which they referred to as dogfish. She described dogfish as brown, ugly-looking bottom dwellers with long tails like an eel. She and her brother regularly fished for them to harvest the intact egg sac, which was a special treat. The eggs were prepared fresh by frying in lard or canned for later consumption.[110]

Although most of the foods Métis families ate were prepared with ingredients harvested from the natural environment, they also purchased and traded for staple items such as flour, baking powder and soda, sugar, tea, salt and pepper, and sometimes canned milk or canned meat. Flour, used in making bannock, was particularly important. A staple in Métis households, bannock was served at nearly every meal. If times were tough and food scarce, bannock was often the only thing Métis families had to eat. Some women also made a lot of bread if the ingredients and supplies were available. Norma Welsh's mother made at least fifteen loaves a week to feed their growing family.[111] However, many preferred bannock because it was easier to make than bread, took less time, and involved fewer ingredients. Tea was also particularly important to the Métis. A cup of hot tea was served with every meal, and it was, like a pot of soup or piece of bannock, always ready and offered to company. Staple items were available from merchants in the immediate vicinity at Lebret, Indian Head, and Balcarres, which the Métis purchased on credit and paid with cash received from their employers.[112] Into the 1920s and 1930s, as Métis poverty intensified during the Depression, the Municipality of North Qu'Appelle No. 187 provided limited staple goods as relief rations for all residents, including the Métis.[113] However, the bulk of staple items consumed by Métis families came from the farmers or settlers who employed them.[114]

As farm labourers in the 1940s, Métis also sporadically had access to beef and pork, as well as eggs, milk, and cream that they received in exchange for work. Some families also managed to keep a few cattle, pigs, or chicken, which provided some of what they consumed. Joe Parisien recalled that they often traded cordwood to farmers for eggs, chicken, or other meat.[115] When farmers were ready to butcher, farm hands helped, as did their wives, again demonstrating the way in which Métis families worked as an economic unit. Margaret Harrison recalled her mother and grandmother helped settler farm wives with butchering cattle and pigs, often in exchange for some of the meat.[116] With this meat, they adapted their menu, processing it differently from the wild game they regularly ate, to make dishes like blood sausage and head cheese.[117] They also canned beef and pork and made their own butter from any milk or cream they received.[118] One of the most important items families received was pork fat, which they cooked down and rendered into lard. While they used lard made from other meat fats, lard made from pork fat was preferred, especially if it was for baking, cooking, and spreading on bannock.[119] Margaret Harrison recalled a treat called *gratons* made from finely chopped pork or pork rinds, cooked with fat and roasted in the oven until crispy.[120] Her family also referred to them as *cracklins* and sometimes served them sprinkled with sugar.[121]

Other than the berries they harvested, fruits were also available from local merchants or seasonally from itinerant produce merchants. Merchants carried fruit such as dried apples, figs, and raisins year-round while fresh fruit was available seasonally. Norma Welsh and Pauline Anderson remember getting bananas and fresh apples as a special treat when in season.[122] Even in season, fresh fruit was cost prohibitive. As a result, if families were to purchase fruit, it was often overripe at a reduced price.[123] Margaret Harrison recalled her family collecting discarded soda bottles to trade with an itinerant merchant who peddled his produce throughout the Valley. He would pull his truck over on the side of the road, and people would come from all over the Valley to purchase his fruit.[124] Overwhelmingly, Métis families rarely engaged in a cash economy, instead bartering or trading with foods they harvested, items they made such as hooked rugs, or goods such as discarded bottles that they collected and used as currency.

Holiday Celebrations and Sharing of Food

Sharing food brought people together and was integral to all Métis gatherings and celebrations. As had always been the case, Métis families looked after one another, and shared food and resources with family members who had less. Sharing of food was a critical means of acknowledging and maintaining kinship relationships and responsibilities. The social aspect of sharing your home and food, and making guests feel welcome, was paramount. Even when visiting others in their homes, Margaret Harrison recalled that families "helped one another in that sense, you always took something along be it extra meat, canned meat, canned chickens."[125]

For Métis families visiting, dancing, music, and feasting were inseparable. Dances were frequently held in people's homes, with the furniture pushed aside or moved out to make room. Local fiddle players played long into the night as people danced the Red River Jig, the reel of four, the reel of eight, the duck dance, the rabbit dance, and other traditional Métis dances. Roy Poitras recalled that dances and card playing occurred frequently in their home, except during Lent. When company came, his mother always cooked for visitors. Even if it was just a simple soup, tea, and bannock, it was the hospitable act of sharing food that was important. "We were poor, but I thought we were rich, because when company came, we always had lots of food."[126]

Holiday celebrations centred on New Year's rather than Christmas. Carried over from the buffalo hunt winter camps of the mid- to late nineteenth century, the tradition of celebrating New Year's continued well into the mid-twentieth century. In Qu'Appelle communities, visiting started in early morning New Year's Day, beginning first at the home of the family's oldest members. Upon arrival, each guest received a blessing from the family patriarch before sharing a meal and then moving on to the next house. This celebrating continued until Epiphany or All Kings Day on 6 January.[127] At each house, tables were loaded with food prepared for the occasion, including dishes of boulettes and beignes, grens, pouchine dans le sac, tourtière, pies, cakes, and cookies. Pouchine dans le sac is a pudding made with finely chopped suet, flour, milk, brown sugar, raisins, and currants, steamed in a cotton bag and served with a sweet rum sauce.[128] George Klyne and Bob Desjarlais recalled that all the women made fruit cakes for New Year's celebrations.[129] Cakes would be prepared up to a month beforehand and stored wrapped in a tight cloth until the New Year's celebrations began. Often, there was a friendly competition over who made the best cakes.[130] Even when families had very little, they saved what they could to make holiday meals special.

Among the Métis, New Year's was a celebration of feasting, visiting, and dancing. Agnes Pelletier described her own memories of these celebrations from the late 1940s or early 1950s. These were social times with always a lot of food to share, despite being poor. In some instances, these celebrations also included alcohol or *li piquette,* in Michif. She recalled the food and festivities warmly:

> We sure had a lot of fun when New Year's came around. We used to eat, have a little bit to drink. We had a lot of fun on New Year's, and we went around visiting, and this was how we celebrated for seven days from January 1st to 7th. And I don't know where they got all the groceries or all the food, but they seemed to manage . . . they used to make meatballs and they'd make pies. You'd have raisin pie, prune pie. They used to also cook the apricots first and then they'd make them in the form of a pie. We used to also eat crushed chokecherries. They used to also make pemmican . . . and some people would put saskatoons

> or they would put some raisins in the pemmican. They would dry the saskatoons and would use in the place of currants. When they crushed the chokecherries in it, they also used to make a pudding. They put flour and water, and this was how they'd thicken it, and this was how you made your pudding.[131]

J.Z. Larocque described similar celebrations in the *Regina Leader Post* in 1948 and 1955.[132] Le Jour l'An, or New Year's Day, is an annual custom celebrated by Métis families. The 1948 Le Jour l'An event Larocque described as an "enthusiastic" annual gathering celebrated across extended families because the Métis had been blessed with good weather, abundant vegetable gardens, and a good crop of wild berries that year, which improved their financial situations.[133] The celebration began following a moment of silence and prayer for three Old People, Melanie Delorme, Mrs. François Desmarais, and Simon Desjarlais, who had passed away that year. At age 102, Elise Klyne Kavanaugh acted as the matriarch of the event and sat with St. Pierre Blondeau at the head table to receive visitors. Blondeau shared stories of hunting buffalo on the plains, followed by several short speeches before the fiddle playing and dancing began. The evening closed with benediction or blessings from the patriarchs.[134] This annual event celebrated the holiday and their successful bounty over the previous year, paid their respects to those who passed away, and honoured the Old People still present. It was also a time for socializing, dancing, visiting, and sharing stories of their history. Sharing of food was, as always, central to this activity.

For Métis families in the Qu'Appelle Valley, sharing of food was integral to how they understood and reinforced their kinship relationships. Visiting solidified the act of food sharing and was an important part of all social activities. Visiting was not just for having fun, dancing, playing cards, and gossiping, but to maintain relationships, work out any family and community differences, and check in on one another. It was through these social activities that families honoured their Old People, recounted their history, and expressed their values, in which sharing food with kin was foundational. At New Year's in particular, these celebrations ensured that all families would have enough to eat and could take part in the family and community festivities, even if their own pantries were bare.

On the road allowance, Métis worked hard to feed their families. All members of the family contributed, often as a family unit, in harvesting the natural environment and producing the foods necessary. In this economic unit, women harvested, grew, and preserved food for their families, while children learned at a young age how to contribute to the family economy. Their work was crucial to the survival of the immediate and extended family as food played a significant role in maintaining and reinforcing kinship relationships and obligations.

Into the 1940s, the Métis did not engage in a cash economy to any great extent but harvested or produced the foods they required, and traded and bartered for additional staple items, using their labour in place of currency. Regardless, they harvested, prepared, and preserved as much as they could despite economic limitations, using food to socialize and celebrate events important to them. The sharing of food remained a well-recognized cultural convention among Métis families, despite their poverty.

Over the course of their lives, women's roles in the family evolved, but the respect they garnered for their wisdom, skills, and expertise did not diminish. Rather, older women held respected positions, acting as community matriarchs and valued for their cultural and practical knowledge related to land use and the Valley environment. Women, including older women, played a significant role in cultural reproduction and knowledge transmission, ensuring that children learned important skills and lessons. This was necessary if they were to be successful in engaging in a subsistence lifestyle that aligned with Métis values. This included the transmission of stories, and the values and ideals that privileged reciprocal obligations and responsibilities to the natural environment and to animal and human relations. These kinship relationships and responsibilities remained central to how the Métis understood themselves despite changes in the world around them.

Chapter 8

Contesting Government Intervention into Harvesting Spaces

> Families would get together, and they would go fishing but they would fish at night and put the net in and it was hush-hush kind of thing, nobody mentioned it. So, for me, that tells me that they couldn't afford licences and they needed an amount of fish, right. So, when they did that, there was all the men would get together and all of them would take fish. Then everybody would have [fish] in the winter and get enough fish to eat for everybody. . . . They would net them at night and then everybody would get them and then you wouldn't hear about it for a while and then you would hear that they are going out again and also you'd know [because] the women would be fixing the nets.[1]

IN THIS SHORT story Margaret Harrison shares her family's experience fishing in the 1940s during an era of intensifying fish and wildlife regulation and conservation measures. Her story demonstrates how fisheries regulation, imposed in the late nineteenth century, and escalating into the twentieth, interrupted and interfered with Métis harvesting activities and autonomy over food production. The federal and later both federal and provincial government's conservation measures created conflict over the resources and disrupted local economies and livelihoods. Enforcement of such measures often manifested as a clash between state agents and Métis subsistence harvesters. For Métis who relied on fish and game to feed their families, they found their subsistence activities criminalized. Margaret's story, however, also reveals the precariousness and adaptiveness of Métis harvesting practices and persistence in continuing these activities in a changing social order despite risks or conflict with settlers, government, and lawmakers. It exposes the impact of reconfiguring Métis spaces as government or private settler spaces, which happened with the introduction and intensification of fisheries, wildlife, and conservation measures in the late nineteenth century. Consequently, families increasingly came under the watchful eye of colonial agents and settlers where suspicion, disdain, and racism shaped their interactions. Métis resource users met and resisted these challenges to maintain their subsistence economy in an environment that increasingly oppressed, regulated, and criminalized their harvesting activities. Qu'Appelle Métis individually and collectively acted in both overt and covert ways to resist increasing government control and regulation of their lives. They continued to regularly, and collectively, petition all levels of government as they had in the 1870s, not for specific recognition of their land rights but for continued and increased access to the food resources the land provided. They modified their harvesting practices to skirt regulation and evade government agents, and closely monitored the activity of local agents who enforced the regulations. These actions demonstrated Métis insistence on maintaining their food harvesting practices and family and community responsibilities despite increased government intrusion.

The Canadian state introduced wildlife conservation and preservation measures immediately following Confederation. By this time, federal, provincial, and territorial legislators already had a well-developed frame of reference for such measures, influenced by British ideas and values around hunting and sportsmanship.[2] Despite this, conservation policy began haphazardly because the government was slow to realize the importance of such efforts.[3] Government's lack of concern over conservation and preservation resulted from various factors, including the belief in the superabundance of wildlife in these vast regions and ideas about the presence of a wilderness frontier; the Macdonald government's National Policy that focused on exploitation and development of lands and resources; and the terms of the British North America Act (1867), which positioned natural resources under provincial jurisdiction.[4] Throughout this period, however, Ottawa retained control over public lands and natural resources in the North-West Territories. Similarly, conservation policies enacted in western Canada were also both fragmented and locally based. Individuals or interest groups, such as the HBC or smaller hunting and fishing clubs, interested in conserving wildlife resources for subsistence, commercial, and recreational purposes, initially carried out these measures.[5]

Government agencies and conservationists perceived wildlife in western and northern Canada as "abundant, self-regulating and self-perpetuating," requiring little protective legislation.[6] They used these ideas of wildlife abundance, or "superabundance," to promote western expansion and exert control over Indigenous economies. It was in this new era of Canadian expansion that long-held ideas of the North-West changed from that of an inhospitable wilderness dominated by the fur trade to a rich agricultural garden, images of which were used to meet the goals of rapid western expansion and development.[7] Predicated on these ideas, wildlife was promoted as a metaphor describing the richness of the West's natural resources and depicting the region as an Eden.[8] Game was a resource to be both exploited and protected until an agricultural economy was fully developed.

Government efforts focused on hunting control and assertion of state control over both wildlife populations and access to such resources by subsistence-based communities.[9] Conservation policies did not, and were not meant to, reflect Indigenous peoples' year-round reliance on wildlife resources.[10] From the beginning, these efforts marginalized local customary uses of wildlife, aiding in the colonization of rural and northern Canada.[11] Regulations set out morally and legally acceptable methods and types of hunting. They also began to generally legislate over-hunting, regulate access to game limits, set closed seasons and seasonal limits, and set out permitted hunting methods and restrictions. Wildlife legislation was directed toward the conservation of species, particularly those that safeguarded the long-term survival of animals to ensure their continued subsistence, commercial, or recreational use by humans.[12] State intervention increased while Indigenous control and access to resources gradually eroded, affecting traditional hunting activities as well as community, kinship, and social relationships within and between Indigenous communities.

Although the British North America Act included no formal legislation over the care and protection of game resources, "wildlife," considered as part of the new country's vast natural resources, fell within the Dominion's legislative authority and responsibility as did jurisdiction over marine and inland fisheries.[13] The federal government dealt with fisheries separately through the Fisheries Act (1868) and the new Department of Marine and Fisheries. The Act applied to both ocean and inland fishing, regulated fishing seasons and net sizes, and set limits on catches. Initially, it applied only to fishing in the eastern provinces, but as settlement advanced across the prairies, so too did the federal application and enforcement of legislation.

In 1875, the government delegated authority over game resources to the territorial North-West Council.[14] The North-West Council was the governing body for the North-West created following the transfer of Rupert's Land in 1870. A series of ordinances, which underwent revision and amendment over time, dealt with game regulations. These ordinances set out seasons on big game such as elk, caribou, antelope, and deer; birds and waterfowl such as swans, geese, ducks, grouse, partridge, and prairie chicken; as well as seasons on other fur-bearing animals such as otter, beaver, fisher, and muskrats.[15] Later ordinances included provisions that restricted the disturbing, injuring, or gathering of wildfowl eggs. Consequences for violating these regulations, even being in possession of any bird or animal during the closed season, could result in a fine ranging from five to fifty dollars or a jail sentence of up to two months. Game guardians had the authority to enforce ordinances, including the ability to search personal property. Often, North-West Mounted Police officers, and their successors the Royal Canadian Mounted Police, acted as *ex-officio* game guardians with the authority to enforce the regulations. Conversely, provisions also allowed an individual in need to take any animal or bird to satisfy immediate want. The provisions, however, included no criteria of "immediate want," suggesting it was likely determined at the game guardian's discretion.[16] With the creation of the province of Saskatchewan in 1905, Ottawa retained jurisdiction over what it felt most valuable for facilitating western settlement, public lands, and natural resources, while the province received authority over fur-bearing and game animals.[17] In 1930, the prairie provinces gained jurisdiction over their natural resources, including fisheries, in the Natural Resources Transfer Agreement.

Implementation of federal fishery regulations in the Qu'Appelle Lakes region began in 1884 with the appointment of Frederick Charles Gilchrist as the region's first fisheries overseer.[18] With explicit instruction from the federal Department of Marine and Fisheries, he was responsible for issuing licences or permits; monitoring commercial and domestic fishing activity and enforcing fisheries regulations, particularly those related to fishing without a licence; fishing during the closed season; and stipulations related to the size of gill net mesh for certain kinds of fish. Soon after this appointment, Gilchrist began noting the frequency, intensity, and challenges of Métis and First Nation fishing.[19] In 1885, he noted that First Nations and Métis in the Qu'Appelle district did a "great deal" of fishing, estimating they took over 150,000 pounds of fish from the lakes and rivers for domestic consumption and small-scale commercial sale. Half of this number, he estimated, were whitefish; the remainder, northern pike and walleye. The Department of Indian Affairs purchased much of the local commercial catch, which they used as rations on the surrounding First Nations reserves. Regional settlers purchased the remainder for about six cents per pound.[20]

The intensity of Indigenous fishing in the region and the risk of overfishing the Qu'Appelle Lakes and River was a consistent concern for Gilchrist because, despite their abundance, a large population was dependent upon the fish resources of the Qu'Appelle Lakes.[21] Being that there were few other lakes in the region, he argued that it was necessary to strictly enforce fishing regulations.[22] A year later, he continued to call for urgent and immediate attention to fish populations in all of the lakes within his region, including the Qu'Appelle Lakes.[23] By 1892, he reported that Mission Lake in the chain of Qu'Appelle Lakes was quickly becoming overfished because of intense fishing by Métis and First Nations from the File Hills reserves, but that Katepwa Lake continued to have a sizable supply of tullibee, northern pike, walleye, perch, and whitefish.[24]

Gilchrist's inability to collect accurate statistics on the quantity of fish caught exacerbated alarm regarding Indigenous overfishing. On multiple occasions, he reported to the minister that it was consistently almost impossible to collect accurate returns from Indigenous fishers.[25] In particular, it was most difficult to ascertain catch numbers from the Métis, who, he noted, were very reluctant to cooperate.[26] Métis fishermen, being illiterate, were "averse to keeping or giving an account of their catch, making it very difficult to get at the correct figures."[27] Gilchrist did not perceive the Métis refusal to provide him with an account of their catches as resistance to government surveillance of their fishing activity, but it likely was. Refusal to cooperate with the government in this manner was not an uncommon resistance strategy for many Métis affronted by government intervention and surveillance of their activity. Indeed, as described earlier, W.A. Clark faced the same challenges when reporting the Métis' economic situation in the Qu'Appelle and File Hills settlements in 1886.[28] Regardless, concern for overfishing of the Qu'Appelle Lakes brought about by the concentration of fishing activity, combined with Gilchrist's inability to collect accurate catch numbers, intensified conservation enforcement.

Collecting accurate catch statistics continued to be a challenge for state agents well into the 1910s. In 1912, E.W. Miller, inspector of fisheries for the Qu'Appelle region, expressed difficulty in assessing the Métis catch, noting that "their guess at it is not likely to be nearly so correct as an estimate by the Fishery Guardian."[29] Three years later, it remained a concern that there was no accurate way of arriving at the amount of fish taken each year, or the number of individuals engaged in fishing. As a solution, Chief Inspector G.S. Davidson proposed that First Nations and Métis fishermen receive free permits to fish for their own use, provided they complete a year end statement that accurately reflected their total catch. This, Davidson believed, would be a way to collect accurate statistics and would be a "step in the proper direction."[30]

Throughout his tenure Gilchrist regularly rationalized that Qu'Appelle Lakes fish resources needed protection not only because of increasing regional settlement but also because of First Nations and Métis' continued reliance on fish resources. In his reports to the minister, Gilchrist lamented the need to enforce conservation and prevention measures in ways that would not cause the Métis undue hardship or put additional pressure on government to provide support for them.[31] Consequently, state agents both high in the bureaucracy and on the ground found themselves unsure of how to balance the need for fisheries protection with the needs of Indigenous peoples. Gilchrist reasoned that fisheries could provide a solution to Métis poverty, not just in the Qu'Appelle Valley but in other areas across the North-West Territories. If well protected and restocked, fisheries could when necessary provide "a never-failing supply of wholesome food" whereby the Métis could earn "a very fair livelihood" if they approached fishing "systematically and with intelligence."[32] In the interim, enforcing conservation measures might cause some hardship but Gilchrist cautioned that it was better that the fish be protected rather than risk depletion, at which point the Métis would be starved out of their communities and left with no other option but to seek government support.[33]

Throughout the late 1880s and into the 1890s, the question of how best to deal with Métis fishermen proved complex.[34] Often referred to as the "Halfbreed Question," what to do with the Métis across the North-West plagued government officials. This label would follow the Métis well into the twentieth century. How could the government enforce the regulations in a way that did not cause the Métis additional hardship? If not enforced, state agents reasoned, "greater hardships will fall to the lot of these people, and the Government will have a large board bill to pay."[35] The question was further complicated by the differences in how fishing regulation applied to Métis and First Nations. First Nations had treaty-protected fishing rights; the Métis did not. Because of such differences, government agents questioned, how could they force the Métis to purchase a licence and observe fishery obligations, and restrict them from fishing during the closed season while at the same time not enforcing the same on First Nations fishermen? Indeed, how could they expect the Métis to simply "stand aside and serenely watch the Indians doing what they are told not to do?"[36]

Indigenous fishing practices combined with the character of the Métis, Gilchrist argued, prompted overfishing and did little to prevent their hardship. The Métis, he argued "had a bad way of doing things," as their practice of gathering their winter supply of fish during breeding season not only depleted fish stocks at a crucial time of year, but contributed to their poverty.[37] During the winter, he maintained, the Métis would not attempt fishing with nets because it was too labour intensive and so it was "doubtful whether they would be able to catch enough fish at that time of the year with which to keep themselves alive."[38] The Métis were so destitute, he contended, they would "often resort to rifles in small streams at the approach of spring, for the purpose of catching suckers for food, as they run up stream preparing for spawning."[39] Although he believed the Métis often preserved enough fish to last the winter, their irresponsible and careless nature resulted in their fish stores being exhausted long before spring. This resulted in the Métis being forced to appeal to the Church, the local Indian agent, or anyone else to provide them with food.[40] To combat this, Gilchrist proposed that Métis fishermen use nets and lines at different times during the winter. Nets could be used until the water became too cold for the fish to be active. When the weather changed and water became more moderate, fishermen could use angling lines in place of nets. These practices, he argued, would keep the fisheries from being depleted and perhaps most importantly, rehabilitate the Métis from their "present state of lazy, improvident helplessness" and keep them from starving, thereby removing any burden placed on fisheries agents and the state.[41]

Government officials believed fishing was an economic last resort and that the Métis would eventually abandon it for more permanent economic opportunities. Giving up their "aimless existence," Gilchrist reasoned, would enable the Métis "to gain a livelihood for themselves and some security for their children."[42] It would also alleviate some concern for overfishing. Gilchrist's successor as overseer, E.W. Miller, anecdotally noted a clear connection between demand for labour brought about by the increase in settlement and a reduced reliance on Métis fishing. In his 1899 report on the Qu'Appelle district, Miller observed that all of the local officers had reported the fisheries' favourable condition in the North-West Territories and a "falling off in the amount of fishing done in the more settled districts owing principally to the great demand for labour in other branches of industry."[43] According to Miller, the number of Métis south of the Saskatchewan River dependent on fishing was decreasing because of economic activity in the more settled areas, and as a result, the most serious risk of fish stock exhaustion was fading.[44] In the following years, this trend continued in the Qu'Appelle Valley, but also in regions further afield.

Fisheries agents such as Gilchrist and Miller regularly encountered First Nations and Métis as they were fishing. If fisheries officers caught Métis fishing "illegally," it meant they fished without the required licence, during the closed season, or with nets of the wrong mesh size. The basis of these legal transgressions was because Métis could not afford to purchase the required two-dollar domestic licence for fishing with a gill net or dip net, or the twenty-five-dollar commercial licence for fishing with a seine. In 1887, the local newspaper, *Qu'Appelle Vidette*, printed a warning from the fisheries overseer that he would be watching for people fishing for sale or barter without a licence. He would also be watching for parties having any fish in their possession during the closed season. If caught, they risked a fine or imprisonment.[45] Fishing without a licence criminalized Métis harvesting activity and created the risk of a penalty most could not afford but did little to deter Métis fishermen. These restrictions and risk of punishment help explain why few Métis had any fish stored for the winter when Clark surveyed families in the Qu'Appelle Valley and File Hills in 1886.

Recognizing Métis' poverty, state agents rarely handed out financial penalties.[46] Rather, fisheries overseers seized fishermen's nets, confiscated catches or simply handed out reprimands and warnings. On one occasion, in late October 1888, Gilchrist spotted Clem Peltier on the south side of Katepwa Lake fishing out of season. When Gilchrist attempted to apprehend him, Peltier dropped his net and fled. The overseer followed him home where he found a large catch of fish. He forced Peltier to forfeit his licence and nets, give up his catch and pay a twenty-five-dollar fine.[47] Two years later, Gilchrist again apprehended Peltier and confiscated his net for fishing during the closed season, but did not give him a fine.[48] The same year, Gilchrist seized at least twelve nets from other fishermen during the closed season, five of which he returned.[49] The flexibility in which Gilchrist applied fishing regulations suggests that in some instances, state agents were sensitive to practical realities over strict law enforcement.

In his formal correspondence to the Minister of Fisheries, Gilchrist generally applauded Métis and European settler fishermen for observing both the closed season and the net mesh size and noted significant gains in First Nations fishermen's adoption of smaller meshed nets. His daily journal, however, tells a different story, providing a more comprehensive description of his frequent dealings with Métis fishermen, both men and women, and their determination to continue fishing despite the threat of having their nets or catch seized or the risk of financial penalty.[50] On another occasion, Gilchrist confiscated six nets sisters Marie Klyne Bellegarde and Madeleine Klyne Desjarlais had between them for fishing out of season. It is unclear whether Gilchrist eventually returned Desjarlais's two nets, but he did return Bellegarde's four nets. Married to Joseph Bellegarde from Little Black Bear reserve north of the Valley, Marie Klyne had gained Treaty Indian status under the Indian Act when she married and so benefited from the treaty right to fish out of season.

Recognizing the need for flexibility in the application of fishing legislation, the deputy minister of fisheries directed Gilchrist, in 1886, to allow the most destitute Métis to fish during the closed season but only with one gill net per family per day.[51] He immediately issued free permits to five Métis fisherman and gave assurances that they might "set their nets once in a while" during the closed season despite contravention of the legislation. He also issued free permits to two widowed Métis women who had no means of support or means of paying for a licence and a permit to an old woman responsible for the care of her blind adult son.

The fisheries overseer was responsible for enforcing fisheries regulation, but he was unmistakably also sympathetic to Métis hardship.[52] In one instance, Gilchrist confiscated nets of a woman fishing illegally but upon hearing her misfortune was convinced to return her nets, allowing her to fish "once in a while." She was a widow from the 1885 Resistance, with two small children to feed. She had no means of support and no horses or cattle. Similarly, Gilchrist was kind toward a fisherman referred to as "Old Fayant" whose nets he had seized. Learning of the man's poor circumstances and his wife's poor state of health, Gilchrist hoped to avoid creating additional hardship for Fayant's family so returned his nets with only a warning. As a state agent, Gilchrist attempted to balance conservation regulation with the needs of local Métis. He acted benevolently toward Métis fishermen, recording their interactions in his daily logs, but rarely reporting or fining them, and returning their nets so that they could continue to support themselves. His efforts were not unlike J.Z. Larocque's actions toward the Métis in the 1930s, where on occasion he tended to act with compassion toward Métis hunters and trappers who had few options but to contravene game regulations to feed their families.

Throughout Gilchrist's tenure, many Métis continued to request his permission to fish during the closed season, and when necessary, petitioned his supervisors in pursuit of such concessions. In 1888, Simon Blondeau unsuccessfully petitioned the Department of Fisheries requesting that they allow the Métis to each fish one net during the closed season.[53] This type of political advocacy and the petitioning for rights to subsistence activity was not a new strategy for Qu'Appelle Métis as they had unsuccessfully petitioned the federal government throughout the 1870s and early 1880s. However, Blondeau's petitioning of the distant federal government rather than working to have their needs met by local officials suggests a disconnect between local and federal government authority and that the Métis were determined to receive assurances of their continued access to fish resources.

Recognizing the reliance on fish resources by Métis not only in the Qu'Appelle Valley but across the North-West, the legislative assembly of the territories adopted a resolution on 14 September 1893 to address the issue. The resolution advocated for changes to Fisheries regulations in the North-West, allowing Métis fishermen permits to fish for their own sustenance, to fish for whitefish during the closed season, and to fish for sturgeon in the Saskatchewan and Battle Rivers.[54] When referred to the federal minister of Marine and Fisheries, the Privy Council maintained that the two-dollar domestic licences must remain a requirement for all fishermen and that regulation enforcement continue, especially when fish were spawning during the closed season.[55] However, due to the resolution made by the legislative assembly, the federal government agreed to issue free licences to those settlers and residents who relied upon fish resources and to permit fishing during the closed season, but only at the discretion of the local fishery overseer. This included cases when the overseer was satisfied that a genuine need existed and that individuals were fishing for domestic consumption and not for barter, trade, or export. If fishermen breached these provisions, the overseer was to cancel licences and impose financial penalties. For the Métis, this access to fish and free fishing licences was based on need, and not on any pre-existing rights, placing them in a rather precarious situation vulnerable to the decisions of the fisheries overseer.

Receiving notification of the changes, Gilchrist worked quickly to acquaint the Métis with the government's intention to issue free permits.[56] Gilchrist invited Métis men of the settlement to meet at the Lebret Mission, with the priest as an interpreter. He shared his plan to grant permits to a few of the neediest and then wait to grant permission to the rest when he was satisfied that most of the fish in the Qu'Appelle Lakes had finished spawning. Irritated with Gilchrist's proposal, the Métis replied that they could not wait to "put up" their winter catch, a phrase they used to describe the catching, hanging, drying, and storing of fish, because without it they would likely starve as only ten to twelve families had any potatoes stored for the winter. In addition, after hearing that fishing was going to be free again, many Qu'Appelle Métis returned from faraway lakes without having put up their winter catch. They asked that Gilchrist grant permits according to their needs and to fish throughout the entire closed season. As a conservation measure, the Métis offered to "watch one another and see that no one used small, meshed nets or put up more fish than he would actually require for the use of himself and family." Gilchrist refused their suggestion, believing they would "fish just as they pleased." He remained adamant that free permits meant the Métis "must act squarely" or be refused any privileges. The Métis agreed to Gilchrist's plan, whereupon he informed them that these concessions were only granted for the current year and that in the next year, the regulations would be enforced. This meeting was not the first time that the priest facilitated interactions between the Métis and the fisheries overseer. He often acted as translator and interpreter between the predominately French- and Michif-speaking Métis and the English-speaking overseer, communicating details regarding fishing regulations, the opening and closing of fishing seasons, and advocating to the overseer on the Métis' behalf when caught fishing illegally.

The Métis may have agreed to Gilchrist's plan for dispensing free licences, but that did little to stop those without licences from fishing. In the days immediately following his October 1894 public meeting, Gilchrist travelled throughout the area visiting Métis homes to assess their existing need, and to monitor and police their fishing activities.[57] Echoing Clark's similar findings less than a decade earlier, in general Gilchrist found the Métis to be "a miserable outfit but not in such bad shape as [he] was led to believe." The Métis were obviously poor, but he found many to have at least a few cattle, horses, or pigs. Some, he noted, abided by the provisions outlined at the meeting, while others simply refused to wait, disregarding his directive and fishing without a permit or the overseer's permission. Gilchrist recalled one instance, whereupon learning of an old woman who fished to support her family, he travelled to her home intent on granting her a free permit. When he reached her home, he found that she had not waited for his approval but had closed her house and set off with her two daughters across Katepwa Lake to fish. Likewise, just days after being given the warning that permits were to be granted for personal use only, Gilchrist became aware that some Métis he had allowed to fish were selling or trading their catch locally. Confronting one of the fishermen, Gilchrist warned that the permits were granted for personal use only and that fish must not be provided to anyone other than family or the permit would have to be forfeited. He also informed the Métis and the mission priest that if the Métis accepted fish from others, they would not be eligible for a free permit. And, once the season started, he would not allow nets with meshes of less than five inches extension or of more than 300 yards in length. Undeniably, fishing permits for the Métis may have been free, but they were not without restrictions.

As Gilchrist made his rounds throughout the Valley region, he used these visits as an opportunity to examine the Métis' catches.[58] He found many of the whitefish had not yet finished their spawning and questioned the Métis' character and their knowledge of fish spawning. Inspecting a catch of whitefish, pike, and tullibee, he reasoned that it was evident that the Métis knew little about spawning of the whitefish. Inspecting fish from many different catches, he found the whitefish in various stages of spawning and so determined that the fishing could potentially start as early as 26 October. Word quickly spread and, on that day, without any official word of the start of the season, the Métis began setting their nets. A few days later, Gilchrist still had not yet announced the start of the season when he apprehended three fishermen with nearly 800 whitefish in their possession. Subsequently, Jules Cardinal and François Boucher came forward to state that they too had been fishing without a permit, catching about 250 fish each.[59] They fished because they desperately needed to feed their families and because they had heard that the season was open. Gilchrist reprimanded them, clarifying that the season had not yet opened, and so not only were they breaking the law but also "injuring their own and their neighbor's chances of getting favors from the Department."[60] Pleased that they had come forward, Gilchrist agreed to overlook their actions and continued to issue free permits to the poorest families, with an added caveat that they only fish within one mile of their house on the main shore of whichever lake they lived closest to.[61] These examples demonstrate that Gilchrist had flexibility in not only how he distributed licences but also in how he enforced regulation.

By 1905, fisheries officials in the new province of Saskatchewan were beginning to see the impact of increased fishing activity on fish stocks. In 1908, federal fisheries inspector for the provinces of Saskatchewan and Alberta, E.W. Miller, noted that they had reached the maximum number of licences safely issued without fear of depleting fish stocks.[62] These provincial numbers did not include Métis across the province who fished without the required licence. The pressure on provincial fisheries caused by licensed fishing, combined with First Nations and Métis fishing activities, attracted the attention of the federal department which, in response, implemented a Dominion of Alberta and Saskatchewan Fisheries Commission in 1910 and 1911. The commission was to report on the conditions and requirements of the fisheries and make recommendations for improvement.[63] In their findings was the continued question of how best to deal with Indigenous peoples' reliance on fishing. The commission made a special recommendation regarding the current licensing system in both provinces, suggesting that First Nations and Métis, whom they considered one and the same, be annually granted one free permit per family to fish with no more than sixty yards of net. The Commission made this decision regardless of the complex history of distinction between First Nations and Métis made through application of the Indian Act, treaty, and scrip policy but based on First Nations and Métis reliance on fishing for their livelihood. These permits allowed holders to fish during the closed season, provided if for their own daily consumption and not to preserve for the future. The recommendation was made despite the request of Indigenous fishermen from northern Saskatchewan and Alberta who asked for special consideration and stressed their desire to take all the fish they required during the whitefish spawning period, not only to meet their daily needs but also for their winter consumption.[64]

The following year, the fisheries department began implementing some of the commission's recommendations including those that increased protection for lakes in the more settled parts of the province, shortened the fishing season on lakes fished for whitefish, and restricted use of nets in smaller lakes to domestic use only.[65] Selective in what it acted on, the department took no immediate action to provide free permits to Indigenous fishermen.[66] A year later, it issued free permits to First Nations and Métis fishermen, provided fishermen complete a form accurately detailing their catch at the end of the year.[67] Consequently, the question of what to do with the Métis remained unanswered at the same time fisheries conservation and preservation efforts increased. After 1905 and increasing after the commission's 1911 recommendations, Métis fishermen faced intensified regulation and enforcement efforts and intrusion into their livelihoods. Interactions with government agents were increasingly shaped by paternalistic attitudes about whether Métis were poor enough to require free fishing licences.

Throughout the remainder of the 1910s and most of the 1920s, the government continued issuing free fishing permits to Métis they deemed most destitute.[68] The decision on whether to issue permits was inconsistent, and Métis continued to advocate for their own interests. They also continued to fish despite regulation. They found ways to challenge the rule of law, resist increased intrusion into their livelihoods, and harvest despite the risks or consequences. Consequently, Métis continued to fish because it was what they knew, but also because they relied on it to feed their families.

In 1930, the National Resources Transfer Agreement (NRTA) transferred responsibility for natural resources to the provinces; it was now, for the first time, up to the provinces to regulate fisheries within their boundaries. Saskatchewan's Department of Natural Resources was created and a new minister, inexperienced in dealing with the complex regulation and conservation of fisheries, was appointed.

By this time, local governments in the Qu'Appelle Valley were feeling the strain of Métis poverty, as municipal budgets increasingly stretched to support relief. In late October 1930, the Fort Qu'Appelle Village Council and the Rural Municipality of North Qu'Appelle No. 187 worked in tandem advocating for amendments to fishery regulations as a means of providing Métis relief. Indeed, free fishing permits would allow Métis families to sustain themselves, reducing the amount of relief they required. Both councils separately requested that the provincial deputy minister of the Department of Natural Resources, John Barnett, extend the fishing season and increase the number of free licences granted in the district. They also requested that the department reduce the allowed net length per individual from 600 yards to 300 yards and that only those who had resided within the immediate area for at least three months receive licences.[69] According to N.E. Rose, secretary for the municipal council, the Métis numbered close to 200 in the municipality, and were for the most part unemployed, relying on relief, and subsisting mostly on fish.[70] As a result, the Municipality of North Qu'Appelle argued that the Métis, as indigent and transient squatters, were a provincial, not municipal, responsibility. The number of Métis living within the municipality had increased with the free licensing, as many moved from far distances toward the lakes, creating an extra financial burden for the village and the municipality.[71] The provision that Métis be required to reside in the municipality for a set time before receiving assistance would hopefully curtail further movement to the region, and thus not further strain municipal budgets.

The response from the provincial Department of Natural Resources, Fisheries Branch was clear: there would be no changes to the regulations.[72] The department took a conservationist position on the residency restriction request and disregarded the request to reduce net yardage as unnecessary. The deputy minister, on the advice of Fisheries Branch Supervisor G.C. MacDonald, refused to implement the residency restriction, noting that the fisheries were a public interest and not for the benefit of any one community. The distance one lived from a lake should not restrict their access to it. Those living further from the lakes should have the same benefit as those who lived in proximity to such lakes.[73] Further, the department pointed out that reduction of net yardage was unwarranted, given that 600 was the maximum for commercial licences, not the domestic licence that the municipality sought.

Two months later, in January 1931, the Fort Qu'Appelle village council requested a two-week extension to the winter fishing season. They argued that fishing alleviated the burden of relief for the village and extending the season until the end of February would potentially eliminate the need for providing relief. They also rationalized that the season extension would not deplete the fish stocks.[74] After again consulting MacDonald, this time about the current size of fish stocks in the Qu'Appelle Lakes, the deputy minister agreed to the extension.[75]

In late spring, the municipal council passed another motion to request a two-week extension to the season.[76] The extra time, they argued, would be enough for unemployed Métis to secure food for their families and alleviate financial pressure on the municipality. Forwarding the municipality's request to the deputy minister's office, Secretary Rose asked for the reinstatement of the free fishing permits and that the Métis not be "unduly penalized" by having to pay the two-dollar domestic licence fee.[77] Three weeks later, the department responded, stating that there would be no further free permits or permission to fish during the closed season. Upholding fishing regulations would protect the fisheries and ultimately benefit Métis who relied on fish resources.[78] By this time, however, the season had already closed so the decision was of little consequence.

Unhappy with the department's response, Métis fishermen employed a familiar political strategy. Petitioning government as they had in the late nineteenth century, Métis heads of families collectively advocated for their rights to maintain their subsistence livelihood. Baptiste Robillard and forty-six others lobbied the provincial government for free permits to fish for their own use, arguing that they were out of work, destitute, and required this relief to avoid starvation.[79] Not coincidently, many of the signatories to this 28 May 1931 petition were children of those who had advocated for land, hunting, and fishing rights in previous petitions of the 1870s to 1880s. Raised listening to the oral histories and stories of their parents, grandparents, aunts, and uncles, these signatories would have recognized petitions as a legitimate avenue through which to advocate on their own behalf and have their voices heard.

The timing of this petition corresponded to the increased politicization of Métis across Saskatchewan, who began organizing in the late 1920s, forming the Halfbreeds of Saskatchewan, later renamed the Saskatchewan Métis Society.[80] By the early 1930s, a handful of Métis from southern Saskatchewan organized around Métis land rights, education, and relief.[81] Métis political organization provided a voice for the Métis, and was a vehicle to "pressure the government to improve the conditions of the Métis—to help them get jobs, relief and education for their children, and to press their land claims."[82] The political efforts of Métis fishermen in petitioning government served as a precursor to more formalized political organization of the Métis Society. A noted and significant departure from earlier Métis petitions was the inclusion of twenty-three women signatories.[83] Thirteen of these women signed alongside their husbands, while ten signed independently, suggesting that they were single or widowed. The presence of women as fishers was not only indicative of the significance of fishing to the maintenance of female-headed households and women's roles in their families, but also reflective of Métis women's burgeoning political activism through the newly formed provincial Métis organizations.[84]

Unlike the previous unanswered petitions, the provincial government took some action on the Métis' request, directing the fisheries inspector to contact the signatories and create a list of only those most destitute and elderly should the department decide to issue free permits. The deputy minister warned the inspector to be very careful of the names he submitted, including only those unable to work or in advanced age.[85] Not all Métis were to receive free permits, only those the fishery inspector determined most indigent.

Four months after the Métis submitted their petition, the municipality again reached out to the Department of Natural Resources, reiterating their position. In September 1931, they asked to receive free permits due to the sizable population in the region that relied on fishing, compounded by the municipality's inability to provide direct or indirect relief in the form of employment. Additionally, the municipality argued that if the department was actively promoting summer sport angling amongst the increasing number of visitors and tourists to the Qu'Appelle Lakes, they should also consider the extraordinary situation that the Métis found themselves in. Restricting their fishing to the open season and requiring that they purchase a domestic licence would inflict undue hardship on an already poor population that had few options.[86]

In the days immediately following the municipality's request, the Métis again drafted a petition for a restoration of the free permits, arguing that they had little means of supporting themselves and that without the means to fish they would have to apply to the municipality or the provincial relief commission for support.[87] Sixty-eight heads of families, representing 277 individuals, signed the petition. The municipal council formally endorsed the Métis position before forwarding it, along with a copy of the council's resolution, to the Minister of Natural Resources.[88] This petition represented a greater number of individuals than the petition in May had done and included forty-nine additional signatories. Unlike the earlier petition, however, only eight women signed on, all identifying as widows. Six of the eight women signed both petitions.

The reply from the new and inexperienced provincial minister's office was not positive. The Department of Natural Resources argued that as a provincial agency, they could do nothing to alter the federal fishing regulations and that there had been no direction from the federal Department of Marine and Fisheries to provide Métis with free permits. As a solution, they suggested that the municipality or the provincial relief commission cover the costs of providing Métis with the two-dollar domestic licence so that they could continue to fish in a "legal manner."[89] The provincial minister held firm in his opinion. The Métis would not be provided free fishing permits, rather they were to be treated as other settlers and made to purchase a domestic licence.[90] After this final decision, the municipality took no further action until two years later, when it engaged in a different strategy. This time, the municipality advocated to have the lakes restocked with whitefish, the Métis' principal food.[91] No sooner had the request been submitted to the province when another Métis petition arrived requesting free permits and a municipal endorsement on their behalf to the provincial Department of Natural Resources.[92] Neither the Métis nor the municipality were ready to give up.

Métis across Saskatchewan also employed similar advocacy strategies, writing letters and submitting petitions, advocating for free permits.[93] Each time the department responded consistently—free permits would be issued only to those under treaty, and it remained necessary for Métis fishermen to purchase a two-dollar domestic fishing licence.[94] Provincial Fisheries Supervisor MacDonald reiterated that his department had no authority over the matter of free licences. If Métis received free licences, then all settlers across the province would have to receive the same privilege. Further, he cautioned, if Métis received permission to fish during the closed season it would increase the risk of depleting fish resources.

The shift in responsibility for fisheries from the federal government to the province under the NRTA in 1930 intensified a jurisdictional and racial divide between Treaty First Nations and the Métis. It was clear, the Métis would not receive licences based on their rights as Indigenous peoples, but would be treated the same as settlers, thereby cementing the erasure of Métis indigeneity. And so, province-wide Métis political advocacy to maintain their fishing livelihoods failed in the 1930s.

The village of Fort Qu'Appelle and the Municipality of North Qu'Appelle No. 187 were not the only local bodies feeling the financial pressure to provide Métis and settler relief. In 1933 and 1934, both the municipalities of Last Mountain Lake and Grayson, in the Qu'Appelle Valley at Crooked Lake, made requests to the Department of Natural Resources for free permits to Métis within their boundaries.[95] Yet again the province remained adamant that doing so was beyond the scope of their department to act contrary to Dominion fishing regulations. Changes to federal regulations not only required an order-in-council, but any changes made would apply to the entire province and not just to selected areas. The minister refused to make this request.[96]

In the years that followed, the provincial Department of Natural Resources and the Saskatchewan Relief Commission worked out an administrative arrangement whereby the commission would, in some areas, cover costs of domestic fishing permits to Métis receiving direct relief. Working with the commission, the new provincial agency responsible for fishing regulation demonstrated its growth and experience in how to respond to the very real and complex issue Métis fishing, and their poverty, presented. This was good news to Qu'Appelle municipality, which had continued to pressure the provincial government to take over their financial burden of Métis relief.[97] It was also welcome news to the Lebret Union of the Unemployed who, in 1939, under the leadership of President Thomas Majore and Secretary Ray Fisher, appeared before municipal council asking that they advocate to the provincial government for free fishing permits for the Métis and days later pressed the provincial Department of Natural Resources to provide free permits.[98] The Union of the Unemployed was a political lobby group formed to advocate for employment and relief during the 1930s. The organization had a loose affiliation with the national Communist Party, of which both Majore and Fisher were members.[99] Both Métis, they joined the lobby group in 1936 hoping to advance Métis interests through the organization.[100] They were also founders of, and active in, the Saskatchewan Métis Society during this time.

In winter 1939, provincial Department of Natural Resources officials issued 106 free permits to Métis throughout the Qu'Appelle Valley.[101] Of those issued, eighty-six were in the immediate area surrounding the Qu'Appelle Lakes. According to G.C. MacDonald, the caveat on these permits was that they were to be issued to "destitute half-breeds" (emphasis in original) on direct relief who could not afford to pay the required fee.[102] They were not to be issued to those on some other form of financial assistance such as Old Age Pension.[103] In 1942, the provincial field officers W.A. Brownlee and J.Z. Larocque issued at least thirty-six free permits to Métis in the Qu'Appelle Valley, billed to the relief commission.[104] These permits did not provide complete freedom to fish in the Qu'Appelle Lakes; rather, individual permits were specific to Katepwa, Mission, or Echo Lakes. This was undoubtedly done as a conservation measure to protect from overfishing and depletion of fish resources on any specific lake. Of these permits granted, several went to individuals who had signed the 1931 Qu'Appelle petitions, four of whom were women.

In addition to collectively petitioning local, provincial, and federal governments for changes to fishing regulations, Métis fishers and their families also worked in individual and covert ways to continue subsistence activity outside the watchful eye of state agents. Métis modified fishing and food preparation practices, taking notice of the game guardian's regular patrols, and spreading word of his movement to other members of the community. In addition, if fishing in the closed season or without a licence, Métis fishers often adapted their practices and fished at night to avoid detection.[105] They also worked in small groups, setting the nets and bringing in the catch so that work happened quickly. Working with others, rather than alone, also allowed the use of more nets and resulted in larger catches. This ensured that families were able to continue sharing the proceeds of their labour and reduce their individual risk.[106] Fishing regulation did not stop the Métis from fishing or from the cultural practice of sharing food across families, but it did encourage adapting their practices to avoid detection.

Early conservation measures in western Canada focused on exerting control over Indigenous economies. As the new Dominion government began implementing fish conservation regulation in the late nineteenth and early twentieth centuries, intervention into Métis livelihoods increased, challenging and criminalizing their subsistence activities. With the creation of the province in 1905 and the subsequent fisheries commission, regulation of Métis fishing intensified. Conservation policy, as it was applied to the Métis, was largely paternalistic and concerned with the intensity of Indigenous fishing and the potential this raised for overfishing and the depletion of fish stocks. In 1930, responsibility for natural resources was transferred to the provincial government and there was increased intervention by the province into Métis livelihoods. In response, the provincial government became the focus of Métis petitioning efforts, as well as of municipalities that singled out Métis relief recipients and advocated for fishing licences to reduce the municipal burden of providing Métis relief.

Despite increased interference and regulation, Métis maintained harvesting practices, acting in individual and collective ways to resist intrusion into their spaces. Métis fishermen responded by refusing government requests to document the size of their catches and by regularly fishing without a licence, challenging the authority of fisheries agents. They adapted harvesting practices to skirt surveillance of government agents and continued to harvest despite the risk of violating regulation. Amidst the renewed politicization of Métis across Saskatchewan,

Qu'Appelle Métis used familiar political strategies such as writing petitions. And, for the first time, signatories included women, demonstrating their growing public role alongside the men in their families and communities, but also that they were not afraid of challenging increased state intrusion into their lives.

Within this environment, fisheries agents such as Gilchrist and Miller appear as agents of state surveillance and enforcement and as intermediaries advocating for Métis interests. They exercised flexibility and at times made decisions not exclusively based on regulation, but with compassion and benevolence if or when they deemed enforcement would be cruel or unfair. For the Métis, they remained in a precarious position with decisions about their livelihoods made often at the whim of individual enforcement officers influenced by identified Métis need but also often by their disdain toward the Métis' perceived character. Local governments acted on behalf of Qu'Appelle Métis, making a concerted and sometimes seemingly coordinated effort to advocate for policy amendments to not just meet Métis needs, but also to mitigate their own financial burden in providing relief. The provincial government sporadically acquiesced to these requests and made temporary concessions, only according to immediate need. As a result, the government remained plagued by the question of how best to deal with Métis needs in a way that was sympathetic to their economic situation but also in the best interests of the province's conservation mandate.

Chapter 9

"This Is a Michif Road": Métis Labour and Relief

All this road here, all the way down here [in the Valley], this was all made by hand, so to speak, with horses. [They] cut all these banks down and oh yes, that was a real job you know at that time, but like I said there probably must have been fifty guys working here. They made the road right from Katepwa to Lebret.

My dad was there, yes, my dad was there. My father-in-law was there and two or three of my uncles. Oh, more than two or three. There was uncle Joe Klyne and Uncle Sam Klyne, they were my uncles. Uncle Pete [Desjarlais] was there and Uncle Rene [Amyotte] and Uncle Fred Fayant. Oh, there was lots of them and old Henry Klyne he was there too. They were all old guys, and the younger guys they worked on the road here too.... Can you imagine what they paid these guys to work on the road here, probably about three or four dollars a day and they probably worked anywhere from eight to ten hours a day, maybe more.

> My father told me that after they finished making the road they turned around and graveled it with the horses and the wagons and those guys with shovels and rakes and stuff, they would rake the big stones off. There was lots of labour and I guess it took them all summer long to do this work but there was, oh there was lots of them. I wouldn't even [guess], there was probably fifty guys working there. But they had guys with shovels and guys with picks and the whole works, they didn't all have horses but the guys that had horses were hired with their horses. ... They got a little bit more; I think they got two dollars a day for their horses.... The Métis people sweated all summer long making this road ... this is a Michif road.[1]

THE 1930S WERE difficult for all prairie residents as the Depression intensified. They were particularly challenging for Qu'Appelle Métis, who already dealt with limited and dwindling economic opportunities and increasing poverty. Out of necessity, most sought relief from the local municipal government, adding pressure to already strained municipal and provincial relief budgets. Like many other local governments across the province, the Rural Municipality of North Qu'Appelle No. 187 viewed the Métis not only as a social and economic problem but a financial burden.[2] On the road allowance, the Métis did not own the land they lived on, nor did they contribute to the municipal tax base. While simultaneously petitioning the provincial government for free fishing licences and concessions for the Métis to be able to continue fishing to feed themselves, the municipal council sought out various relief measures to unburden themselves of financial responsibility for the Métis living within their boundaries, ultimately seeking ways to remove families from the road allowance.

The municipality, funded in partnership with various branches of the provincial government, including the Saskatchewan Relief Commission, the Department of Municipal Affairs, and the Bureau of Labour and Public Welfare, made multiple forms of relief available to municipal residents. In addition to direct relief of food and supplies, support came in the form of road-building work, as Bob Desjarlais describes above, and farm employment programs initially designed to provide relief for urban residents in rural spaces. Relief measures also included creating and operating a cooperative farm for Métis at Lebret. This farm became a rehabilitative effort of the Cooperative Commonwealth Federation government under the leadership of Tommy Douglas in the 1940s to curb social assistance expenditures on the Métis, with the idea to remake them into self-sustaining farmers and remove them from the road allowance. Pressure from the municipal and provincial governments to reduce relief expenditures on the Métis, the continued poverty and lack of employment Métis faced, combined with increased government surveillance and the creation of provincial rehabilitation measures, contributed to the dissolution of Qu'Appelle Valley road allowance communities by mid-century.

The 1930s Great Depression was a worldwide economic and environmental event with national, provincial, and local impacts. When entering the Depression, Canada was economically vulnerable because of weak wheat export markets in the years leading up to the 1929 stock market crash.[3] Although all Canadian provinces suffered, conditions were most severe in Saskatchewan.[4] Poor wheat prices, a collapse in demand for farm products, and grasshopper infestations combined with prolonged and widespread drought to destroy millions of acres of wheat, causing massive crop failures, economic depression, and widespread unemployment in both urban and rural areas. Saskatchewan had the highest decline in provincial per capita incomes among the prairie provinces. While Canada's average per capita income fell 48 percent between 1928 and 1933, Saskatchewan's fell 72 percent compared to Alberta at 61 percent and Manitoba at 49 percent.[5] In the same period, the income of prairie farmers dropped by 94 percent, compared to the total national income, which dropped by 40 percent. By 1931, Saskatchewan's net farm income was negative thirty-one million dollars, forcing farm families to live off any capital they may have acquired or abandon their farms.[6] The economic impacts of the Depression were devastating: by 1937 to

1938, the worst years of the Depression for the prairies, two-thirds of Saskatchewan's farm population was destitute.[7]

All levels of the Canadian government struggled to address the desperate economic conditions and prevent a large-scale famine, responding by providing necessary but expensive unemployment relief and public works projects. Before the Depression, relief was a provincial responsibility administered by the municipalities. Local governments provided health services, police, and fire protection, including services for protecting human life such as disease control, maintenance of hospitals, provision of medical care, assistance to indigent persons, and direct relief to needy municipal residents. By the 1930s, municipalities needed help maintaining essential services and rising relief costs.[8] Financial pressure quickly overwhelmed municipal governments, who desperately sought increased support from the provincial and federal governments. In 1931, the provincial government created the Saskatchewan Relief Commission to administer the province's rural relief program. The commission was a temporary stopgap measure to support provincial citizens requiring relief. It was disbanded in 1934 when the provincial Department of Municipal Affairs created the Bureau of Labour and Public Welfare to administer relief in the province.[9] The federal government responded by providing grants to aid the provinces, who then worked directly and sporadically with municipal governments. Municipalities could appeal to their provincial governments for support but were offered little except for emergencies.[10] When received, support was often temporary or of an ad hoc nature requiring regular renegotiation at annual or monthly intervals. Consequently, relief measures were seen as "too little, too late" to deal with the crisis effectively.[11]

Municipal governments funded and administered direct and indirect relief. Direct relief provided the bare minimum necessities of life, including food, clothing, fuel, and shelter. In contrast, indirect relief was aimed mainly at farmers, providing seed, animal feed, binder twine, and some mechanical and farm supplies. The provincial government also funded public works projects such as constructing roads, buildings, and bridges to put the large number of unemployed men to work. These projects kept people working but required material and labour, making them expensive. The government quickly abandoned these large-scale projects except for road building after it became apparent that the Depression had set in. Most rural municipalities resorted to providing direct food and clothing relief to their most disadvantaged residents.[12] Relief was not charity but a loan requiring recipients to sign a promissory note agreeing to pay back at least a portion of what they received. After all, rural residents, generally farmers, had land and farm assets and, therefore, could reimburse the government for some of the relief they received. Most, however, were not collected.

There were four classes of relief recipients—residents; transients; the physically fit, single, and homeless unemployed; and the physically unfit, single, and homeless unemployed. Municipalities were responsible for direct relief of those they considered their bona fide residents. To qualify as a municipal resident, an individual had to demonstrate residence for a set period. The period was initially six months but in September 1934 was changed to twelve consecutive months of residence.[13] In 1936, the residence clause was amended to twelve cumulative months over three years. Those who could not meet the residence qualifications were deemed transients and granted relief at the expense of the provincial governments, who were also responsible for relief for the physically fit, single, homeless unemployed. While not required to pay for transient relief, municipalities were responsible for the administrative and medical expenses for transients and the physically unfit, single, homeless unemployed.

The process of granting relief ensured that municipal agents had a significant degree of autonomy and decision-making authority over who received relief. Initially, under the direction of the Saskatchewan Relief Commission, municipalities worked with a local relief officer and struck a relief committee comprised of the municipal reeve and two councillors. Potential relief recipients made their case before the relief officer and completed a paper application. The relief committee reviewed applications and made recommendations to the municipal council, who had the power to grant, refuse, or rescind relief. Council then passed their decisions on to the Relief Commission.

Like so many other prairie residents, Qu'Appelle Métis struggled during the Depression. Métis families relied heavily on fishing as well as other wild foods that they hunted, trapped, harvested, and grew for themselves, but environmental conditions also impacted food production and labour opportunities. Seasonal and day labour opportunities working for settler farmers dried up as most farmers could no longer afford to hire additional labour, nor did they have the crops that required such expense. Some Métis left the Valley, finding work on the railroad, while others, primarily single men, left the community, travelling on the train to look for work.[14] A handful of men also worked as an inexpensive and temporary labour force for the municipality, building and repairing roads, cutting brush in preparation for road building, digging ditches, and shovelling snow. This was labour-intensive work where men earned meagre wages for a ten-hour day in the hot summer sun or icy winter temperatures. Others made a few dollars poisoning or trapping coyotes, for which they received a small one-dollar bounty.[15]

As Métis poverty continued to intensify, so did their health care and relief needs. Those who were eligible attempted to survive on their meagre Mother's Allowance or Old Age Pension or looked to municipal governments for relief and financial support in accessing medical care. Until this time, many Qu'Appelle Métis had intermittently received support from the North Qu'Appelle No. 187 municipal council but in a much less organized or systematic way. Some appealed directly to the council where, if deemed desperate enough, they might receive a dollar amount of relief redeemable for food and supplies at a local merchant or support in the form of payment for health care services, including doctor's visits and hospital stays.

The municipal council was challenged by the number of Métis reliant on them for medical care and looked to the provincial government to assume these expenses. They also introduced several internal measures to keep municipal costs down and proposed methods to recoup expenditures. For instance, the council authorized medical doctors to perform only a single visit per patient. If the patient required an additional visit, a hospital stay, or certain medical procedures, the doctor was first to present the case to council for approval.[16] The municipal council also notified doctors and hospitals in Fort Qu'Appelle and Regina that they would not be financially responsible for any patients living in their municipality unless hospital care was first authorized by the provincial medical health officer or the municipal council.[17] If the council became aware that an individual might be able to pay for their medical care, they took measures, such as placing a lien on the individual's property, to recoup costs.[18] For most Métis, this mattered little because most no longer owned land. In 1931, the council even suggested creating a poll tax for non-ratepayers like the Métis as a medical and hospital relief fund.[19] Municipal responsibility for relief and medical care costs increased surveillance of Métis private lives, making their social and economic situation and their health conditions part of the public record, which did little to dispel the racism they already faced from their settler neighbours.

Racial tension had been growing in the province and intensified into the 1920s, coinciding with the growth of the Ku Klux Klan in Saskatchewan. The Klan established itself in the province in 1926 and quickly gained momentum, selling memberships, operating through public meetings, and hosting charismatic lecturers.[20] Their first public demonstration, held in Moose Jaw on 7 June 1927, attracted over 7,000 people from communities across southern Saskatchewan.[21] This was the first time the Klan burned a cross in the province. A year later, with a provincial membership estimated at 25,000, the Klan burned crosses and held gatherings in communities across Saskatchewan in honour of Empire Day, 24 May, a day to celebrate the British Empire and commemorate the birthday of Queen Victoria.[22] At the May 1928 gathering in Melfort, Klan speakers declared before seven to eight thousand people that demonstrations were being held in 161 Saskatchewan communities that day.

A distinct Klan presence was increasingly being felt in southern Saskatchewan, in and near the Qu'Appelle Valley.[23] Although the Klan never outwardly targeted Indigenous peoples, they were decidedly anti-Catholic and anti-French, which may have placed the Qu'Appelle Métis within the Klan's sights. On 22 May 1928, two days before the province-wide Empire Day rallies, a cross was erected and burned on the valley hillside at Lebret, burning the small Catholic shrine and accompanying statuary to the ground.[24] While the Métis may not have been outwardly targeted, they certainly would have understood these anti-Catholic acts as an assault on their cultural and religious ideals, and would have recognized that many of their settler neighbours considered themselves members, or at the very least, supporters of the Klan.

The Klan in Saskatchewan differed from the iteration prevalent in the United States. In Saskatchewan, the Klan was decidedly Protestant and dedicated to keeping Canada British. As such, they were anti-Catholic, anti-French, and anti-Chinese. They believed themselves to be largely non-violent and pursued a moral campaign against alcohol, gambling, and vice. They drew members predominately from the upper working class and the lower middle classes and from those who were seen as neither the elite nor the marginalized or unemployed. Members included those working in service industries and building trades, as well as skilled workers and small business owners. Members were also drawn from those working in municipal governments including mayors, village overseers, reeves, secretary-treasurers, and councillors, who coincidently had control over relief decisions pertaining to the Métis.[25]

Métis reliance on relief and the increasing cost of their medical care was clearly concerning for municipal administrators, who, along with some residents, viewed the Métis as unable to care for their own affairs and, at the very least, as a nuisance.[26] Even before the Depression set in, the municipal council was anxious about the Métis' "rapidly deteriorating" economic situation, arguing that they had already paid out large sums of relief and could not afford or did not wish to continue paying such costs.[27] The Métis, the council reasoned, had little hope of supporting themselves as they were not "endowed by nature with the ability to farm successfully," evidenced by their inability to hold on to the land many had once owned.[28] Back in September 1924, the municipal council even proposed making an urgent appeal to the federal government to set aside a tract of land for the Métis to continue to fish, trap, and hunt so they might be self-supporting, and later, as has been described, actively petitioned the provincial government to provide free fishing licences and extend fishing seasons at specific times throughout the year so that the Métis could be more self-reliant.[29]

By 1930 to 1931, there were approximately 250 Métis in the municipality, the majority requiring relief.[30] By this time, municipal council had brought the Métis situation to the provincial government's attention several times but received no assistance.[31] They continued petitioning the government, arguing that the municipality was "particularly penalized" because of the large number of Métis in their district and the increasing costs of supplying medical care and relief.[32] They had provided relief to many of these families during the previous winter and offered them employment to help them repay this support. Cost-recovery efforts failed, however, as the council blamed the Métis' character, claiming it was "almost impossible" to recoup any of the money spent as most Métis refused work, even when offered reasonable wages.[33]

Frustrated with increasing costs and the lack of provincial support, the municipal council voted in early September 1930 to stop paying for Métis relief without the direct assistance of the provincial government. This was a direct contravention of the Rural Municipalities Act (1929), which outlined municipal responsibility for providing care for sick and destitute residents.[34] While the Métis may have lived within the rural municipality for the required length of time to qualify as residents, most were not landowners and did not contribute to the municipal tax base. As such, they were considered "squatters, transients and non-ratepayers" from which the municipality could not recoup relief or medical costs; therefore, they should be a provincial, not municipal, responsibility.[35]

Looking for support, municipal council requested funding from the provincial Department of Labour and Industries for a roadwork project specifically to employ the Métis. In early 1931, they received the first of several roadwork relief grants, cost-shared with the province.[36] The first roadwork grant was for $400, with the municipality contributing $100. A month later, the council entered into another agreement with the Department of Labour and Industries for $1,000, of which the municipality was to contribute $100.[37] This grant put a crew of at least thirteen Métis men and two non-Métis foremen to work building and repairing municipal roads and bridges. These grants were a critical but temporary solution. By the summer of 1931, the municipal council remained concerned about how they would continue to pay for Métis relief. They requested an additional $15,500 in road grants from the provincial government, estimating that this was only a portion of the $25,000 required to support the Métis through the winter and until the 1932 crop was harvested.[38] To strengthen their proposal, they invited the provincial Minister of Labour J.A. Merkely to visit and tour the Métis settlement at Lebret to witness their living conditions and review the proposed roadwork locations.[39] The minister must have been convinced as the Department of Labour granted the municipality $7,500, only a portion of the total estimate, for roadwork in various places as approved by the minister. A few weeks later, the council made another urgent plea for support, this time to the provincial Department of Highways asking for the remainder of the required funds, stressing the "extreme urgency of putting these people [the Métis] to work at once, in order that they may not starve."[40]

These roadwork relief measures, specifically for the Métis, continued throughout the 1930s. They were renegotiated annually, with the provincial government assuming some financial responsibility for Métis relief.[41] As Bob Desjarlais describes in his story above, men worked in road gangs alongside relatives and friends, building roads throughout the Qu'Appelle Valley for paltry wages. In 1933, general labourers earned two dollars for a ten-hour workday while those also supplying horses or working on road building equipment earned slightly more.[42] Although providing a team of horses guaranteed a higher daily wage, it also included additional costs.[43] By 1938, municipal roadwork rates of pay had increased to $2.50 per day for a general labourer.[44]

The Métis worked hard building roads and earned little. Some also viewed road building as a "make-work project" created "just to make the poor people work."[45] Instead of earning cash payments, they received credit redeemable with local merchants for food or clothing.[46] Working in this type of economy was not new to the Métis, who, as seasonal farm labourers, had worked in a barter economy. George Klyne, whose father built roads during the 1930s, recalled that when the municipality paid his father, they held back some of his earnings, providing the remainder in credit at a local store.[47] George also suggests that the Métis, like his father, were so accustomed to being paid in food and goods rather than cash that they may not have understood this roadwork as a relief measure.

While the roadwork program helped alleviate the municipality's financial responsibility for Métis relief, they were still responsible for direct relief expenditures to their bona fide residents. Early in the Depression, the municipal council approached the Saskatchewan Relief Commission to help with direct relief to all residents in the municipality that required such support.[48] The commission refused. Unhappy with the decision and unable to afford the cost, the municipality urged them to reconsider.[49] The commission acquiesced, agreeing to pay for Métis relief with a few caveats: first, Métis relief was only to consist of flour, tea, lard, baking powder, and clothing in an amount not to exceed $2,000 over a six-month period. Second, that relief was not to be given out to single individuals, only those with spouses and children to support. They were emphatic about this, stating that "NO RELIEF TO BE GRANTED TO OTHER THAN HALF-BREED FAMILIES" (emphasis in original).[50] Third, that the municipal council pass a bylaw allowing them to enter into an agreement with the relief commission whereby it would advance Métis relief as above, provided the municipality assume 30 percent of the total amount of relief advanced.[51] Eager to receive the provincial government's support, the council quickly passed a bylaw to that effect.[52]

Following on the heels of this arrangement, the relief commission began pressuring the municipality to either reduce the number of Métis families on relief to approximately forty families or reduce the amount of relief each received.[53] This was part of a more significant push by the commission to reduce relief allocations to all recipients, not just the Métis. They reasoned that practically all applicants in the rural municipality had enough livestock to care for their meat and dairy requirements, and some likely had a surplus they could sell. When this was taken into consideration, they reasoned, the monthly food allowance should be reduced considerably.[54] It was not just the Rural Municipality of North Qu'Appelle that was to reassess and reduce their relief advances, but all Saskatchewan municipalities. The relief commission advised a 50 percent reduction for the spring as recipients should require less with "hens laying and cows freshening."[55] If municipalities believed a 50 percent reduction in food allotments would cause suffering amongst recipients, the relief commission agreed to consider a lesser reduction on a case-by-case basis.

The municipal council was eager to reduce relief when appropriate.[56] However, they were not now prepared to do so as most Métis recipients, they argued, had neither cattle nor chickens to help feed their families. The council requested that the commission continue providing Métis relief for April 1933 and that a decision from council regarding a May extension would be forthcoming.[57] The council requested an extension in May because the Métis "did not enjoy more than a meagre existence" because of a lack of spring work, but their request was ignored.[58] Instead, the relief commission pressed for further reductions and encouraged the municipality to cancel relief if any recipient could take care of their own requirements.[59] One avenue the municipal council pursued was to request a list from government indicating who in the municipality received Mother's Allowance or Old Age Pension and in what amount. This list, the council argued, would help it reduce relief allotments accordingly.[60]

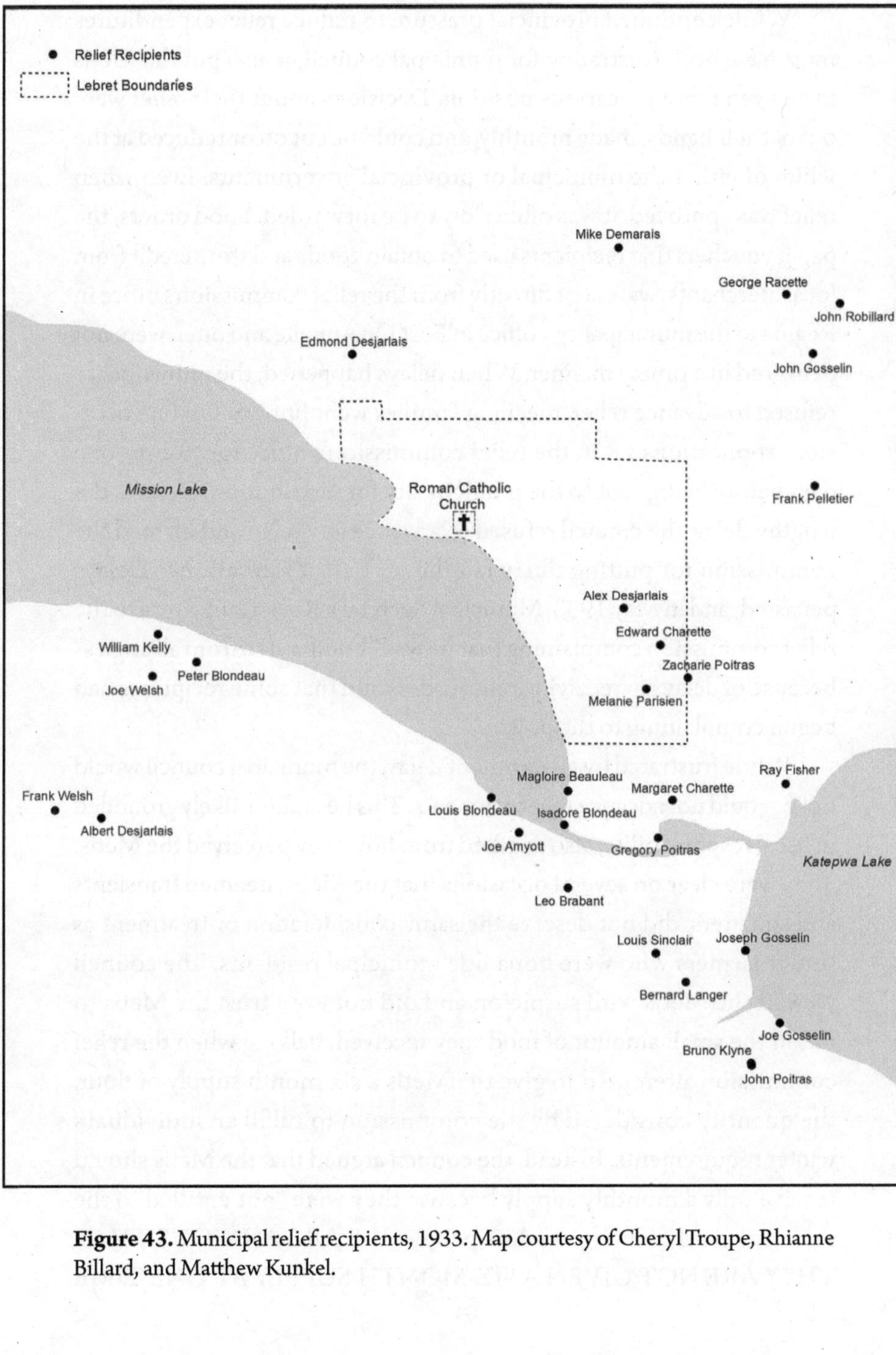

Figure 43. Municipal relief recipients, 1933. Map courtesy of Cheryl Troupe, Rhianne Billard, and Matthew Kunkel.

While continued provincial pressure to reduce relief expenditures must have been frustrating for municipal council, it also put the Métis in an even more precarious position. Decisions about their relief were out of their hands, made monthly, and could be cut off or reduced at the whim of either the municipal or provincial governments. Even when relief was approved, it was often slow to be forwarded. Food orders, the paper vouchers that recipients used to obtain goods and store credit from local merchants, were sent directly from the relief commission's office in Regina to the municipality's office in Fort Qu'Appelle and often were not delivered in a timely manner. When delays happened, the municipality refused to advance relief, meaning families went hungry. On one occasion, applications sat in the relief commission's office for twenty-one days before being sent to the municipality for distribution. Despite the lengthy delay, the council refused to advance any relief and blamed the commission for putting thirty families at risk of starvation.[61] Delays persisted, and in May 1933, Municipal Secretary Rose again wrote to the relief commission complaining that he was "bombarded from all angles" because of delays in receiving relief orders and that some recipients had begun complaining to the police.[62]

While frustrated by government delay, the municipal council would not or could not advance relief payments. This hesitation, likely grounded in fiscal responsibility, also resulted from how they perceived the Métis. They were clear on several occasions that the Métis, deemed transients and squatters, did not deserve the same consideration or treatment as settler farmers who were bona fide municipal residents. The council viewed the Métis with suspicion and did not even trust the Métis to ration the small amount of food they received, balking when the relief commission attempted to give the Métis a six-month supply of flour, the quantity considered by the commission to fulfill an individual's winter requirements. Instead, the council argued that the Métis should receive only a monthly supply because they were "not entitled to the same standard of living as white people. WE ARE ANXIOUS THAT THEY ARE NOT GIVEN A SIX-MONTH SUPPLY AT ONE TIME

AS WAS DONE LAST YEAR" (emphasis in original).[63] The municipal council must have believed that the Métis would waste their flour rations. They also alleged that many were abusing their relief on liquor and were consequently responsible for increased petty crime in the community. They even wrote to the province's deputy attorney general requesting access to the business records of Lebret and Fort Qu'Appelle stores that sold liquor to determine if the Métis were in fact exchanging their food relief for the purchase of alcohol.[64] The deputy attorney general refused the request, claiming no provision in the provincial Liquor Act permitted such an inspection except under subpoena.[65] The municipal council was also concerned about perceived Métis thievery in the village of Lebret and the municipality.[66] In response, they passed a motion to have a police officer "take charge, even for a short time and put the fear of the law into these Métis as it is [they] that are the culprits."[67] It is unknown if any charges were laid. The council continued to monitor the Métis situation closely, believing the Métis could not be trusted. Four years later, still concerned about the situation and hearing reports that some businesses may have been providing cash payments to Métis road workers, the council advised local businesses to be cautious in dealing with Métis on relief. Under no circumstances were the Métis to receive compensation other than credit redeemable for goods and supplies. If this continued, they warned, the municipality would stop issuing relief orders for redemption at offending stores.[68] Consequently, the municipal council had very clear racist ideas about the character of their Métis neighbours: the Métis were wasteful, untrustworthy, and prone to drinking and thievery.

Métis relief was becoming a complex economic problem, not easily solved. Cost sharing with the province helped alleviate but not eliminate the municipality's financial pressure. The provincial government simultaneously provided funds and consistently encouraged the municipality to find ways to cut costs and reduce the number of Métis on relief. At the very least, they argued, the Métis, like those working building roads, should be required to earn their relief. This pressure forced the council to explore other measures of support, including campaigning for free fishing permits for the Métis and encouraging them to work cutting and selling ice from the Qu'Appelle Lakes.[69] They also requested the federal Department of Indian Affairs provide work for local relief recipients in the reconstruction of the Qu'Appelle Industrial School at Lebret. Despite their efforts, by late 1934 to 1935, financial concerns remained. In November 1934, the municipal council passed a motion instructing that only after the Métis had committed their labour would they receive any relief. A few months later, they struck a committee to survey the Métis regarding their food requirements and maintained that they would only disperse relief as "absolutely necessary."[70] The message was clear, the municipality must find a way to reduce the cost of Métis relief. The Métis should be made to work for relief and be given only what was essential. This was in stark comparison to the direct food relief and seed grain advances consistently provided to non-Métis municipal farmers without a requirement to exchange their labour.

In addition to relief costs, the council was also concerned with costs incurred in providing for Métis hospital and medical care. In 1936, 25 percent of the municipality's total revenue was used to cover Métis medical expenses.[71] Municipal responsibility for "this class of indigent," they reasoned, was beyond the scope of the Rural Municipality Act. If the province was responsible for Métis relief, which they demonstrated through cost-sharing relief, they should also be responsible not only for the Métis' unpaid medical debts, but also for all their future medical and hospital costs.[72] Throughout the year, they continued to press the provincial government on the issue of Métis health and medical costs and the cost of food for the winter, seeking out Premier William Patterson and his cabinet in late 1936 to discuss what they termed the "Half-Breed Situation."[73] The label Half-Breed Situation or "Métis Problem," used to describe Métis social and economic conditions, would follow the Métis in dealing with municipal and provincial governments well into the mid-century.

Always looking for support, municipal council also sought help from the Catholic priest at Lebret to pressure the provincial and federal governments. In May 1936, Father Alfred Beaudin of the Oblate Order of Mary Immaculate wrote to Prime Minister Mackenzie King, outlining circumstances in the Qu'Appelle Valley, and suggested creating a farm colony to make the Métis self-sufficient.[74] The Métis, because of their lack of education and poor social and economic situation, he reasoned, have been the victim of misunderstanding and racial prejudice by the settler community. Many are unable to find work or provide for themselves, forcing them to apply unwillingly for relief which the municipality can ill afford. The municipality, he stressed, can no longer aid even the most destitute of Métis families, despite any "favourable intentions" to do so.

The proposed farm colony, Father Beaudin suggested, could be supervised by the federal government until the Métis could provide for themselves. In the priest's plan, the government was to provide financial support, but the Métis would have some decision-making authority. A council comprised of elected Métis residents, under the supervision of federal authorities, would administer farm affairs and the Métis, guided by the Church, would maintain the right to regulate education. Four months later, Beaudin sent a similar letter to Premier Patterson reminding him of the Métis situation in the Valley, informing him of the letter sent to the federal government, and outlining what he envisioned as the province's role in this plan. In his request, the province was to take full fiscal responsibility for relief, medical care, and education until the Métis could "live honourably" without relying on provincial aid.[75] It is unclear what conversations transpired between the municipal council and the oblate order that prompted these letters, or if the farm colony was in fact the priest's idea. For several years, the order had operated a farm a few miles from the village of Lebret that regularly employed Métis farm labour. Regardless, the fact that Father Beaudin references W. Bushell, the reeve for the Rural Municipality of North Qu'Appelle, in his letters suggests that discussion had decidedly occurred.

Premier Patterson quickly responded, advising that the Métis situation not only in the Qu'Appelle Valley but across the province was indeed troubling. Relief costs increasingly put pressure on all municipalities, particularly in locations with a significant Métis population. By 1937 to 1938, there were estimated to be 6,000 Métis across the province, of which most were estimated to be on relief.[76] Admitting that government had given the issue considerable thought but had not yet been able to come up with a satisfactory solution, Patterson reassured Father Beaudin that he would not forget about the Métis.[77]

Patterson's response to the Métis was no doubt influenced by the findings of the 1934 Royal Commission to Investigate the Conditions of the Half-Breeds of Alberta. Known as the Ewing Commission, the Commission's mandate was to examine the health, education, and general welfare of Alberta Métis. The Commission's recommendations were included in the 1938 Métis Population Betterment Act in Alberta. Understood at the time as the most advanced legislation in Canada relating to the Métis, the Act set aside land specifically for the Métis and was seen as a solution to the economic problems they faced.[78] The Act created a series of colonies where Métis residents could continue a subsistence lifestyle of hunting, trapping, and fishing and not be reliant on municipal or provincial relief. Importantly, the Act also defined who was considered Métis, but did so through a lens of poverty, limiting its meaning to those who were indigent with no consideration or acknowledgement of Métis rights.

Indeed, Patterson did not forget them. Early in 1937, the government began pursuing the purchase of land for the creation of a farm as Father Beaudin had suggested. The province advanced the municipality a deposit to purchase a working farm on Section 35–Township 21–Range 13, which already had significant infrastructure, including a garage, several wood and steel granaries, a large log barn, a stable, a chicken house, two sheds, and a single-storey frame house.[79] The municipal council set up a Métis Rehabilitation Committee to administer and oversee the farm. As farm administrators, the municipality could use funds from the sale of farm crops to help cover municipal relief expenses. This committee quickly began purchasing additional machinery and set a meeting with a delegation of Métis to convince them of the farm's potential.[80] The farm went ahead, and the committee selected Métis Ed Majore and Geo Desjarlais, who both had the necessary horses, equipment, and experience to lead planting and put in the 1937 crop. The farm operated as a work-for-wages program and would pay Majore and Desjarlais from the crop sales. The municipality collected 50 percent of sales, and once they deducted Majore and Desjarlais's expenses, they divided the remainder on a sixty–forty basis between the municipality and participating Métis farmers.[81] The following year, Albert Majore joined Desjarlais and Majore on the farm. The committee agreed to give fifty bushels of oats to each of the three farmers for their spring work and a food allotment, which they would reduce once the cows started producing.[82] The provincial government took over operation of the farm in 1939 on the condition that the municipality was refunded the initial advanced price and costs for equipment and seed.[83] By 1940, the farm supported seventeen people in four families.[84] While this measure provided relief to these few families and alleviated some of the financial pressure on the municipality, it did little for the remaining thirty to thirty-five Métis families resident in the Valley region.

Eager to take advantage of any provincial measures to reduce their expenditures, the municipality participated in a food aid program and a farm employment program. The delivery of railcars of potatoes and other vegetables to hungry relief recipients was a province-wide measure aimed at food relief and helping keep municipal costs down temporarily. In 1937 to 1938, during the most difficult years of the Depression, railcars transported food aid to the provinces' hardest-hit areas, most of which were in southern Saskatchewan. The first carload was distributed in the Qu'Appelle Valley in October 1937. In this shipment, 444 bags of potatoes were distributed to forty-five families, but only four were Métis.[85] One of the few Métis recipients, Thomas Desjarlais, wrote to the municipal council expressing his gratitude and declaring his family's further need of vegetables and clothing.[86] Days later, Desjarlais and his wife Virginia applied again for relief and were made to sign a promissory note, promising to pay back the value of potatoes and vegetables the family had received before being considered for more relief. This was likely because Virginia was also receiving twenty dollars in monthly Mother's Allowance from the provincial government, which she could use to reimburse the government for the advance of relief.

In early November, a railcar delivered 600 bags of potatoes to Lebret: 470 bags for residents of the Rural Municipality North Qu'Appelle No. 187 and 130 bags for residents of the neighbouring Rural Municipality of Abernathy No. 186.[87] This time, the Métis received much of the produce. Sixty-one of 163 recipients were Métis, each receiving one ninety-pound bag of potatoes per family member. In April, another shipment of potatoes was allocated to the municipality.[88] The potatoes arrived in late July and August, bringing 600 bags to Fort Qu'Appelle, 600 to Lebret, and 400 to Dysart, north of the Valley, helping to feed hungry Métis families.[89]

Early in the Depression, the municipality also administered a Farm Employment Program, cost-shared between the provincial and federal governments, that began as a winter work project for urban single, homeless, and unemployed men over sixteen in need of relief and to support struggling farm families. The program expanded in 1935 to include unemployed men and women so that women and married couples could participate.[90] Workers were paid five dollars per month while farmers received a government allowance of five dollars monthly to assist with their employees' food and shelter.[91] Once the worker was employed, food relief in their home was reduced because of their absence, but the food quota in the farmer's home did not increase.[92] This was a way of helping keep costs of direct relief down.

To enter the program, labourers had to qualify and prove to municipal administrators that they were destitute. Owning your own farm, even a failing farm, disqualified you from working in the program. Applications could also be rejected if an individual did not have sufficient previous employment to be classified as an unemployed individual, or if farmers required labourers to provide more than unskilled labour.[93] In one instance, the program rejected a Valley farmer's application because the potential employee owned a farm and was considered a "bona fide farmer" and not a labourer. Regardless of their own farm's failure, they were not considered homeless or destitute despite any preference they may have had for farm work rather than direct relief.[94] When implemented in the Valley, most of the program's participants were not Métis. However, by 1937 to 1938 the program employed fifteen Métis, including five women working for settler farmers.[95] Métis were not excluded from hiring farm labourers, but extremely few, if any, had the means to qualify as farmers.

Program administrators closely policed Métis labour. Farmers were expected to keep in regular contact with municipal administrators and notify them of any issues or changes to the worker's employment.[96] The municipality also kept a close eye on Métis labourers, ensuring they remained actively employed, and therefore off municipal relief rolls. On one occasion, Joseph Poitras was reprimanded by the council for being absent from work and was advised to return immediately or be reported to the provincial administrators to take "whatever action they think necessary."[97] Poitras was also threatened that if cut off from the farm employment program, he would not be eligible for municipal relief, nor would his mother be given any additional relief to support him. This program offered another opportunity like municipal roadwork for Métis to work for any relief received. It also put them in direct view of municipal administrators, ever eager and quick to reduce expenditures on the Métis. Like so many other relief measures, this program was renegotiated between the provincial and federal governments on an annual basis, which often meant delays or that it might not be renewed for each successive year.

By 1938 the municipality had reached a breaking point and could no longer afford to pay for Métis relief. In May they passed a motion to reduce the number of non-Métis relief recipients by one-third and to cut off relief to any Métis who worked. Only widows and those unable to work would remain eligible.[98] Two months later, council moved to discontinue all direct relief except for widows or the sick at the discretion of the Municipal Reeve.[99] By September, the council could not make payment to the provincial government for relief advances they received for March to July 1938.[100] Since 1 January 1927, the municipality had paid out $10,500 to cover Métis hospital and medical costs and still owed $2,500 on that debt. They were now in a position where it was impossible to pay these debts and outstanding accounts for 1938 and be able to guarantee any further medical or hospital aid to the Métis for the following year. They continued pressuring government, meeting with Premier Patterson and the attorney general to plead their case for shifting fiscal responsibility from the municipality to the provincial government.[101] Again, they argued that the Métis should be a provincial government responsibility because of their "continued impoverished conditions" and because they were squatters, transients, and non-ratepayers.[102] There were sixty-two Métis families in the municipality that the council believed would be seeking relief during the winter, in addition to forty-fifty non-Indigenous families that would also likely require support.[103] These sixty-two families represented 289 individuals, likely the entire Métis population in the region.

The municipality continued to seek out any additional grants from the provincial government to cover medical and hospital relief and wrote to the director of relief reminding him that local hospitals and medical practitioners were pressuring the municipality to pay for fees they incurred in treating the Métis.[104] The municipality had received $1,000 per year to cover these costs, but needed more.[105] The council went so far as to endorse a proposed Métis hospital at Lebret on the understanding that it would not conflict with a resident doctor at Fort Qu'Appelle and to inquire with the doctor at the First Nations hospital at Fort Qu'Appelle about treatment for non-First Nations patients.[106]

The municipal council continued to insist that the provincial government take responsibility for the Métis. In the same period, the Lebret Relief Committee and the Union of the Unemployed, as discussed earlier, pressured the municipality to do more for the Métis. In February 1938, Fanny Gibson, chairperson of the Lebret Relief Commission, wrote to council asking for clothing and food relief, including more railcars of potatoes.[107] She implored that every day people came to her door begging for food and clothing, and, as a result, many children did not go to school because they had nothing to eat. A year later, in spring 1939, the Union of the Unemployed pressed for municipal support in advocating to the province for free fishing licences, a strategy the municipality had embraced as early as 1931 to offset relief costs. By the fall of 1939, sixty-five Métis were receiving either roadwork or direct relief.[108] Twelve of these received direct relief, while fifty-three received relief through roadwork exclusively. Of those on direct relief, seven were women. Seven additional women also received relief through roadwork. Likely these were women whose sons were old enough for roadwork but too young to be considered for individual relief. Even if the council were in financial straits, they would continue, or be made to continue, to fund Métis relief to some degree.

Throughout 1939 to 1940, the municipality and the province continued to cost-share relief, with the municipality receiving provincial grants annually and sometimes monthly to fund relief.[109] Recognizing the immense need of specific communities and municipalities with high Métis populations across the province, the provincial government inched toward taking full responsibility for the Métis by making a special concession to cover all Métis relief costs in specific municipalities.[110] This was, however, renegotiated on an annual and sometimes monthly basis.

The province's commitment to taking on Métis relief in specific areas, even if negotiated sporadically, prompted them to reconsider the Métis farm as a possible solution to the "Métis Problem." This provincial action also encouraged the Qu'Appelle municipality's resolve to remove Métis from the road allowance. The municipality considered the physical relocation of Métis families from their homes on the road allowance a further means of reducing expenditures. If the Métis could be convinced or made to move into towns or villages, they would no longer be the rural municipality's responsibility but that of the town or village in which they lived. This was an attractive idea that might solve some of the municipality's financial problems, but it certainly would not eliminate

Métis poverty. Municipal council had periodically discussed removal throughout the 1930s but took no specific action.[111] When confronted with removing an individual family, they deemed it was unfair to remove one family unless they were ready to remove "all other trespassers."[112] However, when the municipality found itself to be in dire financial straits in the fall 1937, they proposed to write to all the Métis "squatters" advising them that their houses must be removed from the road allowances by 1 May 1938 and that no houses were to be erected on municipal road allowances in the future.[113] It is unclear if they delivered this message, but it mattered little because even if the Métis had received such a letter, they were without economic means to move and had nowhere to go. A month after the deadline, council raised the issue again but quickly tabled it for the following meeting.[114] The idea was not raised until a year later, when council again insisted that the Métis be made to remove their homes from the road allowance, instructing the municipal secretary to write to one Métis individual directing him to remove his house by 15 November or the house would be destroyed.[115] Council's position on removal had decidedly changed, and they were now willing to single out and remove individual families while others remained.

By 1940, the provincial government was convinced of the potential for a Métis farm project, as only the year prior, it had taken over responsibility for the operation of the municipal farm project. In June, the Patterson government began negotiating with the Catholic Oblate Order at Lebret to lease a section of land as a Métis farm colony.[116] The jointly run project was to be a model farm to encourage and teach agricultural pursuits while providing would-be Métis farmers with the necessary equipment, direction, and supervision to succeed. It would provide homes and livelihoods for those Métis families chosen by the Oblates, with the approval of the minister of municipal affairs, to live there.

The Oblates had a long-standing relationship with the devoutly Catholic Métis, and they agreed with the province because of concern for their parishioners' social and economic welfare. Located on the north side of Mission Lake, adjacent to the residential school, the section of land was ideal for the Métis as it was close to both the Church and school at Lebret. Some were also familiar with this land, as they had earlier worked the section as farm labourers for the Church.

The province paid the Oblate Order $5,000 to cover the costs of equipment and initial operation, including wages for a farm manager and building expenses for several suitable houses and other necessary outbuildings. The Oblates provided supervision, management, and direction in the use of equipment and farm operation. The Oblate brothers' training at the seminary on Mission Lake's south side provided some labour. The Church provided instruction in domestic and household sciences and was responsible for farm residents' spiritual advancement. Farm proceeds were to cover operating expenses, necessary improvements, and, perhaps most importantly, the maintenance of residents. The provincial Department of Municipal Affairs was to pay for seeds and necessary medical attention, including any essential drugs or hospitalization of farm residents, as part of direct relief. If farm proceeds were not enough to cover costs, costs were not to be charged against the land. The initial agreement was for five years, ending 31 March 1945. Upon termination, title and ownership of all property, including produce raised on the farm, remained with the province. At the same time, the Oblates retained ownership of the land and any permanent improvements made during the length of the agreement. The farm did not operate long before the parties amended the lease agreement to include a second parcel of nearby land, owned by the provincial Department of Natural Resources.[117] Like the province, the Oblates were pleased with the farm's success and confident that the farm project "based on discipline, kindness and religious education [was] the proper system to inculcate the principles of civilization and protect the [Métis] from subversive doctrines and bring them up to the standard of true and reliable citizens."[118]

Two years later, the parties remained confident in the project's success, making a second amendment to the agreement and rescinding the June 1940 version.[119] A new twenty-one-year agreement outlined the creation of a four-member advisory committee to guide the farm overseer and manager. The committee was to consist of one member appointed by each of the interested parties, including the minister of municipal affairs, the Oblates, the Métis residents, and one selected by the Saskatchewan Association of Rural Municipalities, who was to be either the secretary-treasurer or a member of the municipal council from any of the neighbouring rural municipalities, including the Rural Municipality of Indian Head No. 156, Abernathy No. 186, North Qu'Appelle No. 187, or Tullymet No. 216. The inclusion of a Métis representative on this committee was an important addition, but it is unclear what, if any, influence, they may have had.

The committee came together quickly, reporting on the farm's success only a month later.[120] The extensive report detailed the construction of several homes and farm outbuildings, the land under cultivation, and livestock raised on the farm. There were nine homes for Métis families, a large granary, pigpen, and chicken house. There were sufficient horses and machinery to operate the farm properly, and farmers had cultivated enough grass to feed their livestock. The committee estimated that enough feed was grown the previous year to provide all their livestock, including twenty-five head of cattle, sixteen horses, 220 chickens, and fifty pigs for a year, perhaps even longer. Several families had progressed in agricultural training and might soon be ready to establish their own farms if government assistance and supervision were provided. While the committee declared the project's potential as a permanent solution to the "Métis Problem," there were also several improvements to be made to further support farm success, including building additional houses for more Métis residents, another pigpen, and horse and cow barns to keep increased livestock numbers. Homes and outbuildings were all erected on Section 15 owned by the Oblates, and not on Section 35, added by government. If the agreement was terminated, the committee recommended that the houses be moved but that farm buildings remain on the Oblate land. They also suggested that all stock and machinery be divided amongst the farm's Métis residents. The report indicated that the health of Métis residents was good and improving, attributed to better housing and access to sufficient food, including milk, eggs, and vegetables produced on the farm. Last, the committee recommended that the provincial government continue to cover medical and hospital expenses for farm residents to the financial benefit of the municipalities that would have otherwise been responsible. If this was not possible, they asked that the provincial government consider hiring a local doctor to provide required medical attention on a monthly salaried basis. The parties drew up another agreement to implement the report's findings, but there was a change in government before implementation could begin.[121]

The CCF and Métis Rehabilitation

In July 1944, the CCF government led by Thomas Clement Douglas came to power, running on a platform of "humanity first" and social democracy. Douglas and the CCF could not ignore the Métis' poverty and worked to shift provincial policy toward their "rehabilitation."[122] This included the creation of the Department of Social Welfare and Rehabilitation to oversee the delivery of social aid programs, including those specifically for the Métis.[123] The department instituted several rehabilitation measures in line with CCF principles of cooperation, aimed at the Métis. This included creating several colonies across the province, run as cooperative farms where Métis could live and farm together. If they removed the Métis from the road allowances, relocated them to farms, and trained them to become farmers, they would be self-reliant.[124] By the late 1940s, colonies at Crescent Lake, Crooked Lake, Lestock, Baljennie, Willow Bunch, Duck Lake, Glen Mary, Green Lake, and Lebret were home to almost 2,500 Métis residents.[125] Initially seen as a success, the colonies were plagued with administrative and structural problems and by the late 1950s, were being abandoned by the CCF. Regardless, at their inception, the provincial government saw these colonies as an important step in addressing the "Métis Problem" and alleviating Métis poverty. For the Métis, movement to these colonies may have provided some economic opportunity to learn and apply farming skills and may have ensured some continued connection to the land. However, removing people from the road allowance and their extended family kinship networks may have weakened or even severed these relationships and hastened movement of Métis families into urban areas.

Early in the CCF's tenure, the new government attempted to consolidate Lebret Métis farm holdings, offering to purchase the Oblate-owned section.[126] Concerned about whether the province had executed the revised twenty-one-year agreement, the Oblates sought a legal opinion before proceeding but were willing to cooperate with the government provided the farm continued to be used to the Métis' benefit.[127] The parties struck a deal that sold the farm to the province and by 1945, the farm was supporting fifty-eight people in nine families.[128] While this was an increase from the three families the farm initially supported, there remained close to 350 Métis individuals in more than seventy families in the Valley in this period.[129]

Following the purchase, the province hired a new farm manager and invested in farm modernization, including power equipment.[130] They built a new modern pig barn to increase hog production, a garage workshop for teaching farm mechanics, and, in 1948, a community hall. They were raising about sixty head of cattle and started a purebred herd. They built a new chicken brooder house to expand their poultry program and began raising bees. In 1946, they produced over 300 pounds of honey to sell to residents and the public. The number of residents and employees fluctuated, but there remained homes on the farm for nine families, as well as a home for the farm manager in the village of Lebret. Heads of families were employed on a salary basis and were advanced farm produce, which they repaid at a nominal rate. The farm also regularly employed teenage boys part-time until age eighteen, allowing them to work when not in school. The farm initially had several successful crop years and raised enough vegetable produce to meet resident's needs and a surplus they could sell back to the government or the public.[131]

Purchase of the Lebret Métis Farm was part of Douglas's provincial plan for Métis rehabilitation. However, it was first necessary to evaluate the Métis' social and economic situation, prompting the Department of Social Welfare and Rehabilitation to conduct a broad survey of Métis across the province to determine their need for rehabilitation. This included surveying Métis settlements at Crescent Lake, Crooked Lake, Duck Lake, Canwood, Baljennie, Lestock, Glen Mary, Willow Bunch, and Green Lake. For the Fort Qu'Appelle and Lebret areas, the Department relied on surveys conducted in the summer of 1943 by E.J. Brandt, superintendent of schools for the Department of Education.[132] While demonstrating significant Métis poverty across the province, these surveys also laid bare the racism and discrimination Métis faced from their non-Indigenous neighbours.

Brandt found seventy-seven Métis families in the Qu'Appelle region, including ninety-three individuals at Fort Qu'Appelle and 257 in the Rural Municipality of North Qu'Appelle No.187, and Lebret.[133] He reported on general living conditions, social relationships with neighbours, employment and education opportunities, and potential rehabilitation opportunities.[134] He recorded his biases and captured the general attitude of local business owners, school teachers, the RCMP stationed in Fort Qu'Appelle, the secretary-treasurer of the municipality, and the Catholic priest at Lebret. Overwhelmingly, they blamed the Métis character and home life for their economic and social situation. The Métis, Brandt reported, were seen by their settler neighbours as lazy, untrustworthy, petty thieves, unable to learn, prone to drinking and violence, and that they should not be trusted to handle their own financial affairs.[135] He concluded that the Métis "problem [was] not entirely welfare as much as health and home management, with education." Brandt's conclusions, while damning, are not surprising considering the similar perception of Métis by the municipal council or in other settler spaces during this period.[136]

Undeniably, Brandt provided a condemning view of the Métis, typical of the racist stereotypes of Indigenous peoples prevalent in all the surveys. He found at least a dozen families living on the road allowance at Katepwa Lake, with about forty school-aged children. He described

Figure 44. Lebret Métis Farm, R-A26083. Photograph courtesy of Provincial Archives of Saskatchewan.

Figure 45. Lebret Métis Farm, R-B12457-18. Photograph courtesy of Provincial Archives of Saskatchewan. The family shown was not identified.

Figure 46. Lebret Métis Farm, R-B 12457-22. Photograph courtesy of Provincial Archives of Saskatchewan.

Figure 47. Lebret Métis Farm, R-B 12457-31. Photograph courtesy of Provincial Archives of Saskatchewan.

their living conditions as "deplorable," with large families living in one or two rooms. He claimed that most homes were untidy, and the people were dirty despite Métis insistence they were consistently busy with housework. Further he noted that the Métis lacked personal pride and were gullible. They lacked acceptable social manners and took advantage of friendships with those not Métis. As a result, most local citizens, he reported, refused to engage with them in social circles. The Métis lacked interest in any recreation, preferring to take "taxis" and "car rides" rather than walking. They were prone to drinking alcohol and partying and had little interest in education.[137]

Further, Brandt reported that the Métis were poor students, and many could not learn. The children did not speak English "even reasonably well," nor could they read or write in English.[138] At the Lebret school, approximately one-third of the student body was Métis. He noted problems with health, cleanliness, and poor attendance, and an added financial burden on schools with a high number of Métis students because most of their parents did not contribute to the tax base that supported the schools.[139] The Fort Qu'Appelle school principal told Brandt that the home environment was to blame for the Métis lack of interest in education. Sister Olive at the Lebret school concurred, blaming Métis students' inability to learn on their diet, as most did not have enough to eat and what they did have was not nourishing.

Brandt reported that the Métis did not socialize with their non-Indigenous neighbours and that alcohol was a significant issue amongst them. Some attended Church socials, but the majority spent their time visiting friends and relatives. There were few recreational opportunities, encouraging men to spend their free time drinking, especially on Saturday nights, where they were accepted by local bar owners, at least until they spent all their money. The RCMP constable stationed at Fort Qu'Appelle and the parish priest relayed that the Métis misused the Mother's Allowance, Old Age Pension, and other forms of social aid to purchase alcohol. This prompted both to suggest public supervision of Métis funds as beneficial in ensuring they could only purchase food and clothing. This, the priest remarked, would be an important step in helping the Métis, but very difficult to administer.[140] The RCMP constable agreed, noting that "it was not unusual for the hotel (the only source of beer) to have upward of $3,000 in cheques cashed by the hotel keeper for the men of the community. It is a well known fact that the family allowance is abused, and the women are beaten by the men to get it, but they refuse to prosecute. Everyone is aware of this but cannot stop the situation."[141]

Brandt recounted that employment was becoming increasingly scarce for the Métis. There was no work in the winter, but casual labour opportunities in road building and with the railway existed in the summer. There was also some employment opportunity, mainly for young women, as domestics and skilled help at the nearby federal Department of Indian Affairs hospital and the provincial tuberculosis sanatorium. But these opportunities mattered little, as Brandt implied that it was the Métis' character that kept them unemployed. They could not be relied upon by their employers, as they had a habit of working for a brief time and quitting once they got paid. Mr. Hiebert, a local business owner, was asked about employing Métis; he responded that the Métis were a "lazy bunch working for a short time earning enough for a few drinks and quitting." Similarly, Mr. Rose, secretary-treasurer of the rural municipality, who had ample experience dealing with Métis relief, was unsympathetic, calling them "a lazy bunch that exist on little or nothing" that only work when forced to.[142]

Finally, Brandt reported prospects for Métis rehabilitation including expanding the Métis Farm and continuing to train the Métis to become independent, self-reliant farmers. He also suggested creating a cooperative market garden or a fish filleting plant, or encouraging the Métis to engage in commercial fishing or cutting and selling ice in the winter.[143] For women, the priest noted that a cottage industry for producing rugs might continue to exist during the summer, marketing to the tourist traffic around the lakes. Regardless, the priest noted, the possibility of Métis "success must be based on a long-term effort aimed at changing their entire mode of living."[144]

Additional questionnaires used to survey individual Métis families provide a less biased and perhaps more accurate representation of their lives at this time.[145] Most families grew vegetable gardens to produce what they needed for the winter. Some had a surplus of potatoes that they sold to a local merchant to purchase supplies and pay off debts, while others with less had to purchase potatoes. Several indicated they were at least seasonally employed, working as farm labourers and on the railway. Others commercial fished in the winter, did odd jobs and carpentry in the summer, or worked at the sanatorium or as caretakers at local beaches that lined the Qu'Appelle Lakes. By the mid-twentieth century a vibrant resort economy had developed in the region, drawing weekend tourists and cottagers, many from the city of Regina. Métis women found seasonal work cleaning cottages, or more year-round employment at the local hotel or café or as domestics for farm families. Few admitted they were on social aid, while others divulged that they would like relief and steady employment if they could get it.

The Department of Social Welfare and Rehabilitation hoped the surveys would help determine a further course of action to help the Métis.[146] The need for economic support and concerns for public health supervision, child welfare, and education demonstrated a need for rehabilitation. But the question that the government had remained: if the Métis were not industrious, if their homes and yards were not clean and tidy, their children unkempt and poorly fed, and the men prone to drinking and laziness, could they even be successfully rehabilitated?

The surveys did little to assist the provincial government create a coherent plan to help the Métis, except for expanding their efforts to include other farm colonies and community development projects at Crescent Lake, Crooked Lake, Duck Lake, Glen Mary, Willow Bunch, and others. In July 1946, Saskatchewan Métis Society leaders and about thirty Métis from across the province met with Premier Douglas, Minister of Social Welfare O.W. Valleau, and other government members to discuss solutions to the Métis issue. Several Qu'Appelle Valley Métis were present, including J.Z. Larocque, who were seemingly influenced by the outcome of the Ewing Commission in Alberta, and advocated for the government to implement a Royal Commission or committee to study the Métis situation in Saskatchewan, take a census of Métis and compile statistics of their social and economic status. Most importantly, however, Métis leaders advocated that tracts of land be set aside for the Métis, each big enough to accommodate twenty to fifty families where they could farm.[147]

Although Douglas had assured the Métis that his government was sympathetic to their situation and were looking for strategies to help the Métis help themselves, later actions of the premier's legal adviser Dr. Morris Shumiatcher demonstrated government's frustration. Communicating to all provincial ministers, Shumiatcher maintained the difficulty in planning for Métis rehabilitation because of the lack of information about their numbers, location, needs, and problems.[148] Despite the recent surveys and advice of Métis leaders, the government remained ill-informed and took only piecemeal action.[149]

Provincial measures helped, but the Rural Municipality of North Qu'Appelle continued to struggle with what to do about the Métis. They again considered a campaign to move the Métis off the road allowance and out of the municipality altogether. They had considered the large-scale movement of Métis before, as early as February 1930, when they met with neighbouring rural municipalities facing similar challenges and struck a committee to study the issue and petition the government to urge Métis relocation to northern Saskatchewan.[150] Now in 1948, the municipal council was again considering relocation. They passed a motion to relocate the Métis to northern Saskatchewan where they would have access to land and where fishing and trapping were more favourable.[151] Council likely made this motion in response to a resolution made at the annual Saskatchewan Association of Rural Municipalities (SARM) Convention only a month prior, where representatives from rural municipalities across the province discussed the increasing financial burden of Métis aid. SARM passed two resolutions regarding the Métis. First, they requested the province take full responsibility for the Métis, and second, that the province relocate the Métis to locations where they could become self-sufficient, responsible citizens.[152] By the late 1940s, the Rural Municipality of North Qu'Appelle was one of thirty-nine across the province dealing with the Métis issue, many of which were considering similar resettlement.[153]

The government reviewed these resolutions and presented them to representatives of the three prairie provinces at a meeting convened 13 July 1949, to discuss shared challenges each faced in dealing with the Métis. K.F. Forster, director of social aid for Saskatchewan, outlined the province's actions in creating farm and community development projects, to which Minister of Social Welfare J.H. Sturdy maintained that the Métis situation was not improving but getting worse despite government intervention. Representatives of the three provinces agreed to each strike an inter-departmental committee within their government to create a plan for the Métis in their respective provinces, which they would circulate to each other at a later meeting.[154] Forster and Sturdy spoke in depth about the actions taken in Saskatchewan to address the Métis issue, addressing the recent relocation of twenty-one Métis families, or about 100 people, from the road allowances near Lestock, north of the Qu'Appelle Valley, to Green Lake in north central Saskatchewan.[155] Green Lake was home to a large Métis rehabilitative colony created under the Patterson government and quickly endorsed by Tommy Douglas's government when elected in 1944. The colony served as a model for additional Métis farms across southern and central Saskatchewan, including the farm at Lebret. Historian F. Laurie Barron argues the Green Lake colony was to be "an administrative experiment in social engineering through which various provincial services would be delivered to a specific disadvantaged group."[156] It was to provide 125 Métis families, most but not all from the immediate Green Lake area, with forty-acre plots of land on a ninety-nine-year lease as well as assistance in farming and building homes. A large central farm, under the control of the provincial government, was also part of the plan, established with necessary farm machinery and supervision to train Métis in farming and raising livestock.[157]

While advertised as a supportive rehabilitative measure in line with CCF socialist philosophy, the forced removal to Green Lake was a pivotal, and traumatic, moment for Lestock Métis and for all Métis across the province, including those in the Qu'Appelle Valley. Removal ensured that the Métis were no longer a financial burden to the Lestock municipality, but it did little to benefit the families, who, familiar with farm labour and the prairie landscape, reached Green Lake ill-prepared for the upcoming winter and the parkland and forested environment. The relocation broke apart extended family groupings and ultimately dispersed the community, signalling to Métis across southern and central Saskatchewan the lengths provincial and municipal governments were willing to take in addressing what these governments perceived as the "Métis Problem." Former Métis leader Jim Sinclair, who experienced the move as a child, notes that the removal was motivated by the provincial government's shame, guilt, and embarrassment about the Métis situation. Although done under the guise of helping the Métis, it was "really to clear the land of our people. [To] try to shift us where no one was.... It was to get rid of us and put us in the North. Whether we survived or not, they didn't care." [158] This relocation, he reminds, was "a government experiment" to solve the provincial government's "Problem" of what to do with the Métis.[159]

Preparing to make the trip, families loaded their meagre possessions, sometimes including their horses and wagons, into train cars for the trip north.[160] Most took only what they could, leaving behind equipment, tents, furniture, and even sentimental items, believing that they could return to their homes if things did not work out in Green Lake.[161] This was a mistake as municipal agents lit the Métis' homes on fire before the train even left the station, ensuring, and sending a message to the Métis that they could not return.[162] Sinclair and others described the removal process, the burning of homes, and the scorn with which the Métis were treated.[163] According to Sinclair, "they moved all our little belongings into the boxcars. I remember that as a boy and one of the things that really bothered me and it still bothers me today, our people lived in tar paper shacks, you know and, very little shelter and as these people left their community with all their stuff piled on their wagons and chairs and the little bit they had, the houses were purposely set on fire as they were leaving, as if to say it to them, these people 'Don't ever come back here again.'"[164]

Isador Pelletier, who grew up in the Lestock road allowance community they called the Chicago Line, remembered the community's forced removal in 1949 and the shock of watching their homes burn. This was an extremely difficult time, where provincial and municipal agents moved through the community, coercing families to relocate to Green Lake with promises of employment opportunities, education for children, land, and houses.[165] Families were divided on whether or not to relocate. Many were reluctant to move and unsure of why they were being pressured to leave. Many were skeptical of the move because "there was so much propaganda about this Green Lake move, and how things were going to change and how people would own land and how people would find a way of life they'd be, you know, they'd be happy with."[166] Isador Pelletier similarly recalled the uncertainty and hesitation many felt. The situation was made worse, he recalled, by the fact that select Métis individuals were solicited by the government to help convince families to move. Not wanting to name names, Isador noted a certain individual who worked hard to convince families to move, promising them education for their children, which ultimately encouraged many to move. Others, Henry Pelletier and Myrtle Lafontaine suggest, were encouraged by the promise of forty acres of land, assistance to set up their farms and build houses, or simply in hopes of a better life at Green Lake.[167]

The skepticism many felt was warranted. When they reached Green Lake, the Métis quickly realized that not all was as promised. Government workers provided little assistance, instead disparagingly judging the Métis character, calling them lazy and treating them poorly.[168] Families were given little support in finding homes or jobs, and the Métis already present in Green Lake were not overly receptive to the newcomers. Isador Pelletier recalled his father faced significant challenges finding a job, housing, or even supporting the family by trapping.[169] Southern Métis competed with northern locals for scarce available jobs, and there were few, if any, traplines that were not already being worked by northerners. There was little housing available, which forced most to live in tents until they could build their own homes. However, families soon realized they needed permits and would be required to pay for each log that they cut, something they could not afford. Perhaps most significantly, the land they had been promised was solid bush that needed clearing before it could be worked. Living in the north proved different, difficult, and extremely frustrating for southern Métis, prompting most to abandon Green Lake. Dispersed from the road allowance, these families had nowhere to go. Some returned to the road allowances near Lestock where they found their homes and possessions destroyed, while others attempted to start over in other communities. Many, like Isador Pelletier's and Jim Sinclair's families, eventually made their way to Regina in search of economic opportunity, where they took up residence on the outskirts of the city, in makeshift tent villages in the city's nuisance grounds.[170] Ultimately, the CCF's Lestock-Green Lake removal scheme was short-sighted and failed the Métis. While it removed them from the road allowance and from municipal view, it did not solve the social, financial, or political problem they posed for the provincial government; rather, it only dispersed these families once again to other marginalized spaces.

Unlike the Lestock municipality, the Qu'Appelle municipal council took no immediate action on relocation, despite having passed a motion in 1948 to do so.[171] By 1950, they remained concerned about the financial burden of the Métis and continued to pressure government for solutions. They attempted once more to work through the Saskatchewan Association of Rural Municipalities, asking for a special meeting at their annual convention to deal with the Métis issue. They also appealed to the Liberal MP for the nearby Melville constituency, V.P. Deshaye, to raise the matter with the premier and ask that the province accept full financial responsibility for the Métis. Deshaye did write to the premier but got nowhere with the municipality's request.[172] Instead, Douglas reminded Deshaye that the government's plan to help the Métis included removal and relocation and then reprimanded Deshaye for publicly opposing such a movement while privately asking the government to act.[173] Days earlier, Deshaye had challenged the Department of Social Welfare's Lestock relocation plan in the legislature, citing the relocation's failure. As a result, the Qu'Appelle municipality's request to the premier died with Deshaye.

Despite the municipal council's many and varied attempts at alleviating its financial responsibility for the Métis, challenges remained. Neither the municipality nor the province took action to move Métis from Qu'Appelle Valley road allowances to the north, although it had been considered more than once. For now, the Lebret Métis Farm supported at least a small segment of the Métis population, easing some financial stress on the municipality. A model of success for the province, it offered Métis families employment opportunities and was one of a confluence of factors that removed Qu'Appelle Métis from the road allowance.

The "Métis Problem" in the Qu'Appelle Valley, as municipal and provincial governments perceived it, had been building for decades. The 1930s Depression ushered in an era of intensified poverty, already widespread amongst the Métis. Municipal relief efforts brought some support, but the sheer numbers of Métis reliant on relief taxed already stretched municipal budgets. Direct relief and work-for-wages programs, including road building and farm employment programs, were cost-shared between municipal, provincial, and federal governments, and required regular and sometimes constant renegotiation. This increasingly brought public attention to the Métis situation, creating tension and debate between municipal and provincial governments over who was fiscally responsible.

The election of T.C. Douglas and the CCF in 1944 ushered in an era of new public policy that adopted the language of rehabilitation and created a series of work colonies, including the Lebret Métis Farm, aimed at removing the Métis from the road allowances, training them to become farmers, and making the Métis economically self-sustaining.

The farm provided homes and employment for several families, but many more remained in their road allowance communities. These relief and rehabilitation measures increased municipal and provincial surveillance of the Métis, propelling their social, economic, and health concerns into public view and exacerbating the racism the Métis faced from municipal administrators and their settler neighbours.

By the 1940s, Qu'Appelle Métis found it increasingly difficult to make a living, especially for those living on the road allowances who, before the Depression, were accustomed to casual and seasonal farm labour. Some left the community searching for employment, while others, including women, found work in the burgeoning cottage and tourist industry growing up around the Qu'Appelle Lakes by the 1950s.

By mid-century, the Rural Municipality of North Qu'Appelle, like others across southern Saskatchewan, contemplated widespread removal and relocation of the Métis that did not materialize. Those who remained reliant on municipal or provincial social aid were seen as a nuisance and an impediment to development. The Métis' continued poverty garnered little public sympathy. Municipal and provincial governments became a looming presence in Métis lives, intervening to an unprecedented extent and making their private lives public in ways not seen before. This left the Métis with few choices and little autonomy. Limited options combined with the lure of employment and educational opportunities in nearby cities encouraged movement of Métis off the road allowance and, for many, out of the Qu'Appelle Valley into the 1950s.

Conclusion

MÉTIS FAMILIES FIRST came to the Qu'Appelle Valley region as buffalo hunters in the mid-nineteenth century. Families originally occupied wintering camps on a seasonal basis, but as the dwindling herds moved further westward, a year-round settlement grew around the Roman Catholic Mission and along the Qu'Appelle Lakes. By the late 1860s, there was a significant and growing number of Métis calling the Qu'Appelle Valley home. These families maintained a subsistence lifestyle, relying initially on buffalo, supplemented by hunting, and trapping other wild game, harvesting wild plants, and engaging in small-scale gardening and agriculture to varying degrees. This routine was carried over from their experience with the Hudson's Bay Company posts or their time in the Red River region. For these families, the buffalo hunt defined social, economic, and political structures. Hunt organization reflected Métis extended family kinship relationships, self-governance, and understandings of the prairie landscape where they lived and hunted in extended family groupings and organized themselves to strategically utilize all available environmental resources. The very structure of the large annual summer hunts demonstrated the way Métis privileged kinship relationships in responding to changing environmental and economic conditions. Within the hunt, there were clearly defined gender roles within which men and women worked in complementary ways as part of an integrated family economic unit. Women were responsible for buffalo processing, requiring intensive amounts of labour and expertise in the production of pemmican, meat, hides, and robes.

Métis women, like other Indigenous women across western Canada, contributed their labour to the functioning of the fur posts, working alongside their husbands and providing their labour in complementary ways. In exchange for rations and supplies, women provided gendered domestic services, and worked in planting and harvesting the post's gardens. The collaborative nature of men's and women's work in the posts' gardens, much like during the buffalo hunt, reveals few distinctions between gender roles; rather it was more important that all contribute their labour when necessary. This also applied when there were limited provisions at the fur posts. During these times, gender roles in supplying the posts with food were flexible, allowing women to supply small game, fish, and wild plants they harvested, contributing to the diet of their families and the HBC employees. As a result, women's labour contributions and expertise were essential not only to family subsistence and economic exchange in the success of the buffalo hunt, but also to feeding the trade itself.

The collapse of the buffalo herds forced the Métis to economically adjust. In the same way that seasonal occupation on the prairies had been an environmental adaptation in response to movement of the buffalo herds, the shift toward year-round occupation of land along the Qu'Appelle Lakes in the late 1860s was a response to changing resource availability. When taking up land on a permanent year-round basis, Métis families followed recognizable land tenure practices, utilizing land in a river-lot system and along kinship lines as they had always done. The role of female kinship in defining these settlement patterns was significant. Often families settled along female kinship lines, making decisions about how to maintain cultural connectedness, remain within the Valley environment, and provide for their families while at the same time adapting to economic change.

As the buffalo economy came to an end, Qu'Appelle Métis increasingly integrated into the settler economy. They took work where they could, gathering buffalo bones, picking rocks, or cutting wood, harvesting Seneca root and berries, and selling fish and the handmade products of women's labour to maintain their economic independence while also preserving their connections to the land. Compensation for their work was often in food or supplies families did not produce themselves, as they lived within a complex barter economy. In this work, Métis carried familiar labour roles forward and continued to work in an integrated family economy where all members contributed. Engaging in these types of wage-labour activities provided some economic stability and allowed Métis to continue their subsistence economy and remain living within an intimately understood and familiar environment. Most took on wage labour when available and some looked to agriculture to provide for their families. Though families farmed to varying degrees, there were examples where individuals achieved some success. Others practised very little or no agriculture other than gardening. For most, they continued to rely on a subsistence lifestyle, supplementing their income with seasonal wage labour, and using their knowledge of the Valley landscape, not as landowners but as labourers in a settler economy.

When families moved, they did so according to recognizable community formation patterns. When taking up scrip and homestead in the Qu'Appelle Valley and at Ste. Delphine in the File Hills region, or when moving on to the road allowances within the Valley region, families made decisions about how to remain and re-establish themselves along familiar extended kinship lines. Living in these family clusters reveals how Métis families sustained a worldview that privileged kinship relationships and connections to the land despite challenges of a new social, economic, and political order. How these families spatially organized themselves and utilized Valley resources was crucial to their understandings of identity and occupancy of this space.

As families increasingly immersed themselves in a settler economy, they felt the pressure of government policy, encroaching settlement, and continued economic changes. Métis families recognized and responded in individual and collective ways to the imposition of settler colonialism, government surveillance, and regulation over their lands and livelihoods. They vigorously advocated for access to lands and resources that would allow them to maintain their subsistence livelihoods and for recognition of their rights and title to land. Despite the government refusing to recognize Métis rights, they continued to petition various government agents looking to secure individual property ownership, advocating for access to resources, and, most importantly, recognition of their rights. This was a familiar political strategy used consistently by Qu'Appelle Métis to have their collective voices heard. The nature and frequency of this petitioning reveals the growth of a Métis political consciousness and reinforced collective identity amongst Qu'Appelle Métis not only regionally, but on the national scale. In their petitioning, Qu'Appelle Métis recognized and advocated for their own issues, but also larger issues facing Métis across the west.

When the federal government refused to act in dealing with Métis rights and grievances, Qu'Appelle Métis petitioned as a means of political action but also as a demonstration of sovereignty over their territory. The Métis well understood the changes that had taken place in Manitoba leading to the creation of the province in 1870 and the implementation of scrip to extinguish Métis title to land, as well as changes resulting closer to home with the negotiation of Treaty Four, the impending Dominion Land Survey, and unavoidable settlement. They feared encroachment on their plots of land and pursued means to be successful in safeguarding their livelihood while also adapting to a new order. Métis responded to these changes and found ways to voice their concerns and advocate for their rights, in individual and collective ways. They used petitioning throughout the 1870s and 1880s to have their rights recognized and to seek protections over their land tenure practices and livelihoods. The maintenance of these practices ensured families would live in proximity to one another and continue to rely on kinship relationships. In addition, such protections would ensure Métis maintained private ownership over their plots of land as well as collective access to hunting and fishing territory within the Valley environment. When faced with the imposition of unsympathetic and foreign Dominion Land and homestead policy that artificially divided Métis land holdings, they continued to advocate for their rights. Often, they found themselves in a precarious position, and in a three-way contest with First Nations and government for access to land in the Qu'Appelle Valley. With treaty signing, and the refusal of Métis petitions to enter treaty, the government recognized distinctions between First Nations and Métis that they applied to their dealings with Métis rights. According to the government, Métis landholders were viewed as regular settlers and did not have any pre-existing Indigenous land title, which forced Métis to register their pre-existing claims according to homestead policy. Although this did protect their private property interests, tensions remained high because it did nothing to recognize Métis rights, title, or access to lands and resources in the Valley.

Many were able to secure land title to the plots of land they occupied prior to survey. Their efforts to secure title were more so to remain in the Valley region than to take up agriculture on an increased scale. Instead of farming for themselves, many chose to work as labourers for new landowners. This was likely because they did not have the capital to invest in the required machinery and implements but also because they wanted to remain in their close-knit extended family groupings rather than take up land away from the community.

By 1885, as tensions were erupting across the North-West, the government chose to act on Métis claims. Through the North-West Half-Breed Claims Commission, Métis would finally have their rights and title recognized. In the implementation of the scrip process, Qu'Appelle Métis found themselves embedded in a foreign and bureaucratic administrative process, often unsympathetic to their needs. They were, however, astute in initially negotiating and securing provisions for what they believed would benefit them, including the rights to purchase their pre-existing or waterfront properties and the right to withdraw from treaty and access scrip. Administrative issues plagued the scrip process; most claimants ended up selling their scrip to land speculators for a fraction of their value. Selling their scrip provided Métis with an influx of short-term cash. The ultimate shortcoming of the scrip system, however, was that the exchange of land and money scrip differed and ultimately encouraged speculation and the removal of land from the Métis. Despite this, there were instances where Métis benefited on a more long-term basis. Some were able to exchange their scrip certificates for homestead land in the File Hills where families once again reorganized themselves along recognizable cultural patterns and kinship lines. In a few short decades the community of Ste. Delphine developed, and some individuals had some success farming and ranching. Most, however, struggled economically and ultimately sold or lost their lands, returning to the Qu'Appelle Valley. Here, they joined extended family members in the same economic situation: displaced within the Qu'Appelle Valley by increased settlement, these families took up residence on the road allowances along township lines and the lakeshores. For most Métis, scrip and homestead policy did little to change the Métis economic situation or secure long-term land tenure.

Qu'Appelle Métis resisted settler colonialism, demonstrating acts of sovereignty, and politically claiming their spaces despite challenges, disregard, and government refusal to recognize Métis rights. But it gradually seeped into almost all aspects of Métis life. When confronted with fisheries regulation, they challenged government agents and authorities so they could continue to make a living and practise their subsistence economy. As government intervention into Métis lives and livelihoods increased into the twentieth century, regulation of Métis fishing intensified. The Métis responded with continued collective political action, petitioning both the federal Department of Fisheries and the provincial government to provide relief in the form of free fishing licences. Throughout this period of increased surveillance, Métis maintained and adapted harvesting practices and resisted intrusion into their spaces by government agents. In the 1930s, petition signatories included women for the first time, demonstrating a growing politicization of Métis and the role of women in their communities. Within this environment, the local municipal government and state agents on occasion acted benevolently toward the Métis. However, as Métis needs intensified during the Depression, the Rural Municipality of North Qu'Appelle advocated to abdicate their financial responsibility for the Métis. Métis on the road allowance, they argued, were squatters who did not contribute to the local tax base and therefore should be a provincial, not municipal, responsibility. By the 1940s, disputes over financial responsibility brought Métis lives and poverty into public view revealing the dark underbelly of contempt, disdain, and racism the Métis faced in settler society. Government sporadically yielded to Métis needs, but only on a temporary basis according to what was most immediate and fiscally prudent. The provincial government and the local rural municipality remained burdened by the financial cost of Métis within their jurisdictions and considered various measures to remove the Métis from the road allowance. This included the creation of the Lebret Métis Farm as a rehabilitative measure to train Métis to become farmers and assimilate into mainstream society. While early years on the farm indicated that it could become a success, it supported only a small portion of Qu'Appelle families. As such, there proved to be no easy or uncomplicated solutions for the Métis and by the early 1950s, most had moved off the road allowances into nearby villages, towns, and cities, looking for education and employment.

As Qu'Appelle Métis adapted to changing economic conditions, they maintained an integrated family economy where roles were complementary and defined by gender yet flexible in response to labour demands and immediate needs. Their economy shifted over time from buffalo hunting to wage labour, but they continued to rely on the land they knew to make a living. For many Métis on the road allowance, they no longer owned the land they lived on but still utilized their knowledge of the Valley environment in providing their labour to other farmers. In this shifting economy, all members contributed their labour and women continued to have important roles in feeding the family. As ever, Métis engaged in land-use activities and labour to ensure the well-being of their families and community.

Métis women recognized the essential role of food production to their economy, but also the social and political commitments that food facilitated. Women were responsible for feeding their families by gathering, preparing, and preserving wild foods as well as by growing large vegetable gardens. Métis women engaged in a variety of activities, using their skills and expertise related to land use and food production that they had learned from their own mothers and grandmothers. They demonstrated decision making and were flexible in their activities and in their contribution to the family economy.

The food women prepared was an important part of all Métis social gatherings and celebrations. On these occasions, Métis women served the finest food available and worked diligently to treat all guests hospitably. These women understood the impact a fine meal, hospitality, and generosity could have on social, political, and economic relationships. Women were creative and flexible in adding variety to their diet and in preparing appetizing and flavourful dishes from simple, and often very few, ingredients.

Métis women found opportunity to engage in a cash economy outside of the home, working as domestics in the homes of their husbands' employers or by selling the products of their labour. They did this while also remaining responsible for domestic responsibilities within the family. In many instances, women marketed their traditional artistic and sewing skills, handed down to them over generations, to bring additional income and necessary food and supplies into the home. Women's roles in the family changed as they aged, but the respect they received for their knowledge and skills did not diminish. These women played a significant role in cultural continuity including the transmission of cultural values, practices, and understandings to younger generations.

Métis families did not fully engage in a cash economy but harvested or produced for themselves many of the foods they required. They also traded and bartered for additional staple items, using their labour as currency. Families took advantage of economic opportunities and adapted to the growing settler agrarian economy in ways that were recognizable and familiar. Even when forced out of necessity to seek out Depression-era relief, the Métis traded their labour for what little relief they did receive. They did not completely accept a foreign and imposed way of life but were selective in how they adapted and what elements of their worldview and subsistence economies they maintained.

When families moved, they resettled along past community formation practices that privileged kinship and followed familiar land-use patterns. For Qu'Appelle Métis families, kinship relationships were central to their worldview and how they understood themselves in this space. They made choices about how to remain in extended family groupings and remain within traditional territory to reaffirm cultural connectedness, relationships, and family. They made choices to live as an extended family rather than relocate, disperse, or move to a different area, at least initially. Métis settlement in the Valley was a continuation of past community organizational structures and occupancy patterns. Each time these families moved within their territory, they resettled along extended family groupings and adapted to changing economic, social, and political situations.

The overarching story of the Qu'Appelle Métis is a story of change and adaptation, but also of stability, resistance, and resilience. This work traces Qu'Appelle Valley Métis economic activity and changes in land occupancy from the 1850s to 1950, with a focus on food production and gender roles. When faced with economic and political change, Qu'Appelle Métis relied upon recognizable community formation patterns and understandings of kinship relationships when making decisions about how to remain within familiar territory. When trying to maintain occupancy of this territory, they responded in individual and collective ways to the increasing settler colonialism and government surveillance they faced. Despite their best efforts, the noose of colonialism tightened around their necks in the early decades of the twentieth century as racism toward the Métis normalized, solidifying their erasure and their removal from the road allowance.

Viewing this history through the lens of family, gender, resistance, and resilience connects individual and community stories to the Qu'Appelle Valley and fixes commonly held values, community practices, protocols, and mutual responsibilities to this place. Métis Old People regularly repeated the phrase "Down there in the Valley" as they began their stories. In its repetition, this phrase links these families and their stories to the Qu'Appelle Valley landscape and imbues it with meaning, confirming that escalating government intervention, surveillance, and settler colonialism did not sever Métis connections to the land. Supplementing these stories with family genealogies and Historical Geographic Information Systems methodologies links people and their stories to the spaces that are important to them, privileging Métis value systems and perspectives. This is particularly important for telling Indigenous stories so deeply rooted in local landscapes. The Qu'Appelle Valley, "their Valley," remains central to how these families and communities continue to understand themselves and their history. These stories, then, constitute a narrative framework that explains Métis road allowance communities and Métis presence in the Valley region historically and contemporarily. These stories illuminate social, economic, and cultural activity where Métis lived according to a worldview defined by extended family networks, the responsibility individuals had to one another in both their immediate and extended family, as well as their relationship to the Valley landscape, revealing how road allowance communities were and are spaces of both resistance and resilience.

Notes

Introduction

1 Sealey and Lucier, *The Métis*; McLean, *Home from the Hill*. In the Dominion Land Survey, meridian and range lines run north-south, converging at the poles. Due to the earth's curvature, township lines at the northern boundary of each township measure slightly less then at its base. Consequently, moving north, each township gets slightly smaller. If no corrections were made, townships would get significantly smaller the further north they were measured from the 49th parallel. To keep townships consistent in size and compensate for the converging range lines, surveyors created corrections lines in the second township north of the 49th parallel and at every fourth township thereafter. At each correction line, the township was slightly displaced. This made the township slightly larger than the township directly south of it, compensating for the convergence. For more information, see McKercher and Wolfe, *Land Survey System*.

2 Campbell, *Road Allowance People*.

3 The North-West Territories was transferred to the Canadian government in 1870 at the same time as Rupert's Land. A federal territory, it was administered by the Department of the Interior that had been created in 1873. The region covered a vast area, stretching west from Labrador, across the northern portions of present-day Quebec and Ontario, through the Prairies to British Columbia, and north from the 49th parallel to the Arctic Ocean. The province of Manitoba was carved out of the territory in 1870 followed by Saskatchewan and Alberta in 1905. The remaining territory was renamed the Northwest Territories in 1906.

4 Located in southeast Saskatchewan, the Qu'Appelle Valley formed as a glacial spillway 14,000 years ago. Water filled the Valley as the glacier retreated. As the water receded, the valley became rich with plants, fish, and game resources. In some places, the Valley is 180 metres deep and varies in width from 1.6 to 3.2 kilometres. The north-facing slopes have a thick covering of various species of trees and shrubs, while the drier south-facing slopes have fewer trees and short dry grass

ground cover. The Valley bottom is a mixed riparian environment and was at one time largely covered in native prairie grasses, at least until broken by the plough in the late nineteenth and early twentieth centuries. The Qu'Appelle River flows through the Valley and has been a vital transportation network. The river flows east from Lake Diefenbaker, to join the Assiniboine River in Manitoba, south of Lake of the Prairies, connecting people and goods throughout the Great Plains. The river feeds six major lakes: Pasqua, Echo, Mission, and Katepwa Lakes—known as the Qu'Appelle Lakes or the Fishing Lakes—and Crooked and Round Lakes further east.

5 There are no true buffalo native to North America. The species commonly referred to as buffalo is either Plains bison (*Bison bisòn Bison*) or Wood bison (*Bison bison Athabascau*). I choose to use the term bison and buffalo interchangeably as buffalo was the term used during the period being studied.

6 Macdougall and St-Onge, "Rooted in Mobility."

7 The Qu'Appelle Valley territory has, at different times, been dominated by the A'aninin, Nakota, Nêhiyawak, and Métis. From the 1690s to 1790s it was occupied by the A'aninin with the Nakoda and Nêhiyawak beginning to move in. By 1821, the Nakota continued to be centred in the Souris River and Qu'Appelle River regions, while the Nêhiyawak moved into the Touchwood Hills region, north of the Qu'Appelle. After 1821, the Nakota moved out of the area, gravitating towards the international border in response to contracting buffalo herds and to trade at American fur posts. As they vacated the territory, the Nêhiyawak moved southward into the Souris River and Qu'Appelle River regions. See Ray, *Indians in the Fur Trade.*

8 Vrooman, *"The Whole Country was . . . 'One Robe'"*; Thompson, *Red Sun.*

9 Milloy, *The Plains Cree*; Vrooman, *"The Whole Country was . . . 'One Robe.'"*

10 Morton, "The Battle of Grand Coteau."

11 Cunfer and Waiser, eds, *Bison and People*; Flores, "Bison Ecology"; Sherow, "Workings of the Geodialectic High Plains Indians and Their Horses"; Dobak, "Killing the Canadian Buffalo; Hämäläinen, "The First Phase of Destruction; Colpitts, "Provisioning the HBC."

12 Cunfer, "Overview," 18–24.

13 Dorion and Préfontaine, "Deconstructing Métis Historiography"; Ens, *Homeland to Hinterland*; Ens, "Dispossession or Adaptation?"; Mailhot and Sprague, "Persistent Settlers."

14 Ray, Miller, and Tough, eds. *Bounty and Benevolence*; Miller, *Compact, Contract, Covenant*; Daschuk, *Clearing the Plains.*

15 Payment, "Batoche After 1885"; Payment, *Free People.*

16 McKay, "The Liberal Order Framework," 1154.

17 Payment, "Batoche After 1885"; Payment, *Free People.*

18 Campbell, "Foreword," xiv.

19 Sealey and Lucier, *The Métis*, 5; McLean, *Home From the Hill*, 7; Barron, *Moccasins*; Barron, "The CCF and the Development of Métis Colonies."

20 Sealey and Lucier, *The Métis*, 144.
21 Barron, *Moccasins*, 7.
22 Barron, 7.
23 Campbell, "Foreword," xiv. The forced removal and burning of homes are widely discussed in Métis oral histories from the Lestock and Punnichy areas of southern Saskatchewan. See also Zeilig and Zeilig, *Ste. Madeleine*.
24 Campbell, *Halfbreed*; Zeilig and Zeilig, *Ste. Madeleine*; Waiser, *Saskatchewan's Playground*; St. Pierre, *Remembering*; Massie, *Forest Prairie Edge*; Herriot, *Towards a Prairie Atonement*.
25 There are numerous oral histories and oral history collections held by the Gabriel Dumont Institute of Native Studies and Applied Research (www.metismuseum.ca) and the Provincial Archives of Saskatchewan relating specifically to the Métis experience in Saskatchewan. There is also a growing body of autobiographies, oral stories, memoirs, and community histories based on this oral history, relating more broadly to Métis experiences across the prairie provinces. One of the first, and most significant in its documentation of the Métis experience in the early to mid-twentieth century in Saskatchewan, is Maria Campbell's autobiography *Halfbreed*. See Campbell, *Halfbreed;* Adams, *Prison of Grass;* Zeilig and Zeilig, *Ste. Madeleine;* Campbell, *Road Allowance People;* Belcourt, *Walking in the Woods;* St. Pierre, *Remembering;* Moine Trottier, *Remembering Will Have to Do;* Pelletier, *Lebret*. Recently, literary author Trevor Herriot has documented Ste. Madeleine Métis experiences in Herriot, *Towards a Prairie Atonement*. There is also a growing body of academic scholarship that utilizes oral histories demonstrating Métis experiences following 1885. See St-Onge, "Memories of Métis Women of St. Eustache"; LaVallée, *St. Laurent*; Payment, *Free People*; Payment, "Batoche After 1885"; Payment, "'La Vie en Rose?'"
26 Michif is the language spoken by Métis peoples in Manitoba, Saskatchewan, North Dakota, and Montana. It is a combination of Nêhiyaw and French, but also borrows from English and other Indigenous languages. Métis from Michif-speaking communities commonly use the term as a marker of Indigenous identity.
27 Van Kirk, *Many Tender Ties;* Brown, *Strangers in Blood;* Carter, Erickson, and Roome, "Introduction," 4.
28 Kubik and Marchildon, *Women's History,* 1; Smillie, "The Invisible Workforce"; Millions, "Breaking the Mould."
29 Carter, *Imperial Plots*; Carter, "Daughters of British Blood"; Carter, *Lost Harvest;* Carter, "First Nations Women of Prairie Canada"; Carter, *The Importance of Being Monogamous.* Carter's recent work, *Imperial Plots,* shifts the focus away from men, adding a complicated gendered perspective to Western Canadian historiography, and to the roles women, including Indigenous women, played in agricultural settlement of the west. This work however limits Indigenous women's agricultural experiences to the period prior to the Dominion Land Survey and does not address their exclusion from these settlement processes.
30 St-Onge, "Memories," 46–47.

31 McCallum, *Indigenous Women*, 6.

32 McCallum, 5.

33 McCallum, 6.

34 Farrell Racette, "Sewing Ourselves"; Farrell Racette, "Sewing for a Living."

35 White, *Land Use, Environment and Social Change*; Cronon, *Changes in the Land*; Pyne, *Fire in America*; Boyd, *Indians, Fire and The Land*; Vale, ed., *Fire, Native Peoples, and the Natural Landscape.*

36 The term "Valley" used throughout refers to the Qu'Appelle Valley.

37 Belasco, "Food Matters," 2.

38 Belasco, 4.

39 Loo, *States of Nature*; Calliou, "Losing the Game"; Thorpe, *Tangled Wild;* Colpitts, *Game in the Garden*; Sandlos, *Hunters at the Margins*; Jacoby, *Crimes Against Nature;* Foster, *Working for Wildlife*; Gulig, "'We Beg the Government.'"

40 This idea of the Qu'Appelle Valley builds on environmental historian Geoff Cunfer's assessment of the Great Plains as neither a story of progress or decline, but as a sort of middle ground where human interaction with the environment is much more nuanced, complex, and ambiguous. See Cunfer, *On the Great Plains.*

41 Payment, "Batoche After 1885"; Payment, "'La Vie en Rose?'"; St-Onge, "Memories"; LaVallée, *St. Laurent*; Macdougall, *One of the Family*; Peters, Stock, and Werner, *Roostertown.*

Chapter 1. "Down There in the Valley": Introducing Bob and Margaret

1 Welsh, "Voices of the Grandmothers," 18.

2 Basso, *Wisdom Sits in Places.*

3 Basso, 74.

4 Cavendar Wilson, "Grandmother to Granddaughter."

5 *Li Vyeu* means "Old Person" or "Elder" in the Michif language. I use the terms Old People, cultural teacher, and Knowledge Keeper to recognize those that hold various forms of knowledge in the Métis community. These are terms selected by individuals I have worked with throughout this study to describe the types of knowledge they possess. This includes cultural and spiritual knowledge, teachings, oral stories, songs, ceremonies, land-based knowledge, community and family history, community genealogical knowledge, and artistic practice. The term *Elder* has been used if requested by the individual.

6 Hooked rugs were a common art practice of Métis women in the early twentieth century. Made from scrap material and old cloths, these rugs were regularly made and sold by women, bringing income into the home. The practice is described in more detail in the following chapter.

7 Jacqueline Pelletier describes a similar research experience she had with Bob Desjarlais in her Master's thesis. See Pelletier, "The First of All Things."

8 Margaret Harrison, personal communication with author, 9 July 2009.

9 Gaudet, "Keeoukaywin." Indigenous scholars have increasingly emphasized relationality and the practice of visiting and storytelling as a decolonizing research practice. See also Smith, *Decolonizing Methodologies*; Kovach, *Indigenous Methodologies*; Wheeler, "Social Relations"; Archibald, *Indigenous Storywork;* Wilson, *Research Is Ceremony*; Absolon, *How We Come To Know;* Brown and Strega, eds., *Research as Resistance;* McGregor, Restoule, and Johnston, *Indigenous Research*; Andersen and O'Brien, *Sources and Methods in Indigenous Studies*; Anderson, *Life Stages of Native Women.*

10 Gaudet, "Keeoukaywin."

11 Wheeler, "Social Relations," 199–200.

12 Wheeler, 199–203; Campbell, *Road Allowance People,* 2.

13 Campbell, *Road Allowance People,* 2.

14 I also relied heavily on the Gabriel Dumont Institute's large collection of oral history interviews available on the Virtual Museum of Métis History and Culture (www.metismuseum.ca). This collection is invaluable, and undoubtedly the most comprehensive archival oral history collection reflecting the Saskatchewan Métis experience. Giving voice to Métis people and Métis women more specifically, these are valuable sources of evidence, revealing the racial prejudice and social and economic challenges road allowance Métis faced in the first half of the twentieth century.

15 Payment, *Free People*; Ens, *Homeland to Hinterland*; Devine, *People Who Own Themselves*; Foster, *We Know Who We Are*; Macdougall, "Wahkootowin"; Troupe, "Métis Women"; Macdougall, *One of the Family*; Brown, "Women as Centre."

16 I created a HGIS data set from available archival records, including Saskatchewan Homestead records, Dominion Land Survey maps, and federal census records capturing individual and household data relating to occupation, household size and composition, place of current and last residence, date of occupancy, length of residence on specific land locations, and types and scale of land improvements, including acres broken, fenced, and cropped.

17 Bodenhamer, Corrigan, and Harris, *Deep Maps and Spatial Narratives;* Ridge, Lafreniere, and Nesbit, "Creating Deep Maps and Spatial Narratives"; Fisher-Fiskin, "'Deep Maps"; Oxx, Brimicombe, and Rush, "Envisioning Deep Maps."

18 *Koohkoom* is Michif for Grandmother. Maross was a nickname for Emerance Bellegarde. She was married to Charlie Racette, while Flora Allary was married to Norbert Racette. Bob's paternal grandfather, Louis Racette, was Charlie and Norbert's brother.

19 Bob Desjarlais, interview, 15 May 2002.

20 Bob Desjarlais, interview, 3 July 2002. A coulee is a geological term used to describe a gully or ravine that was created by water erosion.

21 Delphine's parents were Jean Racette and Fred Fayant. Jean was the daughter of Florence Allary and Norbert Racette. Margaret's mother was Adeline Pelletier dit Racette, daughter of Louis Pelletier dit Racette and Marguerite Brabant.

22 Margaret Harrison and Mary Desnomie, interview, 30 March 2007; Margaret Harrison, interview, 10 July 2009; Margaret Harrison, interview, 12 February 2010; Margaret Harrison, interview, 24 February 2014; Margaret Harrison, interview, 9 July 2014; and Margaret Harrison, interview, 13 March 2022.

23 Margaret Harrison, interview, 12 February 2010.

24 Archer, ed. *Lake Katepwa*, 48.

25 Bob Desjarlais, interview, 15 May 2002.

26 Stooking grain is a method of harvesting, where cut-grain stalks or sheaves in the field are arranged upright to keep the grain heads off the ground and dry until threshing.

27 Norma Welsh and Joe Welsh, interview, 7–8 February 2004. Portions of this interview are available on the Gabriel Dumont Institute's Virtual Museum of Métis History and Culture, www.metismuseum.ca.

28 I have not been able to definitively determine when the original dam was built, but it was before 1911. In 1957, the provincial government constructed a more modern dam on Katepwa Lake, again upgraded in 2005.

29 The Katepwa School was built in 1887. A new school was constructed in 1919.

Chapter 2. Daughters of the Country: Women's Labour in the Métis World

1 Freed, *Daughters of the Country.*

2 Colpitts, *Pemmican Empire.*

3 Colpitts, 7–8.

4 Weekes, *Last Buffalo Hunter*, 60.

5 Cunfer and Waiser, eds., *Bison and People*; Dobak, "Killing the Canadian Buffalo"; Colpitts, "Provisioning the HBC."

6 Colpitts, *Pemmican Empire*, 148–88.

7 Colpitts, 199–200, 216.

8 Ross, *Red River*, 244.

9 Colpitts, *Pemmican Empire*, 214.

10 Ens, *Homeland to Hinterland.*

11 Beaudoin, "A Bison's View of the Landscape"; Brink, "Hunter's Quest."

12 Weekes, *Last Buffalo Hunter*. Norbert Welsh provides a list of the members of the buffalo hunting brigade under the leadership of Charles Trottier in the 1860s. The organization and history of this brigade is examined in more detail in: Troupe, "Métis Women," and Macdougall and St-Onge, "Rooted in Mobility."

13 Troupe, "Métis Women"; Brown, "Women as Centre"; Payment, *Free People*; Foster, *We Know Who We Are*; Macdougall and St-Onge, "Rooted in Mobility."

14 White Horse Plains or the parish of St. François Xavier is located approximately fifteen kilometres west of present-day Winnipeg. Pembina is located south of the Red River Settlement, at the confluence of the Red and Pembina Rivers.

15 St-Onge, Podruchny, and Macdougall, eds., *Contours of a People*; Macdougall and St-Onge, "Rooted in Mobility."

16 Colpitts, *Pemmican Empire,* 155–59.
17 Ross, *Red River,* 249.
18 Provincial Archives of Saskatchewan (PAS), Patrice Fleury Collection, File A-515.
19 Charette, *Vanishing Spaces,* 27; Weekes, *Last Buffalo Hunter,* 58.
20 Ross, *Red River,* 249–50.
21 Erasmus, *Buffalo Days,* 228–29.
22 Belcourt, "Buffalo Hunt," 16.
23 Giraud, *Métis in the Canadian West,* 134.
24 Belcourt, "Buffalo Hunt," 16.
25 Carpenter, *Fifty Dollar Bride,* 35; Callihoo, "Buffalo Hunts," 25. Marie Rose Smith (neé Delorme) was the daughter of Urbain Delorme Jr. and Marie Desmarais. She was born in October 1861 in St. François Xavier and spent most of her early life living with her parents and siblings, moving back and forth between Red River and the western prairies.
26 Giraud, *Métis in the Canadian West,* 149.
27 Carpenter, *Fifty Dollar Bride,* 36.
28 Charette, *Vanishing Spaces,* 56.
29 Troupe, *Expressing Our Heritage,* 56.
30 The word *shaganappi* comes from the Nêyihaw language. It describes the thin strips or laces made from buffalo rawhide.
31 PAS, Patrice Fleury Collection, File A-515.
32 Colpitts, *Pemmican Empire,* 171.
33 "The Fall Hunt," *Nor'Wester,* 15 November 1861, Gabriel Dumont Institute, Virtual Museum of Métis History and Culture, accessed 14 August 2024, https://www.metismuseum.ca/media/document.php/14337.Hunt%20Sept%201861.pdf.
34 Colpitts, *Pemmican Empire,* 171–73.
35 PAS, Patrice Fleury Collection, File A-515.
36 PAS, Patrice Fleury Collection, File A-515.
37 Brink, "Hunter's Quest."
38 Charette, *Vanishing Spaces,* 49.
39 Weekes, *Last Buffalo Hunter,* 58.
40 Charette, *Vanishing Spaces,* 50–55.
41 Weekes, *Last Buffalo Hunter,* 43.
42 Weekes, 43.
43 Weekes, 76–77.
44 Cowie, *Company of Adventurers,* 329.
45 Cowie, 329.
46 Callihoo, "Buffalo Hunts," 24.
47 Giraud, *Métis in the Canadian West,* 153.
48 University of Saskatchewan, University Archives and Special Collections, A.S. Morton Collection, MSS C511/6/1, MG 437, "Journal of Daily Occurrences, Fort Ellice," 1856–1876. See also Ens, *Homeland to Hinterland,* 78–79; Cowie, *Company of Adventurers,* 421; and Giraud, *Métis in the Canadian West,* 155.

49 University of Saskatchewan, University Archives and Special Collections, A.S. Morton Collection, MSS C511/6/1, MG 437, "Journal of Daily Occurrences, Fort Ellice," 1856–1876.

50 University of Saskatchewan, University Archives and Special Collections, A.S. Morton Collection, MSS C511/6/1, MG 437, "Journal of Daily Occurrences, Fort Ellice," 1856–1876. Freemen such as Antoine Gingras, Adott Antoine Gladu, F. Delorme, François Garneau, Joseph Hamelin, Gabriel Frederich, George Fisher and brother, Daniel and brother Alexander Geroux McGillis, John Sinclair, Joseph Tomma, Paul Desnomie, and a young man listed only by his surname Breland were among those who moved through the Fort Ellice region on their way to the Qu'Appelle Lakes. This is likely Pascal Breland. Others such as George Racette senior and son, George "Shaman" Racette, Alex Fisher, and Joseph and John Desmarais visited Ellice on their way to Broken Shell Creek, and William Daniel, Akapow, John McKay, John Fisher, Laframboise and son, Marshall Desjarlais, and Gabriel LaBoucan stopped at the fort on their way to High Pond.

51 Glenbow Archives, M-1531, "Journal of Qu'Appelle Lake Post," 1857–1858. This included Métis traders John Dease, George Fisher, and Daniel and Geroux [*sic*] McGillis.

52 Glenbow Archives, M-1531, "Journal of Qu'Appelle Lake Post," 1857–1858. These include freemen listed only by surname Belguard, LaPierre, Bon Guardipe, and Davis as well as John Fisher, Michel Fridmand, and Narcipe Green.

53 For a detailed examination of Métis women's production of decorative leather clothing and goods, see Farrell Racette, "Sewing Ourselves."

54 Hudson's Bay Company Archives (HBCA), Fort Ellice, Report on Districts. B.63/b/1, "Archibald McDonald to James Graham," 13 June 1874.

55 For a detailed examination of the Desjarlais family, see Devine, *People Who Own Themselves,* 130–33; Devine, "Les Desjarlais." Fort Desjarlais was home to about seventy individuals, most of whom were related to Antoine Desjarlais and Susanne Catherine Allary.

56 University of Saskatchewan, University Archives and Special Collections, A.S. Morton Collection, MSS C511/6/1, MG 437, "Journal of Daily Occurrences, Fort Ellice," 1856–1876.

57 University of Saskatchewan, University Archives and Special Collections, A.S. Morton Collection, MSS C511/6/1, MG 437, "Journal of Daily Occurrences, Fort Ellice," 1856–1876.

58 University of Saskatchewan, University Archives and Special Collections, A.S. Morton Collection, MSS C511/6/1, MG 437, "Journal of Daily Occurrences, Fort Ellice," 1856–1876; Cowie, *Company of Adventurers,* 423.

59 Glenbow Archives, M-1531, "Journal of Qu'Appelle Lake Post, 1857–1858," 4 February 1858.

60 Glenbow Archives, M-1531, "Journal of Qu'Appelle Lake Post, 1857–1858," 4 March 1858.

61 University of Saskatchewan, University Archives and Special Collections, A.S. Morton Collection, MSS C511/6/1, MG 437, "Journal of Daily Occurrences, Fort Ellice, 1856–1876," 31 March 1863.

62 HBCA, Fort Ellice Account Books, B.63/d./5, "List of Servants 1851–52."

63 HBCA, Fort Ellice Account Books, B.63/d/4-11. Records indicate that William Birston, Narcisse Cardinalle, Antoine Desjarlais, François Ducharme, Joseph Letendre, Charles Racette, and Edward Sayer were long-term HBC employees, while Antoine Desjarlais, Simon Blondeau, François Desmarais, John Fisher, Narcisse Cardinalle, and William Birston left the HBC, choosing to live as freemen.

64 Into the 1860s, York boats, each manned by six to eight men, were the preferred means of transportation moving goods from the inland posts to York Factory, the HBC's main shipping depot located at the mouth of the Hayes River on Hudson Bay.

65 For more information on the role of Métis guides in these expeditions, see Spry, *The Palliser Expedition;* Southesk, *Saskatchewan and The Rocky Mountains;* Butler, *The Great Lone Land;* Cheadle, *Cheadle's Journal of Trip Across Canada;* Youle Hind, *Narrative of the Canadian Red River Exploring Expedition.*

66 Cowie, *Company of Adventurers,* 220; Library and Archives Canada (LAC), RG15-D-II-8-b, Reel C-14938, Vol. 1327, Alexander Fisher, Scrip Claim 3636.

67 Long, *Fort Pelly,* 108–128; University of Saskatchewan, University Archives and Special Collections, A.S. Morton Collection, MSS C511/6/1, MG 437, "Journal of Daily Occurrences, Fort Ellice, 1856–1876," December 1863; Cowie, *Company of Adventurers,* 213.

68 University of Saskatchewan, University Archives and Special Collections, A.S. Morton Collection, MSS C511/6/1, MG 437, "Journal of Daily Occurrences, Fort Ellice, 1856–1876," December 1863. Mudding and thatching refers to materials and techniques used to waterproof building roofs. Long grasses were layered on the roof and secured with a mixture of mud and clay. The grasses created a water-resistant barrier and helped to insulate the building, keeping it cool in warm summer months and warm during the winter. Mudding may also have referred to the process where a mixture of mud, clay, and grass was applied between the horizontal logs of buildings. Once applied, the mixture hardened and kept out wind, water, and bugs. It was applied by hand and required regular maintenance, often on an annual or semi-annual basis. The Métis also call this "chinking."

69 Yale University, Beinecke Collection, Hudson's Bay Company Collection, Fort Pelly Scroll Book, "Fort Pelly Rations, Winter 1870–1871."

70 Munro, *Fur Trade Letters,* 41.

71 Cowie, *Company of Adventurers,* 427–28.

72 Cowie, 214–15.

73 Long, *Fort Pelly,* 114–15.

74 Cowie, *Company of Adventurers,* 246.

75 Cowie, 210–14.

76 Cowie, 213–14.

77 Cowie, 286.

78 University of Saskatchewan, University Archives and Special Collections, A.S. Morton Collection, MSS C511/6/1, MG 437, "Journal of Daily Occurrences, Fort Ellice, 1856–1876," September 1867.

79 University of Saskatchewan, University Archives and Special Collections, A.S. Morton Collection, MSS C511/6/1, MG 437, "Journal of Daily Occurrences, Fort Ellice, 1856–1876," March 1859.

80 University of Saskatchewan, University Archives and Special Collections, A.S. Morton Collection, MSS C511/6/1, MG 437, "Journal of Daily Occurrences, Fort Ellice, 1856–1876," 23 February 1869.

81 University of Saskatchewan, University Archives and Special Collections, A.S. Morton Collection, MSS C511/6/1, MG 437, "Journal of Daily Occurrences, Fort Ellice, 1856–1876," March 1863.

82 University of Saskatchewan, University Archives and Special Collections, A.S. Morton Collection, MSS C511/6/1, MG 437, "Journal of Daily Occurrences, Fort Ellice, 1856–1876," March 1863.

83 Cowie, *Company of Adventurers,* 189.

84 Cowie, 300.

85 Weekes, *Last Buffalo Hunter,* 110.

86 Weekes, 109–10.

87 Brink, "Hunter's Quest," 90.

88 Delphine Desjarlais, interview, 8 July 2014.

89 Weekes, *Last Buffalo Hunter*; Charette, *Vanishing Spaces*; Carpenter, *Fifty Dollar Bride*; Callihoo, "Buffalo Hunts."

90 Erasmus, *Buffalo Days,* 232.

91 Weekes, *Last Buffalo Hunter,* 3, 29; Long, *Fort Pelly* 112–18; Yale University, Beinecke Collection, Hudson's Bay Company Collection, Fort Pelly Scroll Book, Outfit 1868.

92 Klimko and Hodges, *Last Mountain House,* 43; Klimko, *The Archaeology and History of Fort Pelly,* 83–84. At Last Mountain House, fourteen different patterns of Spode and W.T. Copeland white earthenware were identified, while at Fort Pelly, thirty-seven were identified.

93 Weekes, *Last Buffalo Hunter,* 103; Klimko and Hodges, *Last Mountain House,* 43; Klimko, *The Archaeology and History of Fort Pelly,* 90.

94 Charette, *Vanishing Spaces,* 43.

95 University of Saskatchewan, University Archives and Special Collections, A.S. Morton Collection, MSS C511/6/1, MG 437, "Journal of Daily Occurrences, Fort Ellice, 1856–1876."

96 Cowie, *Company of Adventurers,* 390.

97 Cowie, 391.

98 Carpenter, *Fifty Dollar Bride,* 28.

99 Cowie, *Company of Adventurers,* 412–15.

100 Cowie, 425.

101 Cowie, 412–15.
102 Cowie, 425.
103 Weekes, *Last Buffalo Hunter*, 74.

Chapter 3. Petitioning for Rights and Taking Up Agriculture

1 LAC, *Sessional Papers, 1885*, Papers and correspondence in connection with half-breed claims and other matters relating to the North-West Territories, No. 116e, "Half-Breeds of the Qu'Appelle to Alexander Morris, Lieutenant-Governor, North-West Territories," 11 September 1874.

2 Cowie, *Company of Adventurers*, 482.

3 For a detailed examination of the movement of Métis out of the Red River region, see Sprague and Frye, *The Genealogy of the First Métis Nation;* and Ens, *Homeland to Hinterland.*

4 Cowie, *Company of Adventurers*, 230; Weekes, *Last Buffalo Hunter*, 60. Male children in nineteenth-century Métis families were often given the name St. Pierre. Bestowed by the priest during baptism, the name may have been given to remind the child and their family to have faith and observe religious devotion throughout their lives. There were at least six individuals with the first name St. Pierre listed as living in the Qu'Appelle region in the 1881 Census including: St. Pierre Poitras (age forty-five), St. Pierre Racette (age thirty-five), St. Pierre Racette (age ten), St. Pierre Blondeau (aged fourteen), St. Pierre Klyne (age seven), and St. Pierre LaPierre (age three). PAS, Canada Census, The Territories, Qu'Appelle, District 192, Sub-District H, 1881.

5 Weekes, *Last Buffalo Hunter*, 96.

6 The St. Florent Mission was often referred to as the Qu'Appelle Mission. In 1885 the settlement was renamed Lebret after Father Louis Lebret who had become the parish priest in 1884.

7 LAC, *Sessional Papers, 1885*, Papers and correspondence in connection with half-breed claims and other matters relating to the North-West Territories, No. 116e, "Half-Breeds of the Qu'Appelle to Alexander Morris, Lieutenant-Governor, North-West Territories," 11 September 1874. Petition signatories included Augustin Brabant, Baptiste Davis, Michel Desjarlais, Michael Klyne, Peter Lapierre, Antoine Larocque, Francis St. Dennis, Norbert Delorme, Thomas Kavanaugh, Pierre Peltier [Pelletier], Michael Desmarias, Simon Blondeau, Pierre Poitras, Jean Monet, Joseph Peltier [Pelletier], Corbert Seigneur, John Fisher, Al Fisher, Alex Swain, François Seignoir, Pierre Flammand, Patrice Monet, Moise Ouellette, Joseph McKay, Joseph Poitras, Antoine Ouellette, Antoine Flavin, Antoine Hamelin, Louison Flammand, Pierre Desnonme, and André Flammand.

8 Close to sixty heads of families along with at least fifty of their adult children signed the 1881 petition: LAC, *Sessional Papers, 1885*, Papers and correspondence in connection with half-breed claims and other matters relating to the North-West Territories, No. 116e, "Pierre LaPierre, Simon Blondin [Blondeau],

John Fisher, Alexander Fisher, John Simpson, Xavier Desnomme, and others, The Half-breeds of Qu'Appelle Settlement to the Marquis of Lorne, Governor General of Canada," 2 September 1881. Signatories included Peter LaPierre, two of his sons, Thomas and Theophile, and son-in law Toussaint [Thomas] Gallarneau; Simon Blondin [Blondeau] and eight of his sons, Zachary, John, Louison, Simon Jr., Napoleon, St. Pierre, Ambroise, and Joseph; John Fisher, his three sons George, Pierre, and William as well as two sons-in-law, Gregoire Ledoux and Lazarus Laliberté; Alexander Fisher and son Alfred; John Simpson, Jr; Xavier Denommil [Desnomme]; Joseph Blion [Blayone]; Elie Blion [Blayone], Pierre Bonnotte [Bonneau] Sr. and sons Pierre Jr., Julien, and Charles; Hilaire Boucher; Augustin Brabant, Sr. and sons Augustin Jr. and Edward; William Daniel and sons Joseph and William Jr; Modeste Daniel; Jean Baptiste Dauphinais; Joseph Delorme; Baptiste Desjarlais and sons Pierre and Isadore; Charles Desjarlais; Mathias Desjarlais; Michel Desjarlais and sons Edbert [Exupert], Michel, and Stanislas; Thomas Desjarlais; François Desmarais; Daniel Dumas; Antoine Fayant Sr. and sons William, Antoine Jr. and Jean Louis; George Fisher Sr; Louison Flammand, sons André and Maxim and son-in-law Samuel Turcotte; James Grant and son Joseph James; Napoleon Hamelin; Alexis Henéré; Archil [Michel] Klyne and his brothers Andrew and Theofile, as well as brothers-in-law Thomas Kavanaugh (on behalf of his wife Elise Klyne) and Thomas Kelly (on behalf of his wife Veronique Klyne); Baptiste Laliberte; Joseph LaPierre; Isadore La Plante; Antoine Larocque Sr. and sons Antoine Jr., Alex, and William; Joseph Marion and son R.T. [Roderick]; Alexis McKay; Baptiste, Camile, François, and Xavier Morin; Joseph Parisien and son-in-law Clément Peltier; Joseph Pellerton Bouvette [Pelletier]; Alex Pelletier; Napoleon Pelletier; Xavier Plante; Iseaid Poitras; brothers Joseph and St. Pierre Poitras, as well as St. Pierre's son Pierre; Charles Racette Sr., son Joseph Sr., and grandson Joseph; Baptiste Robillard; Roderick Ross and sons Roderick Jr., Urbain, and Pierre, and son-in-law Pierre Pelletier; Matthias Sansregret; John Sinclair Sr. and two sons, Thomas and John; François St. Dennis Sr. and son François Jr.; Cuthbert St. Dennis; Edouard St. Germain; Moise Vallee; Norbert Welsh; as well as Father Hugonard and Louis Boucher.

9 PAS, Canada Census, The Territories, Qu'Appelle, District 192, Sub-District H, 1881.

10 Antoine Desjarlais and his second wife Susanne Catherine Allary, Pierre Pelletier and Angelique Comtois, François Fayant and Madeline Lemire, François Falcon and Euphrosine Poitras, Charles Pelletier and Suzanne Bercier, François Amyotte and Louise Hamelin, Antoine Larocque and Françoise Laliberte and Baptiste Davis and Julie Desnomme and others are listed together in the 1850 Census. Susanne Allary is sometimes referred to as Catherine Allary. *Federal U.S. Census, Pembina County, Minnesota Territory, 1850,* accessed 10 August 2024, http://www.usgwarchives.net/mn/pembina/census/1850/.

11 Foster, *We Know Who We Are,* 61–62.

12 Foster, 78–79.

13 Payment, *Free People*; Payment, "Batoche After 1885"; Devine, *The People Who Own Themselves*; Macdougall, *One of the Family*; Macdougall, "Wahkootowin"; Troupe, "Métis Women"; Foster, *We Know Who We Are*; Thorne, *The Many Hands of My Relations.*

14 Cowie, *Company of Adventurers*; PAS, Saskatchewan Homestead Files, File 290.8, "Alexander Fisher, Application for Patent," 3 October 1883; PAS, Saskatchewan Homestead Files, File 290.26, "Elizabeth Fisher, Application for Patent," 22 September 1883.

15 LAC, RG15-D-II-8-c, Vol 1357, Julie Lemire, Scrip Claim 1235.

16 PAS, Saskatchewan Homestead Files, File 290.22, "Simon Blondeau, Application for Patent," 24 March 1884; PAS, Saskatchewan Homestead Files, File 290.4, "Baptiste Desjarlais, Application for Patent," 16 July 1883; PAS, Saskatchewan Homestead Files, File 290.32, "Michel Desjarlais, Application for Patent," 4 June 1884.

17 LAC, RG15-D-II-8-b, Vol. 1325, Simon Blondeau, Scrip Claim 2 and 148; LAC, RG15- D-II-8-b, Vol. 1327, Françoise Desjarlais, Scrip Claim 33.

18 PAS, Saskatchewan Homestead Files, File 326.33, "James Grant, Application for Patent," 4 January 1886.

19 LAC, RG15-D-II-8-b, Vol. 1329, Catherine Ledoux, Scrip Claim 1512; LAC, RG15-D-II-8-b, Vol. 1329, Helene Ledoux, Scrip Claim 1513.

20 Brown, "Women as Centre"; Foster, *We Know Who We Are*; Macdougall, "Wahkootowin"; Payment, *Free People*; Payment, "Batoche After 1885"; Troupe, "Métis Women."

21 PAS, Canada Census, The Territories, Qu'Appelle, District 192, Sub-District H, Household 23, "Simon Blondeau," 1881.

22 PAS, Canada Census, The Territories, Qu'Appelle, District 192, Sub-District H, Household 24, "Simon Blondeau Jr.," 1881; PAS, Canada Census, The Territories, Qu'Appelle, District 192, Sub-District H, Household 25, "John Blondeau," 1881; PAS, Canada Census, The Territories, Qu'Appelle, District 192, Sub-District H, Household 26, "Zacharie Blondeau," 1881; PAS, Canada Census, The Territories, Qu'Appelle, District 192, Sub-District H, Household 27, "Louison Blondeau," 1881.

23 PAS, Canada Census, The Territories, Qu'Appelle, District 192, Sub-District H, Household 19, "Jean Baptiste Robillard," 1881.

24 PAS, Canada Census, The Territories, Qu'Appelle, District 192, Sub-District H, Household 28, "Baptiste Desjarlais," 1881.

25 PAS, Canada Census, The Territories, Qu'Appelle, District 192, Sub-District H, Household 80, "Michel Desjarlais," 1881.

26 LAC, RG15, D-II-1, Vol. 447, Work for Half-Breeds in Qu'Appelle, Letter from Norbert Welsh, File No. 118650, "W.A. Clark, Survey of Half-Breeds in Qu'Appelle and File Hills Districts," 3 December 1886.

27 Foster, *We Know Who We Are*, 41–42.

28 PAS, Canada Census, The Territories, Qu'Appelle, District 192, Sub-District H Household 38, "Madeleine Klyne," 1881.

29 PAS, Canada Census, The Territories, Qu'Appelle, District 192, Sub-District H, Household 73, "André Klyne," 1881; PAS, Canada Census, The Territories, Qu'Appelle, District 192, Sub-District H, Household 39, "Theophile Klyne," 1881; PAS, Canada Census, The Territories, Qu'Appelle, District 192, Sub-District H, Household 78, "Michel Klyne," 1881; PAS, Canada Census, The Territories, Qu'Appelle, District 192, Sub-District H, Household 36, "Thomas Kavanaugh," 1881; PAS, Canada Census, The Territories, Qu'Appelle, District 192, Sub-District H, Household 37, "Thomas Kelly," 1881; PAS, Canada Census, The Territories, Qu'Appelle, District 192, Sub-District H, Household 35, "Thomas Desjarlais," 1881.

30 For a detailed examination of Métis resettlement, see Code, "Les Autres Métis"; Payment, *Free People*.

31 LAC, RG15, D-II-3, Vol.171, Enclosing Indian Branch File No.4145 covering Rev. Pere DeCorby's Explanation re: Manners in which Half-breeds have relocated, File HB 61, "Father DeCorby, Qu'Appelle Mission to David Laird, Minister of the Interior," 1 October 1874.

32 Ens, "Métis Agriculture"; Clark, "The Place of the Métis"; Sprenger, "The Métis Nation."

33 Ens, "Métis Agriculture," 242.

34 Ross, *Red River*, 193–95.

35 Cowie, *Company of Adventurers*, 483.

36 Keay, *Lord Lorne's Expedition*, 34.

37 Williams, *Manitoba and the North-West*, 65.

38 PAS, Saskatchewan Homestead Files, File 290.5, Antoine Larocque, Application for Patent, 8 August 1883.

39 Williams, *Manitoba and the North-West*, 65–67.

40 Williams, 68.

41 PAS, Survey Files, No. 226, Report on the Survey of Claims, "T.R. Hewson, Dominion Land Surveyor to the Minister of the Interior," May 1881; PAS, Saskatchewan Homestead Files, No. 290.13, "Thomas Beaulieau, Application for Patent," 31 August 1883; PAS, Saskatchewan Homestead Files, No. 290.13, "Xavier Perreault, Application for Patent," 27 August 1883; PAS, Saskatchewan Homestead Files, File. 290.22, "Simon Blondeau, Application for Patent," 24 March 1884; PAS, Saskatchewan Homestead Files, File 290.31, "Antoine Hamelin, Application for Patent," 4 June 1884; PAS, Saskatchewan Homestead Files, File 290.8, "Alexander Fisher, Application for Patent," 4 October 1883; PAS, Saskatchewan Homestead Files, File 290.6, "St. Pierre Poitras, Application for Patent," 8 August 1883; PAS, Saskatchewan Homestead Files, 290.5, "Antoine Larocque, Application for Patent," 8 August 1883. Thomas Beaulieau, Peter LaPierre, Xavier Perreault, Simon Blondeau, Antoine Hamelin, and George Fisher farmed between ten and twenty acres, and Alexander Fisher, Joseph Poitras, St. Pierre Poitras, Norbert Welsh, and Antoine Larocque farmed more than twenty acres.

42 By 1883 Klyne had eight acres under cultivation and had been farming her plot of land for at least a decade. Klyne's sons André and Michel farmed ten and twenty-four acres, respectively, while her sons-in-law Thomas Kavanaugh and Thomas Desjarlais farmed ten acres and fifteen acres, respectively. Michel's son John farmed five acres. See PAS, Saskatchewan Homestead Files, File 290.68, "Madeleine Klyne, Application for Patent," 20 July 1885; PAS, Saskatchewan Homestead Files, File 290.18, "André Klyne, Application for Patent," 31 August 1883; PAS, Saskatchewan Homestead Files, File 75387, "Marie Klyne, Declaration," 24 October 1884,; PAS, Saskatchewan Homestead Files, File 290.19, "Thomas Kavanaugh, Application for Patent," 10 July 1883; PAS, Saskatchewan Homestead Files, File 348.41, "Thomas Desjarlais, Statement," 5 October 1886; PAS, Saskatchewan Homestead Files, File 479.68, "John Klyne, Homestead Application," 12 June 1893.

43 Owram, *Promise of Eden.*

44 Morton, "Introduction."

45 Scott was an Irish Protestant supporter of the Canada Party. This was an organization led by John Christian Schultz that promoted the annexation of Red River to the Canadian government and the settlement of the region by Protestant settlers from Ontario. Known to be agitators, members of the party, including Scott, engaged in military skirmishes with the Métis at Fort Garry in 1869. Scott was arrested, charged with treason, and executed by Riel's provisional government. Following his execution, Prime Minister John A. Macdonald sent a military force, the Wolseley Expedition, to western Canada to confront Riel and the Métis, which led to Riel's exile. Schultz and other Canada Party supporters exploited Scott's execution to gain support in eastern Canada and to condemn Riel and the Métis. Riel was executed in 1885, not only for his actions in the 1885 North-West Resistance, but also for Scott's execution. Métis lawyer Jean Teillet argues that Scott has been treated as a martyr in this history. From a Métis perspective, Scott's execution must be understood as a court-ordered death sentence for the brutal murder of Métis Norbert Parisien. See Teillet, *The North-West is Our Mother,* 213–20.

46 Morton, "Introduction."

47 Manitoba Act, 1870, Cap. 3, Sec. 31.

48 Métis Association of Alberta et al., *Métis Land Rights,* 88.

49 Augustus, "The Scrip Solution"; Métis Association of Alberta et al., *Métis Land Rights*; Ens, "Métis Land Rights in Manitoba"; Tough, *"As Their Natural Resources Fail"*; Tough and McGregor, "Rights to the Lands"; Milne, "The Historiography of Métis Land Dispersal"; Sprague, *Canada and the Métis.*

50 Stanley, *The Birth of Western Canada,* 191, 244; Sprague, *Canada and the Métis.* Writing in the 1930s, G.F.G. Stanley argued that, although characterized by a spirit of procrastination, "ministerial incompetence, parliamentary indifference and administrative delay," the government acted in good faith and not in conspiracy to defraud the Métis. Stanley's interpretation remained dominant until the 1980s when challenged by historian Douglas N. Sprague, who, based primarily on the

letters and papers of John A. Macdonald, argues that Ottawa had no intention of fulfilling its obligations under the Manitoba Act.

51 Sprague, *Canada and the Métis.*

52 Hayter, "Racially 'Indian,'" 218–19; See also: Milne, "Historiography."

53 LAC, RG15, D-II-3, Vol. 171, File HB 58, "John Fisher and others Fort Qu'Appelle to Alexander Morris, Lieutenant Governor," 3 May 1873. Signatories included: John Fisher, Alexander Fisher, Joseph Desmarais, Pierre Nomme [Desnomme], Pierre Janneault, François Laframboise, Pierre Peltier [Pelletier], St. Pierre Poitras, Joseph Racette, André Protche [Trottier], and Charles Protche [Trottier].

54 Read, "The Red River Rebellion and J.S. Dennis"; Lovell Clark, *Dictionary of Canadian Biography*, John Christian Schultz, last revised 1990, http://www.biographi.ca/en/bio/schultz_john_christian_12E.html.

55 LAC, RG15, D-II-3, Vol. 171, File HB 58, "Alexander Morris to John Fisher and others," 4 June 1873.

56 LAC, *Sessional Papers, 1885*, Papers and correspondence in connection with half-breed claims and other matters relating to the North-West Territories, No. 116e, "Half-Breeds of the Qu'Appelle to Alexander Morris, Lieutenant-Governor, North-West Territories," 11 September 1874.

57 Lynne Champagne, "Pascal Breland," *Dictionary of Canadian Biography*, last revised 1990, http://www.biographi.ca/en/bio/breland_pascal_12E.html.

58 LAC, *Sessional Papers, 1885*, Papers and correspondence in connection with half-breed claims and other matters relating to the North-West Territories, No. 116e, "Half-Breeds of the Qu'Appelle to Alexander Morris, Lieutenant-Governor, North-West Territories," 11 September 1874.

59 Morris, *Treaties of Canada*, 330–38. For an examination of the role of Métis as treaty interpreters, see Stevenson, "The Métis Cultural Brokers." Baptiste Davis, Pierre Poitras, Pierre Desnomme, Joseph McKay, and Pierre LaPierre signed Treaty Four as witnesses.

60 LAC, *Sessional Papers*, 1876, Annual Report of the Department of the Interior for the year 1875, Vol. 7, No. 9, "Lieutenant Governor Morris to the Secretary of State, Special Appendix B," 17 October 1874, xix–xxii.

61 See Devine, *The People Who Own Themselves*; Innes, *Elder Brother*; McNab, "George Gordon First Nations Women." For discussion of the treaty-making process, see Miller, *Compact, Contract, Covenant*; Ray, Miller, and Tough, *Bounty and Benevolence*; Morris, *The Treaties of Canada*; Friesen, "Magnificent Gifts."

62 Devine, *The People Who Own Themselves*, 144.

63 Indian Act, 1868, Cap. 42, Sec. 15.

64 Morris, *Treaties of Canada*, 294.

65 Morris, 295.

66 Innes, *Elder Brother*.

67 McNab, "George Gordon First Nations Women," 50–51.

68 Innes, *Elder Brother*; McNab, "George Gordon First Nations Women," 50–51.

69 Devine, *The People Who Own Themselves,* 144–145; Morris, *Treaties of Canada,* 356–62.

70 Cowie, *Company of Adventurers,* 416–17.

71 Devine, *The People Who Own Themselves,* 144–45.

72 LAC, *Sessional Papers, 1885,* Papers and correspondence in connection with half-breed claims and other matters relating to the North-West Territories, No. 116e, "Lieutenant Governor Alexander Morris to Augustin Brabant, Baptiste Davis, and others, half-breeds of the Lakes Qu'Appelle and environs," 16 September 1874.

73 LAC, *Sessional Papers, 1885,* Papers and correspondence in connection with half-breed claims and other matters relating to the North-West Territories, No. 116e, "Alexander Morris to David Laird, Minister of the Interior, 17 October 1874.

74 LAC, RG15, D-II-3, Vol. 171, File HB 61, "Father DeCorby to David Laird, Minister of the Interior, 1 October 1874.

75 Throughout the 1870s and 1880s, Métis in settlements such as Blackfoot Crossing, Prince Albert, St. Albert, Battleford, Cypress Hills, Edmonton, and the South Branch settlements of St. Laurent, St. Antoine de Padou, and St. Louis de Langevin submitted petitions to the government, see LAC, *Sessional Papers,* 1885, Papers and correspondence in connection with half-breed claims and other matters relating to the North-West Territories, No. 116e.

76 LAC, RG10, Vol. 3637, File 7089, "Half Breeds at Fort Walsh to Inspector James Morrow Walsh," 6 September 1876. Petition signatories: Louis Militaire [Malaterre], Joseph Parisien, Alex Gariepy, François Lafontaine, Jeremie Eden, Joseph Lemire, John Wells, Daniel Ledoux, Joseph Amiot [Amyotte], Peter Leveille, Joseph Ducharme, Alex Gardy, Pierre Ellery, Joseph Amiot [Amyotte], François Amiot [Amyotte] Jr., Louis Amiot [Amyotte], Baptiste Belgarde, Gilbert Belgarde, C. Amelin [Hamelin], Jean Charet, Xavier Fion [Fayant], Louis De Coteau Sr., Louison De Coteau, Humphrey Favel, Louis Leveille, Moise Adam, Alexis Pelltier [Pelletier], Baptiste Pelltier [Pelletier], Bonaventure Gariepy, and Baptiste Larocque.

77 As Minister of the Interior, Laird was also the ex officio Superintendent-General of Indian Affairs. Laird replaced Alexander Morris as Lieutenant Governor in late 1876.

78 LAC, *Sessional Papers,* 1877, Vol 7. No 11, "J.M. Walsh, Special Appendix D, Report of Mr. J.M. Walsh, respecting the payment by him of Annuities under Treaty No. 4, to Indians at Cypress Hills," 12 September 1876.

79 LAC, *Sessional Papers,* 1877, Vol. 7, No. 11, "M.G. Dickieson to the Honorable Minister of the Interior, Special Appendix C," 7 October 1876.

80 LAC, *Sessional Papers,* 1877, Vol. 7, No. 11, "M.G. Dickieson to the Honorable Minister of the Interior, Special Appendix C," 7 October 1876.

81 LAC, *Sessional Papers,* 1877, Vol. 7, No. 11, "M.G. Dickieson to the Honorable Minister of the Interior, Special Appendix C," 7 October 1876.

82 LAC, *Sessional Papers, 1885,* Papers and correspondence in connection with half-breed claims and other matters relating to the North-West Territories, No.

116e, "Métis Blackfoot Crossing to David Laird, Lieutenant Governor," 19 September 1877.

83 LAC, *Sessional Papers, 1885*, Papers and correspondence in connection with half-breed claims and other matters relating to the North-West Territories, No. 116e, "Half Breeds living in the vicinity of Cypress Hills to the Members of the Privy Council of the North-West Territories," 2 August 1878. Approximately 100 of the 280 signatories could be linked to those in the Qu'Appelle Valley.

84 Waiser, "Legislator's View."

85 Weekes, *Last Buffalo Hunter*, 130–31.

86 LAC, *Sessional Papers, 1885*, Papers and correspondence in connection with half-breed claims and other matters relating to the North-West Territories, No. 116e, "Pierre LaPierre, Simon Blondin [Blondeau], John Fisher, Alexander Fisher, John Simpson, Xavier Desnomme, and others, *The Half-breeds of Qu'Appelle Settlement to the Marquis of Lorne*, Governor General of Canada," 2 September 1881.

Chapter 4. Asserting Sovereignty to Secure Land

1 Bob Desjarlais, interview, 3 July 2002.

2 Owram, *Promise of Eden.*

3 For a detailed account of the Dominion Lands Act, see Martin, *Dominion Lands*; Lambrecht, *Administration.*

4 Dominion Lands Act, 1872.

5 Martin, *Dominion Lands;* Lambrecht, *Administration*; McKercher and Wolfe, *Land Survey System*, 1–11; Eagle, *The Canadian Pacific Railway;* Tyman, "Patterns of Western Land Settlement."

6 Martin, *Dominion Lands*, see Chapter 7, "The Free Homestead System: The Background in the United States." Martin, however, contends that the American and Canadian experience differed in relation to "squatters." In Canada, he notes, squatters "were almost negligible." The Selkirk settlers, Métis, and First Nations were already present in the North-West before the extension of Canadian authority, and their rights were recognized in imperial and Canadian legislation. They were not squatters according to American policy definitions but had recognizable rights.

7 Carter, *Imperial Plots*, 40.

8 Carter, 39.

9 The square township survey system aligns with the lines of latitude and longitude. Township lines run east-west and range lines run north-south. Townships are numbered consecutively beginning with the 49th parallel, or the international boundary, and moving north. Ranges are numbered east to west with the First or Principal Meridian located west of Winnipeg, Manitoba. There are smaller townships in some ranges to compensate for the curvature of the earth. These are generally given both an alpha and numeric label. For example, in Range 12 West of the 2nd Meridian, the township north of 18 is not 19, but 19A. Township 19A is made up of 12 sections rather than the standard 36. Township 19 is north of 19A.

10 Each quarter section is given a directional signifier such as northeast (NE), northwest (NW), southeast (SE) or southwest (SW). When referring to a land location, the signifier begins with the Quarter Section followed by the Township (Twp) number, Range (R) number, and location in reference to a meridian. For instance, NE 12–Twp 19–R 12–W 2 refers to the northeast quarter section of township 19 in range 12, west of the second meridian.

11 Sections 11 and 29 were reserved for schools and the Hudson's Bay Company received Section 8 and all of Section 26 except the north-east quarter. In every fifth township the HBC also received all of Section 26.

12 Lehr, Everitt, and Evans, "Making of the Prairie Landscape"; Stunden Bower, *Wet Prairie.*

13 Carter, *Imperial Plots,* 39.

14 Dominion Lands Act, 1872, Cap. 23, Sec. 33.

15 Dominion Lands Act, 1876, Cap. 23, Sec. 33.

16 Indian Act, 1876, Cap 18, Sec. 70.

17 If homesteaders found their land unsuitable for farming, they could file a declaration of abandonment and then take up another 160-acre quarter section.

18 At various times under the Dominion Lands Act homesteaders were given the right to pre-empt the purchase of a second, adjourning quarter section for an additional ten-dollar filing fee. This right was held before or in preference to any other person, but only if certain conditions could be met. The intent of this provision was to enable a settler to acquire property for the expansion of his agricultural operation if he should be able to do so. After receiving patent on the original homestead, the homesteader had three years to purchase their pre-empted land. Pre-emptions were cancelled in 1890 but restored in 1908. In addition, between 1871 and 1918a homesteader could purchase 160 acres within a nine-mile radius of their homestead at a price of three dollars per acre. See Martin, *Dominion Lands*; and Lambrecht, *Administration.*

19 Lambrecht, *Administration,* 12–13.

20 PAS, Survey Files, No. 226, Report on the Survey of Claims, Survey of Township 21 in Ranges 13 and 14, "T.R. Hewson, Dominion Land Surveyor to the Minister of the Interior," May 1881. The largest claims included: Norbert Welsh with 28.9 acres broken; Larocque with 26.99 acres broken; St. Pierre Poitras with 26.14 acres; Joseph Poitras with 26 acres; George Fisher with 15.7 acres; and Peter LaPierre with 10.22 acres broken.

21 LAC, RG15, D-II-3, Vol 172, File HB 188, Half-breed settlers in Qu'Appelle Valley, that surveyors took evidence as to Right and Settlement in 1882 and 1883, "Memorandum," 6 June 1885.

22 PAS, Dominion Land Survey, Township Survey Maps, "Township 19–Range 11–West of the Second Meridian," 10 May 1883; PAS, Dominion Land Survey, Township Survey Maps, "Township 19–Range 12–West of the Second Meridian," April 1883; PAS, Dominion Land Survey, Township Survey Maps, "Township 20–Range 12–West of the Second Meridian," August 1883; PAS, Dominion

Lands Survey, Township Survey Maps, "Township 20–Range 13–West of the Second Meridian," October 1889; PAS, Dominion Land Survey, Township Survey Maps, "Township 21– Range 13–West of the Second Meridian," May 1893; PAS, Dominion Land Survey, Township Survey Maps, "Township 21–Range 14–West of the Second Meridian," 23 November 1887.

23 PAS, Dominion Land Survey, Township Survey Maps, "Township 19–Range 11–West of the Second Meridian," 10 May 1883. Other versions of these maps are sometimes available at other archives, but these versions are held in the Saskatoon office of the Provincial Archives of Saskatchewan.

24 PAS, Dominion Land Survey, Township Survey Maps, "Township 21–Range 13–West of Second Meridian,"15 May 1893. Compiled from surveys by: Clementi and Hewson, 1881; C.C. DuBerger, 1885; W.T. Thompson, 1881; J. Lestock Reid, 1886; Samuel Brodie, 1886; J.F. Garden, 1881; PAS, Dominion Land Survey, Township Survey Maps, "Township 20–Range 13–West of Second Meridian," 30 October 1889. Compiled from surveys by: Clementi and Hewson, 1881; C.C. DuBerger, 1885; W.T. Thompson, 1881; J. Lestock Reid, 1886; Samuel Brodie, 1886; J.F. Garden, 1881; PAS, Dominion Land Survey, Township Survey Maps, "Township 20–Range 13–West of Second Meridian," 30 October 1889. Compiled from surveys by Paul T.C. Dumais, 1882; J.LS. Michaud, 1882; Tom Kains, 1881; W.T. Thompson, 1881; PAS, Dominion Land Survey, Township Survey Maps, "Township 21–Range 14–West of Second Meridian," 23 November 1887. Compiled from surveys by Clementi and Hewson 1881; T.D. Green, 1886.

25 Dick, *Farmers "Making Good,"* 19–21.

26 Dick, *Farmers "Making Good"*; Carter, *Lost Harvests*, 160.

27 Dick, *Farmers "Making Good,"* 22; LAC, Census of the Three Provisional Districts of the North-West Territories—Assiniboia, Saskatchewan and Alberta, 1885, Report of the Statistical Office, Department of Agriculture, accessed 10 August 2024, https://publications.gc.ca/site/eng/9.830814/publication.html.

28 Dick, *Farmers "Making Good,"* 21–23.

29 Dick, 23.

30 LAC, RG15, D-II-3, Vol 172, File HB 188, Half-breed settlers in Qu'Appelle Valley, that surveyors took evidence as to Right and Settlement in 1882 and 1883, "Memorandum," 6 June 1885.

31 LAC, RG15, D-II-3, Vol 172, File HB 188, Half-breed settlers in Qu'Appelle Valley, that surveyors took evidence as to Right and Settlement in 1882 and 1883, "Memorandum," 6 June 1885.

32 PAS, Surveyor Files, I.226, "T.R. Hewson to Lindsay Russell, Surveyor General," 25 August 1881.

33 PAS, Surveyor Files, I.154, "C.C. DuBerger to the Minister of the Interior, Report on Settlers," 4 December 1882.

34 Tough, *As Their Natural Resources Fail*; Augustus, "The Scrip Solution"; Métis Association of Alberta et al., *Métis Land Rights.*

35 PAS, Surveyor Files, I.154, "C.C. DuBerger to the Minister of the Interior, Report on Settlers," 4 December 1882.

36 LAC, *Sessional Papers, 1885*, Papers and correspondence in connection with half-breed claims and other matters relating to the North-West Territories, No. 116e, "Half-breed Settlers to Edgar Dewdney, Lieutenant Governor, North-West Territories," 29 August 1882. Signatories of the 29 August 1882 petition included: Joseph Blayan [Blayone]; Simon Blondeau and five of his sons, Zacharie, Jean, Louison, Simon Jr., and Napoleon; Gustave [Augustin] Brabant and three of his sons, Gustave [Augustin], Alex, and Edouard; Baptiste Dauphine [Dauphinais], Baptiste Desjarlais; Matthias Desjarlais; Joseph Desmarais; Antoine Fayant and two of his sons, Antoine Jr. and William; Louis Flammand and sons André and Maxime; Joe Gosselin; Napoleon and Antoine Amelain [Hamelin]; John A. [André] Klyne; Antoine La Roque [Larocque] and his son Antoine; Joseph Marion; Alphonse Martin; Kenneth McKenzie; Leon Nault; François Perreault and son Xavier, as well as two of Xavier's sons, Camille and Baptiste; Isadore Plante; [St.] Pierre Poitras; Baptiste Robillard, his son Chrysostome, and son-in law John Simpson; Baptiste Roué [Roy]; François and Pierre St. Denis; and Norbert Welsh.

37 Dick, *Farmers "Making Good,"* 15–16.

38 The Qu'Appelle and Long Lake Land Company was the companion to the Qu'Appelle, Long Lake, and Saskatchewan Railway. Company directors included Nova Scotia MP Robert Doull, Senator Thomas Gibbs, and a handful of lawyers from New Brunswick. The only local director was Thomas Wesley Jackson who was a local lawyer, advocate to the Métis, and for a time, the land agent in Fort Qu'Appelle. He became a member of Parliament in 1886 and was also president of the Wood Mountain and Qu'Appelle Railway. The company was not successful in securing settlers but focused on building transportation networks in the region. The law firm of Osler, Hammond, and Nanton were also investors in the company and acted as bankers, scrip dealers, brokers, and sales agents for the company. E.B. Osler was a Conservative MP from Toronto and the largest shareholder in the Ontario and Qu'Appelle Land Company. Other directors included William Mulock, who temporarily relieved Clifford Sifton as Minister of the Interior. Like the Qu'Appelle and Long Lake Land Company, the Ontario and Qu'Appelle Company did not attract the required settlers. By 1894, they had to surrender much of their land back to the CPR. For more on land colonization companies, see Martin-McGuire, *First Nations Land Surrenders on the Prairies.*

39 LAC, *Sessional Papers, 1885*, Papers and correspondence in connection with half-breed claims and other matters relating to the North-West Territories, No. 116e, "Edgar Dewdney to John A. Macdonald, Minister of the Interior," 29 August 1882.

40 LAC, *Sessional Papers, 1885*, Papers and correspondence in connection with half-breed claims and other matters relating to the North-West Territories, No. 116e, "Edgar Dewdney to John A. Macdonald, Minister of the Interior," 29 August 1882.

41 LAC, *Sessional Papers, 1885*, Papers and correspondence in connection with half-breed claims and other matters relating to the North-West Territories, No. 116e, "Edgar Dewdney to John A. Macdonald, Minister of the Interior," 29 August 1882.

42 LAC, *Sessional Papers, 1885*, Papers and correspondence in connection with half-breed claims and other matters relating to the North-West Territories, No. 116e, "Edgar Dewdney to John A. Macdonald, Minister of the Interior," 29 August 1882.

43 Invested in the settlement and development of the region, Jackson was later president of the Wood Mountain and Qu'Appelle Railway Company.

44 PAS, Dominion Lands Branch, File 42479, "T.W. Jackson to Mr. J. Gordon, "13 February 1883.

45 PAS, Dominion Lands Branch, File 42479, "T.W. Jackson to Mr. J. Gordon, "13 February 1883.

46 LAC, *Sessional Papers, 1885*, Papers and correspondence in connection with half-breed claims and other matters relating to the North-West Territories, No. 116e, "Edgar Dewdney, Lieutenant-Governor, North-West Territories to Minister of the Interior," 19 March 1883.

47 LAC, *Sessional Papers, 1885*, Papers and correspondence in connection with half-breed claims and other matters relating to the North-West Territories, No. 116e, "Edgar Dewdney, Lieutenant-Governor, North-West Territories to Minister of the Interior," 19 March 1883.

48 LAC, *Sessional Papers, 1885*, Papers and correspondence in connection with half-breed claims and other matters relating to the North-West Territories, No. 116e, "Edgar Dewdney, Lieutenant-Governor, North-West Territories to Minister of the Interior," 19 March 1883.

49 LAC, *Sessional Papers, 1885*, Papers and correspondence in connection with half-breed claims and other matters relating to the North-West Territories, No. 116e, "John R. Hall, Acting Secretary, Department of the Interior to Edgar Dewdney, Lieutenant Governor of the North-West Territories," 6 July 1883.

50 LAC, *Sessional Papers, 1885*, Papers and correspondence in connection with half-breed claims and other matters relating to the North-West Territories, No. 116e, "John R. Hall, Secretary, Department of the Interior to T.W. Jackson," 13 March 1884.

51 William Pearce was recruited in 1872 by Dominion Surveyor General John Stoughton Dennis (who the Qu'Appelle Métis had objected to in their May 1873 petition) to survey parts of Manitoba and the North-West Territories. In February 1882, he was appointed Inspector of Dominion Lands agencies, which along with the Office of Commissioner of Dominion Lands constituted the newly formed Dominion Lands Board within the Department of the Interior. The Land Board's role was to supervise Land offices as they opened in the North-West and ensure local agents complied with land policy. They were to adjudicate all land disputes and advise government on the development of lands and resources.

In his work, Pearce insisted on strict compliance. In 1883 he investigated the land claims of Métis along the North Saskatchewan River between Battleford and Prince Albert. His failure to complete this task before 1885 was seen by some as being a factor in the 1885 Resistance. For more information, see David Breen, "William Pearce," *Dictionary of Canadian Biography*, last revised 2005, https://www.biographi.ca/en/bio/pearce_william_15E.html.

52 LAC, RG15, D-II-3, Vol 172, HB 188, Half-Breed settlers in Qu'Appelle Valley, that surveyors took evidence as to Right and Settlement in 1882 and 1883, "Memorandum," 6 June 1885.

53 Ken Cruikshank, "Sir David Lewis Macpherson," *Dictionary of Canadian Biography*, last revised 1990, https://www.biographi.ca/en/bio/macpherson_david_lewis_12E.html.

54 LAC, *Sessional Papers, 1885,* Papers and correspondence in connection with half-breed claims and other matters relating to the North-West Territories, No. 116e, "T.W. Jackson to Minister D. Macpherson," 8 December 1883.

55 LAC, *Sessional Papers, 1885,* Papers and correspondence in connection with half-breed claims and other matters relating to the North-West Territories, No. 116e, "John R. Hall, Secretary, Department of the Interior to T.W. Jackson," 13 March 1884.

56 PAS, Canada Census, 1881, The Territories, Qu'Appelle, District 192, Sub-District H.

57 Twenty-three identified strictly as hunters. Sixteen of these households had more than one individual identified as a farmer. In these instances, the sons or grandsons of the head of household, some as young as fourteen or fifteen years of age, were also listed as farmers.

58 PAS, Canada Census 1881, The Territories, Qu'Appelle, District 192, Sub-District H; PAS, Saskatchewan Homestead Files; LAC, RG15, D-II-1, Vol 447, Work for Half-Breeds in Qu'Appelle, Letter from Norbert Welsh, File No. 118650, "W.A. Clark, Survey of Half-Breeds in Qu'Appelle and File Hills Districts," 3 December 1886.

59 Waiser, *Saskatchewan,* 112.

60 Not all 104 claims included this information. Data represents what was available from the 104 applications.

61 PAS, Saskatchewan Homestead Files, File 345.70, "Xavier Desnomme, Statement," 16 August 1886; LAC, RG15, D-II-1, Vol 447, Work for Half-Breeds in Qu'Appelle, Letter from Norbert Welsh, File No. 118650, "W.A. Clark, Survey of Half-Breeds in Qu'Appelle and File Hills Districts," 3 December 1886.

62 PAS, Saskatchewan Homestead Files, File 250503, "Antoine Hamelin, Statement," 19 July 1906.

63 PAS, Saskatchewan Homestead Files, File 567946, "Lionel Charette, Sworn Statement in Support of Jean Baptiste Dauphinais," 4 January 1906.

64 PAS, Saskatchewan Homestead Files, File 240969, "Jean Blondeau, Statement," 13 August 1889; PAS, Saskatchewan Homestead Files, File 330882, "John Blondeau, Sworn Statement for Michel Klyne," 25 May 1914.
65 PAS, Saskatchewan Homestead Files, File 450070, "Norbert Welsh, Statement," 18 November 1899.
66 Burley, "Creolization."
67 Burley, "Creolization."

Chapter 5. Securing Land Tenure: North-West Half-Breed Scrip and Homesteading

1 Dominion Lands Act, 1879, Cap. 31, Sec. 125.
2 Hatt, "North-West Rebellion Scrip Commissions," 191.
3 Dominion Lands Act, 1879, Cap. 31, Sec. 125.
4 LAC, *Canada Sessional Papers*, 1885, Papers and correspondence in connection with half-breed claims and other matters relating to the North-West Territories, No.116e, "David Macpherson, Minister of the Interior to the Privy Council," 26 January 1885.
5 LAC, RG2, Series A-1-d, Volume 2769, "Order in Council 1885-0135," 28 January 1885.
6 LAC, RG2, Series A-1-d, Volume 2769, "Order in Council 1885-0135," 28 January 1885; LAC, RG2, Series A-1-d, Volume 2769, "Order in Council 1885-0688," 30 March 1885.
7 Street, "Commission," 40.
8 Tough and McGregor, "Rights to the Lands," 39, 55.
9 LAC, RG2, Series A-1-d, Volume 2769, "Order in Council 1885-0688," 30 March 1885; Dominion Lands Act, 1883, Vic. 46, Cap.17, Sec.81e.
10 Métis Association of Alberta et al., *Métis Land Rights*, 94.
11 Augustus, "The Scrip Solution."
12 LAC, *Sessional Papers*, 1885, Papers and correspondence in connection with half-breed claims and other matters relating to the North-West Territories, No.116e, "A.M. Burgess to John M. Egan, Western Division Canadian Pacific Railway," 30 March 1885; LAC, *Sessional Papers*, 1885, Papers and correspondence in connection with half-breed claims and other matters relating to the North-West Territories, No.116e, "A.M. Burgess to C. Drinkwater, Secretary, Canadian Pacific Railway," 30 March 30 1885; LAC, *Sessional Papers*, 1885, Papers and correspondence in connection with half-breed claims and other matters relating to the North-West Territories, No.116e, "A.M. Burgess to T.R. Burpé, Secretary of Land Board," 30 March 1885; LAC, *Sessional Papers*, 1885, Papers and correspondence in connection with half-breed claims and other matters relating to the North-West Territories, No.116e, "A.M. Burgess to Lawrence Vankoughnet, Deputy Superintendent General of Indian Affairs," 30 March 1885; LAC, *Sessional Papers*, 1885, Papers and correspondence in connection with half-breed claims and

other matters relating to the North-West Territories, No.116e, "A.M. Burgess to Fred White, Comptroller of the North-West Mounted Police," 30 March 1885.

13 LAC, *Sessional Papers*, 1885, Papers and correspondence in connection with half-breed claims and other matters relating to the North-West Territories, No.116e, "A.M. Burgess, Deputy Minister of the Interior to W.P. Street," 30 March 1885.

14 LAC, *Sessional Papers*, 1885, Papers and correspondence in connection with half-breed claims and other matters relating to the North-West Territories, No.116e, "Lawrence Vankoughnet, Deputy Superintendent General, Indian Affairs to A.M. Burgess Deputy Minister of the Interior," 1 April 1885.

15 Enfranchisement was the process by which a Status Indian legally lost their status and was conferred with the rights and duties of Canadian citizenship. It was a key feature of the Canadian government's policies to assimilate Indigenous peoples, reducing the number of Status Indians and the financial responsibility of the government for such individuals. It was first implemented in the 1857 Act for the Gradual Civilization of the Indian tribes in the Canadas and based on the assumption that First Nations people would voluntarily give up their legal status. If a Status Indian was male, over age twenty-one, literate in English or French, debt-free, and decidedly of good moral character they could be declared enfranchised by Indian Affairs administrators and made to become a citizen. Once enfranchised they were given land from within the reserve boundaries as their personal property, undermining Indigenous collective landholding on the reserve. The Enfranchisement Act of 1869 updated earlier provisions and in 1876, enfranchisement became compulsory under the Indian Act, remaining so until 1961. Under the Indian Act, Status Indians could lose their legal status for serving in the Canadian Armed Forces, getting a university education, becoming a minister, or leaving the reserve for an extended period of time. These activities demonstrated an individual's desire and ability to assimilate. If a man became enfranchised, his wife and children also lost their statuses. Status Indian women also were enfranchised if they married someone other than a Status Indian. The removal of status for women who married non-Indian men was rectified in 1985 with the passing of Bill C-31.

16 Street, "Commission," 45–46.

17 Street, 45.

18 For more on the way in which scrip was administered, see Tough and McGregor, "Rights to the Lands."

19 LAC, RG2, Series A-1-d, Volume 2769, "Order in Council 1885-0688," 30 March 1885; LAC, *Sessional Papers*, 1885, Papers and correspondence in connection with half-breed claims and other matters relating to the North-West Territories, No.116e, "John McGee, Clerk Privy Council to the Minister of the Interior. Certified Copy of a Report of a Committee of the Honorable the Privy Council, approved by His Excellency the Governor General," 30 March 1885.

20 LAC, *Sessional Papers*, 1885, Papers and correspondence in connection with half-breed claims and other matters relating to the North-West Territories, No.116e, "A.M. Burgess to T.W. Jackson," 31 March 1885.

21 LAC, *Sessional Papers,* 1885, Papers and correspondence in connection with half-breed claims and other matters relating to the North-West Territories, No.116e, "W.P. Street to David MacPherson," 4 April 1885.

22 LAC, *Sessional Papers,* 1885, Papers and correspondence in connection with half-breed claims and other matters relating to the North-West Territories, No.116e, "W.P. Street to David MacPherson," 4 April 1885.

23 LAC, *Sessional Papers,* 1885, Papers and correspondence in connection with half-breed claims and other matters relating to the North-West Territories, No.116e, "David Macpherson to W.P. Street," 6 April 1885.

24 LAC, *Sessional Papers,* 1885, Papers and correspondence in connection with half-breed claims and other matters relating to the North-West Territories, No.116e, "David Macpherson to W.P. Street," 6 April 1885.

25 Street, "Commission," 48–49.

26 T.W. Jackson, "Mr. Jackson on Indian and Half-Breed Matters," *Qu'Appelle Vidette,* 21 January 1886.

27 PAS, Amédée E. and Henriette Forget Papers, Half-Breed Claims and Commissions, 1885–1895, Petition, "Qu'Appelle Valley Half-Breeds, Petition," ca.1885. Note: Only part of this document exists in this file. The section listing signatories is missing.

28 T.W. Jackson, "Mr. Jackson on Indian and Half-Breed Matters," *Qu'Appelle Vidette,* 21 January 1886.

29 Mr. Fisher is likely Alexander Fisher or his brother John, both in their sixties at the time.

30 T.W. Jackson, "Mr. Jackson on Indian and Half-Breed Matters," *Qu'Appelle Vidette,* 21 January 1886.

31 Street, "Commission," 48–49.

32 Street, 48–49.

33 Street, 49.

34 LAC, *Sessional Papers,* 1885, Papers and correspondence in connection with half-breed claims and other matters relating to the North-West Territories, No.116e, "W.P. Street to David Macpherson, Minister of the Interior," 6 April 1885; T.W. Jackson, "Mr. Jackson on Indian and Half-Breed Matters, *Qu'Appelle Vidette,* 21 January 1886. Telegram is indicated as undecipherable in the *Sessional Papers,* but Jackson read a copy during his speech documented in the 1885 Qu'Appelle newspaper.

35 LAC, *Sessional Papers,* 1885, Papers and correspondence in connection with half-breed claims and other matters relating to the North-West Territories, No.116e, "W.P. Street to David Macpherson, Minister of the Interior," 6 April 1885; LAC, *Sessional Papers,* 1885, Papers and correspondence in connection with half-breed claims and other matters relating to the North-West Territories, No.116e, "David Macpherson to W.P. Street," 11 April 1885.

36 LAC, *Sessional Papers*, 1885, Papers and correspondence in connection with half-breed claims and other matters relating to the North-West Territories, No.116e, "David Macpherson to W.P. Street," 11 April 1885.

37 LAC, *Sessional Papers*, 1885, Papers and correspondence in connection with half-breed claims and other matters relating to the North-West Territories, No.116e, "David Macpherson to W.P. Street," 13 April 1885; LAC, RG2, Series A-1-d, Volume 2769, "Order in Council 1885-0821," 30 March 1885.

38 Street, "Commission," 49.

39 Street, 49.

40 LAC, RG15-D-II-8-b, C-14939, Vol. 1328, Madeleine Hamelin, Scrip Claim 13.

41 LAC, RG15-D-II-8-b, C-14939, Vol. 1328, Madeleine Hamelin, Scrip Claim 13; LAC, RG15-D-II-8-b, C-14936, Vol. 1325, Isadore Amiot, Scrip Claim 7.

42 Street, "Commission," 49; LAC, RG15-D-II-8-b, C-14939, Vol. 1328, Madeleine Hamelin, Scrip Claim 13; Glenbow Archives, M-8450-463—Lebret Parish Records, Vol. II. 1881–1887, Register of St. Florent Mission of Qu'Appelle Lake, Saskatchewan, Joseph Amyot, deceased 5 April 1885.

43 Street, "Commission," 50.

44 LAC, *Sessional Papers*, 1886, Department of the Interior Annual Return for 1885, No. 45, "Schedule showing the number of Half-Breeds, &c., who proved their claims before the North-West Half-Breed Commission, at the several places where the said Commission held its sittings," 23 March 1885. The number of Métis who proved their claims at Fort Qu'Appelle was 183, including: 48 Half-Breed Heads of Families, of which 27 were male and 21 females; and 135 Children of Half-Breed Heads of Families, of which 80 were male and 55 females. In addition, claims were also proven for: 22 Deceased Half-Breed Heads of Families (14 male, 8 female); and 33 (21 male, 11 female) Deceased Children of Half-Breed Heads of Families who were living on 15 July 1870.

45 LAC, *Sessional Papers*, 1886, Department of the Interior Annual Return for 1885, No. 8, "A.M. Burgess, Deputy Minister of the Interior, Report of the North-West Half-Breed Claims Commission."

46 T.W. Jackson, "Mr. Jackson on Indian and Half-Breed Matters, *Qu'Appelle Vidette*, 21 January 1886.

47 T.W. Jackson, "Mr. Jackson on Indian and Half-Breed Matters, *Qu'Appelle Vidette*, 21 January 1886.

48 LAC, *Sessional Papers*, 1885, Papers and correspondence in connection with half-breed claims and other matters relating to the North-West Territories, No.116e, "D.L. Macpherson, Minister of the Interior to W.P. Street, Commissioner," 10 April 1885.

49 PAS, Saskatchewan Homestead Files, File No. 97132, Jean Baptiste Dauphinais, List of Scrip issued to holders of waterfronts, 1885.

50 PAS, Saskatchewan Homestead Files, File 290.25, "John Simpson, Application for Patent"; LAC, RG15-D-II-8-b, C-14941, Vol. 1332, John Simpson, Scrip Claim 163.

51 John Simpson, Biographical Sheets, Hudson's Bay Company Archives, last revised July 2003, https://www.gov.mb.ca/chc/archives/_docs/hbca/biographical/s/simpson_john.pdf.
52 LAC, RG15-D-II-8-b, C-14941, Vol. 1332, John Simpson, Scrip Declaration, Claim 1561, 14 April 1885.
53 LAC, RG15-D-II-8-b, C-14941, Vol. 1332, John Simpson, Scrip Declaration, Claim 1561, 20 August 1885.
54 LAC, RG15-D-II-8-b, C-14939, Vol. 1328, Antoine Hamelin, Scrip Declaration, Claim 172.
55 LAC, RG15-D-II-8-b, C-14939, Vol. 1328, Antoine Hamelin, Scrip Declaration, Claim 172.
56 PAS, Saskatchewan Homestead Files, File 290.31, "Antoine Hamelin, Application for Patent," 4 June 188.
57 LAC, RG15-D-II-8-b, C-14939, Vol. 1328, Antoine Hamelin, Scrip Declaration, Claim 172.
58 PAS, Saskatchewan Homestead Files, File 250503, "Antoine Hamelin, Affidavit," November 1885.
59 PAS, Saskatchewan Homestead Files, File 250503, "Antoine Hamelin, Affidavit," November 1885.
60 PAS, Saskatchewan Homestead Files, File 290.22, "Simon Blondeau, Application for Patent."
61 LAC, RG15-D-II-8-b, Vol. 1325, Simon Blondeau, Scrip Claim 2 and 148.
62 PAS, Saskatchewan Homestead Files, File 521351, "Simon Blondeau, Last Will and Testament," 20 October 1906.
63 Niemi-Bohum, "Colonial Categories."
64 Niemi-Bohum, "Colonial Categories"; Devine, *The People Who Own Themselves*, 176–78.
65 Niemi-Bohum, "Colonial Categories."
66 Niemi-Bohum, "Colonial Categories," 80.
67 Indian Act 1876, Cap 18, Sec. 3, sub-Sec. 3.
68 Indian Act 1876, Cap 18, Sec. 3, sub-Sec. 3(e).
69 LAC, *Sessional Papers*, 1885, Papers and correspondence in connection with half-breed claims and other matters relating to the North-West Territories, No.116e, "David Laird to the Minister of Interior," 15 November 1878.
70 Indian Act, 1879, Cap. 34, Sec. 1.
71 P.R.E. Group, Indian and Northern Affairs, *Historical Development*, 76–77.
72 P.R.E. Group, 76–77.
73 P.R.E. Group, 76–77.
74 Beal, "Money, Markets and Economic Development."
75 Métis Association of Alberta et al., *Métis Land Rights*. Métis Association of Alberta et al. argues that due to their poverty following the provision of scrip there were several Métis in the North-West that were subsequently readmitted to treaty on condition that they repay the value of the scrip they received.

76 Daschuk, *Clearing the Plains*; Carter, *Lost Harvests*.

77 LAC, RG10, File 24303-2A, "Hayter Reed to Superintendent of Indian Affairs," 26 July 1886. Quoted in: Indian and Northern Affairs, *Admission of Half-Breeds into Treaty*.

78 Niemi-Bohun, "Colonial Categories."

79 LAC, *Sessional Papers, 1887*, Department of the Interior Annual Return for 1886, No. 7, Schedule C: Detailed Schedule of Claims preferred before the North-West Half-Breed Claims Commission, during the season of 1886, Report Respecting Claims of Half-Breeds, 12 January 1887.

80 LAC, *Sessional Papers, 1887*, Department of the Interior Annual Return for 1886, No. 7, Schedule C: Detailed Schedule of Claims preferred before the North-West Half-Breed Claims Commission, during the season of 1886, Report Respecting Claims of Half-Breeds, 12 January 1887.

81 LAC, RG15, D-II-8-c, C-14986, Vol. 1357, Julie Martin, Scrip Certificate and Discharge from Treaty.

82 LAC, RG15, D-II-1, Vol 447, Work for Half-Breeds in Qu'Appelle, Letter from Norbert Welsh, File No. 118650, "W.A. Clark, Survey of Half-Breeds in Qu'Appelle and File Hills Districts," 3 December 1886.

83 LAC, *Sessional Papers*, 1887. Department of the Interior Annual Return for 1886, No.7, "Report on Half-Breed Scrip."

84 LAC, RG15, HB8276, "T.W. Jackson to Thomas White, Minister of the Interior, Petition signed by 34 Half-Breed heads of families of the Qu'Appelle District who have recently left Treaty with a view to taking Scrip," 16 October 1886.

85 LAC, RG15, HB8276, "T.W. Jackson to Thomas White, Minister of the Interior, Petition signed by 34 Half-Breed heads of families of the Qu'Appelle District who have recently left Treaty with a view to taking Scrip," 16 October 1886.

86 Among the signatories to the petition were Julie Martin's sons Joseph, François, William, Xavier, Pierre, Cuthbert, and daughter Julie Larocque, as well as three of Martin's grandchildren: Pierre Jr., son of Pierre Lemire, and Adelaide and Marie Rose Larocque, daughters of Julie and Baptiste Larocque.

87 LAC, RG15, HB8276, "T.W. Jackson to Thomas White, Minister of the Interior, Petition signed by 34 Half-Breed heads of families of the Qu'Appelle District who have recently left Treaty with a view to taking Scrip," 16 October 1886.

88 LAC, RG15, HB8276, "A.M. Burgess to Thomas White, Minister of the Interior, Petition signed by 34 Half-Breed heads of families of the Qu'Appelle District who have recently left Treaty with a view to taking Scrip," 2 November 1886; "Additional Scrip for Half-Breeds," *Qu'Appelle Vidette*, 6 January 1887.

89 "Additional Scrip for Half-Breeds," *Qu'Appelle Vidette*, 6 January 1887.

90 Métis Association of Alberta et al., *Métis Land Rights*, 112.

91 Métis Association of Alberta et al., 103.

92 Tough and McGregor, "Rights to the Lands."

93 Augustus, "The Scrip Solution."

94 Ens and Sawchuk, *From New Peoples to New Nations*, 160.

95 Tough and McGregor, "Rights to Lands"; Tough, *As Their Natural Resources Fail*; Métis Association of Alberta et al., *Métis Land Rights*; Ens and Sawchuk, *From New Peoples to New Nations*.
96 Métis Association of Alberta et al., *Métis Land Rights*, 131; Augustus, "The Scrip Solution," 102–3.
97 Métis Association of Alberta et al., *Métis Land Rights*, 136.
98 Tough, *As Their Natural Resources Fail*, 188.
99 Métis Association of Alberta et al., *Métis Land Rights*, 91–92; Sprague, *Canada and the Métis*; Hatt, "North-West Rebellion Scrip Commissions."
100 Flanagan, *Métis Lands in Manitoba*.
101 Métis Association of Alberta et al., *Métis Land Rights*, 118.
102 "Lieut.-Governor's Visit to Qu'Appelle Half-breeds," *Qu'Appelle Vidette*, 11 February 1886.
103 LAC, RG15, D-II-1, Vol 447, Work for Half-Breeds in Qu'Appelle, Letter from Norbert Welsh, File No. 118650, "Norbert Welsh to Lieutenant Governor Edgar Dewdney," 14 June 1886.
104 LAC, RG15, D-II-1, Vol 447, Work for Half-Breeds in Qu'Appelle, Letter from Norbert Welsh, File No. 118650, "W.A. Clark to Lieutenant Governor Edgar Dewdney," 3 December 1886.
105 LAC, RG15, D-II-1, Vol 447, Work for Half-Breeds in Qu'Appelle, Letter from Norbert Welsh, File No. 118650, "W.A. Clark to Lieutenant Governor Edgar Dewdney," 3 December 1886.
106 LAC, RG15, D-II-1, Vol 447, Work for Half-Breeds in Qu'Appelle, Letter from Norbert Welsh, File No. 118650, "Amédée Forget, Clerk of Council to A.M. Burgess, Deputy Minister of the Interior," 24 June 1886.
107 Dick, *Farmers "Making Good,"* 18–19.
108 LAC, RG15, D-II-1, Vol 447, Work for Half-Breeds in Qu'Appelle, Letter from Norbert Welsh, File No. 118650, "W.A. Clark, Survey of Half-Breeds in Qu'Appelle and File Hills Districts," 3 December 1886; PAS, Canada Census, The Territories, Qu'Appelle, District 192, Sub-District H, 1881.
109 Carter, "Demonstrating Success," 241.
110 PAS, Saskatchewan Homestead Files, File 710304, Joseph Brunet.
111 This included François Perreault and his wife Margaurite Allard. An elderly couple in their seventies, they lived close to their son Xavier Perreault and his wife Isabelle Bonneau. Xavier and Isabelle's own children, daughter Leocadie and son Camile, also lived in the region with their respective spouses, Hilaire Boucher and Mary Racette. Also living here were Isabelle's father Pierre Bonneau, and siblings Pierre and Emerise.
112 Dick, *Farmers "Making Good,"* 18–19.
113 PAS, Saskatchewan Homestead Files, Joseph Gosselin, File 223975, "Homestead Inspector Report to H.H. Smith, Commissioner of Dominion Lands," 15 August 1885; PAS, Saskatchewan Homestead Files, Joseph Gosselin, File 223975, "Joseph Gosselin, Statement," 4 September 1885.

114 PAS, Saskatchewan Homestead Files, John Klyne File 901341, "Homestead Inspector Report to H.H. Smith, Commissioner Dominion Lands Winnipeg," 14 August 1885.
115 PAS, Saskatchewan Homestead Files, Napoleon Blondeau, File 97893, "Homestead Inspector to Dominion Lands Agent," 5 August 1885.
116 PAS, Saskatchewan Homestead Files, Napoleon Blondeau, File 97893, "Homestead Inspector to Dominion Lands Agent," 5 August 1885.
117 PAS, Saskatchewan Homestead Files, Napoleon Blondeau, File 97893, "Napoleon Blondeau, Statement," 9 July 1884.
118 PAS, Saskatchewan Homestead Files, Napoleon Blondeau, File 97893, "Homestead Inspector to Dominion Lands Agent," 5 August 1885.
119 PAS, Saskatchewan Homestead Files, Chrysotome Robilllard, File 481066.
120 PAS, Saskatchewan Homestead Files, File 222646, "Napoleon Blondeau, Declaration," 9 June 1909.
121 PAS, Saskatchewan Homestead Files, Jean Blondeau, File 240969, "Homestead Inspectors Report."
122 PAS, Saskatchewan Homestead Files, Zacharie Blondeau, File 504182, "Homestead Inspectors Report," 29 August 1884.
123 PAS, Saskatchewan Homestead Files, Zacharie Blondeau, File 504182, "Zacharie Blondeau, Declaration, 20 November 1893.
124 PAS, Saskatchewan Homestead Files, Eustache Brabant, File 130220, "T.W. Jackson to A. Walsh, Commissioner of Lands Branch," 6 July 1884.
125 PAS, Saskatchewan Homestead Files, Cuthbert St. Denis, File 182988.

Chapter 6. "We Got Our House Built by Seneca Roots": Life on the Road Allowance

1 Bob Desjarlais, interview, 3 July 2002. Select portions of this chapter have been published as "Métis Stories an Women's Artistic Labour in Margaret Pelletier Harrison's Margaret's Rug," in Michele Hardy, Timothy Long, and Julia Krueger, eds., *Prairie Interlace: Weaving, Modernisms, and the Expanded Frame, 1960–2000.* Calgary: University of Calgary Press, 2023.
2 Payment, "Batoche After 1885," 173–88; Payment, *Free People.*
3 Marles et al., *Aboriginal Plant,* 216–17.
4 Payment, *Free People,* 232; Payment, "Batoche After 1885," 174–75.
5 Barnett, "Big Business," 20; Pallister, "The Bone Hunters." Sugar manufacturers used crushed bison bones to filter impurities out of sugar cane juice, leaving a clear liquid that, when dried, produced pure white sugar. For an examination of communal buffalo hunting and the creation of buffalo bone beds, see: Walker, "An Overview of Prehistoric Communal Bison Hunting on the Great Plains."
6 Payment, *Free People,* 230–31.
7 St-Onge, "Memories," 62.
8 St-Onge, "Memories," 62.

9 LaVallée, *St. Laurent.*
10 Barnett, "Big Business," 22–23.
11 Hogue, *Métis and the Medicine Line,* 176.
12 Potyondi, *In Palliser's Triangle,* 35–36; "Communications," *Qu'Appelle Vidette,* 11 July 1889.
13 Barnett, "Big Business," 24–25.
14 Barnett, 24–25.
15 Barnett, 21.
16 Barnett, 21.
17 Joe Blondeau, interview, 19 August 1982.
18 Barnett, "Big Business," 21.
19 Agnes Amyotte Fisher and Celina Amyotte Poitras, interview, 3 August 1982.
20 Binnie-Clark, *Wheat and Women,* 130–31.
21 John Joe Larocque, interview, 13 August 1982.
22 Stooking is the arrangement of fresh cut-grain stalks into sheaves while still in the field. Arranging cut stalks this way kept the grain heads off the ground, allowing the grain to dry and protecting it from vermin before it was threshed. Stooks could remain in the field for days or even weeks before the grain was dry enough for storage. Wheat, barley, and oats were typically arranged into stooks prior to threshing.
23 John Joe Larocque, interview, 13 August 1982.
24 Caroline Henry, interview, 15 August 1982.
25 Margaret Harrison and Adeline Pelletier dit Racette, interview, 23–24 May 2002; Margaret Harrison, interview, 9 July 2014.
26 Margaret Harrison and Adeline Pelletier dit Racette, interview, 23–24 May 2002.
27 Margaret Harrison, interview, 9 July 2014; Jimmy Larocque with Guy Blondeau, interview, 10–11 January 2004.
28 Josephine Tarr, interview, 27 February 1984.
29 Norma Welsh and Joe Welsh, interview, 7–8 February 2004.
30 Bob Desjarlais and George Klyne, interview, 6–7 December 2003.
31 Bob Desjarlais and George Klyne, interview, 6–7 December 2003.
32 Caroline Henry, interview, 15 August 1982; Agnes Amyotte Fisher and Celina Amyotte Poitras, interview, 3 August 1982; Agnes Poitras Pelletier, interview, 30 May 2003.
33 Agnes Poitras Pelletier, interview, 30 May 2003.
34 Caroline Henry, interview, 15 August 1982; Agnes Amyotte Fisher and Celina Amyotte Poitras, interview, 3 August 1982.
35 Caroline Henry, interview, 15 August 1982.
36 Agnes Amyotte Fisher and Celina Amyotte Poitras, interview, 3 August 1982.
37 Agnes Amyotte Fisher and Celina Amyotte Poitras, interview, 3 August 1982.
38 Bob Desjarlais and George Klyne, interview, 6–7 December 2003.
39 Bob Desjarlais and George Klyne, interview, 6–7 December 2003; PAS, Canada Census Returns, 1916, Sub-District 20, Qu'Appelle, District 26, Saskatchewan, Government of Canada.

40 Bob Desjarlais and George Klyne, interview, 6–7 December 2003; George Klyne, interview, 31 March 2007; George Klyne, interview, 4 August 2014; Bob Desjarlais, interview 15 May 2002; Stanley Racette, interview, 11 August 1983.
41 Bob Desjarlais, interview, 15 May 2002.
42 George Klyne, interview, 4 August 2014.
43 Bob Desjarlais, interview, 15 May 2002; George Klyne, interview, 4 August 2014.
44 George Klyne, interview, 4 August 2014.
45 George Klyne, interview, 31 March 2007.
46 Bob Desjarlais, interview, 15 May 2002; Bob Desjarlais, interview 3 July 2002.
47 George Klyne, interview, 4 August 2014.
48 PAS, Department of Social Welfare and Rehabilitation, Rehabilitation Branch, Lebret Métis Farm, R85-308, R933 File III 33b, "J.S. White to Mrs. A. Jakeman," 4 June 1960; PAS, Department of Social Welfare and Rehabilitation, Rehabilitation Branch, Lebret Métis Farm, R85-308, R933 File III 33b, "K. Forster, Director of Rehabilitation to J.S. White, Deputy Minister," 30 June 1960; PAS, Department of Social Welfare and Rehabilitation, Rehabilitation Branch, Lebret Métis Farm, R85-308, R933 File III 33b, "J.S. White to H.S. Meldrun, QC, Deputy Attorney General," 7 July 1961; PAS, Department of Social Welfare and Rehabilitation, Rehabilitation Branch, Lebret Métis Farm, R85-308, R933 File III 33b, "K. Forster to J.S. White, 20 September 1960. The Department of Social Welfare and Rehabilitation was unsure of how to interpret Skinner's term "retired Métis" and how to best proceed in a way that would benefit them. Far from any town or village, the parcel of land was east of Lebret on the north side of the Valley. A portion of the property fronted the water, but the majority was hillside, covered in grass and a few trees. The Director of Rehabilitation, K. Forster, saw no logical reason to accept the gift even if there were no restrictions on its use. He considered refusing it and pursued the option to sell, providing the proceeds be used to purchase land for the Métis near Lebret or for the cooperative housing projects at Lestock or Crooked Lake.
49 PAS, Department of Social Welfare and Rehabilitation, Rehabilitation Branch, Lebret Métis Farm, R85-308, R933 File III 33b, 20 September 1960.
50 Stanley Racette, interview, 11 August 1983; Agnes Poitras Pelletier, interview, 30 May 2003.
51 Bob Desjarlais and George Klyne, interview, 6–7 December 2003.
52 Josephine Tarr, interview, 27 February 1984.
53 Caroline Henry, interview, 15 August 1982.
54 Caroline Henry, interview, 15 August 1982.
55 Lux, *Medicine That Walks*, 99.
56 Lux, 99.
57 McNab, "George Gordon First Nations Women," 85–86; Brass, *I Walk in Two Worlds*, 37.
58 Bob Desjarlais and George Klyne, interview, 6–7 December 2003.
59 Bob Desjarlais and George Klyne, interview, 6–7 December 2003.

60 Bob Desjarlais and George Klyne, interview, 6–7 December 2003.
61 Bob Desjarlais and George Klyne, interview, 6–7 December 2003.
62 Joe Blondeau, interview, 19 August 1982.
63 Weekes, *Last Buffalo Hunter*, 172–73.
64 Farrell Racette, "Sewing Ourselves."
65 Farrell Racette, "Nimble Fingers and Strong Backs."
66 PAS, Saskatchewan Homestead Files, M. Blondeau, File 521351, "Simon Blondeau, Last Will and Testament," 20 October 1906. When Simon Blondeau died in 1906, he left his first homestead (SE3–Twp21–R13–W2) to his unmarried daughter Melanie and second homestead (SW14–Twp25–R12–W2) located north of the Valley in the settlement of Ste. Delphine to his son, Pierre.
67 Farrell Racette, "Sewing Ourselves," 244.
68 Paget, *People of the Plains*.
69 Quoted in Farrell Racette, "Sewing Ourselves," 244; LAC, RG10, Vol. 7908, File 40,000-9, Amelia M. Paget, "Report on the Qu'Appelle Agencies," 1913.
70 Quoted in Farrell Racette, "Sewing Ourselves," 244; LAC, RG10, Vol. 7908, File 40,000-9, Amelia M. Paget, "Report on the Qu'Appelle Agencies," 1913.
71 Farrell Racette, "Sewing Ourselves," 246.
72 Agnes Amyotte Fisher and Celina Amyotte Poitras, interview, 3 August 1982; Joseph Moran, interview, 22 August 1983; Bob Desjarlais and George Klyne, interview, 6–7 December 2003; Bob Desjarlais, interview, 15 May 2002; Bob Desjarlais, interview, 3 July 2002; Margaret Harrison and Adeline Pelletier dit Racette, interview, 23–24 May 2002; Margaret Harrison, interview, 24 February 2014; Margaret Harrison, interview, 9 July 2014.
73 Agnes Amyotte Fisher and Celina Amyotte Poitras, interview, 3 August 1982.
74 Margaret Harrison, interview, 9 July 2014.
75 Bob Desjarlais and George Klyne, interview, 6–7 December 2003; Bob Desjarlais, interview, 15 May 2002; Bob Desjarlais, interview, 3 July 2002; Margaret Harrison and Adeline Pelletier dit Racette, interview, 23–24 May 2002; Margaret Harrison, interview, 24 February 2014; Margaret Harrison, interview, 9 July 2014.
76 Joseph Moran, interview, 22 August 1983; Bob Desjarlais and George Klyne, interview, 6–7 December 2003; Bob Desjarlais, interview, 15 May 2002; Bob Desjarlais, interview, 3 July 2002; Margaret Harrison and Adeline Pelletier dit Racette, interview, 23–24 May 2002; Margaret Harrison, interview, 24 February 2014; Margaret Harrison, interview, 9 July 2014.
77 Margaret Harrison and Adeline Pelletier dit Racette, interview, 23–24 May 2002; Margaret Harrison, interview, 24 February 2014; Bob Desjarlais, interview, 15 May 2002.
78 Josephine Tarr, interview, 27 February 1984.
79 Joseph Moran, interview, 22 August 1983.
80 Joseph Moran, interview, 22 August 1983.
81 Margaret Harrison, interview, 9 July 2014; Margaret Harrison and Adeline Pelletier dit Racette, interview, 23–24 May 2002.

Chapter 7. Going Hunting Rabbits: Women's Labour in Feeding the Family

1 George Klyne, interview, 4 August 2014; Bob Desjarlais and George Klyne, interview, 6–7 December 2003. This is not a verbatim transcript of the story.

2 A version of this story has recently been transcribed by Klyne's grandson Jesse Rae Archibald Barber and published. George Klyne, "The Trapper and the Snare."

3 LAC, RG15, D-II-1, Vol 447, Work for Half-Breeds in Qu'Appelle, Letter from Norbert Welsh, File No. 118650, "W.A. Clark, Survey of Half-Breeds in Qu'Appelle and File Hills Districts," 3 December 1886.

4 Stanley Racette, interview, 11 August 1983.

5 Stanley Racette, interview, 11 August 1983.

6 Moise Vallee had 100 pounds and Michel Klyne 700 pounds.

7 The size of flour sacks is not recorded, but it is likely these were forty-nine-pound quarter barrel sacks, which were commonly used in this period.

8 LAC, RG15, D-II-1, Vol 447, Work for Half-Breeds in Qu'Appelle, Letter from Norbert Welsh, File No. 118650, "W.A. Clark, Survey of Half-Breeds in Qu'Appelle and File Hills Districts," 3 December 1886, Suzanne Pelletier, Household 44.

9 LAC, RG15, D-II-1, Vol 447, Work for Half-Breeds in Qu'Appelle, Letter from Norbert Welsh, File No. 118650, "W.A. Clark, Survey of Half-Breeds in Qu'Appelle and File Hills Districts," 3 December 1886, Madeleine Bourassa, Household 62; LAC, RG15, D-II-1, Vol 447, Work for Half-Breeds in Qu'Appelle, Letter from Norbert Welsh, File No. 118650, "W.A. Clark, Survey of Half-Breeds in Qu'Appelle and File Hills Districts," 3 December 1886, Madeleine Klyne, Household 51.

10 LAC, RG15, D-II-1, Vol 447, Work for Half-Breeds in Qu'Appelle, Letter from Norbert Welsh, File No. 118650, "W.A. Clark, Survey of Half-Breeds in Qu'Appelle and File Hills Districts," 3 December 1886, Suzanne Pelletier, Household 44.

11 PAS, Canada Census, The Territories, Qu'Appelle, District 192, Sub-District H, Household 52, "Joseph Pelletier," 1881; PAS, Canada Census, The Territories, Qu'Appelle, District 192, Sub-District H, Household 55, "Roderick Ross," 1881; LAC, RG15, D-II-1, Vol 447, Work for Half-Breeds in Qu'Appelle, Letter from Norbert Welsh, File No. 118650, "W.A. Clark, Survey of Half-Breeds in Qu'Appelle and File Hills Districts," 3 December 1886, Cuthbert Pelletier, Household 42; LAC, RG15, D-II-1, Vol 447, Work for Half-Breeds in Qu'Appelle, Letter from Norbert Welsh, File No. 118650, "W.A. Clark, Survey of Half-Breeds in Qu'Appelle and File Hills Districts," 3 December 1886, Roderick Ross, Household 43.

12 PAS, Canada Census, The Territories, Qu'Appelle, District 192, Sub-District H, Household 59, "Suzanne Pelletier," 1881; LAC, RG15, D-II-1, Vol 447, Work for Half-Breeds in Qu'Appelle, Letter from Norbert Welsh, File No. 118650, "W.A. Clark, Survey of Half-Breeds in Qu'Appelle and File Hills Districts," 3 December 1886, "Suzanne Pelletier, Household 44."

13 LAC, RG15, D-II-1, Vol 447, Work for Half-Breeds in Qu'Appelle, Letter from Norbert Welsh, File No. 118650, "W.A. Clark, Survey of Half-Breeds in Qu'Appelle

and File Hills Districts," 3 December 1886, "Edouard Pelletier, Household 15"; LAC, RG15, D-II-1, Vol 447, Work for Half-Breeds in Qu'Appelle, Letter from Norbert Welsh, File No. 118650, "W.A. Clark, Survey of Half-Breeds in Qu'Appelle and File Hills Districts," 3 December 1886, "Alphonse Pelletier, Household 11"; LAC, RG15, D-II-1, Vol 447, Work for Half-Breeds in Qu'Appelle, Letter from Norbert Welsh, File No. 118650, "W.A. Clark, Survey of Half-Breeds in Qu'Appelle and File Hills Districts," 3 December 1886; LAC, RG15, D-II-1, Vol 447, Work for Half-Breeds in Qu'Appelle, Letter from Norbert Welsh, File No. 118650, "W.A. Clark, Survey of Half-Breeds in Qu'Appelle and File Hills Districts," 3 December 1886, "Joseph Pelletier, Household 13."

14 Madeleine Beauchemin Klyne was the daughter of Charlotte Pelletier, Charles Pelletier's sister.

15 LAC, RG15, D-II-8-c, Vol. 1337, "Madeleine Bourassa, as heir of Jean Baptiste Bourassa, Scrip Claim 143," 2 May 1885.

16 LAC, RG15, D-II-1, Vol. 496, "Madeleine Bourassa, Declaration," 15 June 1900; LAC, RG15-D-II-8-c, Vol. 1337, "Bella Bourassa, Claim 1271."

17 Glenbow, Department of Indian Affairs, Hobbema Agency, File 845, "List of Halfbreeds who have Withdrawn from Treaty," 1 June 1888; LAC, RG10, Vol. 3912, File 111,716, "Assistant Secretary to Superintendent General, Department of Indian Affairs," 26 February 1894.

18 LAC, RG15, D-II-1, Vol 447, Work for Half-Breeds in Qu'Appelle, Letter from Norbert Welsh, File No. 118650, "W.A. Clark, Survey of Half-Breeds in Qu'Appelle and File Hills Districts," 3 December 1886, "Mrs. Jean Baptiste Bourassa," Household 62.

19 LAC, RG15, D-II-1, Vol 447, Work for Half-Breeds in Qu'Appelle, Letter from Norbert Welsh, File No. 118650, "W.A. Clark, Survey of Half-Breeds in Qu'Appelle and File Hills Districts," 3 December 1886, "Madeleine Bourassa, Household 62."; LAC, RG15, D-II-8-b, Vol. 1325, "Mrs. Jean Baptiste Bourassa, Claim 169," 1 May 1885. Families living on Section 8-Township 21-Range 13 included: Joseph Vilbrun, Joseph Lambert, George Fisher, Marshall Vivier, Mrs. Louis Duscharme, Gabriel Fisher, and Alphonso Martin. In neighbouring sections were Simon Blondeau Sr., and Mrs. Pete LaPierre and her son Thomas LaPierre.

20 LAC, RG15, D-II-8-c, Vol 1337, "Baptiste Bourassa, Claim 2225"; Glenbow, Department of Indian Affairs, Hobbema Agency, File 845, "List of Halfbreeds who have Withdrawn from Treaty," 1 June 1888. Baptiste Bourassa had taken treaty at Cote reserve with his first wife. His second wife, Harriet, was a member of the Keeseekoose when the family discharged from treaty in 1886.

21 LAC, RG15, D-II-8-c, Vol. 1363, "Norbert Pelletier, Claim 1135."

22 LAC, RG15, D-II-8-b, Vol. 1325, "Patrice Bourassa, Claim 74"; LAC, RG15, D-II-8-c, Vol. 1347, "Pierre Flammand, heir to his deceased children, Claim 589"; LAC, RG15, D-II-8-c, Vol. 1363, "Norbert Pelletier, Claim 1135."

23 PAS, F.C. Gilchrist, "Diary of a Homesteader and Fisheries Inspector, 1883–1896."

24 PAS, Saskatchewan Homestead Files, Madeleine Klyne, Files 290.68 and 115261.

25 Margaret Harrison, interview, 24 February 2014.
26 Bob Desjarlais, interview, 15 May 2002.
27 Margaret Harrison, interview, 9 July 2014; Bob Desjarlais, interview, 15 May 2002.
28 Portt et al., *A Review of Fish Sampling Methods.*
29 Portt et al., *A Review of Fish Sampling Methods.*
30 Margaret Harrison, interview, 9 July 2014.
31 Delphine Desjarlais, interview, 8 July 2014.
32 Like many other ground squirrels, Richardson's ground squirrels (*Urocitellus richarsonii,* formerly *Spermophilus richardsonii*) are colloquially called gophers. They are burrowing rodents that dig extensive underground tunnels. Their habitat stretches throughout the northern U.S. and western Canada. During hard times, they provided food when there were few other options. Gail R. Michener and Josef K. Schmutz, "Richardson's Ground Squirrel, *Spermophilus richardsonii,*" accessed 10 August 2024, http://www.albertapcf.org/rsu_docs/prairie_notes_2.pdf.
33 Snares were made from thin wire fashioned into a loop and attached to a stick. The wire loop acts like a trip wire that tightens into a noose, killing the animal when it enters the loop and trips the wire.
34 Anderson, *Life Stages of Native Women.*
35 Delphine Desjarlais, interview, 8 July 2014.
36 Pauline Anderson, Billie Robison, and Norma Welsh, interview, 2004.
37 Bob Desjarlais, interview, 3 July 2002.
38 Bob Desjarlais, interview, 3 July 2002.
39 Bob Desjarlais and George Klyne, interview, 6–7 December 2003; Bob Desjarlais, interview, 15 May 2002.
40 Bob Desjarlais, interview, 15 May 2002.
41 Bob Desjarlais, interview, 15 May 2002.
42 Bob Desjarlais and George Klyne, interview, 6–7 December 2003.
43 Roy Poitras, interview, 4 July 2015.
44 Bob Desjarlais, interview, 15 May 2002; Bob Desjarlais and George Klyne, interview, 6–7 December 2003.
45 For a discussion of game law regulation and enforcement, see Chapter 8.
46 Bob Desjarlais and George Klyne, interview, 6–7 December 2003.
47 Bob Desjarlais and George Klyne, interview, 6–7 December 2003; Campbell, *Halfbreed.*
48 Roy Poitras, interview, 4 July 2015.
49 Roy Poitras, interview, 4 July 2015.
50 PAS, Department of Natural Resources, N.R.3, Correspondence with Field Offices and District Superintendents – J.Z. Larocque, Lebret, 1935–1938, A.4.2. "J.Z. Larocque, Field Officer, to Commissioner John R. Hill, Department of Natural Resources," 1 May 1936.
51 Following his employment with the provincial government, Larocque actively politicized Métis across southern Saskatchewan becoming one of the founders and first presidents of the Saskatchewan Métis Society. He was well respected by

many in the community, serving as a public notary and often as an intermediary for community members when they had legal affairs that needed attention. He actively wrote and spoke publicly on Métis issues and history. For more on J.Z. Larocque, see Devine, "J.Z. Larocque."

52 Jimmy Larocque with Guy Blondeau, interview, 10–11 January 2004; Bob Desjarlais and George Klyne, interview, 6–7 December 2003.

53 Bob Desjarlais, interview, 15 May 2002; Bob Desjarlais and George Klyne, interview, 6–7 December 2003.

54 PAS, Department of Natural Resources, N.R.3, Correspondence with Field Offices and District Superintendents—J.Z. Larocque, Lebret, 1935–1938, A.4.2. "J.Z. Larocque, Field Officer, to Commissioner E. Forsythe, Department of Natural Resources," 18 July 1937.

55 Bob Desjarlais and George Klyne, interview, 6–7 December 2003.

56 Hourie and Carriére-Acco, "Métis Families."

57 Margaret Harrison, interview, 9 July 2014; Delphine Desjarlais, interview, 8 July 2014; Bob Desjarlais, interview, 3 July 2002.

58 Bob Desjarlais and George Klyne, interview, 6–7 December 2003.

59 Manitoba Maples (*Acer negundo*) are found in the Qu'Appelle Valley and across the western prairies, not the Sugar Maples (*Acer saccharum*) commonly found in Quebec. Manitoba Maples produce a light-coloured syrup, less sweet than the syrup made from sugar maple sap.

60 J.Z. Larocque, "Maples Tapped for 100 Years," *Regina Leader Post*, 9 May 1946.

61 Lucy Desjarlais Whiteman, interview with Rita Schilling, in Schilling, *Gabriel's Children*, 92.

62 Lawrence Welsh, Pauline Anderson, Billie Robison, Pat Sullivan, and Norma Welsh, interview, 2004.

63 Lawrence Welsh, Pauline Anderson, Billie Robison, Pat Sullivan, and Norma Welsh, interview, 2004.

64 Bob Desjarlais, interview, 3 July 2002; Margaret Harrison, interview, 24 February 2014; Roy Poitras, interview, 4 July 2015; Bob Desjarlais and George Klyne, interview, 6–7 December 2003; Campbell, *Halfbreed*; Campbell, "Foreword."

65 Roy Poitras, interview, 4 July 2015.

66 Bob Desjarlais, interview, 3 July 2002.

67 Delphine Desjarlais, interview, 8 July 2014.

68 Bob Desjarlais, interview, 3 July 2002.

69 Norma Welsh and Joe Welsh, interview, 7–8 February 2004.

70 Bob Desjarlais and George Klyne, interview, 6–7 December 2003; Norma Welsh and Joe Welsh, interview, 7–8 February 2004.

71 Brown and Brightman, *"The Orders of the Dreamed,"* 197.

72 Brass, *Medicine Boy and Other Cree Tales.*

73 Norma Welsh and Joe Welsh, interview, 7–8 February 2004.

74 Lawrie Barkwell, "Métis Folklore: People, Ma-ma-kwa-se-sak or Memequayiwahk," accessed 10 August 2024, http://www.metismuseum.ca/media/document.php/14521.Métis%20Folklore.pdf
75 Norma Welsh and Joe Welsh, interview, 7–8 February 2004.
76 Norma Welsh and Joe Welsh, interview, 7–8 February 2004.
77 Norma Welsh and Joe Welsh, interview, 7–8 February 2004.
78 Joseph Parisien, interview, 8 August 1983.
79 Bob Desjarlais, interview, 15 May 2002.
80 Caroline Henry, interview, 15 August 1982.
81 Margaret Harrison, interview, 24 February 2014.
82 The Rural Municipality of North Qu'Appelle No. 187 was incorporated in 1919 and governed by a reeve (a position similar to a mayor), and council. In the early years of the twentieth century Saskatchewan, local governments or rural municipalities were financially responsible for medical and relief provided to their poor or "indigent" residents. For a further discussion of relief, see Chapter 9.
83 Bob Desjarlais and George Klyne, interview, 6–7 December 2003.
84 Margaret Harrison, interview, 24 February 2014.
85 Bob Desjarlais and George Klyne, interview, 6–7 December 2003.
86 Margaret Harrison, interview, 9 July 2014.
87 Norma Welsh and Joe Welsh, interview, 7–8 February 2004.
88 Margaret Harrison, interview, 9 July 2014.
89 Margaret Harrison, interview, 24 February 2014.
90 Bob Desjarlais and George Klyne, interview, 6–7 December 2003.
91 Delphine Desjarlais, interview, 8 July 2014.
92 Margaret Harrison, interview, 24 February 2014.
93 Bob Desjarlais and George Klyne, interview, 6–7 December 2003; Margaret Harrison, interview, 9 July 2014; Joseph Moran, interview, 22 August 1983.
94 Delphine Desjarlais, interview, 8 July 2014; Margaret Harrison, interview, 9 July 2014.
95 Joe Blondeau, interview, 19 August 1982.
96 Roy Poitras, interview, 4 July 2015.
97 Norma Welsh, interview, 16 February 2014.
98 Burley, Horsfall, and Brandon, *Structural Considerations of Métis Ethnicity.*
99 Margaret Harrison, interview, 9 July 2014.
100 John Arcand, personal communication, 15 January 2017.
101 Margaret Harrison, interview, 9 July 2014; Billie Robison, interview, 15 March 2000; Agnes Pelletier, interview, 30 May 2003.
102 Weekes, *Last Buffalo Hunter,* 110.
103 Payment, *Free People,* 49.
104 Lawrence Welsh, Pauline Anderson, Billie Robison, Pat Sullivan, and Norma Welsh, interview, 2004.
105 Agnes Poitras Pelletier, interview, 30 May 2003.

106 Josephine Tarr, interview, 27 February 1984; Mary Desnomie, interview, 23 February 2010; Norma Welsh, interview, 16 February 2014; Margaret Harrison, 12 February 2010.

107 Billie Robison, interview, 15 March 2000.

108 Margaret Harrison, interview, 9 July 2014.

109 Billie Robison, interview, 15 March 2000.

110 Margaret Harrison, interview, 9 July 2014.

111 Lawrence Welsh, Pauline Anderson, Billie Robison, Pat Sullivan, and Norma Welsh, interview, 2004.

112 Roy Poitras, interview, 4 July 2015.

113 PAS, Rural Municipality of North Qu'Appelle No. 187, R2.739, Relief Records 1921–1955.

114 Bob Desjarlais, interview, 15 May 2002.

115 Joseph Parisien, interview, 8 August 1983.

116 Margaret Harrison, interview, 24 February 2014.

117 Margaret Harrison, interview, 24 February 2014.

118 Lawrence Welsh, Pauline Anderson, Billie Robison, Pat Sullivan, and Norma Welsh, interview, 2004.

119 Margaret Harrison, interview, 24 February 2014.

120 Payment, *Free People*, 49.

121 Margaret Harrison, interview, 24 February 2014.

122 Pauline Anderson, Billie Robison, and Norma Welsh, interview, 2004.

123 Roy Poitras, interview, 4 July 2015.

124 Margaret Harrison and Adeline Pelletier dit Racette, interview, 23–24 May 2002.

125 Margaret Harrison, interview, 24 February 2014.

126 Roy Poitras, interview, 4 July 2015.

127 Epiphany is a Catholic holiday celebrated January 6 to mark the coming of the three wise men to visit the baby Jesus.

128 Hourie, et al., "Métis Foods," 130.

129 Bob Desjarlais and George Klyne, interview, 6–7 December 2003.

130 Bob Desjarlais and George Klyne, interview, 6–7 December 2003.

131 Agnes Poitras Pelletier, interview, 30 May 2003.

132 Joseph Z. Larocque, "Métis celebrate Le Jour de l'An," *Regina Leader Post,* 8 January 1948; Joseph Z. Larocque, "Traditional Religious Theme for Métis Yule Observance," *Regina Leader Post*, 24 December 1955.

133 Joseph Z. Larocque, "Métis celebrate Le Jour de l'An," *Regina Leader Post,* 8 January 1948.

134 Joseph Z. Larocque, "Métis celebrate Le Jour de l'An," *Regina Leader Post,* 8 January 1948.

Chapter 8. Contesting Government Intervention into Harvesting Spaces

1 Margaret Harrison, interview, 9 July 2014.

2 For more on the influence of British values of hunting and wildlife, on Canadian conservation and wildlife regulation see Loo, *States of Nature*; Gillespie, *Hunting for Empire;* Calliou, "Losing the Game."
3 Foster, *Working for Wildlife*, 3.
4 Foster, 4.
5 Loo, *States of Nature*, 6.
6 Foster, *Working for Wildlife*, 8–9.
7 Colpitts, *Game in the Garden*, 39; Owram, *Promise of Eden.*
8 Colpitts, *Game in the Garden*, 165.
9 Colpitts, 67; Sandlos, *Hunters at the Margins.*
10 Calliou, "Losing the Game," 155.
11 Loo, *States of Nature*, 6.
12 Loo, 4–6.
13 Foster, *Working for Wildlife*, 8; Waiser, "Legislator's View," 255.
14 Waiser, "Legislator's View," 255.
15 A fisher is a member of the weasel family and resembles a large mink.
16 North-West Territories, *Ordinances of the North-West Territories.*
17 Gulig, "We Beg the Government."
18 D.H. Bocking, "Gilchrist, Frederick Charles," *Dictionary of Canadian Biography*, last revised 1990, http://www.biographi.ca/en/bio/gilchrist_frederick_charles_12E.html.
19 For instance, in 1889, he noted the presence of about twenty Halfbreed and Indian families, or 100 people, fishing north of the Qu'Appelle Valley at Long Lake, with about 140 gill nets.
20 LAC, *Sessional Papers*, 1886, Department of Marine and Fisheries, No. 11, Annual Report for Department of Marine and Fisheries for 1885.
21 LAC, *Sessional Papers*, 1888, Department of Marine and Fisheries, No. 6, Annual Report of the Department of Marine and Fisheries, 1887.
22 LAC, *Sessional Papers*, 1888, Department of Marine and Fisheries, No. 6, Annual Report of the Department of Marine and Fisheries, 1887.
23 LAC, *Sessional Papers*, 1889, Department of Marine and Fisheries, No. 8, Annual Report of the Department of Marine and Fisheries, 1888.
24 LAC, *Sessional Papers*, 1893, Department of Marine and Fisheries, No. 10A, Annual Report of the Department of Marine and Fisheries, 1892.
25 LAC, *Sessional Papers*, 1887, Department of Marine and Fisheries, No. 16, Annual Report of the Department of Marine and Fisheries, 1886.
26 LAC, *Sessional Papers*, 1893, Department of Marine and Fisheries, No. 10A, Annual Report of the Department of Marine and Fisheries, 1892.
27 LAC, *Sessional Papers*, 1888, Department of Marine and Fisheries, No. 6, Annual Report of the Department of Marine and Fisheries, 1887.
28 LAC, RG15, D-II-1, Vol 447, Work for Half-Breeds in Qu'Appelle, Letter from Norbert Welsh, File No. 118650, "W.A. Clark, Survey of Half-Breeds in Qu'Appelle and File Hills Districts," 3 December 1886.

29 LAC, *Sessional Papers*, 1913, Department of Marine and Fisheries, No. 22, Annual Report of the Department of Marine and Fisheries, 1912, "Appendix No.9, Saskatchewan—Report on the Fisheries of the Province by Inspector E.W. Miller, Fort Qu'Appelle."

30 LAC, *Sessional Papers*, 1916, Department of Marine and Fisheries, No. 39, Annual Report of the Department of Marine and Fisheries, 1915, "Appendix No. 6. Saskatchewan and Alberta—Report on the Fisheries of the Provinces by Chief Inspector G.S. Davidson, Indian Head, Saskatchewan."

31 LAC, *Sessional Papers*, 1893, Department of Marine and Fisheries, No. 10A, Annual Report of the Department of Marine and Fisheries, 1892.

32 LAC, *Sessional Papers*, 1895, Department of Marine and Fisheries, No. 11A, Annual Report of the Department of Marine and Fisheries, 1894, "Appendix No. 12, North-West Territories—Annual Report for the Year 1894, on the Fisheries of the North-West Territories, by Inspector F.C. Gilchrist."

33 LAC, *Sessional Papers*, 1894, Department of Marine and Fisheries, No. 11, Annual Report of the Department of Marine and Fisheries, "Appendix No. 10, North-West Territories—Annual Report for the Year 1893, on the Fisheries of the North-West Territories, by Inspector F.C. Gilchrist."

34 LAC, *Sessional Papers*, 1893, Department of Marine and Fisheries, No. 10A, Annual Report of the Department of Marine and Fisheries, 1892, "Appendix No. 12."; LAC, *Sessional Papers*, 1895, Department of Marine and Fisheries, No. 11A, Annual Report of the Department of Marine and Fisheries, 1894.

35 LAC, *Sessional Papers*, 1893, Department of Marine and Fisheries, No. 10A, Annual Report of the Department of Marine and Fisheries, 1892.

36 LAC, *Sessional Papers*, 1893, Department of Marine and Fisheries, No. 10A, Annual Report of the Department of Marine and Fisheries, 1892.

37 LAC, *Sessional Papers*, 1894, Department of Marine and Fisheries, No. 11, Annual Report of the Department of Marine and Fisheries, "Appendix No. 10, North-West Territories—Annual Report for the Year 1893, on the Fisheries of the North-West Territories, by Inspector F.C. Gilchrist."

38 LAC, *Sessional Papers*, 1894, Department of Marine and Fisheries, No. 11, Annual Report of the Department of Marine and Fisheries, "Appendix No. 10, North-West Territories—Annual Report for the Year 1893, on the Fisheries of the North-West Territories, by Inspector F.C. Gilchrist."

39 LAC, *Sessional Papers*, 1894, Department of Marine and Fisheries, No. 11, Annual Report of the Department of Marine and Fisheries, "Appendix No. 10, North-West Territories—Annual Report for the Year 1893, on the Fisheries of the North-West Territories, by Inspector F.C. Gilchrist."

40 LAC, *Sessional Papers*, 1894, Department of Marine and Fisheries, No. 11, Annual Report of the Department of Marine and Fisheries, "Appendix No. 10, North-West Territories—Annual Report for the Year 1893, on the Fisheries of the North-West Territories, by Inspector F.C. Gilchrist."

41 LAC, *Sessional Papers*, 1894, Department of Marine and Fisheries, No. 11, Annual Report of the Department of Marine and Fisheries, "Appendix No. 10, North-West Territories—Annual Report for the Year 1893, on the Fisheries of the North-West Territories, by Inspector F.C. Gilchrist."

42 LAC, *Sessional Papers*, 1895, Department of Marine and Fisheries, No. 11A, Annual Report of the Department of Marine and Fisheries, 1894, "Appendix No. 12."

43 LAC, *Sessional Papers*, 1900, Department of Marine and Fisheries, No. 11A, Annual Report of the Department of Marine and Fisheries, 1899.

44 LAC, *Sessional Papers*, 1901, Department of Marine and Fisheries, No. 22, Annual Report of the Department of Marine and Fisheries,1900, "Appendix No. 7, North-West Territories—Report on the Fisheries of the North-West Territories, for the Year 1899, by Inspector E.W. Miller."

45 *Qu'Appelle Vidette*, 21 April 1877.

46 In a review of Canada Sessional Papers Annual Reports from the Department of Marine and Fisheries from 1886 to 1900 there are only a handful on instances where Métis fisherman were apprehended and fined.

47 LAC, Sessional Papers, 1889, Department of Marine and Fisheries, No. 8, Annual Report for the Department of Marine and Fisheries, 1888, "Appendix No.7"; PAS, F.C. Gilchrist, "Diary of a Homesteader and Fisheries Inspector, 1883–1896."

48 PAS, F.C. Gilchrist, "Diary of a Homesteader and Fisheries Inspector, 1883–1896."

49 PAS, F.C. Gilchrist, "Diary of a Homesteader and Fisheries Inspector, 1883–1896."

50 PAS, F.C. Gilchrist, "Diary of a Homesteader and Fisheries Inspector, 1883–1896"; Métis fishers Baptiste Desjarlais, Simon Blondeau, Alex Fisher, Baptiste Robillard, Jules Cardinal, François Boucher, "Old Fayant," and others including several Métis women, such as Madeleine Klyne and her daughters Elise Klyne Kavanaugh, Madeleine Klyne Desjarlais, and Marie Klyne Bellegarde, regularly came into conflict with state agents.

51 PAS, F.C. Gilchrist, "Diary of a Homesteader and Fisheries Inspector, 1883–1896."

52 PAS, F.C. Gilchrist, "Diary of a Homesteader and Fisheries Inspector, 1883–1896."

53 PAS, F.C. Gilchrist, "Diary of a Homesteader and Fisheries Inspector, 1883–1896."

54 North-West Territories, *Journals of the Legislative Assembly*, 83–84.

55 PAS, Department of the Interior, Fisheries Regulation, John Mcgee, Clerk Privy Council to Lieutenant Governor, Certified Copy of a Report of a Committee of the Honourable Privy Council, Approved by his Excellency the Governor General in Council, on the 28th of October 1893.

56 PAS, F.C. Gilchrist, "Diary of a Homesteader and Fisheries Inspector, 1883–1896."

57 PAS, F.C. Gilchrist, "Diary of a Homesteader and Fisheries Inspector, 1883–1896."

58 PAS, F.C. Gilchrist, "Diary of a Homesteader and Fisheries Inspector, 1883–1896."

59 PAS, F.C. Gilchrist, "Diary of a Homesteader and Fisheries Inspector, 1883–1896."

60 PAS, F.C. Gilchrist, "Diary of a Homesteader and Fisheries Inspector, 1883–1896."

61 PAS, F.C. Gilchrist, "Diary of a Homesteader and Fisheries Inspector, 1883–1896."

62 LAC, *Sessional Papers*, 1909, Department of Marine and Fisheries, No. 22, Annual Report of the Department of Marine and Fisheries by Inspector E.W. Miller, for the Year Ending March 30, 1908, "Appendix No. 9."

63 Canada, *Dominion Alberta and Saskatchewan Fisheries Commission*, 22.

64 Canada, 29.

65 LAC, *Sessional Papers, 1914*, Department of Marine and Fisheries, No. 22, Annual Report of the Department of Marine and Fisheries, "Appendix No. 9. Saskatchewan and Alberta—Report on the Fisheries of the Provinces, by Chief Inspector E.W. Miller, Fort Qu'Appelle," 1912.

66 LAC, *Sessional Papers, 1915*, Department of Marine and Fisheries, No. 39, Annual Report of the Department of Marine and Fisheries, "Appendix No. 7. Saskatchewan and Alberta—Report on the Fisheries of the Provinces, by Chief Inspector E.W. Miller, Fort Qu'Appelle," 1913.

67 LAC, *Sessional Papers, 1916*, Department of Marine and Fisheries, No. 39, Annual Report of the Department of Marine and Fisheries, "Appendix No. 6. Annual Report of the Department of Marine and Fisheries," 1915.

68 For instance, Métis at Lac Pelletier in southern Saskatchewan were given free fishing permits from at least 1924 to 1929. See PAS, Department of Natural Resources, F-300-RR, Fisheries NR1-1 Fisheries: Rules and Regulations, 1930–31, "G.C. MacDonald, Supervisor of Fisheries to John Barnett, Deputy Minister, Department of Natural Resources," 8 October 1930.

69 PAS, Department of Natural Resources, F-300-RR, Fisheries NR1-1, Fisheries: Rules and Regulations, 1930–31, "Village of Fort Qu'Appelle to Minister of Natural Resources, Department of Natural Resources," 23 October 1930; PAS, Department of Natural Resources, F-300-RR, Fisheries NR1-1, Fisheries: Rules and Regulations, 1930–31, "Rural Municipality of North Qu'Appelle No. 187 to Minister of Natural Resources, Department of Natural Resources," 6 November 1930.

70 PAS, Department of Natural Resources, Fisheries Branch, NR.13 7, Licenses, Free to Halfbreeds and Destitute Settlers and closed season fishing, 1931–1942, "N.E. Rose, Secretary Treasurer, Municipality of North Qu'Appelle No. 187 to John Barnett, Deputy Minister of Natural Resources," 5 May 1931. At this time, the municipality estimated that there were at least thirty-five to forty Métis families or 200 individuals living within their boundaries.

71 PAS, Department of Natural Resources, Fisheries Branch, NR.13 7, Licenses, Free to Halfbreeds and Destitute Settlers and closed season fishing, 1931–1942, "N.E. Rose, Secretary Treasurer, Municipality of North Qu'Appelle No. 187 to John Barnett, Deputy Minister of Natural Resources," 5 May 1931.

72 PAS, Department of Natural Resources, F-300-RR, Fisheries NR1-1, Fisheries: Rules and Regulations, 1930–31, "John Barnett, Deputy Minister Natural Resources to N.E. Rose, Secretary Treasurer, Municipality of North Qu'Appelle No. 187," 20 November 1930.

73 PAS, Department of Natural Resources, F-300-RR, Fisheries NR1-1, Fisheries: Rules and Regulations, 1930–31, "G.C. MacDonald, Supervisor of Fisheries to John Barnett, Deputy Minister Natural Resources, Department of Natural Resources," 28 October 1930.

74 PAS, Department of Natural Resources, F-300-RR, Fisheries NR1-1, Fisheries: Rules and Regulations, 1930–31, "M.A. Harrison, Secretary Treasurer, Village of Fort Qu'Appelle to John Barnett, Deputy Minister Natural Resources," 26 January 1931.

75 PAS, Department of Natural Resources, F-300-RR, Fisheries NR1-1, Fisheries: Rules and Regulations, 1930–31, "John Barnett, Deputy Minister Natural Resources to M.A. Harrison, Secretary Treasurer, Village of Fort Qu'Appelle," 13 February 1931.

76 PAS, Rural Municipality of North Qu'Appelle No. 187, R2.739, Relief Records 1921–1955, Municipal Council Minutes, 4 May 1931.

77 PAS, Department of Natural Resources, Fisheries Branch, NR.13, 7, Licenses, Free to Halfbreeds and Destitute Settlers and closed season fishing, 1931–1942, "N.E. Rose Secretary Treasurer, Municipality of North Qu'Appelle No. 187 to John Barnett, Deputy Minister of Natural Resources," 5 May 1931.

78 PAS, Department of Natural Resources, Fisheries Branch, NR.13, 7, Licenses, Free to Halfbreeds and Destitute Settlers and closed season fishing, 1931–1942, "G.C. MacDonald, Supervisor of Fisheries to N.E. Rose, Secretary Treasurer, Municipality of North Qu'Appelle No. 187."

79 PAS, Department of Natural Resources, Fisheries Branch, NR.13, 7, Licenses, Free to Halfbreeds and Destitute Settlers and closed season fishing, 1931–1942, "Baptiste Robillard and 46 others," 28 May 1931.

80 On the political organization of the Saskatchewan Métis Society, see Dobbin, "Métis Struggles of the Twentieth Century: Part One," 16–19; Dobbin, "Métis Struggles of the Twentieth Century: Part Two," 10–13; Barron, *Moccasins*; Schilling, *Gabriel's Children*.

81 Thomas Major, interview, 14 March 1978; Joe Amyotte, interview, 11 August 1977. In Thomas Major's interview transcript his name is spelled Major. In other archival documents, including those he wrote, it is spelled Majore. I have used the spelling Majore when referring to him and his wife, Marie. Marie Major's interview transcript cited later also spells their name as Major.

82 Dobbin, "Métis Struggles of the Twentieth Century: Part One," 17.

83 PAS, Department of Natural Resources, Fisheries Branch, NR.13, 7, Licenses, Free to Halfbreeds and Destitute Settlers and closed season fishing, 1931–1942, "Baptiste Robillard and 46 others," 28 May 1931. Petition signatories included: Baptiste Robillard, Alex Desjarlais, Mrs. Alex Desjarlais, Isadore Blondeau, Mrs. Isadore Blondeau, Thomas St. Denis, Mrs. [Philomena] Clement Brabant, John Larocque, Mrs. John Larocque, W.J. Fisher, Mrs. W.J. Fisher, Jean Baptiste Larocque, Mrs. M.L. Larcoque, Joseph Amyotte, Mrs. Joseph Amyotte, Mr. Jack Blondeau, Mrs. Chris Robillard [Françoise Blondeau], Mrs. Gaspard Jeannotte [neé Blondeau], Mrs. Solomon Parisien [Melanie Liza Majore], Mrs. Jennie Parisien, John Kelly, Leo Parisien, Mrs. Leo Parisien, Ray Fisher, Maurice Parisien, Mrs. Gregoire Poitras [Celina Parisien], Gregoire Poitras, Thomas Poitras, Alex Brabant, William Kelly, Joseph Peltier, Mike Desjarlais, Mrs. Mike Desjarlais, Mrs. Tobie Brabant [Marie Fisher], Simon Desjarlais, Mrs. E. Shanite, Mrs. Baptiste Robillard, Charles Pelletier, Joe Pelletier, Mrs. Joe Pelletier, Albert Klyne, Mrs. A Klyne, John Charette, Mrs. J. Charette, Mrs. Louis Sinclair, Louis Sinclair, Mrs. Margaret Charette, and Leo St. Dennis.

84 Troupe, "Métis Women."

85 PAS, Department of Natural Resources, Fisheries Branch, NR.13, 7, Licenses, Free to Halfbreeds and Destitute Settlers and closed season fishing, 1931–1942, "G.C. MacDonald, Supervisor of Fisheries to P.S. Pettit, Fishery Inspector, Fort Qu'Appelle," 12 June 1931.

86 PAS, Department of Natural Resources, Fisheries Branch, NR.13, 7, Licenses, Free to Halfbreeds and Destitute Settlers and closed season fishing, 1931–1942, "G.M. Bushell, Reeve, Municipality of North Qu'Appelle No. 187 to Supervisor of Fisheries," 4 September 1931.

87 PAS, Department of Natural Resources, F-300-RR, Fisheries NR1-1, Fisheries: Rules and Regulations, 1930–31, "Lebret Métis to J.T.M. Anderson, Minister of Department of Natural Resources, Fisheries Branch, Petition," 19 September 1931. Petition signatories included: William Fisher, J. Morin, Alex St. Dennis, Fred Klyne, Clyne Wright, Frank Morin, Joe Morin, Mike Desmarias, George Racette, Leo Brabant, Ray Fisher, Albert Dazé, Moise Dazé, Peter Blondeau, William J. Kelly, Thomas Desjarlais, J.B. Larocque, Isadore Blondeau, M. Blondeau, Bruno Klyne, J.B. Poitras, Rene Page St., W.J. Fisher, Henri Parisien, Mrs. T. Brabant, J.B. Parisien, John Parisien, Alex Brabant, Simon Desjarlais, J.B. Blondeau, Joe Delorme, Joe Desjarlais, Stanley Desjarlais, Isadore Desjarlais, G. Jannott [Jeanotte], Alfred Majore, Edmond Majore, William Desjarlais, Adolphe Pelletier, Mrs. Margaret Charette, Mr. Allan Larocque, Walter Harper, J.B. Robillard, John Larocque, Alex Desjarlais, Zachary Poitras, Corbett St. Denis, Joe Adrian St. Dennis, Joe Pelletier, Louis St. Clair [Sinclair], John Kelly, Mrs. Soloman Parisien, Mrs. Justine Page, Mrs. Jennie Parisien, Johnny Blondeau, Mrs. C. Robillard, Zachary Blondeau, Mike Beaulieau, Gregory Poitras, Paul Bruno, Joe. Z. Larocque, Mrs. Adeline Delorme, Mrs. C. Brabant, Geo Poitras, Geo Amyotte, F.X, Welsh, and Joe Welsh.

88 PAS, Department of Natural Resources, F-300-RR, Fisheries NR1-1, Fisheries: Rules and Regulations, 1930–31, "N.E. Rose, Secretary, Rural Municipality of North Qu'Appelle, No. 187 to J.T.M. Anderson, Minister, Department of Natural Resources, Fisheries Branch," 19 October 1931.

89 PAS, Department of Natural Resources, F-300-RR, Fisheries NR1-1, Fisheries: Rules and Regulations, 1930–31, "Department of Natural Resources to N.E. Rose, Secretary-Treasurer, Rural Municipality of North Qu'Appelle No. 187," 26 October 1931.

90 PAS, Department of Natural Resources, Fisheries Branch, NR.13, 7, Licenses, Free to Halfbreeds and Destitute Settlers and closed season fishing, 1931–1942, "G.C. Macdonald, Supervisor of Fisheries to Louis Sangret, Turtleford," 10 November 1931.

91 PAS, Rural Municipality of North Qu'Appelle No. 187, R2.739, Relief Records 1921–1955, Municipal Council Minutes, 2 October 1933.

92 PAS, Rural Municipality of North Qu'Appelle No. 187, R2.739, Relief Records 1921–1955, Municipal Council Minutes, 7 October 1933.

93 PAS, Department of Natural Resources, Fisheries Branch, NR.13, 7, Licenses, Free to Halfbreeds and Destitute Settlers and closed season fishing, 1931–1942, "Baptiste Parenteau, Duck Lake to Supervisor of Fisheries, Department of Natural Resources," 4 June 1931; PAS, Department of Natural Resources, Fisheries Branch, NR.13, 7, Licenses, Free to Halfbreeds and Destitute Settlers and closed season fishing, 1931–1942, "W.J. Tait, Saskatoon to Supervisor of Fisheries, Department of Natural Resources," 13 June 1931; PAS, Department of Natural Resources, Fisheries Branch, NR.13, 7, Licenses, Free to Halfbreeds and Destitute Settlers and closed season fishing, 1931–1942, "J.B. Ouellette, St. Laurent to Supervisor of Fisheries, Department of Natural Resources," 23 June 1931; PAS, Department of Natural Resources, Fisheries Branch, NR.13, 7, Licenses, Free to Halfbreeds and Destitute Settlers and closed season fishing, 1931–1942, "Louis Sangret, Turtleford," 4 November 1931; PAS, Department of Natural Resources, Fisheries Branch, NR.13, 7, Licenses, Free to Halfbreeds and Destitute Settlers and closed season fishing, 1931–1942, "J.B. Arcand, Debden to Supervisor of Fisheries, Department of Natural Resources," 18 November 1931; PAS, Department of Natural Resources, Fisheries Branch, NR.13, 7, Licenses, Free to Halfbreeds and Destitute Settlers and closed season fishing, 1931–1942, "Aime Thibeault, Fairholme to Supervisor of Fisheries, Department of Natural Resources," 15 December 1931; PAS, Department of Natural Resources, Fisheries Branch, NR.13, 7, Licenses, Free to Halfbreeds and Destitute Settlers and closed season fishing, 1931–1942, "M. Martell, Halfbreeds at Cochin to John Barnett, Deputy Minister," 1 November 1931; PAS, Department of Natural Resources, Fisheries Branch, NR.13, 7, Licenses, Free to Halfbreeds and Destitute Settlers and closed season fishing, 1931–1942, "M. Martell and Halfbreeds at Cochin to John Barnett, Deputy Minister, Department of Natural Resources, Petition," 1 November 1932.

94 PAS, Department of Natural Resources, Fisheries Branch, NR.13, 7, Licenses, Free to Halfbreeds and Destitute Settlers and closed season fishing, 1931–1942, "G.C. MacDonald, Supervisor of Fisheries to M. Martell, Cochin," 8 November 1932.

95 PAS, Department of Natural Resources, Fisheries Branch, NR.13, 7, Licenses, Free to Halfbreeds and Destitute Settlers and closed season fishing, 1931–1942, "M. Hocking Secretary Treasurer, Rural Municipality of Last Mountain Lake, No. 250 to Deputy Minister, Department of Natural Resources," 18 December 1933; PAS, Department of Natural Resources, Fisheries Branch, NR.13, 7, Licenses, Free to Halfbreeds and Destitute Settlers and closed season fishing, 1931–1942, "S.

MacDonald, Secretary Treasurer, Rural Municipality of Grayson No. 184 to W.W. Amos, Deputy Minister, Department of Natural Resources," 9 November 1934.

96 PAS, Department of Natural Resources, Fisheries Branch, NR.13, 7. Licenses, Free to Halfbreeds and Destitute Settlers and closed season fishing, 1931–1942, "G.C. MacDonald, Supervisor of Fisheries to M. Hocking, Secretary Treasurer, Rural Municipality of Last Mountain Lake, No. 250," 4 January 1934; PAS, Department of Natural Resources, Fisheries Branch, NR.13, 7, Licenses, Free to Halfbreeds and Destitute Settlers and closed season fishing, 1931–1942, "W.W. Amos, Deputy Minister, Department of Natural Resources to S. MacDonald, Secretary Treasurer, Rural Municipality of Grayson No. 184," 14 November 1934.

97 PAS, Rural Municipality of North Qu'Appelle No. 187, R2.739, Relief Records 1921–1955, Municipal Council Minutes, 4 November 1935; PAS, Rural Municipality of North Qu'Appelle No. 187, R2.739, Relief Records 1921–1955, Municipal Council Minutes, 7 November 1935.

98 PAS, Rural Municipality of North Qu'Appelle No. 187, R2.739, Relief Records 1921–1955, Municipal Council Minutes, 6 March 1939; PAS, Department of Natural Resources, Fisheries Branch, NR.13, 7, Licenses, Free to Halfbreeds and Destitute Settlers and closed season fishing, 1931–1942, "Thomas Majore and Ray Fisher, Union of the Unemployed to Department of Natural Resources," 16 March 1939.

99 Thomas Major, interview, 14 March 1978.

100 Thomas Major, interview, 14 March 1978.

101 PAS, Department of Natural Resources, Fisheries Branch, NR.13, 7. Licenses, Free to Halfbreeds and Destitute Settlers and closed season fishing, 1931–1942, "G.C. MacDonald, Supervisor of Fisheries to J.R. Hill, Deputy Minister, Department of Natural Resources," 5 May 1939.

102 PAS, Department of Natural Resources, Fisheries Branch, NR.13, 7, Licenses, Free to Halfbreeds and Destitute Settlers and closed season fishing, 1931–1942, "G.C. MacDonald, Supervisor of Fisheries to V. E. Lefebvre, Field Officer, Whitewood," 8 June 1939.

103 PAS, Department of Natural Resources, Fisheries Branch, NR.13, 7, Licenses, Free to Halfbreeds and Destitute Settlers and closed season fishing, 1931–1942, "O. Bright, Supervisor of Fisheries to J.Z. Larocque, Field Officer," 12 December 1942; PAS, Department of Natural Resources, Fisheries Branch, NR.13, 7, Licenses, Free to Halfbreeds and Destitute Settlers and closed season fishing, 1931–1942, "O. Bright, Supervisor of Fisheries to A.L. Spencer, Acting Superintendent, Fish Hatchery, Fort Qu'Appelle," 15 December 1942.

104 PAS, Department of Natural Resources, Fisheries Branch, NR.13, 7, Licenses, Free to Halfbreeds and Destitute Settlers and closed season fishing, 1931–1942, "O. Bright, Supervisor of Fisheries to J.E. Tanner, Chief Accountant," 4 March 1932; PAS, Department of Natural Resources, Fisheries Branch, NR.13, 7, Licenses, Free to Halfbreeds and Destitute Settlers and closed season fishing, 1931–1942, "O. Bright, Supervisor of Fisheries to J. E. Tanner, Chief Accountant," 8 April 1942;

PAS, Department of Natural Resources, Fisheries Branch, NR.13, 7, Licenses, Free to Halfbreeds and Destitute Settlers and closed season fishing, 1931–1942, "J. Z. Larocque, Field Officer to O. Bright, Supervisor of Fisheries," 17 December 1942.

105 Lawrence Welsh, Pauline Anderson, Billie Robison, Pat Sullivan, and Norma Welsh, interview, 2004; Margaret Harrison, interview, 9 July 2014.

106 Margaret Harrison, interview, 9 July 2014.

Chapter 9. "This Is a Michif Road": Métis Labour and Relief

1 Bob Desjarlais, interview, 3 July 2002.

2 Barron, "The CCF"; Barron, *Moccasins,* 46.

3 Sirois and Rowell, Report, 144.

4 Sirois and Rowell, 169.

5 Table 50—The Decline in Provincial Per Capita Incomes, 1928–29 to 1933 in Sirois and Rowell, Report, 150.

6 Marchildon, "Introduction," 1.

7 Sirois and Rowell, 169.

8 Sirois and Rowell, 163–64.

9 PAS, General Files of the Provincial Auditor, Relief Files—Miscellaneous. Box 16, "First Annual Report of the Bureau of Labour and Public Welfare," 1935.

10 Alma Lawton, "Relief Administration," 41.

11 Marchildon, "Introduction," 2.

12 Lawton, "Relief Administration," 42.

13 PAS, General Files of the Provincial Auditor, Relief Files—Miscellaneous. Box 16, "Bureau of Labour and Public Welfare, Department of Municipal Affairs to all Municipalities," 10 November 1934.

14 Marie Major, interview, 20 August 1982; John Joe Larcoque, interview, 13 August 1982.

15 PAS, Rural Municipality of North Qu'Appelle No. 187, R2.739, Relief Records 1921–1955, Municipal Council Minutes.

16 PAS, Rural Municipality of North Qu'Appelle No. 187, R2.739, Relief Records 1921–1955, Municipal Council Minutes, 2 September 1930.

17 PAS, Rural Municipality of North Qu'Appelle No. 187, R2.739, Relief Records 1921–1955, Municipal Council Minutes, 8 September 1925.

18 PAS, Rural Municipality of North Qu'Appelle No. 187, R2.739, Relief Records 1921–1955, Municipal Council Minutes, 8 November 1927.

19 PAS, Rural Municipality of North Qu'Appelle No. 187, R2.739, Relief Records 1921–1955, Municipal Council Minutes, 2 November 1927; PAS, Rural Municipality of North Qu'Appelle No. 187, R2.739, Relief Records 1921–1955, Municipal Council Minutes, 7 December 1931.

20 Pitsula, *Keeping Canada British,* 109.

21 Pitsula, 20; "Huge Cross Burned as Klan Hold Big Meet at Moose Jaw," *Regina Leader Post,* 8 June 1927, 1.

22 Pitsula, *Keeping Canada British*, 91, 99.
23 Pitsula, 91, 99; Benson, "... taken in hand by Indians," 93.
24 "Statuary and Shrine Razed on Lebret Hill," *Regina Leader Post*, 23 May 1928, 12.
25 Pitsula, *Keeping Canada British*, 105–6.
26 PAS, Rural Municipality of North Qu'Appelle No. 187, R2.739, Relief Records 1921–1955, Municipal Council Minutes, 27 March 1927; PAS, Rural Municipality of North Qu'Appelle No. 187, R2.739, Relief Records 1921–1955, Municipal Council Minutes, 1 August 1927.
27 PAS, Rural Municipality of North Qu'Appelle No. 187, R2.739, Relief Records 1921–1955, Municipal Council Minutes, 8 September 1924.
28 PAS, Rural Municipality of North Qu'Appelle No. 187, R2.739, Relief Records 1921–1955, Municipal Council Minutes, 8 September 1924.
29 PAS, Rural Municipality of North Qu'Appelle No. 187, R2.739, Relief Records 1921–1955, Municipal Council Minutes, 8 September 1924.
30 PAS, Rural Municipality of North Qu'Appelle No. 187, R2.739, Relief Records 1921–1955, Municipal Council Minutes, 6 July 1931. This number shows an increase from the 5 May 1931 letter from N.E. Rose, Secretary Treasurer, Municipality of North Qu'Appelle No. 187 to John Barnett, Deputy Minister of Natural Resources estimating that there were at least thirty-five to forty Métis families or 200 individuals living within their boundaries.
31 PAS, Rural Municipality of North Qu'Appelle No. 187, R2.739, Relief Records 1921–1955, Municipal Council Minutes, 2 September 1930.
32 PAS, Rural Municipality of North Qu'Appelle No. 187, R2.739, Relief Records 1921–1955, Municipal Council Minutes, 2 September 1930.
33 PAS, Rural Municipality of North Qu'Appelle No. 187, R2.739, Relief Records 1921–1955, Municipal Council Minutes, 2 September 1930.
34 PAS, Rural Municipality of North Qu'Appelle No. 187, R2.739, Relief Records 1921–1955, Municipal Council Minutes, 2 September 1930.; The Rural Municipality Act, 1928-29, c.34, s.1; R.S.S. 1930, c.106, s.1.
35 PAS, Rural Municipality of North Qu'Appelle No. 187, R2.739, Relief Records 1921–1955, Municipal Council Minutes, 6 September 1938.
36 PAS, Rural Municipality of North Qu'Appelle Np. 187, R2.739, Relief Records 1921–1955, Municipal Council Minutes, 3 February 1931.
37 PAS, Rural Municipality of North Qu'Appelle No. 187, R2.739, Relief Records 1921–1955, Municipal Council Minutes, 7 April 1931.
38 PAS, Rural Municipality of North Qu'Appelle No. 187, R2.739, Relief Records 1921–1955, Municipal Council Minutes, 6 July 1931.
39 PAS, Rural Municipality of North Qu'Appelle No. 187, R2.739, Relief Records 1921–1955, Municipal Council Minutes, 12 August 1931; PAS, Rural Municipality of North Qu'Appelle No. 187, R2.739, Relief Records 1921–1955, Municipal Council Minutes, 22 August 1931.
40 PAS, Rural Municipality of North Qu'Appelle No. 187, R2.739, Relief Records 1921–1955, Municipal Council Minutes, 8 September 1931.

41 PAS, Rural Municipality of North Qu'Appelle No. 187, R2.739, Relief Records 1921–1955, Municipal Council Minutes, 10 November 1937.
42 PAS, Rural Municipality of North Qu'Appelle No. 187, R2.739, Relief Records 1921–1955, Municipal Council Minutes, 6 March 1933.
43 Stanley Racette, interview, 11 August 1983.
44 PAS, Rural Municipality of North Qu'Appelle No. 187, R2.739, Relief Records 1921–1955, Municipal Council Minutes, 2 May 1938.
45 Stanley Racette, interview, 11 August 1983.
46 PAS, Rural Municipality of North Qu'Appelle No. 187, R2.739, Relief Records 1921–1955, Municipal Council Minutes, 13 July 1936; PAS, Rural Municipality of North Qu'Appelle No. 187, R2.739, Relief Records 1921–1955, Municipal Council Minutes, 2 May 1938.
47 Bob Desjarlais and George Klyne, interview, 6–7 December 2003.
48 PAS, Rural Municipality of North Qu'Appelle No. 187, R2.739, Relief Records 1921–1955, Municipal Council Minutes, 7 November 1932.
49 PAS, Rural Municipality of North Qu'Appelle No. 187, R2.739, Relief Records 1921–1955, Municipal Council Minutes, 5 December 1932.
50 PAS, Rural Municipality of North Qu'Appelle No. 187, R2.739, Relief Records 1921–1955, "Field Services Branch, Saskatchewan Relief Commission to Secretary-Treasurer N.E. Rose," 10 December 1932.
51 PAS, Rural Municipality of North Qu'Appelle No. 187, R2.739, Relief Records 1921–1955, "Field Services Branch, Saskatchewan Relief Commission to Secretary-Treasurer N.E. Rose," 10 December 1932.
52 PAS, Rural Municipality of North Qu'Appelle No. 187, R2.739, Relief Records 1921–1955, Municipal Council Minutes, 3 January 1933.
53 PAS, Rural Municipality of North Qu'Appelle No. 187, R2.739, Relief Records 1921–1955, "General Manager of Food Department to Secretary-Treasurer N.E Rose," 7 February 1933.
54 PAS, Rural Municipality of North Qu'Appelle No. 187, R2.739, Relief Records 1921–1955, "General Manager of Food Department to Secretary-Treasurer N.E Rose," 7 February 1933.
55 PAS, Rural Municipality of North Qu'Appelle No. 187, R2.739, Relief Records 1921–1955, "General Manager of Food Department to All Municipalities in Receipt of Food Relief," 23 February 1933. Freshening is a term used to describe a cow that has recently given birth and is producing milk.
56 PAS, Rural Municipality of North Qu'Appelle No. 187, R2.739, Relief Records 1921–1955, "N.E. Rose to General Manager, Food Department, Saskatchewan Relief Commission," 27 February 1933.
57 PAS, Rural Municipality of North Qu'Appelle No. 187, R2.739, Relief Records 1921–1955, Municipal Council Minutes, 6 March 1933; PAS, Rural Municipality of North Qu'Appelle No. 187, R2.739, Relief Records 1921–1955, "N.E. Rose to Field Services Branch, Saskatchewan Relief Commission," 21 April 1933.

58 PAS, Rural Municipality of North Qu'Appelle No. 187, R2.739, Relief Records 1921–1955, Municipal Council Minutes, 1 May 1933; PAS, Rural Municipality of North Qu'Appelle No. 187, R2.739, Relief Records 1921–1955, "N.E. Rose to Saskatchewan Relief Commission," 8 May 1933.

59 PAS, Rural Municipality of North Qu'Appelle No. 187, R2.739, Relief Records 1921–1955, "General Manager of Saskatchewan Relief Commission to N.E. Rose," 11 May 1933.

60 PAS, Rural Municipality of North Qu'Appelle No. 187, R2.739, Relief Records 1921–1955, "N.E. Rose to Commissioner, Saskatchewan Relief Commission," 21 January 1933.

61 PAS, Rural Municipality of North Qu'Appelle No. 187, R2.739, Relief Records 1921–1955, "N.E. Rose to Field Services Branch, Saskatchewan Relief Commission," 4 January 1932.

62 PAS, Rural Municipality of North Qu'Appelle No. 187, R2.739, Relief Records 1921–1955, "N.E. Rose to Field Services Branch, Saskatchewan Relief Commission," 4 January 1932.

63 PAS, Rural Municipality of North Qu'Appelle No. 187, R2.739, Relief Records 1921–1955, "N.E. Rose to A. Kendell, Field Services Branch, Saskatchewan Relief Commission," 22 December 1932.

64 PAS, Rural Municipality of North Qu'Appelle No. 187, R2.739, Relief Records 1921–1955, "N.E. Rose to A. Kendell, Field Services Branch, Saskatchewan Relief Commission," 22 December 1932.

65 PAS, Rural Municipality of North Qu'Appelle No. 187, R2.739, Relief Records 1921–1955, "Deputy Attorney General to N.E. Rose," 28 December 1932.

66 PAS, Rural Municipality of North Qu'Appelle No. 187, R2.739, Relief Records 1921–1955, Municipal Council Minutes, 5 June 1933.

67 PAS, Rural Municipality of North Qu'Appelle No. 187, R2.739, Relief Records 1921–1955, Municipal Council Minutes, 5 June 1933.

68 PAS, Rural Municipality of North Qu'Appelle No. 187, R2.739, Relief Records 1921–1955, Municipal Council Minutes, 5 January 1937.

69 PAS, Rural Municipality of North Qu'Appelle No. 187, R2.739, Relief Records 1921–1955, Municipal Council Minutes, 3 January 1933.

70 PAS, Rural Municipality of North Qu'Appelle No. 187, R2.739, Relief Records 1921–1955, Municipal Council Minutes, 5 November 1934; PAS, Rural Municipality of North Qu'Appelle No. 187, R2.739, Relief Records 1921–1955, Municipal Council Minutes, 2 December 1935; PAS, Rural Municipality of North Qu'Appelle No. 187, R2.739, Relief Records 1921–1955, Municipal Council Minutes, February 1935.

71 PAS, Rural Municipality of North Qu'Appelle No. 187, R2.739, Relief Records 1921–1955, Municipal Council Minutes, 2 March 1936.

72 PAS, Rural Municipality of North Qu'Appelle No. 187, R2.739, Relief Records 1921–1955, Municipal Council Minutes, 2 March 1936.

73 PAS, Rural Municipality of North Qu'Appelle No. 187, R2.739, Relief Records 1921–1955, Municipal Council Minutes, 5 October 1936; PAS, Rural Municipality of North Qu'Appelle No. 187, R2.739, Relief Records 1921–1955, Municipal Council Minutes, 2 November 1936; PAS, Rural Municipality of North Qu'Appelle No. 187, R2.739, Relief Records 1921–1955, Municipal Council Minutes, 21 November 1936.

74 University of Saskatchewan, University Archives and Special Collections, F.L. Barron fonds, Fonds MG 233, 2. Writing and Research, Archives Deschatelets, L282 M27 T3, "Father Alfred Beaudin, Lebret, to Prime Minister Mackenzie King," 15 May 1936.

75 University of Saskatchewan, University Archives and Special Collections, F.L. Barron fonds, Fonds MG 233, 2. Writing and Research, Archives Deschatelets, L282 M27 T3, "Father Alfred Beaudin, Lebret, to William Patterson 10 September 1936.

76 PAS, Department of Education, Ed. Addendum, File 48, Métis Schools, "Memorandum for Dr. McKechnie, Deputy Minister of Education," 26 October 1938.

77 University of Saskatchewan, University Archives and Special Collections, F.L. Barron fonds, Fonds MG 233, 2. Writing and Research, Archives Deschatelets, L282 M27 T3, "William Patterson to Father Alfred Beaudin," 5 October 1936.

78 O'Byrne, "'No other weapon except organization'"; Métis Association of Alberta et al., *Métis Land Rights*, 215–42.

79 PAS, Rural Municipality of North Qu'Appelle No. 187, R2.739, Relief Records 1921–1955, Municipal Council Minutes, 15 March 1937.

80 PAS, Rural Municipality of North Qu'Appelle No. 187, R2.739, Relief Records 1921–1955, Municipal Council Minutes, 8 March 1937; PAS, Rural Municipality of North Qu'Appelle No. 187, R2.739, Relief Records 1921–1955, Municipal Council Minutes, 15 March 1937.

81 PAS, Rural Municipality of North Qu'Appelle No. 187, R2.739, Relief Records 1921–1955, Municipal Council Minutes, 8 September 1937.

82 PAS, Rural Municipality of North Qu'Appelle No. 187, R2.739, Relief Records 1921–1955, Municipal Council Minutes, 5 April 1938.

83 PAS, Rural Municipality of North Qu'Appelle No. 187, R2.739, Relief Records 1921–1955, Municipal Council Minutes, 6 February 1939.

84 Gabriel Dumont Institute, Beverly Worsely Collection, Lebret Métis Harm History (01) Southeast Area Community Service Co-Operative, Association of Métis and Non-Status Indians, 1970s–80s, accessed 10 August 20024, https://www.metis-museum.ca/resource.php/148911.

85 PAS, Rural Municipality of North Qu'Appelle No. 187, R2.739, Relief Records 1921–1955, "N.E. Rose to Director of Relief, Bureau of Labour and Public Welfare," 23 October 1937; PAS, Rural Municipality of North Qu'Appelle No. 187, R2.739, Relief Records 1921–1955, "Recipients, Voluntary Car Distribution," 29 October 1937.

86 PAS, Rural Municipality of North Qu'Appelle No. 187, R2.739, Relief Records 1921–1955, "Thomas Desjarlais to N.E. Rose," 16 October 1937.

87 PAS, Rural Municipality of North Qu'Appelle No. 187, R2.739, Relief Records 1921–1955, "N.E. Rose to Bureau of Labour and Public Welfare," 3 November 1937.

88 PAS, Rural Municipality of North Qu'Appelle No. 187, R2.739, Relief Records 1921–1955, "N.E. Rose to Director of Relief, Bureau of Labour and Public Welfare," 11 April 1938.

89 PAS, Rural Municipality of North Qu'Appelle No. 187, R2.739, Relief Records 1921–1955, "N.E. Rose to Director of Relief, Bureau of Labour and Public Welfare," 25 July 1938; PAS, Rural Municipality of North Qu'Appelle No. 187, R2.739, Relief Records 1921–1955, "N.E. Rose to Director of Relief, Bureau of Labour and Public Welfare," 10 August 1938; PAS, Rural Municipality of North Qu'Appelle No. 187, R2.739, Relief Records 1921–1955, "N.E. Rose to Director of Relief, Bureau of Labour and Public Welfare," 19 August 1938.

90 Danysk, "No Help for the Farm," 140–48.

91 PAS, General Files of the Provincial Auditor, Relief Files—Miscellaneous. Box 16, "First Annual Report of the Bureau of Labour and Public Welfare," 1935.

92 PAS, Rural Municipality of North Qu'Appelle No. 187, R2.739, Relief Records 1921–1955, "Director of Relief to N.E. Rose," 5 November 1937.

93 PAS, Rural Municipality of North Qu'Appelle No. 187, R2.739, Relief Records 1921–1955, "Commissioner of Labour and Public Welfare to Orval Cavan, Fort Qu'Appelle," 1 December 1937.

94 PAS, Rural Municipality of North Qu'Appelle No. 187, R2.739, Relief Records 1921–1955, "J.H. Hamilton to Thomas M. Molloy, Bureau of Labour and Public Welfare," 6 November 1937.

95 PAS, Rural Municipality of North Qu'Appelle No. 187, R2.739, Relief Records 1921–1955, "Director of Relief to N.E. Rose," 21 October 1937; PAS, Rural Municipality of North Qu'Appelle No. 187, R2.739, Relief Records 1921–1955, "Director of Relief to N.E. Rose," 5 November 1937; PAS, Rural Municipality of North Qu'Appelle No. 187, R2.739, Relief Records 1921–1955, "Director of Relief to N.E. Rose," 31 January 1938; PAS, Rural Municipality of North Qu'Appelle No. 187, R2.739, Relief Records 1921–1955, "Director of Relief to N.E. Rose," 18 February 1938. Women included Annie Fisher, Annie Gosselin, Mrs. Helen Majore, Nora Larocque, and Mary St. Denis.

96 PAS, Rural Municipality of North Qu'Appelle No. 187, R2.739, Relief Records 1921–1955, "N.E. Rose to John Charbaneau," 2 December 1937.

97 PAS, Rural Municipality of North Qu'Appelle No. 187, R2.739, Relief Records 1921–1955, "N.E. Rose to Joseph Poitras," 2 December 1937.

98 PAS, Rural Municipality of North Qu'Appelle No. 187, R2.739, Relief Records 1921–1955, Municipal Council Minutes, 2 May 1938.

99 PAS, Rural Municipality of North Qu'Appelle No. 187, R2.739, Relief Records 1921–1955, Municipal Council Minutes, 4 July 1938.

100 PAS, Rural Municipality of North Qu'Appelle No. 187, R2.739, Relief Records 1921–1955, Municipal Council Minutes, 6 September 1938.

101 PAS, Rural Municipality of North Qu'Appelle No. 187, R2.739, Relief Records 1921–1955, Municipal Council Minutes, 3 October 1938.

102 PAS, Rural Municipality of North Qu'Appelle No. 187, R2.739, Relief Records 1921–1955, Municipal Council Minutes, 6 September 1938.

103 PAS, Rural Municipality of North Qu'Appelle No. 187, R2.739, Relief Records 1921–1955, Municipal Council Minutes, 13 October 1938; PAS, Rural Municipality of North Qu'Appelle No. 187, R2.739, Relief Records 1921–1955, Municipal Council Minutes, 18 November 1938.

104 PAS, Rural Municipality of North Qu'Appelle No. 187, R2.739, Relief Records 1921–1955, Municipal Council Minutes, 4 November 1940.

105 PAS, Rural Municipality of North Qu'Appelle No. 187, R2.739, Relief Records 1921–1955, Municipal Council Minutes, 3 December 1936.

106 PAS, Rural Municipality of North Qu'Appelle No. 187, R2.739, Relief Records 1921–1955, Municipal Council Minutes, 3 February 1941; PAS, Rural Municipality of North Qu'Appelle No. 187, R2.739, Relief Records 1921–1955, Municipal Council Minutes, 3 January 1942.

107 PAS, Rural Municipality of North Qu'Appelle No. 187, R2.739, Relief Records 1921–1955, "Fanny E. Gibson, Lebret Relief Commission to N.E. Rose," 28 February 1938.

108 PAS, Rural Municipality of North Qu'Appelle No. 187, R2.739, Relief Records 1921–1955, Municipal Council Minutes, 20 November 1939.

109 PAS, General Files of the Provincial Auditor, 1940–1944, Relief-Misc. R-281.3, Box 16-18.

110 Barron, *Moccasins*, 15–16.

111 PAS, Rural Municipality of North Qu'Appelle No. 187, R2.739, Relief Records 1921–1955, Municipal Council Minutes, 7 March 1927; PAS, Rural Municipality of North Qu'Appelle No. 187, R2.739, Relief Records 1921–1955, Municipal Council Minutes, 2 June 1930; PAS, Rural Municipality of North Qu'Appelle No. 187, R2.739, Relief Records 1921–1955, Municipal Council Minutes, 3 October 1932; PAS, Rural Municipality of North Qu'Appelle No. 187, R2.739, Relief Records 1921–1955, Municipal Council Minutes, 6 March 1933; PAS, Rural Municipality of North Qu'Appelle No. 187, R2.739, Relief Records 1921–1955, Municipal Council Minutes, 6 June 1933; PAS, Rural Municipality of North Qu'Appelle No. 187, R2.739, Relief Records 1921–1955, Municipal Council Minutes, 2 October 1939.

112 PAS, Rural Municipality of North Qu'Appelle No. 187, R2.739, Relief Records 1921–1955, Municipal Council Minutes, 6 March 1933.

113 PAS, Rural Municipality of North Qu'Appelle No. 187, R2.739, Relief Records 1921–1955, Municipal Council Minutes, 4 October 1937.

114 PAS, Rural Municipality of North Qu'Appelle No. 187, R2.739, Relief Records 1921–1955, Municipal Council Minutes, 6 June 1938.

115 PAS, Rural Municipality of North Qu'Appelle No. 187, R2.739, Relief Records 1921–1955, Municipal Council Minutes, 2 October 1939.

116 University of Saskatchewan, University Archives and Special Collections, F.L. Barron fonds, Fonds MG 233, 2. Writing and Research, Archives Deschatelets, L282 M27 T3, "Lease agreement between Department of Municipal Affairs and Les Congregation des Missionaires Oblats de Marie Immaculee des Territoires Du Nord Ouest," 10 June 1940. The section of land was Section 15–Township 21–Range 13–West of the Second Meridian.

117 University of Saskatchewan, University Archives and Special Collections, F.L. Barron fonds, Fonds MG 233, 2. Writing and Research, Archives Deschatelets, L282 M27 T3, "Lease agreement between Department of Municipal Affairs and Les Congregation des Missionaires Oblats de Marie Immaculee Des Territoires Du Nord Ouest," 25 April 1941. The second section of land was Section 35–Township 21–Range 13–West of the Second Meridian.

118 University of Saskatchewan, University Archives and Special Collections, F.L. Barron fonds, Fonds MG 233, 2. Writing and Research, Archives Deschatelets, L282 M27 T3, "Oblates to W.W. Dawson, Director of Relief, Direct Relief Branch, Department of Municipal Affairs," 22 May 1941.

119 University of Saskatchewan, University Archives and Special Collections, F.L. Barron fonds, Fonds MG 233, 2. Writing and Research, Archives Deschatelets, L282 M27 T3, "Lease agreement between Department of Municipal Affairs and Les Congregation des Missionaires Oblats de Marie Immaculee Des Te4rritories Du Nord Ouest," 1 January 1943.

120 University of Saskatchewan, University Archives and Special Collections, F.L. Barron fonds, Fonds MG 233, 2. Writing and Research, Archives Deschatelets, L282 M27 T3, "Report of Farm Committee to R.J.M. Parker, Minister of Municipal Affairs," 2 February 1943.

121 University of Saskatchewan, University Archives and Special Collections, F.L. Barron fonds, Fonds MG 233, 2. Writing and Research, Archives Deschatelets, L282 M27 T3, "Carl Franke from Edmond C. Bridges," 20 January 1945.

122 Barron, *Moccasins*; Barron, "The CCF and the Development of Métis Colonies."

123 Barron, *Moccasins*, 47.

124 Barron, "The CCF and the Development of Métis Colonies"; Barron, *Moccasins*, 48.

125 Barron, "The CCF and the Development of Métis Colonies," 252.

126 University of Saskatchewan, University Archives and Special Collections, F.L. Barron fonds, Fonds MG 233, 2. Writing and Research, Archives Deschatelets, L282 M27 T3, "J.S. White, Deputy Minister of Social Welfare to Father Lavigne, OMI," 3 January 1945.

127 University of Saskatchewan, University Archives and Special Collections, F.L. Barron fonds, Fonds MG 233, 2. Writing and Research, Archives Deschatelets, L282 M27 T3, "Carl Franke from Edmond C. Bridges," 20 January 1945.

128 PAS, Department of Social Welfare and Rehabilitation, Rehabilitation Branch, Métis Surveys, R85-308, R933 File III 13. Farm residents included Joseph

Blondeau, wife and two children; Louis Blondeau, wife and six children; Maurice Blondeau, wife and seven children; Louis Bourassa, wife and two children; Albert Desjarlais, wife and ten children; August Desjarlais, wife and two children; George Pelletier, wife and three children; Mike Blondeau, wife and two children; Leo Desjarlais, wife and six children for a total of fifty-eight people.

129 PAS, Department of Social Welfare and Rehabilitation, Rehabilitation Branch, Métis Surveys, R85-308, R933 File III 13; PAS, Department of Social Welfare and Rehabilitation, Rehabilitation Branch, Métis Surveys, R85-308, R933 File III 14.

130 PAS, Annual Report of the Department of Social Welfare and Rehabilitation, 1945–1946; PAS, Annual Report of the Department of Social Welfare and Rehabilitation, 1946–1947; PAS, Annual Report of the Department of Social Welfare and Rehabilitation, 1947–1948.

131 PAS, Annual Report of the Department of Social Welfare and Rehabilitation, 1946–1947; "Métis Run Their Own Farm," *Regina Leader Post,* 24 February 1948, 3.

132 PAS, Department of Education, Ed. Addendum, File 48, Métis Schools, "E.J. Brandt, Superintendent of Schools, Department of Education, Special Report Re: Métis children," 30 July 1943.

133 PAS, Department of Social Welfare and Rehabilitation, Rehabilitation Branch, Métis Surveys, R85-308, R933 File III 13; PAS, Department of Social Welfare and Rehabilitation, Rehabilitation Branch, Métis Surveys, R85-308, R933 File III 14.

134 PAS, Department of Social Welfare and Rehabilitation, Rehabilitation Branch, Métis Surveys, R85-308, R933 File III 13; PAS, Department of Social Welfare and Rehabilitation, Rehabilitation Branch, Métis Surveys, R85-308, R933 File III 15.

135 PAS, Department of Social Welfare and Rehabilitation, Rehabilitation Branch, Métis Surveys, R85-308, R933 File III 13; PAS, Department of Social Welfare and Rehabilitation, Rehabilitation Branch, Métis Surveys, R85-308, R933 File III 14.

136 Peters, Stock, and Werner, *Roostertown.*

137 PAS, Department of Social Welfare and Rehabilitation, Rehabilitation Branch, Métis Surveys, R85-308, R933 File III 13; PAS, Department of Social Welfare and Rehabilitation, Rehabilitation Branch, Métis Surveys, R85-308, R933 File III 15.

138 PAS, Department of Education, Ed. Addendum, File 48, Métis Schools, "E.J. Brandt, Superintendent of Schools, Department of Education, Special Report Re: Métis children," 30 July 1943.

139 PAS, Department of Education, Ed. Addendum, File 48, Métis Schools, "E.J. Brandt to Dr. J.H. Mckechnie, Deputy Minister of Education," 16 February 1943.

140 PAS, Department of Social Welfare and Rehabilitation, Rehabilitation Branch, Métis Surveys, R85-308, R933 File III 13.

141 PAS, Department of Social Welfare and Rehabilitation, Rehabilitation Branch, Métis Surveys, R85-308, R933 File III 13.

142 PAS, Department of Social Welfare and Rehabilitation, Rehabilitation Branch, Métis Surveys, R85-308, R933 File III 13.

143 PAS, Department of Social Welfare and Rehabilitation, Rehabilitation Branch, Métis Surveys, R85-308, R933 File III 13.

144 PAS, Department of Social Welfare and Rehabilitation, Rehabilitation Branch, Métis Surveys, R85-308, R933 File III 13.

145 PAS, Department of Social Welfare and Rehabilitation, Rehabilitation Branch, Métis Surveys, R85-308, R933 File III 14.

146 PAS, Department of Social Welfare and Rehabilitation, Rehabilitation Branch, Métis Surveys, R85-308, R933 File III 14.

147 "Métis Association asks, "better break," *Regina Leader Post*, 31 July 1946; PAS, J.H Sturdy Papers, M14 File 198. "Métis Conference Proceedings," 1946.

148 PAS, T.C. Douglas Papers, Files of the Premier, "Métis" R-33.1, file XL 859 b. (44), "Dr. Morris Shumiatcher to All Provincial Ministers, "10 August 1946.

149 PAS, T.C. Douglas Papers, Files of the Premier, "Métis" R-33.1, file XL 859 b. (44), "T.C. Douglas to Sol Pritchard, Baljennie," 12 June 1947.

150 PAS, Rural Municipality of North Qu'Appelle No. 187, R2.739, Relief Records 1921–1955, Municipal Council Minutes, 3 February 1930; PAS, Rural Municipality of North Qu'Appelle No. 187, R2.739, Relief Records 1921–1955, Municipal Council Minutes, 2 June 1930.

151 PAS, Rural Municipality of North Qu'Appelle No. 187, R2.739, Relief Records 1921–1955, Municipal Council Minutes, 3 April 1948.

152 "Métis Problem Discussed," *Regina Leader Post*, 27 February 1948; PAS, T.C. Douglas Papers, Files of the Premier, "Métis" R-33.1, file XL 859 b. (44), "Interprovincial Meeting on the Métis—Minutes," 13 July 1949.

153 PAS, Rural Municipality of North Qu'Appelle No. 187, R2.739, Relief Records 1921–1955, Municipal Council Minutes, 3 January 1949; "RM's facing Money problems," *Regina Leader Post*, 8 March 1949, 3; Barron, "The CCF" 252.

154 PAS, T.C. Douglas Papers, R-33.2. XXII Indian Affairs 407. (24-6-5) Métis Problem, March–June 1950, "James Macdonald, Saskatchewan Association of Rural Municipalities to T.C. Douglas," 20 February 1950; PAS, T.C. Douglas Papers, Files of the Premier, "Métis" R-33.1, file XL 859 b. (44), "Interprovincial Meeting on the Métis—Minutes," 13 July 1949; PAS, T.C. Douglas Papers, Files of the Premier, "Métis" R-33.1, file XL 859 b. (44),"J.H. Sturdy to Premier T.C. Douglas, W.S. Lloyd, J.H. Brockelbank, I.C. Nollet, L.F. McIntosh," 25 July 1949.

155 PAS, T.C. Douglas Papers, Files of the Premier, "Métis" R-33.1, file XL 859 b. (44), "James Macdonald, Saskatchewan Association of Rural Municipalities to T.C. Douglas," 20 February 1950; PAS, T.C. Douglas Papers, Files of the Premier, "Métis" R-33.1, file XL 859 b. (44), "Interprovincial Meeting on the Métis—Minutes," 13 July 1949; PAS, T.C. Douglas Papers, Files of the Premier, "Métis" R-33.1, file XL 859 b. (44), "J.H. Sturdy to Premier T.C. Douglas, W.S. Lloyd, J.H. Brockelbank, I.C. Nollet, L.F. McIntosh," 25 July 1949.

156 Barron, "The CCF," 250.

157 Barron, "The CCF," 249–50.

158 Jim Sinclair and Jim Durocher, interview, 2004.

159 Jim Sinclair, interview, 2011.

160 Henry Pelletier, interview, 17 March 1978; Isador Pelletier, interview, 23 November 2000; Myrtle Lafontaine, interview, July 1982.

161 Isador Pelletier, interview, 2011.

162 Isador Pelletier, interview, 2011; Henry Pelletier, interview, 17 March 1978; Jim Sinclair, interview, 2011.

163 Jim Sinclair and Jim Durocher, interview, 2004; Jim Sinclair, interview, 2011; Isador Pelletier, interview, 2011; Isador Pelletier, interview, 23 November 2000.

164 Jim Sinclair and Jim Durocher, interview, 2004.

165 Isador Pelletier, interview, 2011; Isador Pelletier, interview, 23 November 2000.

166 Jim Sinclair, interview, 2011.

167 Henry Pelletier, interview, 17 March 1978; Myrtle Lafontaine, interview, July 1982.

168 Jim Sinclair, interview, 2011; Barron, "The CCF."

169 Isador Pelletier, interview, 2011; Isador Pelletier, interview, 23 November 2000.

170 Jim Sinclair, interview, 2011.

171 PAS, Rural Municipality of North Qu'Appelle No. 187, R2.739, Relief Records 1921–1955, Municipal Council Minutes, 3 April 1948.

172 PAS, T.C. Douglas Papers, Files of the Premier, "Métis" R-33.1, file XL 859 b. (44)," V.P. Deshaye to T.C. Douglas," 27 February 1950.

173 PAS, T.C. Douglas Papers, Files of the Premier, "Métis" R-33.1, file XL 859 b. (44), "T.C. Douglas to V.P Deshaye," 7 March 1950.

Bibliography

Archival Collections

Gabriel Dumont Institute, Virtual Museum of Métis History and Culture
Beverly Worsely Collection
Biography and Essay Collection
Oral History Collection
Photograph Collection

Glenbow Library and Archives, Calgary
Department of Indian Affairs, Hobbema Agency
Journal of Qu'Appelle Lake Post, 1857–1858
Photograph Collection
Lebret Parish Records

Hudson's Bay Company Archives, Winnipeg
Biographical Sheets
Fort Ellice Post Records

Legislative Acts
Dominion Lands Act, 1872, 1876, 1879, 1883
Indian Act, 1868, 1876, 1879
Manitoba Act, 1870
Rural Municipality Act, 1928–1929

Library and Archives Canada, Ottawa
Department of Indian Affairs, RG10
Department of the Interior, RG15
Photograph Collection

Privy Council, RG2

Sessional Papers 1876
Sessional Papers 1877
Sessional Papers 1885
Sessional Papers 1886
Sessional Papers 1887
Sessional Papers 1888
Sessional Papers 1889
Sessional Papers 1893
Sessional Papers 1894
Sessional Papers 1895
Sessional Papers 1900
Sessional Papers 1901
Sessional Papers 1909
Sessional Papers 1913
Sessional Papers 1914
Sessional Papers 1915
Sessional Papers 1916

Provincial Archives of Saskatchewan
Department of the Interior, Dominion Land Survey Maps
Department of the Interior, Dominion Lands Branch
Department of the Interior, Dominion Lands Branch, Homestead Files
Department of the Interior, Surveyor Files
T.C. Douglas Papers
Amédée E. and Henriette Forget Papers

Government Record Series:
- Department of Education
- Department of Natural Resources
- Department of Natural Resources, Fisheries Branch
- Department of Social Welfare and Rehabilitation
- General Files of the Provincial Auditor

Manuscript Collection:
- F.C. Gilchrist Files
- Patrice Fleury Files

Photograph Collection

Rural Municipality of North Qu'Appelle No. 187 Records

J.H. Sturdy Papers

Saskatoon Public Library, Local History Room
Photograph Collection

University Archives and Special Collections, University of Saskatchewan
F.L. Barron Fonds
A.S. Morton Collection

Yale University
Beinecke Rare Book Collection, Hudson's Bay Company Records

Published Primary Sources

Government of Canada. "Canada Census Returns, 1916, Sub-District 20, Qu'Appelle, District 26, Saskatchewan." *Library and Archives Canada*. https://library-archives.canada.ca/eng/collection/research-help/genealogy-family-history/censuses/districts/1916-districts/pages/saskatchewan.aspx#q.

———. "Census of the three provisional districts of the North-west Territories, 1884–5." *Library and Archives Canada*. Accessed 10 August 2024. https://publications.gc.ca/site/eng/9.830814/publication.html.

———. "Census Returns, 1881." *Library and Archives Canada*. Accessed 10 August 2024. https://www.bac-lac.gc.ca/eng/census/1881/Pages/about-census.aspx.

———. *Dominion Alberta and Saskatchewan Fisheries Commission, 1910–1911, Report and Recommendations with Appendices*. Ottawa: Government Printing Bureau, 1912.

Indian and Northern Affairs. *Admission of Half-Breeds into Treaty*. Ottawa: Treaties and Historical Research Centre, 1976.

North-West Territories. *Journals of the Legislative Assembly of the North-West Territories.* Regina: J.A. Reid, Government Printer, 1893.

———. *Ordinances of the North-West Territories, Canada*. Regina: Government Printer, 1877–1984.

P.R.E. Group, Indian and Northern Affairs. *Historical Development of the Indian Act.* Ottawa: Treaties and Historical Research Centre, 1978: 76–77.

Sirois, Joseph, and Newton Wesley Rowell. *Report of the Royal Commission on Dominion-Provincial Relations*. Ottawa: King's Printer, 1940. Accessed 10 August 2024. https://epe.lac-bac.gc.ca/100/200/301/pco-bcp/commissions-ef/sirois1940-eng/sirois1940-v1-part2-eng.pdf.

United States. *Federal U.S. Census, Pembina County, Minnesota Territory, 1850*. Accessed 10 August 2024. http://www.usgwarchives.net/mn/pembina/census/1850/.

Newspapers
Nor'Wester
Qu'Appelle Vidette
Regina Leader Post

Interviews

Amyotte, Joe. Interview by Murray Dobbin. Virtual Museum of Métis History and Culture, Gabriel Dumont Institute, 11 August 1977. Transcript. www.metismuseum.ca.

Amyotte Fisher, Agnes, and Celina Amyotte Poitras. Interview by Sharon Gaddie and Margaret Jefferson. Virtual Museum of Métis History and Culture, Gabriel Dumont Institute, 3 August 1982. Transcript. www.metismuseum.ca.

Anderson, Pauline, Billie Robison, and Norma Welsh. Interview by Cheryl Troupe. Virtual Museum of Métis History and Culture, Gabriel Dumont Institute, 2004. Transcript. www.metismuseum.ca.

Blondeau, Joe. Interview by Sharon Gaddie. Virtual Museum of Métis History and Culture, Gabriel Dumont Institute, 19 August 1982.Transcript. www.metismuseum.ca.

Desjarlais, Bob. Interview by Cheryl Troupe and Calvin Racette. Virtual Museum of Métis History and Culture, Gabriel Dumont Institute, 15 May 2002. Transcript. www.metismuseum.ca.

Desjarlais, Bob. Interview by Cheryl Troupe and Leah Dorion. Virtual Museum of Métis History and Culture, Gabriel Dumont Institute, 3 July 2002. Transcript. www.metismuseum.ca.

Desjarlais, Bob, and George Klyne. Interview by Sherry Farrell Racette. Virtual Museum of Métis History and Culture, Gabriel Dumont Institute, 6–7 December 2003. Transcript. www.metismuseum.ca.

Desjarlais, Delphine. Interview by Cheryl Troupe. 8 July 2014. Transcript.

Desnomie, Mary. Interview by Cheryl Troupe. 23 February 2010. Transcript.

Harrison, Margaret. Interview by Cheryl Troupe. 10 July 2009. Transcript.

———. Interview by Cheryl Troupe. 12 February 2010. Transcript.

———. Interview by Cheryl Troupe. 24 February 2014. Transcript.

———. Interview by Cheryl Troupe. 9 July 2014. Transcript.

———. Interview by Cheryl Troupe. 13 March 2022. Transcript.

Harrison, Margaret, and Adeline Pelletier dit Racette. Interview by Leah Dorion and Anna Flaminio. Virtual Museum of Métis History and Culture, Gabriel Dumont Institute, 23–24 May 2002. Transcript. www.metismuseum.ca.

Harrison, Margaret, and Mary Desnomie. Interview by Cheryl Troupe and Maria Campbell. 30 March 2007. Audio.

Henry, Caroline. Interview by Margaret Jefferson. Virtual Museum of Métis History and Culture, Gabriel Dumont Institute, 15 August 1982. Transcript. www.metismuseum.ca.

Klyne, George. Interview by Cheryl Troupe. 4 August 2014. Transcript.

Klyne, George. Interview by Cheryl Troupe and Maria Campbell. 31 March 2007. Audio.

Lafontaine, Myrtle. Interview by Margaret Jefferson. Virtual Museum of Métis History and Culture, Gabriel Dumont Institute, July 1982. Transcript. www.metismuseum.ca.

Larocque, Jimmy, and Guy Blondeau. Interview by Sherry Farrell Racette. Virtual Museum of Métis History and Culture, Gabriel Dumont Institute, 10–11 January 2004. Transcript. www.metismuseum.ca.

Larocque, John Joe. Interview by Joe Ross. Virtual Museum of Métis History and Culture, Gabriel Dumont Institute, 13 August 1982. Transcript. www.metismuseum.ca.

Major, Marie. Interview with Sharon Gaddie. Virtual Museum of Métis History and Culture, Gabriel Dumont Institute, 20 August 1982. Transcript. www.metismuseum.ca.

Major, Thomas. Interview by Murray Dobbin. Virtual Museum of Métis History and Culture, Gabriel Dumont Institute, 14 March 1978. Transcript. www.metismuseum.ca.

Moran, Joseph. Interview by Sharon Gaddie. Virtual Museum of Métis History and Culture, Gabriel Dumont Institute, 22 August 1983. Transcript. www.metismuseum.ca.

Parisien, Joseph. Interview with Nathan Bear. Virtual Museum of Métis History and Culture, Gabriel Dumont Institute, 8 August 1983. Transcript. www.metismuseum.ca.

Pelletier, Henry. Interview by Murray Dobbin. Virtual Museum of Métis History and Culture, Gabriel Dumont Institute, 17 March 1978. Transcript. www.metismuseum.ca.

Pelletier, Isador. Interview with John Arcand and Maria Campbell. Virtual Museum of Métis History and Culture, Gabriel Dumont Institute, 23 November 2000. Video. www.metismuseum.ca.

Pelletier, Isador. Interview by Maria Campbell and Cheryl Troupe, 2011. Transcript.

Poitras Pelletier, Agnes. Interview by Norman Fleury. Virtual Museum of Métis History and Culture, Gabriel Dumont Institute, 30 May 2003. Transcript. www.metismuseum.ca.

Poitras, Roy. Interview by Cheryl Troupe. 4 July 2015. Transcript.

Racette, Stanley. Interview by Sharon Gaddie. Virtual Museum of Métis History and Culture, Gabriel Dumont Institute, 11 August 1983. Transcript. www.metismuseum.ca.

Robison, Billie. Interview by Leah Dorion. Virtual Museum of Métis History and Culture, Gabriel Dumont Institute, 15 March 2000. Transcript. www.metismuseum.ca.

Sinclair, Jim. Interview by Maria Campbell and Cheryl Troupe. 2011. Transcript.

Sinclair, Jim, and Jim Durocher. Interview by Ron Laliberte. Virtual Museum of Métis History and Culture, Gabriel Dumont Institute, 2004. Transcript. www.metismuseum.ca.

Tarr, Josephine. Interview by Victoria Racette. Virtual Museum of Métis History and Culture, Gabriel Dumont Institute, 27 February 1984. Transcript. www.metismuseum.ca.

Welsh, Lawrence, Pauline Anderson, Billie Robison, Pat Sullivan, and Norma Welsh. Interview by Cheryl Troupe. Virtual Museum of Métis History and Culture, Gabriel Dumont Institute, 2004. Transcript. www.metismuseum.ca.

Welsh, Norma. Interview by Cheryl Troupe. 16 February 2014. Transcript.

Welsh, Norma, and Joe Welsh. Interview by Sherry Farrell Racette. Virtual Museum of Métis History and Culture, Gabriel Dumont Institute, 7–8 February 2004. Transcript. www.metismuseum.ca.

Secondary Sources

Absolon, Kathleen. *How We Come To Know: Kaandossiwin.* Winnipeg: Fernwood, 2001.

Adams, Howard. *Prison of Grass: Canada from a Native Point of View.* Toronto: General Publishing, 1979.

Andersen, Chris, and Jean M. O'Brien. *Sources and Methods in Indigenous Studies.* New York: Routledge, 2017.

Anderson, Kim. *Life Stages of Native Women: Memory, Teachings, and Story Medicine.* Winnipeg: University of Manitoba Press, 2011.

Archer, John. ed. *Lake Katepwa: Memories of Yesterday with Notes for Today.* Regina: The Lake Katepwa Historical Society, 1984.

BIBLIOGRAPHY

Archibald, Jo-Ann. *Indigenous Storywork: Educating the Heart, Mind, Body, and Spirit.* Vancouver: UBC Press, 2008.

Augustus, Camie. "The Scrip Solution: The North-West Métis Scrip Policy, 1885–1887." Master's thesis, University of Calgary, 2005.

Barnett, Le Roy. "How Buffalo Bones Became Big Business." *Canadian Geographic Journal*, July/August 1974, 20–25.

Barron, F. Laurie. "The CCF and the Development of Métis Colonies in Southern Saskatchewan During the Premiership of T.C. Douglas, 1944–1961." *Canadian Journal of Native Studies* 10, no. 2 (1990): 243–72.

———. *Walking in Indian Moccasins: The Native Policies of Tommy Douglas and the CCF.* Vancouver: UBC Press, 1997.

Basso, Keith. *Wisdom Sits in Places: Landscape and Language Among the Western Apache.* Albuquerque: University of New Mexico Press, 1996.

Beal, Carl. "Money, Markets and Economic Development in Saskatchewan Reserve Communities." PhD diss., University of Manitoba, 1994.

Beaudoin, Alwynne B. "A Bison's View of the Landscape and the Paleoenvironment." In *Bison and People on the North American Great Plains: A Deep Environmental History*, edited by Geoff Cunfer and Bill Waiser, 51–89. College Station: Texas A&M University Press, 2016.

Belasco, Warren. "Food Matters: Perspectives on an Emerging Field." In *Food Nations: Selling Taste in Consumer Societies*, edited by Warren Belasco and Philip Scranton, 2–23. New York: Routledge, 2002.

Belcourt, G. A. "Buffalo Hunt." *The Beaver*, December 1944, 13–17.

Belcourt, Herb. *Walking in the Woods: A Métis Journey*. Victoria: Brindle and Glass, 2006.

Benson, Sarah. "'... taken in hand by Indians': Jewish-Indigenous Relations in the Early Twentieth-Century Qu'Appelle Valley Region." Master's thesis, University of Saskatchewan, 2023.

Binnie-Clark, Georgina. *Wheat and Women*. Toronto: University of Toronto Press, 2007.

Bodenhamer, David, John Corrigan, and Trevor M. Harris, eds. *Deep Maps and Spatial Narratives*. Bloomington: Indiana University Press, 2015.

Boyd, Robert. *Indians, Fire and the Land in the Pacific Northwest.* Corvallis: Oregon State University Press, 1999.

Brass, Eleanor. *Medicine Boy and Other Cree Tales*. Calgary: Glenbow-Alberta Institute, 1979.

———. *I Walk in Two Worlds*. Calgary: Glenbow Museum, 1987.

Brink, Jack. "A Hunter's Quest for Bison Fat." In *Bison and People on the North American Great Plains: A Deep Environmental History*, edited by Geoff Cunfer and Bill Waiser, 90–121. College Station: Texas A&M University Press, 2016.

Brown, Jennifer S.H. *Strangers in Blood: Fur Trade Company Families in Indian Country.* Vancouver: UBC Press, 1980.

———. "Women as Centre and Symbol in the Emergence of Métis Communities." *The Canadian Journal of Native Studies* 3, no. 1 (1983): 39–46.

Brown, Jennifer S.H., and Robert Brightman. *"The Orders of the Dreamed": George Nelson on Cree and Northern Ojibwa Religion and Myth, 1823.* Winnipeg: University of Manitoba Press, 1990.

Brown, Leslie, and Susan Strega, eds. *Research as Resistance: Critical, Indigenous and Anti-Oppressive Approaches.* Toronto: Canadian Scholars' Press, 2005.

Burley, David V. "Creolization and Late Nineteenth Century Métis Vernacular Log Architecture on the South Saskatchewan River." *Historical Archaeology* 34, no. 3 (2000): 27–35.

Burley, David V., Gayle A. Horsfall, and John D. Brandon. *Structural Considerations of Métis Ethnicity: An Archaeological, Architectural and Historical Study.* Vermillion, SD: University of South Dakota Press, 1992.

Butler, William Francis. *The Great Lone Land: An Account of the Red River Expedition and Other Travels and Adventures in Western Canada.* Rutland, VT: Charles E. Tuttle Company, 1970.

Callihoo, Victoria. "Our Buffalo Hunts." *Alberta Historical Review* 8, no. 1 (Winter 1860): 24–25.

Calliou, Brian. "Losing the Game: Wildlife Conservation and the Regulation of First Nations Hunting in Alberta, 1880–1930." Master of Law thesis, University of Alberta, 2007.

Campbell, Maria. *Halfbreed.* Toronto: McClelland and Stewart, 1973.

———. *Stories of the Road Allowance People.* Penticton: Theytus Books, 1995.

———. "Foreword." In *Contours of a People: Métis Family, Mobility, and History,* edited by Nicole St-Onge, Carolyn Podruchny, and Brenda Macdougall, xiii–xxvi. Norman: University of Oklahoma Press, 2012.

Carpenter, Jock. *Fifty Dollar Bride: Marie Rose Smith, A Chronicle of Métis Life in the 19th Century.* Sidney, BC: Gray's Publishing, 1977.

Carter, Sarah. *Lost Harvests: Prairie Indian Reserve Farmers and Government Policy.* Montreal: McGill-Queen's University Press, 1990.

———. "First Nations Women of Prairie Canada in the Early Reserve Years, the 1870s to the 1920s: A Preliminary Inquiry." In *Women of the First Nations: Power, Wisdom, and Strength,* edited by Christine Miller and Patricia Chuchryk, 51–76. Winnipeg: University of Manitoba Press, 1997.

———. *The Importance of Being Monogamous: Marriage and Nation Building in Western Canada to 1915.* Edmonton: University of Alberta Press, 2008.

———. "'Daughters of British Blood' or 'Hordes of Men of Alien Race': The Homesteads-for-Women Campaign in Western Canada." *Great Plains Quarterly* 29, no. 4 (Fall 2009): 267–86.

———. "Demonstrating Success: The File Hills Farm Colony." In *Immigration and Settlement, 1870–1939*, edited by Gregory P. Marchildon, 235–63. Regina: Canadian Plains Research Center, 2009.

———. *Imperial Plots: Women, Land, and the Spadework of British Colonialism on the Canadian Prairies*. Winnipeg: University of Manitoba Press, 2016.

Carter, Sarah, Lesley Erickson, and Patricia Roome. "Introduction." In *Unsettled Pasts: Reconceiving the West Through Women's History*, edited by Sarah Carter, Lesley Erickson, Patricia Roome, and Char Smith, 1–13. Calgary: University of Calgary Press, 2005.

Cavendar Wilson, Angela. "Grandmother to Granddaughter: Generations of Oral History in a Dakota Family." *American Indian Quarterly* 20, no.1 (1996): 7–13.

Charette, Guillaume. *Vanishing Spaces: Memoirs of a Prairie Métis*. Winnipeg: Bois-Brûlés, 1981.

Cheadle, Walter B. *Cheadle's Journal of Trip Across Canada, 1862–1863*. Rutland, VT: Charles E. Tuttle Company, 1971.

Clark, Leland W. "The Place of the Métis Within the Agricultural Economy of the Red River in the 1840s and 1850s." *Canadian Journal of Native Studies* 3, no. 1 (1983): 69–84.

Code, Paget J. "Les Autres Métis: The English Métis of the Prince Albert Settlement, 1882–1886." Master's thesis, University of Saskatchewan, 2008.

Colpitts, George. *Game in the Garden: A Human History of Wildlife in Western Canada to 1940*. Vancouver: UBC Press, 2002.

———. "Provisioning the HBC: Market Economies in the British Buffalo Commons in the Early Nineteenth Century." *Western Historical Quarterly* 43 (Summer 2012): 179–203.

———. *Pemmican Empire: Food, Trade, and the Last Bison Hunts in the Northern Plains, 1780–1882*. New York: Cambridge University Press, 2015.

Cowie, Isaac. *The Company of Adventurers: A Narrative of Seven Years in the Service of the Hudson's Bay Company During 1867–1874*. Lincoln: University of Nebraska Press, 1993.

Cronon, William. *Changes in the Land: Indians, Colonists and the Ecology of New England*. New York: Hill and Wang, 1983.

Cunfer, Geoff. *On the Great Plains: Agriculture and Environment*. College Station: Texas A&M University Press, 2005.

———. "Overview: The Decline and Fall of the Bison Empire." In *Bison and People on the North American Great Plains: A Deep Environmental History*, edited by Geoff Cunfer and Bill Waiser, 1–29. College Station: Texas A&M University Press, 2016.

Cunfer, Geoff, and Bill Waiser, eds. *Bison and People on the North American Great Plains: A Deep Environmental History.* College Station: Texas A & M University Press, 2016.

Danysk, Cecilia. "No Help for the Farm: The Farm Employment Plans of the 1930s in Prairie Canada." In *Drought & Depression: History of the Prairie West, Vol. 6*, edited by Gregory P. Marchildon, 139–62. Regina: University of Regina Press, 2018.

Daschuk, James. *Clearing the Plains: Disease, Politics of Starvation, and the Loss of Aboriginal Life*. Regina: University of Regina Press, 2013.

Devine, Heather. "Les Desjarlais: The Development and Dispersion of a Proto-Métis Hunting Band, 1785–1870." In *From Rupert's Land to Canada*, edited by Theodore Binnema, Gerhard J. Ens, and R.C. MacLeod, 129–60. Edmonton: University of Alberta Press, 2001.

———. *The People Who Own Themselves: Aboriginal Ethnogenesis in a Canadian Family, 1660–1900*. Calgary: University of Calgary Press, 2004.

———. "J.Z. LaRocque: A Métis Historian's Account of His Family's Experiences during the North-West Rebellion of 1885." In *Finding Directions West: Readings That Locate and Dislocate Western Canada's Past*, edited by George Colpitts and Heather Devine, 59–91. Calgary: University of Calgary Press, 2017.

Dick, Lyle. *Farmers "Making Good": The Development of Abernathy District, Saskatchewan, 1880–1920.* Calgary: University of Calgary Press, 2008.

Dobak, William A. "Killing the Canadian Buffalo, 1821–1881." *Western Historical Quarterly* 27, no. 1 (Spring 1996): 33–52.

Dobbin, Murray. "Métis Struggles of the Twentieth Century: The Saskatchewan Métis Society—1935–1980. Part One: Early Beginnings." *New Breed Magazine*, August 1978.

———. "Métis Struggles of the Twentieth Century: The Saskatchewan Métis Society—1935–1980. Part Two: The Land Issues: Whitemen's Advice and Government Deceit." *New Breed Magazine*, September 1978.

Dorion, Leah, and Darren R. Préfontaine. "Deconstructing Métis Historiography: Giving Voice to the Métis People." In *Métis Legacy: A Métis Historiography and Annotated Bibliography*, edited by Lawrence J. Barkwell, Leah Dorion, and Darren R. Préfontaine, 13–36. Winnipeg: Pemmican Publications, 2000.

Eagle, John. *The Canadian Pacific Railway and the Development of Western Canada.* Kingston-Montreal: McGill-Queen's University Press, 1989.

Ens, Gerhard J. "Métis Land Rights in Manitoba." *Manitoba History* 5 (Spring 1983). Accessed 10 August 2024. http://www.mhs.mb.ca/docs/mb_history/05/metislands.shtml.

———. "Dispossession or Adaptation? Migration and Persistence of the Red River Métis, 1835–1890." *Canadian Historical Papers* 23, no. 1 (1988): 120–44.

———. "Métis Agriculture in Red River During the Transition from Peasant Society to Industrial Capitalism: The Example of St. François Xavier, 1835–1870." In *Swords and Ploughshares: War and Agriculture in Western Canada,* edited by R.C. Macleod, 239–62. Edmonton: University of Alberta Press, 1993.

———. *Homeland to Hinterland: The Changing Worlds of the Red River Métis in the Nineteenth Century.* Toronto: University of Toronto Press, 1996.

Ens, Gerhard J., and Joe Sawchuk. *From New Peoples to New Nations.* Toronto: University of Toronto Press, 2016.

Erasmus, Peter. *Buffalo Days and Nights.* Calgary: Fifth House Publishers, 1999.

Farrell Racette, Sherry. '"Sewing Ourselves Together': Clothing, Decorative Arts and the Expression of Métis and Halfbreed Identity." PhD diss., University of Manitoba, 2004.

———. "Sewing for a Living: The Commodification of Métis Women's Artistic Production." In *Contact Zones: Aboriginal and Settler Women in Canada's Colonial Past,* edited by Katie Pickles and Myra Rutherdale, 17–46. Vancouver: UBC Press, 2005.

———. "Nimble Fingers and Strong Backs: First Nations and Métis Women in Fur Trade and Rural Economies." In *Indigenous Women and Work, From Labor to Activism,* edited by Carol Williams, 148–62. Chicago: University of Illinois Press, 2012.

Fisher-Fiskin, Shelley. "'Deep Maps': A Brief for Digital Palimpsest Mapping Projects (DPMPS, or 'Deep Maps')." *Journal of Transnational American Studies* 3.2 (2011): 1–31.

Flanagan, Thomas E. *Métis Lands in Manitoba.* Calgary: University of Calgary Press, 1991.

Flores, Dan. "Bison Ecology and Bison Diplomacy: The Southern Plains from 1800 to 1850." *Journal of American History* 28, no. 2 (September 1991): 465–85.

Foster, Janet. *Working for Wildlife: The Beginning of Preservation in Canada.* Toronto: University of Toronto Press, 1978.

Foster, Martha Harroun. *We Know Who We Are: Métis Identity in a Montana Community.* Norman: University of Oklahoma Press, 2006.

Freed, Don. "Daughters of the Country." *The Valley of Green and Blue.* Gabriel Dumont Institute, 2007. CD.

Friesen, Jean. "Magnificent Gifts: The Treaties of Canada with the Indians of the North-West, 1869–76." *Transactions of the Royal Society of Canada,* Series V. Vol. 1 (1996): 41–51.

Gaudet, Janice Cindy. "Keeoukaywin: The Visiting Way—Fostering an Indigenous Research Methodology." *Aboriginal Policy Studies* 7, no. 2 (2019): 47–64.

Gillespie, Greg. *Hunting for Empire: Narratives of Sport in Rupert's Land, 1840–1870.* Vancouver: UBC Press, 2007.

Giraud, Marcel. *The Métis in the Canadian West, Volume II,* trans. George Woodcock. Edmonton: University of Alberta Press, 1986.

Gulig, Anthony. "'We Beg the Government': Native People and Game Regulation in Northern Saskatchewan, 1900–1940." *Prairie Forum* 28, no. 1 (Spring 2003): 81–98.

Hämäläinen, Pekka. "The First Phase of Destruction: Killing the Southern Plains Buffalo, 1790–1840." *Great Plains Quarterly* 21 (Spring 2001): 101–14.

Hatt, Ken. "North-West Rebellion Scrip Commissions, 1885–1889." In *1885 and After: Native Society in Transition,* edited by F. Laurie Barron and James B. Waldram, 189–204. Regina: Canadian Plains Research Center, 1986.

Hayter, Jennifer. "Racially 'Indian,' Legally 'White': The Canadian State's Struggle to Categorize the Métis, 1850–1900." PhD diss., University of Toronto, 2017.

Herriot, Trevor. *Towards a Prairie Atonement.* Regina: University of Regina Press, 2016.

Hogue, Michel. *Métis and the Medicine Line: Creating a Border and Dividing a People.* Regina: University of Regina Press, 2015.

Hourie, Audreen, and Anne Carriére-Acco. "Métis Families." In *Métis Legacy II,* edited by Lawrence Barkwell, Leah M. Dorion, and Audreen Hourie, 53–63. Winnipeg and Saskatoon: Pemmican Publications and Gabriel Dumont Institute, 2006.

Hourie, Audreen, Anne Carriére-Acco, Lawrence Barkwell, and Leah Dorion. "Métis Foods." In *Métis Legacy II,* edited by Lawrence Barkwell, Leah M. Dorion, and Audreen Hourie, 119–32. Winnipeg and Saskatoon: Pemmican Publications and Gabriel Dumont Institute, 2006.

Innes, Robert Alexander. *Elder Brother and the Law of the People: Contemporary Kinship and Cowessess First Nation.* Winnipeg: University of Manitoba Press, 2013.

Jacoby, Karl. *Crimes Against Nature: Squatters, Poachers, Thieves and the Hidden History of American Conservation.* Berkeley: University of California Press, 2001.

Keay, Helen Ruth. *Lord Lorne's Expedition to the North-West, Reported by Rev. Dr. James MacGregor, 1881.* Regina: University of Regina Printing Services, 2004.

Klimko, Olga. *The Archaeology and History of Fort Pelly I, 1824–1856.* Regina: Saskatchewan Culture and Recreation, 1983.

Klimko, Olga, and John Hodges. *Last Mountain House: A Hudson's Bay Company Outpost in the Qu'Appelle Valley*. Saskatoon: Western Heritage Services, 1993.

Klyne, George. "The Trapper and the Snare." In *kisiskâciwan: Indigenous Voices From Where The River Flows Swiftly,* edited by Jesse Rae Archibald Barber, 163–64. Regina: University of Regina Press, 2018.

Kovach, Margaret. *Indigenous Methodologies: Characteristics, Conversations, and Contexts.* Toronto: University of Toronto Press, 2009.

Kubik, Wendy, and Gregory P. Marchildon. *Women's History: History of the Prairie West Series* Vol. 5. Regina: University of Regina Press, 2015.

Lambrecht, Kirk N. *The Administration of Dominion Lands, 1870–1930.* Regina: Canadian Plains Research Center, 1991.

LaVallée, Guy. *The Métis of St. Laurent, Manitoba: Their Life and Stories, 1920–1988.* Winnipeg: S.P., 2003.

Lawton, Alma. "Relief Administration in Saskatoon During the Depression." *Saskatchewan History* 22, no. 2 (1969): 41.

Lehr, John C., John Everitt, and Simon Evans. "Making of the Prairie Landscape." In *Immigration and Settlement, 1870–1939,* edited by Gregory P. Marchildon, 13–58. Regina: Canadian Plains Research Center, 2009.

Long, W.H. *Fort Pelly Journal of Daily Occurrences, 1863.* Regina: Regina Archaeological Society, 1987.

Loo, Tina. *States of Nature: Conserving Canada's Wildlife in the Twentieth Century.* Vancouver: UBC Press, 2006.

Lux, Maureen. *Medicine That Walks: Disease, Medicine, and Canadian Plains Native People, 1880–1940.* Toronto: University of Toronto Press, 2001.

Macdougall, Brenda. "Wahkootowin: Family and Cultural Identity in Northwestern Saskatchewan Métis Communities." *The Canadian Historical Review* 87, no. 3 (September 2006): 431–62.

———. *One of the Family: Métis Culture in Nineteenth-Century Northwestern Saskatchewan.* Vancouver: UBC Press, 2010.

Macdougall, Brenda, and Nicole St-Onge. "Rooted in Mobility: Métis Buffalo Hunting Brigades." *Manitoba History* 71 (Winter 2013): 21–32.

Mailhot, P.R., and D.N. Sprague. "Persistent Settlers: The Dispersal and Resettlement of the Red River Métis, 1870–1885." *Canadian Ethnic Studies* 18 (1985): 1–30.

Marchildon, Gregory P. "Introduction." In *Drought & Depression: History of the Prairie West, Vol. 6,* edited by Gregory P. Marchildon, 1–12. Regina: University of Regina Press, 2018.

Marles, Robin J., Christina Clavelle, Leslie Monteleone, Natalie Tays, and Donna Burns. *Aboriginal Plant Use in Canada's Northwest Boreal Forest*. Vancouver: UBC Press, 2000.

Martin, Chester. *"Dominion Lands" Policy*. Edited by Lewis H. Thomas. Toronto: McClelland and Stewart, 1973.

Martin-McGuire, Peggy. *First Nations Land Surrenders on the Prairies, 1896–1911*. Ottawa: Indian Claims Commission, Government of Canada, 1996. Accessed 10 August 2024. http://publications.gc.ca/site/eng/9.833886/publication.html.

Massie, Merle. *Forest Prairie Edge: Place History in Saskatchewan*. Winnipeg: University of Manitoba Press, 2014.

McCallum, Mary Jane Logan. *Indigenous Women, Work, and History, 1940–1980*. Winnipeg: University of Manitoba Press, 2014.

McGregor, Deborah, Jean-Paul Restoule, and Rochelle Johnston. *Indigenous Research: Theories, Practices, and Relationships*. Toronto: Canadian Scholars Press, 2018.

McKay, Ian. "The Liberal Order Framework: A Prospectus for Reconnaissance of Canadian History." *The Canadian Historical Review* 102, Supplement 4 (December 2021): 1133–57.

McKercher, R.B., and B. Wolfe. *Understanding Western Canada's Dominion Land Survey System*. Saskatoon: University of Saskatchewan, 1986.

McLean, Don. *Home From the Hill: A History of the Métis in Western Canada*. Regina: Gabriel Dumont Institute, 1987.

McNab, Miriam. "George Gordon First Nations Women: Partners in Survival." PhD diss., University of Saskatchewan, 2017.

Métis Association of Alberta, Joe Sawchuk, Patricia Sawchuk, and Theresa Ferguson. *Métis Land Rights in Alberta: A Political History*. Edmonton: Métis Association of Alberta, 1981.

Miller, J.R. *Compact, Contract, Covenant: Aboriginal Treaty-making in Canada*. Toronto: University of Toronto Press, 2009.

Millions, Erin. "Breaking the Mould: A Historiographical Review of Saskatchewan Women's History, 1880–1930." *Saskatchewan History* 54 (Fall 2002): 31–49.

Milloy, John. *The Plains Cree: Trade, Diplomacy, and War, 1790–1870*. Winnipeg: University of Manitoba Press, 1990.

Milne, Brad. "The Historiography of Métis Land Dispersal, 1870–1890." *Manitoba History* 30 (Autumn 1995): 30–41.

Moine Trottier, Louise. *Remembering Will Have To Do: The Life and Times of Louise (Trottier) Moine*. Saskatoon: Gabriel Dumont Institute, 2013.

Morris, Alexander. *The Treaties of Canada with the Indians of Manitoba and the North-West Territories*. Toronto: Cole's Publishing, 1979.

Morton, W.L. "Introduction." In *Alexander Begg's Red River Journal and Other Papers Relative to the Red River Resistance of 1869–1870,* edited by W.L. Morton. Toronto: Champlain Society, 1956.

———. "The Battle of Grand Coteau: July 13 and 14, 1851." *Manitoba Historical Society Transactions,* Series 3, 1959–60. Accessed 10 August 2024. http://www.mhs.mb.ca/docs/transactions/3/grandcouteau.shtml.

Munro, Douglas K. *Fur Trade Letters of Willie Traill, 1864–1894.* Edmonton: University of Alberta Press, 2006.

Niemi-Bohum, Melanie. "Colonial Categories and Familial Responses to Treaty and Métis Scrip Policy: The 'Edmonton and District Stragglers,' 1870–1888." *Canadian Historical Review* 90, no. 1 (March 2009): 71–98.

O'Byrne, Nicole. "'No other weapon except organization': The Métis Association of Alberta and the 1938 Métis Population Betterment Act." *Journal of the Canadian Historical Association* 24, no. 2 (Fall 2013): 311–52.

Owram, Doug. *Promise of Eden: The Canadian Expansionist Movement and the Idea of the West, 1856–1900.* Toronto: University of Toronto Press, 1980.

Oxx, Katie, Allan Brimicombe, and Johnathan Rush. "Envisioning Deep Maps: Exploring the Spatial Navigation Metaphor in Deep Mapping." *International Journal of Humanities and Arts Computing* 7, no. 1–2 (2013): 221–27.

Paget, Amelia M. *People of the Plains.* Regina: Canadian Plains Research Center, 2004.

Pallister, Casey. "The Bone Hunters: New Visions of an Ossified Past." *Great Plains Quarterly* 42, no. 3 (Summer 2022): 191–209.

Payment, Diane Paulette. "Batoche After 1885: A Society in Transition." In *1885 and After: Native Society in Transition,* edited by F. Laurie Barron and James B. Waldram, 173–88. Regina: Canadian Plains Research Center, 1986.

———. *The Free People—Otipemisiwak: Batoche 1870–1930.* Ottawa: National Historic Parks and Sites, 1990.

———. "La Vie en Rose"? Métis Women at Batoche, 1870–1920." In *Women of the First Nations: Power, Wisdom, and Strength,* edited by Christine Miller and Patricia Chuchryk, 19–37. Winnipeg: University of Manitoba Press, 1996.

Pelletier, Jacqueline Margaret. "The First of All Things: The Significance of Place in Métis Histories and Communities in the Qu'Appelle Valley, Saskatchewan." Master's thesis, University of Alberta, 2006.

Pelletier, Joan. *Lebret—Looking Back and Beyond: An Autobiography.* Saskatoon: Gabriel Dumont Institute, 2023.

Peters, Evelyn, Matthew Stock, and Adrian Werner. *Roostertown: The History of an Urban Métis Community, 1901–1961.* Winnipeg: University of Manitoba Press, 2018.

Pitsula, James. *Keeping Canada British: The Ku Klux Klan in 1920s Saskatchewan.* Vancouver: UBC Press, 2013.

Portt, C.B., G.A. Coker, D.L. Ming, and R.G. Randall. *A Review of Fish Sampling Methods Commonly Used in Canadian Freshwater Habitats.* Ottawa: Fisheries and Oceans Canada, 2006.

Potyondi, Barry. *In Palliser's Triangle: Living in the Grasslands, 1850–1930.* Saskatoon: Purich Publishing, 1995.

Pyne, Stephen. *Fire in America: A Cultural History of Wildland and Rural Fire.* Princeton: Princeton University Press, 1982.

Ray, Arthur. *Indians in the Fur Trade: Their Role as Trappers, Hunters, and Middlemen in the Lands Southwest of Hudson Bay, 1660–1870.* Toronto: University of Toronto Press, 1998.

Ray, Arthur, Jim Miller, and Frank Tough, eds. *Bounty and Benevolence: A History of Saskatchewan Treaties.* Montreal: McGill-Queen's University Press, 2002.

Read, Colin. "The Red River Rebellion and J.S. Dennis, Lieutenant and Conservator of the Peace." *Manitoba History* 3 (1982). Accessed 10 August 2024. http://www.mhs.mb.ca/docs/mb_history/03/dennis_js.shtml.

Ridge, Mia, Don Lafreniere, and Scott Nesbit. "Creating Deep Maps and Spatial Narratives Through Design." *International Journal of Humanities and Arts Computing* 7, no. 1–2 (1 October 2013): 176–89.

Ross, Alexander. *The Red River Settlement: Its Rise, Progress, and Present State With Some Account of The Native Races and Its General History to the Present Day.* Minneapolis: Ross and Haines, 1957 [1856].

Sandlos, John. *Hunters at the Margins: Native People and Wildlife Conservation in the Northwest Territories.* Vancouver: UBC Press, 2008.

Schilling, Rita. *Gabriel's Children.* Saskatoon: Saskatoon Métis Society, Local 11, 1983.

Sealey, Bruce D., and Antoine S. Lucier. *The Métis: Canada's Forgotten People.* Winnipeg: Pemmican Publishers, 1975.

Sherow, James E. "Workings of the Geodialectic High Plains Indians and Their Horses in the Region of the Arkansas River Valley, 1800–1870." *Environmental History Review* 16, no. 2 (Summer 1992): 61–84.

Smillie, Christine. "The Invisible Workforce: Women Workers in Saskatchewan from 1905 to World War II." *Saskatchewan History* 39, no. 2 (1986): 62–79.

Smith, Linda Tuhiwai. *Decolonizing Methodologies: Research and Indigenous Peoples.* Dunedin: University of Otago Press, 1999.

Southesk, The Earl of. *Saskatchewan and The Rocky Mountains: A Diary and Narrative of Travel, Sport, and Adventure, During a Journey Through the Hudson's Bay Company's Territories, In 1859–1860.* Edmonton: M.G. Hurtig, 1969.

Sprague, D.N. *Canada and the Métis, 1869–1885.* Waterloo: Wilfrid Laurier University Press, 1988.

Sprague, D.N., and R.P. Frye. *The Genealogy of the First Métis Nation: The Development and Dispersal of the Red River Settlement, 1820–1900.* Winnipeg: Pemmican Publications, 1983.

Sprenger, George Herman. "The Métis Nation: Buffalo Hunting versus Agriculture in the Red River Settlement, 1810–1870." In *Native People, Native Lands: Canadian Indians, Inuit and Métis,* edited by Bruce Alden Cox, 120–35. Ottawa: Carleton University Press, 1987.

Spry, Irene M. *The Palliser Expedition: An Account of John Palliser's British North American Exploring Expedition, 1857–1860.* Toronto: Macmillian Company of Canada, 1963.

Stanley, G.F.G. *The Birth of Western Canada: A History of the Riel Rebellions.* Toronto: University of Toronto Press, 1961.

Stevenson, Allyson. "The Métis Cultural Brokers and the Western Numbered Treaties, 1869–1877." Master's thesis, University of Saskatchewan, 2004.

St-Onge, Nicole. "Memories of Métis Women of St. Eustache, Manitoba, 1910–1980." *Oral History Forum* 19–20 (1999–2000): 90–111.

St-Onge, Nicole, Carolyn Podruchny, and Brenda Macdougall, eds. *Contours of a People: Métis Family, Mobility, and History.* Norman: University of Oklahoma Press, 2012.

St. Pierre, Edwin. *Remembering My Métis Past: Reminiscences of Edwin St. Pierre.* Saskatoon: Gabriel Dumont Institute, 2012.

Street, W.P.R. "The Commission of 1885 to The North-West Territories," *Canadian Historical Review,* with Introduction by H.H. Langton, vol. 25, no. 1 (1944): 44–45.

Stunden Bower, Shannon. *Wet Prairie: People, Land, and Water in Agricultural Manitoba.* Vancouver: UBC Press, 2011.

Teillet, Jean. *The North-West Is Our Mother: The Story of Louis Riel's People, the Métis Nation.* Toronto: HarperCollins, 2019.

Thompson, Charles Duncan. *Red Sun: Gabriel Dumont, the Folk Hero.* Saskatoon: Gabriel Dumont Institute, 2017.

Thorne, Tanis. *The Many Hands of My Relations: French and Indians on the Lower Missouri.* Columbia: University of Missouri Press, 1996.

Thorpe, Jocelyn. *Temagami's Tangled Wild: Race, Gender, and the Making of Canadian Nature.* Vancouver: UBC Press, 2012.

Tough, Frank. *"As Their Natural Resources Fail": Native Peoples and The Economic History of Northern Manitoba, 1870–1930.* Vancouver: UBC Press, 1996.

Tough, Frank, and Erin McGregor. "'The Rights to the Lands May be Transferred': Archival Records as Colonial Text—A Narrative of Métis Scrip." In *Natives and Settlers—Now and Then: Historical Issues and Current Perspectives on Treaties and Land Claims in Canada*, edited by Paul W. DePasquale, 33–63. Edmonton: University of Alberta Press, 2007.

Troupe, Cheryl. *Expressing Our Heritage: Métis Artistic Designs*. Saskatoon: Gabriel Dumont Institute, 2001.

———. "Métis Women: Social Structure, Urbanization, and Political Activism, 1850–1980." Master's thesis, University of Saskatchewan, 2010.

Tyman, John L. "Patterns of Western Land Settlement." *Transactions of the Manitoba Historical Society*, Series 3, no. 28 (1971–72). Accessed 10 August 2024. http://www.mhs.mb.ca/docs/transactions/3/landsettlement.shtml.

Vale, Thomas, ed. *Fire, Native Peoples and the Natural Landscape*. Washington: Island Press, 2002.

Van Kirk, Sylvia. *Many Tender Ties: Women in Fur Trade Society, 1670–1870*. Winnipeg: Watson and Dwywer, 1980.

Vrooman, Nicolas C.P. *"The Whole Country was . . . 'One Robe'" The Little Shell Tribe's America*. Helena, MT: Little Shell Tribe of Chippewa Indians of Montana and Drumlummon Institute, 2012.

Waiser, Bill. *Saskatchewan's Playground, A History of Prince Albert National Park*. Saskatoon: Fifth House Publishers, 1989.

———. *Saskatchewan: A New History*. Saskatoon: Fifth House, 2005.

———. "A Legislator's View of Bison Collapse: The 1877 North-West Territories Bison Protection Ordinance." In *Bison and People on the North American Great Plains: A Deep Environmental History*, edited by Geoff Cunfer and Bill Waiser, 245–62. College Station: Texas A&M University Press, 2016.

Walker, Ernest G. "An Overview of Prehistoric Communal Bison Hunting on the Great Plains." In *Bison and People on the North American Great Plains: A Deep Environmental History*, edited by Geoff Cunfer and Bill Waiser, 122–55. College Station: Texas A&M University Press, 2016.

Weekes, Mary. *The Last Buffalo Hunter*. Saskatoon: Fifth House Publishers, 1994.

Welsh, Christine. "Voices of the Grandmothers: Reclaiming a Métis Heritage." *Canadian Literature* 131 (Winter 1991): 15–24.

Wheeler, Winona. "Reflections on the Social Relations of Indigenous Oral Histories." In *Walking a Tightrope: Aboriginal People and Their Representations*, edited by David McNab and Ute Lischke, 189–214. Waterloo: Wilfrid Laurier University Press, 2005.

White, Richard. *Land Use, Environment and Social Change: The Shaping of Island County, Washington*. Seattle: University of Washington Press, 1980.

Williams, W.H. *Manitoba and the North-West: Journal of a Trip from Toronto to the Rocky Mountains Via Lake Superior, Thunder Bay, Rat Portage, Winnipeg, Qu'Appelle, Prince Albert, Battleford, Fort Calgary and Fort McLeod and Return Via Edmonton, Touchwood Hills, Etc.* Toronto: Hunter Rose and Company, 1882.

Wilson, Shawn. *Research Is Ceremony: Indigenous Research Methods.* Black Point, NS: Fernwood, 2008.

Youle Hind, Henry. *Narrative of the Canadian Red River Exploring Expedition of 1857, and of the Assiniboine and Saskatchewan Exploring Expedition of 1858.* Edmonton: M.G. Hurtig, 1971.

Zeilig, Ken, and Victoria Zeilig. *Ste. Madeleine: Community Without a Town, Métis Elders in Interview.* Winnipeg: Pemmican Publications, 1987.

Index

Page numbers in bold indicate tables and figures

I

J

K

Q

R